Communications in Computer and Information Science 883

Commenced Publication in 2007
Founding and Former Series Editors:
Phoebe Chen, Alfredo Cuzzocrea, Xiaoyong Du, Orhun Kara, Ting Liu,
Dominik Ślęzak, and Xiaokang Yang

More information about this series at http://www.springer.com/series/7899

Rafael Valencia-García · Gema Alcaraz-Mármol
Javier Del Cioppo-Morstadt · Néstor Vera-Lucio
Martha Bucaram-Leverone (Eds.)

Technologies and Innovation

4th International Conference, CITI 2018
Guayaquil, Ecuador, November 6–9, 2018
Proceedings

 Springer

Editors
Rafael Valencia-García
Facultad de Informática
Universidad de Murcia
Murcia, Spain

Gema Alcaraz-Mármol
Departamento de Filología Moderna
Universidad de Castilla la Mancha
Ciudad Real, Ciudad Real, Spain

Javier Del Cioppo-Morstadt
Universidad Agraria del Ecuador
Guayaquil, Ecuador

Néstor Vera-Lucio
Universidad Agraria del Ecuador
Guayaquil, Ecuador

Martha Bucaram-Leverone
Universidad Agraria del Ecuador
Guayaquil, Ecuador

ISSN 1865-0929   ISSN 1865-0937 (electronic)
Communications in Computer and Information Science
ISBN 978-3-030-00939-7   ISBN 978-3-030-00940-3 (eBook)
https://doi.org/10.1007/978-3-030-00940-3

Library of Congress Control Number: 2018954766

This Springer imprint is published by the registered company Springer Nature Switzerland AG
The registered company address is: Gewerbestrasse 11, 6330 Cham, Switzerland

CITI 2018 - Preface

The 4th International Conference on Technologies and Innovation (CITI 2018) was held during November 6–9, 2018, in Guayaquil, Ecuador. The CITI series of conferences aims to become an international framework and meeting point for professionals who are mainly devoted to research, development, innovation, and university teaching in the field of computer science and technology applied to any important field of innovation. CITI 2018 was organized as a knowledge-exchange conference consisting of several contributions about current innovative technology. These proposals deal with the most important aspects and future prospects from academic, innovative, and scientific perspectives. The goal of the conference was the feasibility of investigating advanced and innovative methods and techniques and their application in different domains in the field of computer science and information systems, representing innovation in today's society.

We would like to express our gratitude to all the authors who submitted papers to CITI 2018, and our congratulations to those whose papers were accepted. There were 64 submissions this year. Each submission was reviewed by at least three Program Committee (PC) members. Only the papers with an average score of ≥ 1.0 were considered for final inclusion, and almost all accepted papers had positive reviews or at least one review with a score of 2 (accept) or higher. Finally, the PC decided to accept 21 full papers.

We would also like to thank the PC members, who agreed to review the manuscripts in a timely manner and provided valuable feedback to the authors.

November 2018

Rafael Valencia-García
Gema Alcaraz-Mármol
Javier Del Cioppo-Morstadt
Néstor Vera-Lucio
Martha Bucaram-Leverone

Organization

Honorary Committee

Martha Bucaram Leverone	Universidad Agraria del Ecuador, Ecuador
Javier Del Cioppo-Morstadt	Universidad Agraria del Ecuador, Ecuador
Néstor Vera Lucio	Universidad Agraria del Ecuador, Ecuador
Teresa Samaniego Cobo	Universidad Agraria del Ecuador, Ecuador

Organizing Committee

Rafael Valencia-García	Universidad de Murcia, Spain
Gema Alcaraz-Mármol	Universidad de Castilla-La Mancha, Spain
Javier Del Cioppo-Morstadt	Universidad Agraria del Ecuador, Ecuador
Néstor Vera Lucio	Universidad Agraria del Ecuador, Ecuador
Martha Bucaram Leverone	Universidad Agraria del Ecuador, Ecuador

Program Committee

Jacobo Bucaram Ortiz	Universidad Agraria del Ecuador, Ecuador
Martha Bucaram Leverone	Universidad Agraria del Ecuador, Ecuador
Rina Bucaram Leverone	Universidad Agraria del Ecuador, Ecuador
Rafael Valencia-García	Universidad de Murcia, Spain
Ricardo Colomo-Palacios	Ostfold University College, Norway
Ghassan Beydoun	University of Technology Sydney, Australia
Antonio A. López-Lorca	University of Melbourne, Australia
José Antonio Miñarro-Giménez	Medical Graz University, Austria
Catalina Martínez-Costa	Medical Graz University, Austria
Chunguo Wu	Jillin University, China
Siti Hajar Othman	Universiti Teknologi Malaysia, Malaysia
Anatoly Gladun	V.M. Glushkov of National Academy Science, Ukraine
Aarón Ayllón-Benítez	Université de Bordeaux, France
Giner Alor-Hernández	Instituto Tecnológico de Orizaba, Mexico
José Luis Ochoa	Universidad de Sonora, México
Ana Muñoz	Universidad de Los Andes, Venezuela
Miguel Ángel Rodríguez-García	Universidad Rey Juan Carlos, Spain
Lucía Serrano-Luján	Universidad Rey Juan Carlos, Spain
Eugenio Martínez-Cámara	Universidad de Granada, Spain
Gema Alcaraz-Mármol	Universidad de Castilla la Mancha, Spain

Mario Hernández Hernández	Universidad Autónoma de Guerrero, Mexico
Severino Feliciano Morales	Universidad Autónoma de Guerrero, Mexico
Guido Sciavicco	University of Ferrara, Italy
José Aguilar	Universidad de los Andes, Venezuela
Ángel García Pedrero	Universidad Politécnica de Madrid, Spain
Miguel Vargas-Lombardo	Universidad Tecnologica de Panama, Panama
Denis Cedeño Moreno	Universidad Tecnologica de Panama, Panama
Viviana Yarel Rosales Morales	Instituto Tecnologico de Orizaba, Mexico
José Javier Samper-Zapater	Universidad de Valencia, Spain
Claudia Victoria Isaza Narvaez	Universidad de Antioquia, Colombia
Raquel Vasquez Ramirez	Instituto Tecnologico de Orizaba, Mexico
Janio Jadán Guerrero	Universidad Indoamérica, Ecuador
Bernardo Cánovas-Segura	Universidad de Murcia, Spain
Noa Patricia Cruz Díaz	Hospital Universitario Virgen del Rocio, Spain

Local Organizing Committee

Katty Lagos Ortiz (General Coordinator)	Universidad Agraria del Ecuador, Ecuador
Andrea Sinche Guzmán	Universidad Agraria del Ecuador, Ecuador
Vanessa Vergara Lozano	Universidad Agraria del Ecuador, Ecuador
Karina Real Avilés	Universidad Agraria del Ecuador, Ecuador
Mayra Garzón Goya	Universidad Agraria del Ecuador, Ecuador
Evelyn Solis	Universidad Agraria del Ecuador, Ecuador
Raquel Gómez Chabla	Universidad Agraria del Ecuador, Ecuador
María Pilar Avilés	Universidad Agraria del Ecuador, Ecuador
Maritza Aguirre Munizaga	Universidad Agraria del Ecuador, Ecuador
Mariuxi Tejada Castro	Universidad Agraria del Ecuador, Ecuador
Carlota Delgado Vera	Universidad Agraria del Ecuador, Ecuador
Elke Yerovi Ricaurte	Universidad Agraria del Ecuador, Ecuador
Karen Mite Baidal	Universidad Agraria del Ecuador, Ecuador
Jorge Hidalgo Larrea	Universidad Agraria del Ecuador, Ecuador
José Salavarria	Universidad Agraria del Ecuador, Ecuador
Wilson Molina Oleas	Universidad Agraria del Ecuador, Ecuador
Ana Herrera	Universidad Agraria del Ecuador, Ecuador
Johana Ramos	Universidad Agraria del Ecuador, Ecuador
Mitchell Vásquez Bermúdez	Universidad Agraria del Ecuador, Ecuador
Roberto Cabezas Cabezas	Universidad Agraria del Ecuador, Ecuador
Mario Cardenas	Universidad Agraria del Ecuador, Ecuador
Edgar Zuña	Universidad Agraria del Ecuador, Ecuador

Sponsoring Institutions

http://www.uagraria.edu.ec/

http://www.springer.com/series/7899

Contents

Intelligent and Knowledge-Based Systems

E-learning

ICT in Agronomy

An Ontology-Based Decision Support System for Insect Pest Control in Crops

Katty Lagos-Ortiz[1]([⊠]) [iD], José Medina-Moreira[1,2] [iD],
César Morán-Castro[1], Carlos Campuzano[1],
and Rafael Valencia-García[3] [iD]

[1] Facultad de Ciencias Agrarias, Universidad Agraria del Ecuador,
Av. 25 de Julio, Guayaquil, Ecuador
{klagos, jmedina, cmoran}@uagraria.edu.ec,
carloscampozano92@gmail.com
[2] Facultad de Ciencias Matemáticas y Físicas,
Universidad de Guayaquil, Cdla, Universitaria Salvador Allende,
Guayaquil, Ecuador
jose.medimamo@ug.edu.ec
[3] Facultad de Informática, Universidad de Murcia,
Campus Espinardo, 30100 Murcia, Spain
valencia@um.es

Abstract. Agriculture provides most of the world's food that helps to sustain and enhance human life. Diseases infections and insect pest in crops cause considerable economic losses. Diagnosing or defining the type of insect pest or disease that affects the crop is not an easy task for farmers, even more, when the diversity of insects and diseases is quite numerous. There is a need for tools focused on the knowledge management of experts capable of providing guidelines for the diagnosis and prevention of insect pests. This work presents an ontology-based decision support system for insect pest control in sugarcane, rice, soya, and cacao crops. This system takes advantage of Semantic Web technologies to represent the experts' knowledge as well as to apply semantic reasoning to diagnose the insect pest that affects the crop. This system was evaluated to measure its efficacy regarding the diagnosis of the insect pest that affects a crop obtaining encouraging results.

Keywords: Agriculture · Plague · Insect · Prevention · Ontology

1 Introduction

Agriculture provides most of the world's food that helps to sustain and enhance human life. Nowadays, agricultural expansion has allowed the growth of agricultural land [1], which in turn causes an increase in the cultivation of food products. In this area, diseases infections and insect pest in crops can occur, thus causing considerable economic losses [2]. Furthermore, the growth of agricultural lands and the biodiversity decline affect the control of natural enemies [3]. Diagnosing or defining the type of insect pest or disease that affects the crop is not an easy task for farmers, even more,

© Springer Nature Switzerland AG 2018
R. Valencia-García et al. (Eds.): CITI 2018, CCIS 883, pp. 3–14, 2018.
https://doi.org/10.1007/978-3-030-00940-3_1

when the diversity of insects and diseases is quite numerous. Hence, farmers have developed homemade strategies that help them manage and control diseases that affect crops [4].

Many of the damages caused by insects or diseases to the crop are visible to the farmer. Therefore, experienced farmers can diagnose the disease or identify the insect pest that affects the crop and carry out control actions to recover the crop. However, sometimes the disease or plague is so widespread that it causes the loss of the crop. In this sense, it is important that farmers have a wide knowledge and experience on insect pest domain in order to correctly identify that one that affects their crop and perform the correct actions that help them control the pest. The correct identification of an insect pest requires knowledge and experience of professionals or experts in insect pest control since sometimes it is not enough to identify the symptoms of the crop, but also it is necessary to examine the area where the pest was found or to have a sample of it. Furthermore, incorrect pest identification causes considerable time and economic losses.

Agricultural entomology is a multidisciplinary research area that, among other things, studies insect pests. Insects are the most important component of macroscopic biodiversity [5]. There is a great diversity of insects whose impact on the environment can be very significant. Because of this fact, it is necessary that agricultural entomology be integrated into crop monitoring systems to help farmers to make decisions regarding the control, prevention, and management of insect pests. There is a need for tools focused on the knowledge management of experts capable of providing guidelines for the diagnosis and prevention of insect pests, that is, tools that allow addressing unstructured problems [6].

The semantic web has emerged as a new approach which main goal is to provide to Web information with a well-defined meaning and make it understandable not only by humans but also by computers [7]. Thanks to this, computers can automate, integrate and reuse high-quality information from distributed information sources. Ontologies are considered one of the pillars of the Semantic Web. An ontology is a formal and explicit specification of a shared conceptualization [8]. Ontologies aim to turn the web into a self-navigable and self-understood space where searches for information provide results adapted to the desired requirements [9]. Ontologies have been successfully used in domains such as biological sciences [10], biomedicine [11], dietetics and health [12], and plant diseases management [13], among others.

Considering the above-discussed facts, there is a need for tools that provide farmers with recommendations for effectively perform the monitoring of crops and control of insect pest that affect crops, based on experts' knowledge from agricultural entomology. This work presents an ontology-based decision support system for insect pest control in sugarcane, rice, soya, and cacao crops. This system uses ontologies to model the agricultural entomology domain through concepts and properties related to crops, insect pests, and control. This ontology is based knowledge of professionals with a wide experience in insect pests control. The proposed system diagnoses the insect pest affecting the crop based on a set of symptoms provided by farmers. Once the insect pest is diagnosed, the system also provides recommendations for insect pest control. To perform these processes, the system uses a semantic repository and a rule-based inference engine.

The remainder of this paper is structured as follows: Sect. 2 discusses a set of decision support system used in different domains. Then, Sect. 3 details the components of the decision-support system proposed in this work, whereas Sect. 4 addresses the evaluation performed to test the effectiveness of our proposal regarding diagnosis of insect pest. Finally, Sect. 5 discusses the research conclusions and future directions.

2   Related Works

Decision support or support systems (DSS) are computerized information systems that present several alternative solutions to specific problems [14]. The features of DSS are more striking than their definitions [15]. DSSs have been adopted in domains such as medicine. For instance, in [16], the authors proposed a DSS focused on diagnoses process, patient care, therapeutic plans, among others. This system uses a rule-based engine to infer recommendations based on patient's symptoms provided the doctor. In [17], the authors proposed a hybrid DSS that interprets the result of a quantitative simulation model and expert systems to generate recommendations in the agricultural area. This system is composed of four main modules, namely: user interface, simulation models, explanation module, and user model. These modules allow collecting users questions, analyze them and generates individualized explanations necessary to make a more informed decision. Antonopoulou et. al. [18] presented a DSS for agriculture domain based on Web and mobile technologies. This system helps farmers to select alternative crops to increase economic incomes. This system is composed of modules focused on needs of collaboration, information management, crops marketing, simulation and forecasting models, pest control, and crop selection. The architecture of this system allows adding new modules that incorporate functionalities focused on addressing users' needs. On the other hand, Weed Manager [19] is a DSS that allows farmers to control weeds on wheat crops at different seasons. This system is based on heuristic decision models and stochastic dynamic programming. Also, it contains a database of herbicides information used in wheat crops. Weed Manager implements a planning tool for investigating weed control strategies and a rotating planning tool to consider future options. Finally, in [20], the authors proposed an ontology of insects that describes concepts such as morphology, taxonomy, physiology, biology, ecology, entomology, toxicology, and pathology of insects, among others. This ontology allows identifying an insect based on its characteristics as well as diagnosing the disease caused by it, based on a set of symptoms.

The aforementioned literature presented research efforts in the areas of weed control and crop diseases management that contribute to the improvement of different agricultural processes. However, there are no reports of any DSS that allows identifying the insect pest that affects a crop, as well as for providing recommendations for disease control and treatment. This work presents a DSS for insect pest diagnosing in sugarcane, rice, soya, and cacao crops, based on domain knowledge modeled by means of an ontology that is constantly updated by experts in entomology. This system aims to help farmers control diseases caused by insect pest through the provision of recommendations for controlling and treatment of the disease. In the following section, we thoroughly explain and describe the components of our proposal and their interactions.

3 Ontology-Based Decision Support System

Sometimes, diagnosing the insect pest that affects a crop can be easily performed by farmers. Many other times, however, it is required the participation of experienced professionals for a successful diagnosis. Insects can attack several crops and present different symptoms, which could lead to an erroneous diagnosis, and consequently, the use of an incorrect treatment. An incorrect diagnosis can cause considerable economic losses thus making necessary to establish a new strategy for crops management. Due to the proliferation of new insect pest and diseases, it is necessary to improve traditional methods of crops management and disease control and treatment by integrating current technologies supported by experts' knowledge of insect pest control and treatment, including the handling of pesticides. Moreover, the accelerated process of changes occurring in agriculture presupposed a reorientation of current methodologies used for the management and control of agricultural pests.

The DSS presented in this work aims to help farmers diagnose the correct insect pest that affects a crop, to perform the right control actions that avoid the spread of the disease guided by a set of recommendations provided by it. The architecture of system here proposed (see Fig. 1) is composed of three core modules: the ontology of the agricultural entomology domain, a rule-based engine, and a semantic indexing module. In the following sections, we thoroughly explain and describe the components of our proposal.

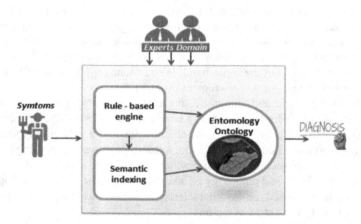

Fig. 1. Architecture of the DSS for insect pest control in crops.

In a nutshell, the DSS here proposed works as follows. First of all, farmer collects a set of symptoms that he/she perceives in the crop and provides this information as input to the DSS. Secondly, the system diagnoses the insect pest based on the data provided. To this end, the system uses a rule-based engine that relies on an ontology that models the agricultural entomology domain. Once the diagnosis process has concluded, the system recommends a set of documents containing insect pest control strategies. These documents are indexed by using semantic technologies in order to retrieve documents with semantically similar terms in an accurate, quick and efficient way. Finally, the system present results to farmers so they can make a more informed decision about insect pest control in sugarcane, rice, soya, and cacao crops. The following sections thoroughly describe the functions of the ontology of the agricultural entomology and the rule-based engine.

3.1 Agricultural Entomology Ontology

Experts' knowledge of insect pest control and treatment, including the handling of pesticides, is required by our proposal to diagnose the insect pest that affects a crop as well as to provide recommendations to control the diagnosed insect pest. In this sense, our proposal uses an ontology that models agricultural entomology domain, specifically, the domain of insect pests in sugarcane, rice, soybeans, and cocoa crops, as well as chemical substances used in crop management. The agricultural entomology ontology was implemented by using the OWL 2 Web Ontology Language [21] and Protégé [22], an open-source editor and framework for building both simple and complex ontology-based applications.

When an ontology models a specific domain, it is known as domain ontology i.e., a conceptualization of a particular domain [20]. This kind of ontology represents a data dictionary with definitions of domain concepts and their relationships. The ontology here proposed belongs to this group i.e., it models the domain of agricultural entomology through concepts related to insect pests control and chemical substances used in crop diseases control and management. The design of this ontology is intended to be reusable. In other words, this ontology aims that the knowledge modeled by it can be shared and reused by other organizations and researchers.

The design and development process of the agricultural entomology ontology is described below.

- First, the scope of the agricultural entomology ontology was defined in conjunction with entomologists. This ontology defines a classification of insects that affect sugarcane, rice, soya, and cacao crops, as well as a classification of chemical substances used in crop diseases control and management. Also, this ontology defines the relationships among diseases, symptoms, insects, and chemical substances.
- The ontology proposed in this work considered already available ontologies. Specifically, it considers the ontologies designed by the Plant Disease Ontology [23]. These ontologies provide a controlled vocabulary for plant's morphological and anatomical structures. Also, it considered the GENIA ontology [24] which covers biological continuants. Finally, it considered already available insects taxonomies.
- We describe all concepts and properties defined by the ontology proposed in this work. Also, we defined the relationships among crop diseases and their symptoms. Finally, we defined the chemical substances that are used for the control of insect pests in sugarcane, rice, soya, and cacao crops.

- Finally, we defined, in conjunction with experts in agricultural entomology domain, the classes and their hierarchies, properties, entities, as well as the relationships among them. Entities were defined in accordance with their order levels, family, and species. In this task, we put special attention to the fact that several crops can be affected by the same insect pests and can present different symptoms.

Figure 2 shows an excerpt of the ontology for the agricultural entomology domain here proposed. As was mentioned, it defines next concepts: (1) a classification of insects that affect sugarcane, rice, soya, and cacao crops; (2) a classification of chemical substances used in crop management; (3) a classification of crops; (4) a classification of diseases, symptoms, treatments and recommendations for crops control and management. Next sections describe the main classes and object properties of the ontology proposed in this work.

Fig. 2. An excerpt of the ontology for agricultural entomology domain.

Classes

The phytopathology ontology defines six main classes, namely: Insect, Crop, Chemical substance, Symptom, Recommendation, and Treatment. These classes are described below.

- Insect. It defines a taxonomy of insects that affect sugarcane, rice, soya, and cacao crops.
- Crop. This class defines a taxonomy of crops. For the purpose of this work, only sugarcane, rice, soya, and cacao crops were considered.
- Chemical substance. It defines a taxonomy of chemical substances used in crop diseases control and management.
- Symptom. It collects symptoms that crops (sugarcane, rice, soya, and cacao) present when are affected by an insect pest.
- Recommendation. It collects a wide set of recommendations for insect pests controlling. These recommendations were defined by domain experts.
- Treatment. It collects treatments for crop diseases caused by an insect pest. A treatment describes how to treat the crop in terms of doses and periodicity of medication.

In this ontology, the chemical substance, recommendation, and treatment classes were defined as disjoint classes i.e. an individual cannot be an instance of more than one of these classes. As mentioned earlier, this ontology has been designed for specific crops (sugarcane, rice, soya, and cacao crops), however, with the help of entomologists and other domain experts, it could be extended in order to integrate and add more crops, insects, diseases, symptoms, treatments, and recommendations.

Properties

Our ontology establishes a set of properties that allow the system to diagnose the insect pest that affects a crop based on the symptoms provided by farmers. These properties are described below.

- isSymptomOf. This property is used to indicate the symptoms of a crop disease caused by an insect pest. For instance, the symptom "wrinkled leaves caused by lack of hydration" is presented in crops that are affected by the "phyllophagous spp" insect.
- isCausedBy. This property is used to relate a symptom presented in crops with the insect that causes it. For instance, the symptom "reduction of the sap in leaves" is caused by the attack of the "bemisia tabaci" insect.
- hasTreatment. This relation is used to indicate the treatment that might be followed by the user to deal with the crop disease caused by an insect pest. As was mentioned, a treatment establishes how to treat the crop in terms of doses and periodicity of medication.

The ontology also specifies some inverse object properties such as hasSymptom for the object property isSymptomOf, CauseOf for the object property isCausedBy, or the property isTreatment which is the inverse of hasTreatment. For example, this means that the "burns in the underside of leaves" symptom is caused by the "diatraea saccharalis" insect, and that the "diatraea saccharalis" insect causes the "burns in the underside of leaves" symptom. Finally, it should be mentioned that the Insect class plays the most crucial role in this ontology since most object properties are associated to it i.e. this class is present in most of domains and ranges of the properties.

3.2 Rule-Based Engine

Aiming to establish the set of rules used by our proposal to diagnose the insect pest that affects a crop, a group of experts in agricultural entomology was interviewed concerning different aspects of crop diseases caused by insect pests that have a greater economic impact in the Costa region of Ecuador. Among the topics that were cover during interviews are the type of crops in the region, crop diseases caused by insect pests, symptoms of crop diseases, chemical substances used in crop diseases control and management, doses and periodicity of medication, recommendations for crop management, among others. Finally, experts were asked to provide a set of treatments and recommendations for the control and management of insect pests in crops from the Costa region of Ecuador.

Once the interviews were performed, the group of experts in agricultural entomology was asked to establish a set of conditions considering the knowledge described by the ontology proposed in this work. These conditions concern relations between the symptoms presented in crops affected by an insect pest and the insect that causes them, as well as the treatments that could be followed by the farmer, including the doses and periodicity of medication.

The set of conditions established by experts allows relating a symptom with the insect that cause it. However, to provide better results, the experts were also asked to rank each symptom according to the insect. This rank helps to deal with the problem arising from the fact that two or more insect pests can share symptoms. For instance, Table 1 presents the symptoms caused by the "Metamasius hemipterus" and "Diatraea saccharalis" insects. As can be observed, these insects share the "Accumulation of sawdust on holes in galleries" symptom. However, when farmers provided this symptom, our proposal will select the "Metamasius hemipterus" insect because the symptom above mentioned has a higher priority.

Table 1. Crop diseases' symptoms ranking example.

Rank	Metamasius hemipterus	Diatraea saccharalis
1	Accumulation of sawdust on holes in galleries	Apical bud death
2	Infected leaves become yellowish	Weight-losing
3	Many larvae invade plant roots	Accumulation of sawdust on holes in galleries
4	Dead sprouts	Juice quality reduction

Once the set of conditions were established by experts, we developed a set of rules based on such information. These rules were defined by using SWRL [25], a proposed language for the Semantic Web that can be used to express rules as well as logic. This set of rules drives the reasoning process, i.e. these rules are used by our proposal to diagnose the insect pest that affects a crop based on the symptoms provided by farmers. These rules follow the format presented in Eq. 1:

$$R_1, R_2, \ldots, R_n \to D \tag{1}$$

Where D is the resulting action when the conditions are fulfilled and Ri, R2, ..., Rn are atomic formulas depicting conditions. When the farmer provides the symptoms presented in the crops, the rule-based engine diagnoses the insect pest that affect it based on the rules established. It must be noted that different rules may be applied to the given symptoms. However, the rank assigned to the symptoms are considered for the final diagnoses. Once the insect pest is diagnosed, the system provides farmer treatments and recommendations for insect pest control and management. This information is obtained based on the properties (isTreatmentOf and isRecommendationOf) defined by the ontology for agricultural entomology domain proposed in this work. In addition to treatments and recommendations provided by the system, our proposal also provides farmers with a set of agricultural entomology documents related to the insect pest diagnosed by the system. The faculty of agricultural sciences of the UAE (Universidad Agraria del Ecuador) provides most of these documents. Also, this document database is continuously updated with recent research works.

4   Evaluation and Results

This section presents the evaluation performed aiming to measure the effectiveness of our proposal in terms of diagnosis of the insect pest that affect a crop. For this purpose, a group consisting of 10 farmers from the Costa region of Ecuador was involved. These farmers were selected because they have sugarcane, rice, soya, and cacao crops. Each farmer taking part in the evaluation process provided different sets of symptoms related to 10 crop diseases caused by insect pests. Sugarcane, rice, soya, and cacao crops were considered in this process. The evaluation process was divided into next phases:

1. Farmers involved in this process provided a set of symptoms that they perceived in their crop when an insect pest affect it. A total of 100 sets of symptoms were collected (10 per farmer).
2. The sets of symptoms collected were provided as input to the DSS.
3. The DSS made a diagnosis for each set of symptoms provided.
4. The insect pest diagnosed by the DSS was compared to the insect pest previously known.
5. Finally, the results were evaluated using the precision, recall [25], and F-measure [26] metrics, where true positives (TP) are the sets of symptoms that were correctly related with a given insect pest i.e. those cases that were correctly diagnosed. False positives (FP) are the sets of symptoms that were incorrectly related to a given crop disease. Finally, false negatives (FN) are the sets of symptoms that were related to a disease other than the correct one.

Evaluation results concerning the diagnosis of the insect pest that affects a crop are presented in Table 2. The evaluation results demonstrate a good efficiency of the DSS concerning the diagnosis of the insect pests that affect a crop. As can be observed in Table 2 there is no a big difference between the scores obtained for each insect. The DSS got an average precision score of 0.78641, an average recall score of 0.7163, and an average F-measure score of 0.77762. The insect with the highest precision was the Diatraea saccharalis, which is present in sugarcane crops, with a score of 0.88000. Meanwhile, the crop disease with worst precision (0.6666) was the Phyllophaga spp, which is present in rice crops.

Table 2. Evaluation results.

Insect	TP	FP	FN	Precision	Recall	F-measure
Sipha flava	18	7	6	0.72000	0.75000	0.73469
Phyllophaga spp	20	8	5	0.71429	0.80000	0.75472
Pseudoplusia includens	19	4	5	0.82609	0.79167	0.80851
Epitrix spp	19	5	7	0.79167	0.73077	0.76000
Diatraea saccharalis	22	3	6	0.88000	0.78571	0.83019
Avg.				0.78641	0.77163	0.77762

5   Conclusions and Future Work

This work presented a DSS that diagnoses the insect pest that affects a crop based on a set of symptoms provided by the farmer. This system takes advantage of Semantic Web technologies to represent the experts' knowledge as well as to apply semantic reasoning to diagnose the insect pest. Our proposal aims to make this kind of systems accessible for farmers so they can perform the correct actions to control the disease and avoid a reduction in agricultural profitability. Our proposal obtained encouraging results with an F-measure of 0.77762 for the diagnosis of insect pests that affects sugarcane, rice, soya, and cacao crops. The main contribution of this work is twofold. First, the design of an ontology for describing crop diseases, their symptoms, the insects that cause them, as well as treatments and recommendations for the control and management of crop diseases. Second, a set of rules that allows diagnosing the insect pest that affects a crop based on a set of symptoms provided by the farmer.

As future work, we plan to design and develop a Web and mobile applications that allow experts to feed the rule-based engine with new rules focused on the diagnosis of insect pests that affect crops different to the considered in this work. In this sense, we also plan to implement a collaborative environment where experts can farmers can collaborate to solve problems, drawing on their different kinds of knowledge. Finally, we plan to integrate image processing technologies that help our system to automatically detect symptoms in crops.

References

1. Macé, K., Morlon, P., Munier-Jolain, N., Quéré, L.: Time scales as a factor in decision-making by French farmers on weed management in annual crops. Agric. Syst. **93**, 115–142 (2007). https://doi.org/10.1016/J.AGSY.2006.04.007
2. Tripathy, A.K., Adinarayana, J., Sudharsan, D., et al.: Data mining and wireless sensor network for agriculture pest/disease predictions. In: 2011 World Congress on Information and Communication Technologies, pp. 1229–1234. IEEE (2011)
3. Bianchi, F.J.J.A., Booij, C.J.H., Tscharntke, T.: Sustainable pest regulation in agricultural landscapes: a review on landscape composition, biodiversity and natural pest control. Proc. Biol. Sci. **273**, 1715–1727 (2006). https://doi.org/10.1098/rspb.2006.3530
4. Mueller, U.G., Gerardo, N.M., Aanen, D.K., et al.: The evolution of agriculture in insects. Annu. Rev. Ecol. Evol. Syst. **36**, 563–595 (2005). https://doi.org/10.1146/annurev.ecolsys.36.102003.152626
5. Gullan, P.J., Cranston, P.S.: The Insects: An Outline of Entomology. Wiley, Hoboken (2014)
6. Coulson, R.N., Saunders, M.C.: Computer-assisted decision-making as applied to entomology. Annu. Rev. Entomol. **32**, 415–437 (1987). https://doi.org/10.1146/annurev.en.32.010187.002215
7. Shadbolt, N., Berners-Lee, T., Hall, W.: The semantic web revisited. IEEE Intell. Syst. **21**, 96–101 (2006). https://doi.org/10.1109/MIS.2006.62
8. Gruber, T.: What is An Ontology?. Springer, Berlin (1993)
9. Hoehndorf, R., Schofield, P.N., Gkoutos, G.V.: The role of ontologies in biological and biomedical research: a functional perspective. Brief. Bioinform. **16**, 1069–1080 (2015). https://doi.org/10.1093/bib/bbv011
10. Ashburner, M., Ball, C.A., Blake, J.A., et al.: Gene ontology: tool for the unification of biology. Nat. Genet. **25**, 25–29 (2000). https://doi.org/10.1038/75556
11. Ruiz-Martínez, J.M., Valencia-García, R., Martínez-Béjar, R., Hoffmann, A.: BioOntoVerb: a top level ontology based framework to populate biomedical ontologies from texts. Knowl. Based Syst. **36**, 68–80 (2012). https://doi.org/10.1016/J.KNOSYS.2012.06.002
12. Lange, M.C., Lemay, D.G., German, J.B.: A multi-ontology framework to guide agriculture and food towards diet and health. J. Sci. Food Agric. **87**, 1427–1434 (2007). https://doi.org/10.1002/jsfa.2832
13. Lagos-Ortíz, K., Medina-Moreira, J., Paredes-Valverde, M.A., Valencia-García, R.: An ontology-based decision support system for the diagnosis of plant diseases. J. Inf. Technol. Res. **10**, 2–3 (2017)
14. Power, D.J., Sharda, R., Burstein, F.: Decision support systems. In: Wiley Encyclopedia of Management, pp. 1–4. Wiley, Chichester (2015)
15. Sprague, R.H.: A framework for the development of decision support systems. Source MIS Q **4**, 1–26 (1980)
16. Silva Layes, M.E., Falappa, M.A., Simari, G.R.: Sistemas de soporte a las decisiones clínicas (2011)
17. Greer, J.E., Falk, S., Greer, K.J., Bentham, M.J.: Explaining and justifying recommendations in an agriculture decision support system. Comput. Electron. Agric. **11**, 195–214 (1994). https://doi.org/10.1016/0168-1699(94)90008-6
18. Antonopoulou, E., Karetsos, S.T., Maliappis, M., Sideridis, A.B.: Web and mobile technologies in a prototype DSS for major field crops. Comput. Electron. Agric. **70**, 292–301 (2010). https://doi.org/10.1016/j.compag.2009.07.024

19. Parsons, D.J., Benjamin, L.R., Clarke, J., et al.: Weed manager—a model-based decision support system for weed management in arable crops. Comput. Electron. Agric. **65**, 155–167 (2009). https://doi.org/10.1016/J.COMPAG.2008.08.007
20. Wu, M., Zhao, H.: Study on the ontology for entomology identification expert system. In: 2009 First International Conference on Information Science Engineering, pp. 2406–2409. IEEE (2009)
21. Mankovskii, S., Gogolla, M., Urban, S.D., et al.: OWL: web ontology language. In: Encyclopedia of Database Systems, pp. 2008–2009. Springer, Boston (2009)
22. Noy, N.F., Crubézy, M., Fergerson, R.W., et al.: Protégé-2000: an open-source ontology-development and knowledge-acquisition environment. AMIA 2003 Open Source Expo (2003)
23. Plant Ontology Consortium: The plant ontology consortium and plant ontologies. Comp. Funct. Genomics **3**, 137–142 (2002). https://doi.org/10.1002/cfg.154
24. Bennett, B., Fellbaum, C., Hahn, U., et al.: From GENIA to BIOTOP Towards a Top-Level Ontology for Biology. IOS Press, Amsterdam (2006)
25. Clarke, S.J., Willett, P.: Estimating the recall performance of web search engines. Aslib Proc. **49**, 184–189 (1997). https://doi.org/10.1108/eb051463
26. Yang, Y., Liu, X.: A re-examination of text categorization methods. In: Proceedings of the 22nd Annual International ACM SIGIR Conference on Research and Development in Information – SIGIR 1999, pp. 42–49. ACM Press, New York (1999)
27. Montoya, J.U.: Sistema inteligente para el control de plagas en cultivos. Rev. Electrón. Fac. Ing. **3**, 28–34 (2016)

Use of Technologies of Image Recognition in Agriculture: Systematic Review of Literature

Carlota Delgado-Vera[1]([✉]) [iD], Karen Mite-Baidal[1] [iD],
Raquel Gomez-Chabla[1] [iD], Evelyn Solís-Avilés[1],
Sergio Merchán-Benavides[2] [iD], and Ana Rodríguez[1] [iD]

[1] Engineering School of Computation and Informatics,
Faculty of Agricultural Science, Universidad Agraria del Ecuador,
Av. 25 de Julio y Pio Jaramillo, P.O. BOX 09-04-100, Guayaquil, Ecuador
{cdelgado,kmite,rgomez,esolis,
arodriguez}@uagraria.edu.ec
[2] Engineering School of Agronomy, Faculty of Agricultural Science,
Universidad Agraria del Ecuador,
Av. 25 de Julio y Pio Jaramillo, P.O. BOX 09-04-100, Guayaquil, Ecuador
smerchan@uagraria.edu.ec

Abstract. In the last decades, the mechanization of productive processes has focused on replacing the tasks performed by people with machines. However nowadays, the integration of software, robots and artificial intelligence point to the automation in agriculture. This is of great importance for the increase of productivity and the economic growth of the country solving in this way the lack of workforce and its associated high costs, offering great benefits to population. Currently, researchers are developing numerous fruit and vegetable classification algorithms, of which essential parameter is color; that allows the detection of nutrient deficiencies, diagnosis of diseases and fruit quality; the same ones that have proven to be accurate and require less time compared to traditional methods. The aim of this article is to provide a systematic review of classifying techniques through machine learning, its components and the utility for the agronomist.

Keywords: Image recognition · Computer vision · Fuzzy ruler
Neural networks

1 Introduction

Digital image processing is a widely used tool in the automation of industrial processes [1, 2], medicine [3, 4], in fish farming [5] for fish recognition, agriculture [6, 7], among other areas due to its reliability, efficiency and speed of processing; with this tool, precision is achieved in agriculture, providing many benefits on real data in different areas of the agricultural field, of which objective is the increase of production and crop management. Accordingly, it is necessary to work with remote sensing tools and systems of agriculture with which the analysis of areas with various agronomic factors-

© Springer Nature Switzerland AG 2018
R. Valencia-García et al. (Eds.): CITI 2018, CCIS 883, pp. 15–29, 2018.
https://doi.org/10.1007/978-3-030-00940-3_2

that are observed in images taken by an unmanned aerial vehicle-is made [8] to obtain a subsequent processing, organizing the visualization and information of the blemishes in the area. Agriculture is aimed at increasing the productivity and quality of food with a reduced cost and with a greater benefit, which recently has received great importance. One of the vital components of the crop is the management in the precise diagnosis and the timely solution of the problem in the field. Diagnosis is a very difficult task to perform manually, since it is a function of a series of parameters such as environment, nutrients, organisms, etc. With the recent advance in the processing of images and recognition of patterns and techniques, classification of crop diseases is possible. Image processing techniques in which semantic information is extracted from images can improve agricultural practices, with higher process precision and consistency while reducing manual monitoring by farmers. It often offers flexibility and effectively replaces farmers' decision-making based on visual stimuli.

This review presents field-based studies and/or laboratory experiments that consisting on the use of applications or computer systems that involve the techniques and/or methods used in image processing. They involve five basic processes acquisition of images, preprocessing, segmentation, object detection and classification. All are relevant in precision agriculture. These data sets can use image processing techniques as a way to help provide high resolution images to be used for decision making.

2 Revisión Sistemática de las Tecnologías de Reconocimiento de Imágenes

From the review of research and projects related to agriculture and computer tools, references have been obtained of the use that can be given to techniques that incorporate the use of technologies towards precision agriculture. In this section, we provide an overview of the steps involved in the process.

2.1 Formalization of Questions

The utility provided by this type of technology in the agricultural field was obtained by the by means of the following question:

How are image recognition technologies used in precisión agriculture?

In this work "technology" is considered as those methods of auto-learning or machine learning within the field of Artificial Intelligence and which have been implemented in research laboratories for the analysis or processing of images of agricultural products, according to the texture, shape, color, size, among others, detecting some pathological disease of the leaf, stem, fruit or vegetable, lack of nutrients, quality, etc. The list of keywords used to discover and responding to the research consisted of: techniques, image processing, methods, machine vision based automatic, artificial neural networks, fuzzy classifier. Additional questions to complement this research, and thus obtain information of great interest, are detailed below: What are the techniques/methods that are used for the processing of images in fruits and vegetables? What are the stages that are realized to obtain image processing? What are the parameters that models need in image recognition? in which area of agriculture are image processing techniques used?

2.2   Selection of Sources

The list of keywords shown in the previous section was combined using the logical connectors "OR" and "AND", to obtain the main search. The search string had the structure P1 and P2 and P3, each part is defined in Table 1 below:

Table 1. Search string and source

Source	Specific search string	Extra options included
Science Direct	Date > 2013 and ((technique or methods) and ("image recognition" or "automatic learning" or "algorithms for image recognition") and "Machine Vision Based Automatic" OR "fuzzy classifier" OR "Artificial Neural Network"))	Computers and electronics in agriculture
IEEE CS	((technique or methods) and ("image recognition" or "automatic learning" or "algorithms for image recognition") and "Machine Vision Based Automatic" OR "fuzzy classifier" OR "Artificial Neural Network"))	Fruits and vegetables
Elsevier	((technique or methods) and ("image recognition" or "automatic learning" or "algorithms for image recognition") and "Machine Vision Based Automatic" OR "fuzzy classifier" OR "Artificial Neural Network"))	Fruits and vegetables
Springer	((technique or methods) and ("image recognition" or "automatic learning" or "algorithms for image recognition") and "Machine Vision Based Automatic" OR "fuzzy classifier" OR "Artificial Neural Network"))	Fruits and vegetables

P1: methods OR techniques in image processing in fruits and vegetables.
P2: stages AND parameters AND components for image recognition.
P3: Machine Vision Based Automatic OR fuzzy classifier OR Artificial Neural Network.

Our research together with this involved finding a large amount of non-useful documents although the maximum number of articles was obtained. However, in line with the research question, the inclusion and exclusion criteria that were designed to obtain only useful works were used as follows: with P1, we aim to obtain all those works related to techniques, algorithms and methods; with P2 and P3 works related to the parameters, stages or components that should be considered when carrying out an image or recognition treatment and in what stages in the cultivation of plants this type of technology is used. Finally, the main sources in the list of initial sources are presented, in which a systematic review will be executed: EL SEVIER, IEEE digital library, Science @ Direct, Springer, Google Scholar, Journal and Conferences International of Engineering and Technology, of Agricultural and Biological Engineering. The combination of these search terms resulted in a collection of publications that provided a first approximation to our research question and allowed us to obtain a primary list of potentially relevant studies; these results had to be filtered to extract those initiatives that had met the conditions of revision with precision. These proposals were reduced through the definition of a set of inclusion and exclusion criteria, which had to be objective in order to reduce the biased results and guarantee the respectability of the review process as shown in Table 2. The subject is a very recent and changing research area, and therefore, the time scope is restricted to the last five years. New initiatives were included considering all proposals published after 2008. Due to language limitations, only studies written in English in this review were considered. An objective criterion was established by relying on an accepted method disseminated by USDA or FAO.

Table 2. Summary of number of studies

Type of model	# of studies
Artificial Vision System (SMV)	10
Artificial Neural Networks (ANN)	11
Fuzzy classifier and function-based rules	10
Others	5
Total	36

In most cases the criteria or guidelines that were used to reduce the initiatives obtained by the first search was to contrast the title and the summary or executive summary with the proposed criteria to decide whether to include or exclude the proposal. However, in case of doubt it was necessary in some cases to analyze the entire text to make an adequate decision.

The quality evaluation of the selection of publications was carried out in the multistage process mentioned above. As stated above, the systematic review was made iteratively, which means that the results were analyzed after each cycle to confirm if we were heading in the right direction.

3   Extraction of Information

There are currently many tools and applications that include techniques and analysis algorithms for the processing/recognition of images linked to high precision agriculture. These techniques include terrestrial/aerial remote sensing which, by capturing images using thermal, hyper spectral, photometric (RGB) cameras [9, 10], among others, are processed and analyzed to solve problems in the following areas of agriculture: crop management; identification of nutrient deficiencies and plant content; inspection, evaluation and classification of the quality of fruits; crop and land estimation [11].

For the processing and analysis of images Zhang et al. [12] establish levels: the low level (basic), which involves the acquisition of images and the image preprocessing; the intermediate level, which is the processing and analysis of images, involving the segmentation of images, extraction of characteristics, representation and description; the high level, which is the key step of the image analysis, implies recognition, and interpretation and classification. It is show in Fig. 1.

To do this, some of the automated learning approaches (machine learning) are used, which are detailed below:

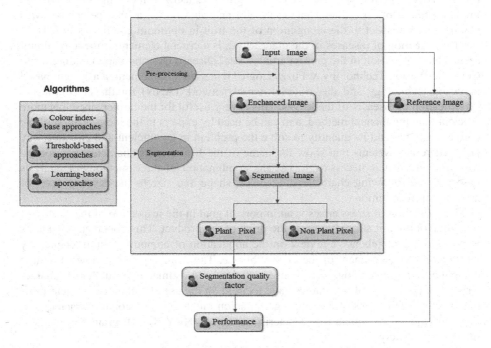

Fig. 1. Processing levels for image recognition

3.1 Artificial Vision System

The applications of computer vision allow to acquire, analyze and process images in order to produce information that is treated by the computer, which uses reliable methods for that. Due to this advantage it is accepted by the agricultural and food industries. At the agricultural level, they aim to estimate one or several characteristics of the product of interest-fruits and vegetables-at a particular time and relate them to quality, which is normally associated with maturity, absence of deformities and imperfections, etc.

The following research "Advances in Machine Vision Applications for Automatic Inspection and Quality Evaluation of Fruits and Vegetables" highlights that in most of these applications, image analysis is used to evaluate characteristics such as color, size, shape, texture and damage [13].

The study "Search for Optimum Color Space for the Recognition of Oranges in Agricultural Fields" proposes the design and implementation of a recognition system based on color. They used OpenCV (Open Source of Computer Vision) which are libraries that provide a set of image processing functions, as well as patterns and functions of image analysis, which used the color segmentation method [14].

The most widely used vision systems for quality inspection of food and agricultural products are three: Traditional artificial vision, hyperspectral and multispectral, where each system has its advantages and disadvantages. In the following research they used a robot to harvest kiwi fruit, which takes the night shots using artificial lighting. With the implementation of an artificial vision system and algorithms, a high percentage was obtained with respect to the recognition of the fruit in optimum conditions [15, 16].

The detection of diseases in the plant leaves is a crucial element in the agricultural sector. For this reason in the present article "Leaf Disease Detection and Grading using Computer Vision Technology & Fuzzy Logic" it has been implemented a system based in vision technology and the artificial neural network (ANN) for the detection and classification of diseases of the leaves. This is very useful for the farmer since it is more efficient than the manual method, and can be used by experts in the identification of the correct pesticide and its quantity to solve the problem in an efficient and effective way [17]. There are systems that show the name of the fruit and its characteristics for the user, for which it is necessary to use the combination of three methods of analysis based on the following characteristics: color, shape and size to increase the level of accuracy in recognition.

The detection of stress crises is an important goal in the inspection of the quality of rice, to avoid that it strongly affects the price of the product. This document [18] aims to provide a comprehensive review on the application of computer vision technology with respect to assessment of the quality of rice. The results of this review show that computer vision technology can be used efficiently to estimate the qualitative characteristics of rice. Most of the studies have focused on the use of techniques to determine the visual specifications of the grain, germination rate and dimensional characteristics, and, consequently, estimating characteristics such as HRY, DOM, grain crack, maturity, purity, variety.

The authors [19] propose an algorithm for the non-destructive automatic classification of tomatoes based on maturity and texture. Using the concept of change in the external color during different stages, two phases are carried out. The first phase classifies the tomatoes in terms of maturity and the second phase qualifies ripe tomatoes in terms of quality. To do this, two classifiers have been combined, improving in this way the calculation, time and precision, which are SMV and KNN.

In the study "Design of an automatic apple sorting system using machine vision" the authors describe an automatic classification system of apples and quality inspection, which is based on real-time processing. The varieties of Golden, Starking Delicious and Granny Smith are classified in different sets according to their color, size and weight. It also detects apples affected by scabies, spots and rot. To analyze the visual properties of the apples, two chambers of identical industrial colors are placed on the roller conveyor. Four images [20] can be captured and processed from any apple rolling on the conveyor using an image processing software in 0.52 s. As a result, the proposed machine can order an average of 15 apples per second using two channels. In the experimental studies, the design of the system was tested using three different speeds of conveyor belt and three apple cultivars to classify and inspect 183 samples with an average classification accuracy rate of 73–96%.

With the use of an expert system for the automatic recognition of different species of plants through the image of the leaf, the authors [21] used a decision-making algorithm called ant colony (ACO), which is used to investigate the best images for the recognition of individual species within the search space. To do so, a set of feasible characteristics such as shape, morphology, texture and color are extracted from the images of the leaves. The selected characteristics are used by the support vector machine (SVM) to classify the species. The effectiveness of the system was tested on around 2050 images of leaves collected from two plant databases and the results of the study achieved an average accuracy of 95.53%, confirming the possibilities of using the proposed system for an automatic classification of several species of plants.

3.2 Systems of Artificial Neural Networks

The technology of image recognition based on neural networks is a widely treated learning paradigm in Artificial Intelligence. Neural networks are inspired by the biological processes of the brain. According to Rajneet & Miss Manjeet Kaur, this technology is based on the strategy for the segmentation of photographs in sheets and background within a variety of sizes and color options that are extracted from each of the RGB and HSI representations of the image. These parameters are finally introduced into the neural networks and the applied mathematical classifiers that are used to confirm the condition of the plant [22].

Among the applications of this system, we find the control of the plant health by identifying deficiencies of iron, zinc and nitrogen and controlling the leaves, detecting and classifying the types of diseases in citrus, as well as various types of mineral deficiencies in the crop. The study "Rice Disease Identification using Pattern Recognition Techniques" [23] presents a proto-type of software for the detection of rice disease based on the infected images of several rice plants. The images of the infected rice plants are captured by a digital camera and processed using image segmentation and growth techniques to detect infected parts of the plants; the infected part of the leaf has been used for classification using a neural network.

For the segmentation of disease spots [24], an algorithm was created using image processing techniques on the leafs of the plant; in this work, a comparison of the effect of the CIELAB, HSI and YCbCr color space in the process of detecting disease spots, and experiments were carried out with different families of leaves of "Monocot" and "Dotoc" plants. In "Mobile Application for Medicinal Plant Identification Based on Leaf Image" [25] the authors propose MedLeaf as a new mobile application for the identification of medicinal plants based on the image of the leaf, running on the Android operating system. It complies with two main functionalities: identification of medicinal plants and information search about the medicinal plant. We use the local binary pattern to extract the texture of the leaf and the probabilistic neural network to classify the image. In this research, we use 30 species of Indonesian medicinal plants and each species consists of 48 digital images of leaves. To evaluate the user satisfaction with the application, they conducted a questionnaire based on the heuristic evaluation. MedLeaf will help botanic gardeners and with the management of natural reserve parks to identify medicinal plants.

There are algorithms that extract a number of textures and color characteristics. The research "Automatic Detection of Nutritional Deficiencies in Coffee Tree Leaves Through Shape and Texture Descriptors" focuses on the automatic identification of nutritional deficiencies of Boron (B), Calcium (Ca), Iron (Fe) and Potassium (K), through the use of descriptors of shape and texture of coffee leaves images. After the acquisition of images containing coffee, the leaves of the trees are subject to a segmentation process using the Otsu method. Then, the Blurred Form Model (BSM) descriptions and the Gray-Level Co-occurrence Matrix (GLCM) are applied to extract shape and texture characteristics. Finally, the image obtained is used to train KNN, Naïve Bayes and neural network classifiers by using the extracted characteristic, to infer the type of deficiency presented in each analyzed image [26–29].

In the following study [30], they determined and classified the best wavelengths to discriminate plants affected by bay wilt in avocado (Lw) due to stress factors. They applied three classification methods, stepwise discriminant analysis (STEPDISC), multilayer perceptron (MLP) and radial basis function (RBF) in the early stage of Lw infestation. The classification results obtained for MLP presented a percentage of classification accuracy as high as 98%, and they were better than those of STEPDISC and RBF. The neuronal network MLP selected certain wavelengths that were crucial to correctly distinguish healthy trees from those with stress. The results showed that there were sufficient spectral differences between laurel wilt, healthy trees and trees that have other diseases; therefore, a teledetection technique could diagnose the level of LW in the early stage of infestation.

A method of detection of diseases, diagnosis and timely management to prevent crops from suffering great losses in cotton [31] consists of pre-processing the input image by means of histogram equalization, increasing the contrast in the image; then K-means is used; it is a grouping algorithm for segmentation that classifies objects based on a set of characteristics and, finally, the classification is made using the neural network.

Zhang et al. [32] implemented a fruit classification system, so that fruit can be recognized more efficiently. This methodology includes the following four steps: pre-processing, secondly, the characteristics were extracted (color, shape and texture), in the third step they used the analysis of the main component to eliminate excessive characteristics; then follows the fruit classification system based on biogeography optimization (BBO) and feedforward neural network (FNN) whose name is BBO-FNN. The experiment used 1653 color fruit images (18 categories) for a five-fold stratified cross-validation. The results showed that the system had an overall accuracy of 89.11%.

3.3   Fuzzy Classifier and Function Based Rules

Abdullah et al. [33] present a study for the identification of diseases of watermelon leaves-critical in Malaysia (diseases of Downy Mildew and Anthracno-se) - through the color RGB, where the images were captured in a standardized and controlled environment. This study involves 200 samples of infected leaves of which diseases were classified using the fuzzy logic technique. Fuzzy Logic was used to handle uncertainty and vagueness, as it provides a means to translate qualitative and imprecise information into quantitative (linguistic) terms. The results have shown that the system can classify both diseases with a precision percentage of more than 67%. Therefore, the application of soft computing techniques such as fuzzy logic should be selected as a classifier in when deciding about systems.

In [34] he used a prototype artificial vision system for the automatic fruit classification according to the level of ripeness and mango quality. The automated system collects video images from the CCD camera placed on the top of a conveyor belt that carries mangoes; then it processes the images to collect several relevant characteristics that are sensitive to the level of maturity and quality. Finally, the qualification system has two inputs (maturity and quality) and one output (qualification). A total of 16 numbers of fuzzy rules are created to classify the mango fruit into four grades.

The authors [35] propose a structure of the classification systems based on fuzzy rules, to estimate the ripeness of tomatoes according to color. The two color representations: the red-green color difference and the red-green color relationship are derived from the extracted RGB color information. Then they are compared with the classification criteria, using a set of rules and decision trees that are automatically generated from the set of characteristics. Preliminary results showed that the system reached precision in a percentage of 94.29% of classification.

In the article "Quality determination of Mozafati dates using Mamdani fuzzy inference system" the author mentions that fuzzy logic provides a methodology to model uncertainty and the human way of thinking, reasoning and perceiving. Besides logic has variables that influence behavior and the system relationships. In the proposed system the values of the output variables are expressed in the linguistic terms "large, medium and small". The relationships are defined in yes-then rules, and the outputs use defuzzification techniques. The accuracy percentage of the system is 91% [36, 37].

The authors [38] of "Thermal imaging with fuzzy classifier for maturity and size based non-destructive Mango (Mangifera indica L.) grading" used a thermal camera together with the Fuzzy inference system for decision making, for the classification of the mango based on its ripeness and size. The prediction of mango ripeness is made through its color and size, and it is based on three parameters, namely weight, eccentricity and area. The fuzzy classifier is used to predict the size function. As for qualification, mango decision making theory is used and classified into two categories: the time needed to qualify a mango is 2.3 s and the accuracy received is 89%.

The authors will develop an intelligent farm system called Smart Farm [39], which is capable of classifying and qualifying tomatoes. This process will be carried out automatically by means of image processing and fuzzy logic. There will be a diffuse inference system that will be established using the MATLAB software to classify and grade the tomato fruit. In the classification, the system will determine if the tomato is damaged or not. On the other hand, the system will distinguish whether a specific fruit or crop is slightly ripe, ripe or too ripe. It is believed that this study is of great help to farmers, high-yield crops and productive plants.

There are systems that simulate the behavior of a human pathologist. In this research [40] the web-based "AgriDiagnose" application is proposed, which consists of an intelligent pathology tool to model the diseases and its mobile application so that Farmers interact with the system to diagnose diseases in the field, correctly determining ill plants. The system is based on dialogues and for decision making it uses a multi-criteria technique that is a hybrid of Analytic. Four measures were used: sensitivity, specificity, precision and accuracy. Preliminary results show an accuracy of 95%.

The detection and elimination of weeds is a vital task to improve the profitability and efficiency of agricultural processes. In the article "Weed detecting robot in sugarcane fields using fuzzy real time classifier" [41], researchers propose a robotic model of weed detection for sugar cane fields in India that uses a real-time fuzzy classifier on the textures of the leaves, which is based on Raspberry Pi microcontroller and suitable input/output subsystems, such as cameras, small lights and motors with energy systems. The prototype control incorporates the weed detection mechanism using a Raspbian operating system and Phyton programming. The system detects weeds with 92.9% accuracy in a processing time of 0.02 s.

4   Discussion of Results

This section provides a discussion on the validity of the results of the systematic review shown in Table 2, which shows the main models/techniques used for image recognition and is used in different areas of agriculture, from growth to finished product. The yield and the quality of the product are important criteria for the farmer, considering that work without the help of technology becomes tedious and tiresome. The computer vision system offers a quantitative method for the estimation of morphological parameters and the quality of agricultural products obtaining faster and more accurate results [24, 25]. Artificial neural networks are more robust for the treatment that is required by interpolating large amounts of data. The systems based on rules, also known as knowledge-based systems, need an expert to establish the rules, so it is not adaptable to the environment. Fuzzy classifiers use decision trees, which provide classification accuracy.

Table 3 shows the parameters that are needed for the recognition systems to perform the processing of the images. The type of characteristics of the image varies according to the species and variety. Likewise, the use of a greater number of characteristics increases the computational cost. The accuracy of this type of system for recognition is 83.87%. This type of methods can be used to recognize the quality in fruit and vegetables, diagnosis of disease, deficiency of nutrients, maturity of the fruit; this allows to have profitability in crop production, to avoid losses and to see quality products.

Table 3. Crop, parameters and best classification methods

Crop	Method	Recognition parameters	Accuracy	Utility
Apple	SVM	Color Texture	93.5%	Classification of fruit
Fruit and vegetables		Color Size Shape Texture	–	Recognition
Orange		Color spaces (HLS), (HSV), (YCrCb), (YUV)	–	Recognition
Kiwi fruit		Color	88.3%	Quality
Citric		Color	92.4%	Disease diagnosis
Viburnum acerifolium		Softness Shape Leaf	89.0%	Disease diagnosis
Cotton		Softness Shape leaf		Disease diagnosis
Rice	(ANN)	Leaf color	92%	Disease diagnosis
"Monocot" and "Dotoc"		Color spaces (HLS), (YCrCb)	–	Disease diagnosis
Biofarmaka ipb, cikabayan ipb		Shape, color and leaf texture	60%	Plant information
Coffee		Shape, color and leaf texture	49.81%	Nutrients
Papaya		Leaf color	97%	Nutrients
Cotton		Leaf color	87.99%	Nutrients
Oil Palm		Color RGB, histogram-based textures RGB and grey	83%	Nutrients
Avocado		Wavelength	98%	Disease
Cotton		Leaf color	89.56%	Disease diagnosis
Different fruit		Color, shape and texture	89.11%	Fruit classification

(continued)

Table 3. (*continued*)

Crop	Method	Recognition parameters	Accuracy	Utility
Watermelon	Fuzzy classificator & function-based rules	Color RGB	67%	Disease
Tomatoes		Color	94.29%	Fruit ripeness
Mango		Video images from CCD Peel Size	–	Ripeness and quality
Tomato		Color	94.29%	Ripeness
Fruit		Size and peel	91.00%	Quality

5 Conclusion

The use of machine learning methods for image processing facilitates the quick and accurate analysis of plagues, nutrient deficiencies and product quality in large areas of crop, managing to replace labor. The complexity of calculation required by this type of systems is of high percentage. The effectiveness of the method depends on the correlation between the measuring parameters and the quality of the image. This allows researchers to develop new and improved techniques for classification and quality of fruits and vegetables.

One factor to be improved is the development of image processing techniques for agriculture with availability of online data sets. There are no available online image databases on food quality evaluation, detection of fruit defects or classification of weeds/crops; this will help in testing and verification of new methods of image processing. Future work will consist of the processing of the images obtained in "A Photogrammetry Software as a Tool for Precision Agriculture: A Case Study" using machine vision techniques in order to identify the possible attack of plague in the crop. Among the techniques to be used are those of morphological filters, Gaussian fuzzy and HSL filtering. On the other hand, it is necessary to carry out the development of a prototype that implements an alternative for the visualization of the information processed by an application for the Android operating system for mobile devices.

References

1. Cubero, S., Aleixos, N., Moltó, E., Gómez-Sanchis, J., Blasco, J.: Advances in machine vision applications for automatic inspection and quality evaluation of fruits and vegetables. Food Bioprocess Technol. **4**, 487–504 (2011)
2. Germain, J.C., Aguilera, J.M.: Identifying industrial food foam structures by 2D surface image analysis and pattern recognition. J. Food Eng. **111**, 440–448 (2012)
3. Bowles, H., Sánchez, N., Tapias, A., Paredes, P., Campos, F., Bluemel, C., Olmos, R.A.V., Vidal-Sicart, S.: Radioguided surgery and the GOSTT concept: from pre-operative image and intraoperative navigation to image-assisted excision. Rev. Esp. Med. Nucl. Imagen Mol. (Engl. Ed.) **36**, 175–184 (2017)

4. Haque, A., Faizi, M.S.H., Rather, J.A., Khan, M.S.: Next generation NIR fluorophores for tumor imaging and fluorescence-guided surgery: a review. Bioorg. Med. Chem. **25**, 2017–2034 (2017)
5. Saitoh, T., Shibata, T., Miyazono, T.: Image-based fish recognition. In: 2015 7th International Conference of Soft Computing and Pattern Recognition (SoCPaR), pp. 260–263. IEEE (2015)
6. Begue, A., Kowlessur, V., Singh, U., Mahomoodally, F., Pudaruth, S.: Automatic recognition of medicinal plants using machine learning techniques. Int. J. Adv. Comput. Sci. Appl. **8**, 166–175 (2017)
7. Kan, H.X., Jin, L., Zhou, F.L.: Classification of medicinal plant leaf image based on multi-feature extraction. Pattern Recognit. Image Anal. **27**, 581–587 (2017)
8. Delgado-vera, C., Aguirre-munizaga, M., Rodr, A.: A photogrammetry software as a tool for precision agriculture: a case study. Technol. Innov. **749**, 282–295 (2017)
9. Muñoz, F.I.I., Comport, A.I.: Point-to-hyperplane RGB-D pose estimation: fusing photometric and geometric measurements. In: 2016 IEEE/RSJ International Conference on Intelligent Robots and Systems (IROS), pp. 24–29 (2016)
10. Chakrabarti, A., Sunkavalli, K.: Single-image RGB photometric stereo with spatially-varying albedo. In: 2016 Fourth International Conference on 3D Vision (3DV), pp. 258–266. IEEE (2016)
11. Chandel, G.S., Singh, P.K.: Digital image processing applications in agriculture: a survey. Int. J. Adv. Res. Comput. Sci. Softw. Eng. **5**, 8–20 (2015)
12. Zhang, B., Huang, W., Li, J., Zhao, C., Fan, S., Wu, J., Liu, C.: Principles, developments and applications of computer vision for external quality inspection of fruits and vegetables: a review. Food Res. Int. **62**, 326–343 (2014)
13. Cubero, S., Aleixos, N., Moltó, E., Gómez-Sanchis, J., Blasco, J.: Advances in machine vision applications for automatic inspection and quality evaluation of fruits and vegetables. Food Bioprocess Technol. **4**, 487–504 (2011)
14. Hernández-Hernández, J.L., Hernández-Hernández, M., Feliciano-Morales, S., Álvarez-Hilario, V., Herrera-Miranda, I.: Search for optimum color space for the recognition of oranges in agricultural fields. In: Valencia-García, R., Lagos-Ortiz, K., Alcaraz-Mármol, G., Del Cioppo, J., Vera-Lucio, N., Bucaram-Leverone, M. (eds.) Communications in Computer and Information Science, pp. 296–307. Springer, Cham (2017). https://doi.org/10.1007/978-3-319-67283-0_22
15. Fu, L.S., Wang, B., Cui, Y.J., Su, S., Gejima, Y., Kobayashi, T.: Kiwifruit recognition at nighttime using artificial lighting based on machine vision. Int. J. Agric. Biol. Eng. **8**, 52–59 (2015)
16. Lü, Q., Cai, J.R., Liu, B., Lie, D., Zhang, Y.J.: Identification of fruit and branch in natural scenes for citrus harvesting robot using machine vision and support vector machine. Int. J. Agric. Biol. Eng. **7**, 115–121 (2014)
17. Rastogi, A., Arora, R., Sharma, S.: Leaf disease detection and grading using computer vision technology & fuzzy logic. In: 2015 2nd International Conference on Signal Processing and Integrated Networks (SPIN), pp. 500–505. IEEE (2015)
18. Zareiforoush, H., Minaei, S.: Potential applications of computer vision in quality inspection of rice: a review. Food Eng. Rev. **7**, 321–345 (2015)
19. Pavithra, V., Pounroja, R., Bama, B.S.: Machine vision based automatic sorting of cherry tomatoes. In: 2015 2nd International Conference on Electronics and Communication Systems (ICECS), pp. 271–275. IEEE (2015)
20. Sofu, M.M., Er, O., Kayacan, M.C., Cetis, B.: Design of an automatic apple sorting system using machine vision. Comput. Electron. Agric. **127**, 395–405 (2016)

21. Ghasab, M.A.J., Khamis, S., Mohammad, F., Fariman, H.J.: Feature decision-making ant colony optimization system for an automated recognition of plant species. Expert Syst. Appl. **42**, 2361–2370 (2015)
22. Kaur, R., Kaur, M.: A brief review on plant disease detection using in image processing. Int. J. Comput. Sci. Mob. Comput. **6**, 101–106 (2017)
23. Phadikar, S., Sil, J.: Rice disease identification using pattern recognition techniques. In: 2008 11th International Conference on Computer and Information Technology, pp. 420–423. IEEE (2008)
24. Chaudhary, P., Chaudhari, A.K., Godara, S.: Color transform based approach for disease spot detection on plant leaf. Int. J. Comput. Sci. Telecommun. **3**, 65–71 (2012)
25. Prasvita, D.S., Herdiyeni, Y.: MedLeaf: mobile application for medicinal plant identification based on leaf image. Int. J. Adv. Sci. Eng. Inf. Technol. **3**, 5–9 (2013)
26. Vassallo-barco, M., Vives-garnique, L., Tuesta-monteza, V., Mejía-cabrera, H.I.: Automatic detection of nutritional deficiencies in coffee tree leaves through shape and texture descriptors. J. Digit. Inf. Manag. **15** (2017)
27. Sartin, M.A., da Silva, A.C.R.: Evaluation of image segmentation and filtering with ann in the papaya leaf. Int. J. Comput. Sci. Inf. Technol. **6**, 47–58 (2014)
28. Sartin, M.A., Da Silva, A.C.R., Kappes, C.: Image segmentation with artificial neural network. **10**, 1084–1093 (2014)
29. Asraf, H.M., Tahir, N., Rizam, S.B.S., Abdullah, R.: Elaeis guineensis nutritional lacking identification based on statistical analysis and artificial neural network. Recent Adv. Syst. Sci. Math. Model. 144–149 (2012)
30. Abdulridha, J., Ehsani, R., de Castro, A.: Detection and differentiation between laurel wilt disease, phytophthora disease, and salinity damage using a hyperspectral sensing technique. Agriculture **6**, 56 (2016)
31. Warne, P.P., Ganorkar, S.R.: Detection of diseases on cotton leaves using K-mean clustering method. Int. Res. J. Eng. Technol. **2**, 425–431 (2015)
32. Zhang, Y., Phillips, P., Wang, S., Ji, G., Yang, J., Wu, J.: Fruit classification by biogeography-based optimization and feedforward neural network. Expert Syst. **33**, 239–253 (2016)
33. Abdullah, N.E., Hashim, H., Yusof, Y.W.M., Osman, F.N., Kusim, A.S., Adam, M.S.: A characterization of watermelon leaf diseases using fuzzy logic. In: 2012 IEEE Symposium on Business, Engineering and Industrial Applications, pp. 1–6. IEEE (2012)
34. Nandi, C.S.: Machine vision based automatic fruit grading system using fuzzy algorithm, pp. 26–30 (2014)
35. Goel, N., Sehgal, P.: Fuzzy classification of pre-harvest tomatoes for ripeness estimation - an approach based on automatic rule learning using decision tree. Appl. Soft Comput. J. **36**, 45–56 (2015)
36. Alavi, N.: Quality determination of Mozafati dates using Mamdani fuzzy inference system. J. Saudi Soc. Agric. Sci. **12**, 137–142 (2013)
37. Papageorgiou, E.I., Kokkinos, K., Dikopoulou, Z.: Fuzzy sets in agriculture. Stud. Fuzziness Soft Comput. **341** (2016)
38. Naik, S., Patel, B.: Thermal imaging with fuzzy classifier for maturity and size based non-destructive Mango (Mangifera indica L.) grading. In: International Conference on Emerging Trends & Innovation, pp. 15–20. IEEE (2017)
39. Dorado, L.C., Aguila, J.I.C., Caldo, R.B.: Smart farm: automated classifying and grading system of tomatoes using fuzzy logic. Laguna J. Eng. Comput. Stud. **3**, 64–72 (2016)

40. Goodridge, W., Bernard, M., Jordan, R., Rampersad, R.: Intelligent diagnosis of diseases in plants using a hybrid multi-criteria decision making technique. Comput. Electron. Agric. **133**, 80–87 (2017)
41. Sujaritha, M., Annadurai, S., Satheeshkumar, J., Kowshik Sharan, S., Mahesh, L.: Weed detecting robot in sugarcane fields using fuzzy real time classifier. Comput. Electron. Agric. **134**, 160–171 (2017)

Monitoring System for Shrimp Farming: A Case Study of CAMASIG S.A.

Raquel Gómez-Chabla(✉) ⓘ, Karina Real-Avilés ⓘ,
Carlota Delgado-Vera, Cristhian Chávez, and Néstor Vera-Lucio

Escuela de Ingeniería en Computación e Informática,
Facultad de Ciencias Agrarias, Universidad Agraria del Ecuador,
Av. 25 de Julio y Pio Jaramillo, P.O. BOX 09-04-100, Guayaquil, Ecuador
{rgomez, kreal, cdelgado, nvera}@uagraria.edu.ec,
cristhian.chavez1994@gmail.com

Abstract. In 2016, Ecuador produced 368,181 tons of shrimp Penaeus vannamei and ex-ported 370,780 tons corresponding to $ 2.58 billion, according to ProEcuador (Institute for Export and Investment Promotion). The shrimp exportation represented 22.76% of the country's non-oil exports. The Ecuadorian shrimp industry invests in technology focused on improving the production of shrimp and the quality of the postlarvae aiming to avoid falls in production, high mortality rates and disparity in the size of shrimp. However, it is necessary that this industry adopts innovative technologies that allow it to improve the quality and production of its products. In this sense, this work presents a case study where a water monitoring system was implemented in a shrimp culture pond of the CAMASIG S.A. company. This system integrates technologies such as Cloud computing, Arduino-based devices, and mobile applications that allow users to remotely monitor a shrimp culture pond, as well as to receive alerts when an out-of-range water parameter (pH, temperature, and dissolved oxygen) is detected. This last module consists of a set of sensors that allows collecting data about the pH, temperature, and dissolved oxygen in the water. This system was evaluated to test its effectiveness in terms of the size, weight, and the percentage of survival of the shrimp achieved when the shrimp culture pond is monitored by this system.

Keywords: Shrimp culture · Monitoring system · Arduino

1 Introduction

In 2016, Ecuador produced 368,181 tons of shrimp Penaeus vannamei [1] and exported 370,780 tons corresponding to $ 2.58 billion, according to ProEcuador (Institute for Export and Investment Promotion). The shrimp exportation represented 22.76% of the country's non-oil exports. In the other hand, in recent years, Ecuador has excelled in the production of postlarvae thanks to the fact that the demand for this product has increased significantly. Therefore, the Ecuadorian shrimp industry invests in technology focused on improving the production of shrimp and the quality of the postlarvae aiming to avoid falls in production, high mortality rates and disparity in the size of shrimp.

© Springer Nature Switzerland AG 2018
R. Valencia-García et al. (Eds.): CITI 2018, CCIS 883, pp. 30–43, 2018.
https://doi.org/10.1007/978-3-030-00940-3_3

Information and Communication Technology (ICT) provides advantages and new possibilities in different domains. For instance, mobile devices have been incorporated in the medical domain for the monitoring [2, 3] and detection of different diseases [4]. In education domain, the continuous evolution of ICT has allowed students to generate ideas and innovative projects with the aim of improving the quality of life of society as a whole [5]. In entertainment domain, mobile devices such as smartphones and electronic tablets have been adopted thanks to their processing and wireless communication capabilities as well as the integration of sensors such as magnetometers, accelerometers, and gyroscopes, among others [6]. On the other hand, in the food industry, embedded systems and sensors have been used in conjunction to collect and analyze information from the environment in order to improve the production and quality of tilapia fish [7]. In [8], the authors describe a system to monitor the degree of freshness of the tilapia fish. This system uses an optical sensor that changes color in response to the pH alteration, which occurs in the presence of alkaline vapors such as volatile amines (TVB-N) produced during the deterioration of fish. Considering the above discussed, it is necessary that the food industry adopts ICT that allow it to improve the quality and production of different food products. Besides, the adoption of ICT could help to reduce obstacles and uncertainty, optimize resources, add value to food production, as well as encourage the entrepreneurship of professionals.

Shrimp farming in Ecuador is an important activity that has been carried out for 40 years. In fact, Ecuador is considered the pioneer of shrimp farming in America. Ecuador produces 2 types of shrimp, namely: (1) white shrimp or Litopenaeus vannamei, which, due to its high resistance to environmental changes in captivity, represents the 95% of the total production; and (2) shrimp Litopenaeus stylirostris, which represents only 5% of the production. Table 1 shows Ecuador's shrimp exports (percentages) from the January–March 2018 according to the National Aquaculture Chamber. These data show that in America, exports of this product have been maintained, meanwhile, in Asia, there has been an increase of 8% compared to January.

Table 1. Exports (percentages) of Ecuadorian shrimp.

Country	January 2018	January–February 2018	January–March 2018
Africa	0%	0%	0%
America	2%	2%	2%
Asia	51%	54%	59%
USA	19%	17%	16%
Europe	28%	27%	23%

In Ecuador, the cultivation of white shrimp is usually done in ponds, which must comply with the optimal parameters of temperature, pH, and oxygen. These parameters are of great importance since they influence the feeding, growth and optimum development of the shrimp. Currently, there is a great boom in the adoption of ICT by shrimp companies, which makes this industry one of the most dynamic in Ecuador.

This work presents a case study where a water monitoring system was implemented in a shrimp culture pond of the CAMASIG S.A. company. This system integrates technologies such as Cloud computing, Arduino, and mobile applications. Also, it sends messages to the user when detects an out-of-range water parameter. The remainder of this paper is structured as follows: Sect. 2 described a set of research efforts related to the monitoring systems. Then, Sect. 3 details the hardware and software components of the water monitoring system presented in this work, whereas Sect. 4 describes the case study. Section 5 presents the evaluation performed to test the effectiveness of this system in terms of the size, weight and the percentage of survival of the shrimp achieved when the shrimp culture pond is monitored [9] by this system. Finally, Sect. 6 discusses our conclusions.

2 Related Works

The ICT plays a very important role in society and specifically in different sectors of the production industry. In this industry, intelligent automation systems that encompass control and supervision tasks have been implemented. These systems aim to guarantee the expected results in the mining and oil, agricultural, aquaculture and forestry sectors [10]. Mining and foreign-currency generation are some of the activities that contribute the most to the gross domestic product of a country. However, mining workplaces are generally located in areas far from urban centers, which requires a series of logistical, planning and security efforts in order to be efficiently performed. In [11], the authors presented a real-time monitoring system that allows controlling a security dam. In addition, this system allows automatically and remotely obtaining pre-alarm information in order to reduce risks and accidents. In [12], the authors present a sheep monitoring system that aims to protect them from attacks by wolves. For this purpose, this system uses sensors to measure the body temperature and heart rate of the sheep. In this way, when there is a drastic change in these parameters, an alarm is sent to the user to he/she carry out the necessary actions. As can be seen from above, technological advances in the development of monitoring systems allow collecting and processing greater amounts of relevant information of animals and their environment with the aim of improving their production, growth, and health [13].

Monitoring systems are also used in the aquaculture domain. For instance, in [14], the authors presented a real-time fish monitoring system that allows measuring the amount of lactic acid in the fish's blood in order to measure their stress levels. In [15], a monitoring system that combines precision aquaculture with open hardware platforms and Artificial Intelligence is presented. This system automatically registers physico-chemical variables of water (dissolved oxygen, temperature and pH), and processes them using fuzzy logic in order to determine the quality of the water. In [16], the authors proposed an automated system for the administration of food in the culture of tilapia fish. This system uses wireless technologies for food administration and a SCADA-type (Supervisory Control And Data Acquisition) program to remotely monitor the status of each food dispatcher. On the other hand, in Machala, Ecuador, a system for measuring the temperature of a pond for the culture of fish was implemented. This system uses a temperature sensor based on the 16F84A PIC controller and provides a LED display that allows the user to view the data captured by the sensor.

In other work, a system for taking water samples is implemented aiming to register and check the quality of water.

Nowadays, mobile applications have been adopted in multiple domains to solve a wide range of problems. However, in Ecuador, there is no a mobile application for shrimp culture that allows monitoring shrimp culture ponds and that provide information on temperature, pH and dissolved oxygen in the water [17]. In this sense, this work presents a water monitoring system that provides an Android-based application that allows users to remotely monitor a shrimp culture pond. Also, this application sends alerts to the users when an out-of-range water parameter is detected by the Arduino-based module. This last module consists of a set of sensors that allows collecting data about the pH, temperature, and dissolved oxygen in the water.

3   Hardware and Software Features

This section describes the hardware and software used for the development of the monitoring system of shrimp culture ponds presented in this work. With respect to hardware platform, this system uses Arduino, an open-source platform for developing electronic prototypes. Arduino allows developing solutions that integrate sensors to obtain various parameters in real time. In this sense, the system presented in this work integrates an Arduino-based solution that allows to measure in real time the temperature, pH, color, proximity, and dissolved oxygen in the water.

Regarding software used in this work, two main development tools were used, namely Android Studio and MySQL. On the one hand, Android Studio is the official integrated development environment (IDE) for the development of Android-based applications. This tool was used to develop the Android-based application that allows users to send commands to the Arduino-based system, as well as visualize the data coming from the sensors integrated into it. On the other hand, we use the MySQL database manager to store the information coming from the sensors. This information is

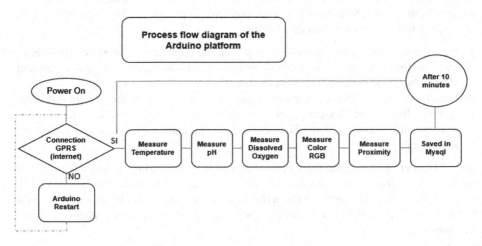

Fig. 1. Flow diagram process.

sent to the MySQL database hosted in the cloud via GPRS devices. The mobile application uses this information to generate alarms when the monitored parameters vary drastically. In addition, this application allows users to view the monitored data and generate reports that support decision making with respect to the tank for shrimp farming.

Figure 1 depicts the flow diagram that describes the monitoring process of the shrimp culture pond. This process goes from obtaining data through sensors to its storage, processing, and transformation into useful information for the end user.

4 Case Study

Despite water monitoring is a relevant task for a successful shrimp culture, the company CAMASIG S.A. does not have technological tools that allow it to obtain data from the pond for shrimp larvae culture, nor to monitor its evolution and maintenance. In addition, this company does not have an application that allows it to store data from water monitoring process to support decisions. This situation generates inconveniences because a simple variation of water parameters might cause diseases in the shrimp and even its death. In order to solve the aforementioned problems, this work presents a water monitoring system based on open source technologies. Specifically, this system offers an Android-based application that allows monitoring the levels of temperature, pH, color, proximity, and dissolved oxygen in the water. Furthermore, this mobile application allows biologists and employees in charge of shrimp culture to control the parameters of the water to which the shrimp are exposed.

4.1 Water Monitoring System Architecture

The water monitoring system described in this work was implemented in a shrimp culture pond of the company CAMASIG S.A. This system integrates Arduino-based technologies to monitor the levels of temperature, pH, color, proximity, and dissolved oxygen in the water. Specifically, the architecture proposed in this paper (see Fig. 2) consists of the three layers described below:

1. Presentation layer. This layer contains the mobile application that allows the user to monitor the water through different forms, as well as receive the corresponding alerts when water parameters vary drastically.
2. Data access layer. This contains the classes that interact with the system database.
3. Devices layer. The devices layer consists of all the electronic devices such as sensors and actuators that allow collecting the parameters of the water to be monitored.

As can be seen in Fig. 2, the architecture of the water monitoring system offers a set of services that support the company business process. In addition, the independence between the layers that compose the architecture enables the continuous evolution of it because this fact allows the addition of new features without affecting basic functionality.

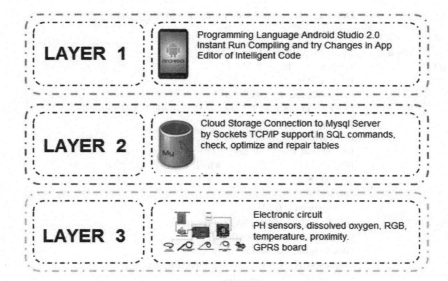

Fig. 2. Monitoring system architecture.

4.2 Morphology of the Monitoring System

As mentioned earlier, the water monitoring system presented in this work provides a module based on Arduino technology that allows collecting all water parameters considered by the system. Specifically, this module uses the hardware described in Table 2. On the other hand, the system was developed by using next software: Android Studio 2.3.3, PHP, MySQL, Java, and Arduino IDE. Finally, it must be mentioned that the database is hosted in the Cloud.

As can be seen in Fig. 3, the Arduino-based module obtains water parameters through the sensors described in Table 2. This data is sent to the MySQL database via Internet. For this purpose, this module uses a GPRS SIM900 studio card and a mobile phone chip. Moreover, the Arduino-based module is powered by a solar panel battery which consists of a 4-m stainless steel bar. This panel is located about 1.5 m from the surface. Meanwhile, the sensors remain submerged in the water.

Figure 4 depicts the data flow between the sensors, the Arduino board, the database, and the mobile application. This data flow is explained below.

First, the sensors obtain the data of temperature, pH, color, proximity and dissolved oxygen in the water of the shrimp culture tank. It is important that the values of these variables are within the ranges established in Table 3 since these variables greatly influence the correct feeding, growth, and development of shrimp.

- The quality of the shrimp depends a lot on the pH of the water. In this sense, the pH sensor indicates how acidic or alkaline water is. On the other hand, the proximity sensor prevents the water level of the tank from reaching the Arduino-based device that contains the sensors. When the water level reaches a distance of less than 10 cm with respect to the device, a motor is driven to maintain the Arduino-based device

Table 2. Hardware used in the monitoring system.

Hardware	Specifications
Arduino Mega 2560	Microcontroller: ATmega2560 Operating voltage: 5 V Input voltage (recommended): 7–12 V Input voltage (limits): 6–20 V Digital I/O pins: 54 (of which 14 provide PWM output) Analog input pins: 16 DC current per I/O pin: 40 mA DC current for 3.3 V pin: 50 mA Flash memory: 256 KB of which 8 KB used by bootloader SRAM: 8 KB EEPROM: 4 KB Clock speed: 16 MHz
GPRS SIM900	Quad-band 850/900/1800/1900 MHz GPRS multi-slot class 10/8 GPRS mobile station class B Transmission power 2 W @850/900 MHz Control via AT commands AT commands for operations with TCP/IP sockets
Sensors	PH sensor, EZO RGB sensor, proximity sensor, temperature sensor, dissolved oxygen sensor
Solar panel and battery	3 solar panels and a double USB Recharge to 2 A Micro USB cable for Android devices

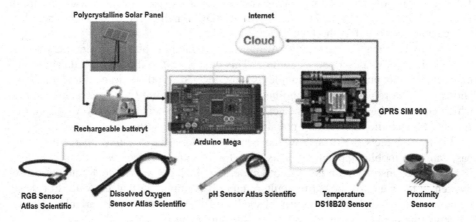

Fig. 3. Monitoring system.

far from the water. Finally, the EZO RGB sensor captures the color of the water. This sensor is capable of recognizing five different colors that determine the characteristics of water. These colors are: Pale green. This color indicates an adequate concentration of algae in the pond.

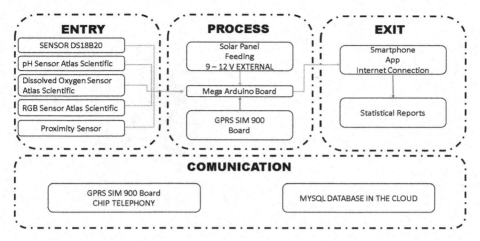

Fig. 4. Data flow of the monitoring system.

Table 3. Parameter settings for shrimp.

Parameter	Value	Scale
Lowest lethal temperature (°C)	14	−50 and 125 (°C)
Optimum temperature (°C)	26–30	−50 and 125 (°C)
Highest lethal temperature (°C)	40	−50 and 125 (°C)
Optimal dissolved oxygen	5–10	2 and 10
Optimal PH	7–9	1–14

- Gray. This color indicates a low concentration of algae in the pond. This situation demands fertilization and changing the pond water.
- Moss green. This color indicates that the algae begin to die. This situation demands to immediately change the pond water.
- Shining green. This color indicates large concentrations of algae. This situation demands to change the pond water to reduce the risk of a decrease in the concentration of oxygen dissolved in the water during the night.
- Brown. This color indicates a large number of dead algae due mainly to the lack of nutrients and excess metabolites. In this case, it is necessary to change the pond water and fertilize the pond.

Figure 5 shows the concentration of pH and dissolved oxygen in the water of a set of samples used in this work. The values 1, 2, and 3 correspond to the colors brown, pale green, and gray respectively. Also, it is observed that when the concentration of oxygen is in an optimum range, the color of the water tends to pale green (2); when there is a low concentration of oxygen, the color of the water tends to brown (1); and, when there is a high concentration of oxygen but not many algae, the color of the water tends to gray (3). Despite these data, it was observed that the color of the water is more related to the turbidity of the water.

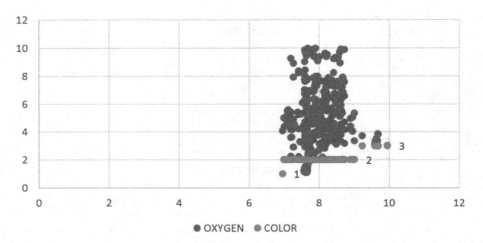

Fig. 5. pH and dissolved oxygen.

The water monitoring system sends email messages to the user when the water parameters are out of range. Figure 6 shows some messages sent by the system. For example, the system sends the messages "The current tank temperature is N" when this parameter is less than 26 or greater than 30; "Oxygen dissolved in water is low" when the value of this parameter is less than 4; and "The pH of the water is N" when this parameter has a value less than 7 or greater than 9.

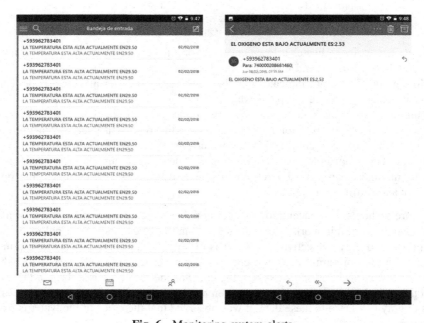

Fig. 6. Monitoring system alerts.

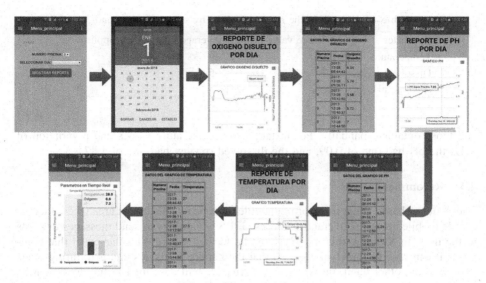

Fig. 7. Reports by day.

Finally, the Android-based mobile application also allows users to generate reports of the different water parameters that are being monitored. Figure 7 shows the mobile interfaces through which the user generates reports by day, week, month, year, as well as a specific period.

4.3 Test Cases

The development process of the water monitoring system presented in this work followed the XP methodology [18]. This methodology is divided into five phases namely: analysis, planning, design, coding, and testing. In addition, this methodology allows performing partial tests with the aim of obtaining a product that meets the needs of the company. Once the water Arduino-based water monitoring system was developed, this was implemented in a shrimp pond of the company CAMASIG S.A. The data collected through this system were stored in a database hosted in the cloud for further analysis.

The water monitoring system presented in this work was used for 120 days by the company. In this period, 3992 samples containing the values of all parameters considered by the system (temperature, pH and dissolved oxygen in the water) were collected. From the collected data set, 480 samples were selected corresponding to the periods from 4:00 to 4:30 and from 16:00 to 16:30. These periods were selected because the shrimp culture pond should be monitored in the morning and in the afternoon to maintain the quality of water in an optimal state [19, 20].

In order to evaluate the effectiveness of the proposed system, the data obtained through this system were compared with those obtained manually by the people in charge of monitoring the pond for shrimp farming. Table 4 presents the average of the results obtained for each of the three parameters considered in this evaluation. As can be seen, there is no great difference between the results obtained through our proposal

Table 4. Average of the results obtained by sensors in the pond 3.

Parameter	Average value manual	Average value of the application
Temperature	27.00	26.63
Dissolved oxygen	7.97	6.5
Average pH	5.12	5.21

and those obtained manually. For instance, the temperature values had a variation of 0.37, the pH had one of 0.09, and the dissolved oxygen had one of 1.47.

4.4   Recommendations

The Arduino-based water monitoring module must be installed in an area where there is a wide mobile network coverage as it uses GPRS technology to send messages or alerts to the user. In addition, this module must be located where the solar panel that composes it can receive direct sunlight so that the battery is always charged during operation. On the other hand, the water monitoring system described in this work can be implemented in any company dedicated to the culture of aquatic species since it allows monitoring the pH, color, temperature and dissolved oxygen in the water, which are the main parameters that should be considered in this domain.

The current version of the monitoring system only considers three water parameters. However, as future work, we are planning to add a salinity sensor and a sensor to measure the turbidity of the water [21]. This will provide more data that support user decisions regarding the quality of water of the shrimp culture pond.

5   Results

Figure 8 shows the number of times that the temperature, pH, and dissolved oxygen values obtained manually and through the application were out of range. As can be seen, the number of times that out-of-range values were obtained by the application is higher than when the data are manually obtained. We ascribe these results to the fact that the sensors used by our proposal allow obtaining more precise values. As can be seen in Fig. 8, there is a big difference between the number of times the system obtained an out-of-range pH value (284) and the number of times that out-of-range pH values were manually obtained (11). Although the difference between the pH values obtained by both methods had an average value of 0.21, our proposal was able to detect more out-of-range pH values and notify the user. The generation of these notifications is very important since a pH value out of range can produce lethal effects in shrimp. With regard to the oxygen parameter, our proposal was able to generate 57 alerts more than the manual method. It should be mentioned that the oxygen parameter varies according to the time of day, being that in the early morning it tends to fall and in the evenings it increases.

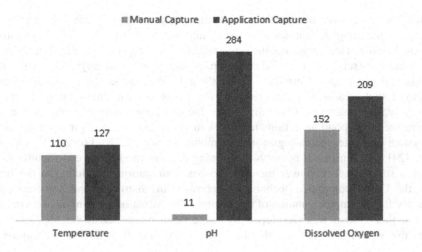

Fig. 8. Alerts obtained manually and through the application.

5.1 Evaluation

The water monitoring system was implemented in the shrimp culture pond number 3 of the CAMASIG company during a complete shrimp farming process (120 days). To evaluate the effectiveness of this system, we compared the length, weight, and percentage of survival of the shrimp cultured in the pond 3, with those cultivated in the pond 2, which was manually monitored. Table 5 presents the results obtained, where it can be seen that the shrimps cultured in pond 3 reached a larger size (9–12 cm) and weight (20 g) than those cultured in the pond 2 (8–10 cm and 17 g, respectively). It is important to mention that the commercial weight of shrimp ranges from 10 to 20 g. This weight is reached between 95 and 120 days after sowing. Hence, our proposal obtained better results for commercial purposes. Finally, the percentage of survival of the shrimp obtained a higher value in the pond where our proposal was implemented.

Table 5. Evaluation metrics used for shrimp farming process.

Metric	Pond 2	Pond 3
Shrimp length (cm)	8–10	9–12
Weight (g)	17	20
% survival	80–90	90

6 Conclusions

This work presents a water monitoring system focused on shrimp culture ponds. The architecture of this system consists of three layers clearly differentiated and independent of each other. This feature will allow adding new features and sensors in order to provide the user with more information that supports their decisions. The most important technologies that are integrated into this system are Cloud computing, Arduino-based devices, and mobile applications. With respect to the mobile application, it allows users to monitor the shrimp culture pond from anywhere. The main benefits that our proposal provides to the shrimp culture process are: (1) the shrimp mortality rate decreases; (2) it can help prevent diseases by alerting the user about out-of-range water parameters; (3) agility, since the real-time monitoring allows users to perform the corresponding actions to deal with risk factors; and (4) innovation, since this system integrates technologies such as mobile devices, GPRS board [22, 23], solar panels [24], and sensors. It is worth mentioning that our proposal is eco-friendly since it uses a solar panel to power the Arduino-based monitoring module. On the other hand, the Cloud computing technology decreases the hardware and software costs necessary for the implementation of this system. This situation, in conjunction with the fact that this system was developed by using open-source hardware and software, makes this system an economical solution for companies dedicated to the culture of aquatic species.

References

1. Campos-Montes, G.R., Montaldo, H.H., Martínez-Ortega, A., Jiménez, A.M., Castillo-Juárez, H.: Genetic parameters for growth and survival traits in Pacific white shrimp *Penaeus* (*Litopenaeus*) *vannamei* from a nucleus population undergoing a two-stage selection program. Aquac. Int. **21**, 299–310 (2013)
2. Schwartz, B., Baca, A.: Wearables and apps – modern diagnostic frameworks for health promotion through sport. Dtsch. Z. Sportmed. **2016**, 131–136 (2016)
3. Haghi, M., Thurow, K., Stoll, R.: Wearable devices in medical internet of things: scientific research and commercially available devices. Healthc. Inform. Res. **23**, 4 (2017)
4. Ozanne, A., Johansson, D., Hällgren Graneheim, U., Malmgren, K., Bergquist, F., Alt Murphy, M.: Wearables in epilepsy and Parkinson's disease-a focus group study. Acta Neurol. Scand. **137**, 188–194 (2018)
5. Universities, C.: Technology's past, present and future role in education. Autumn 41–43 (2017)
6. Virtual Reality Society: Understanding Sensors: Magnetometers, Accelerometers and Gyroscopes - Virtual Reality
7. Gómez-Chabla, R., Aguirre-Munizaga, M., Samaniego-Cobo, T., Choez, J., Vera-Lucio, N.: A reference framework for empowering the creation of projects with Arduino in the Ecuadorian Universities. In: Communications in Computer and Information Science (2017)
8. Domínguez-Aragón, A., Olmedo-Martínez, J.A., Zaragoza-Contreras, E.A.: Colorimetric sensor based on a poly(ortho-phenylenediamine-*co*-aniline) copolymer for the monitoring of tilapia (*Orechromis niloticus*) freshness. Sens. Actuators B Chem. **259**, 170–176 (2018)
9. Viseur, R.: From open source software to open source hardware. **378**, 286–291 (2012)
10. Taylor, P., Gayar, O.F., El-gayar, O.F.: The use of information technology in aquaculture management. Aquac. Econ. Manag. 37–41 (2008)
11. Sun, E., Zhang, X., Li, Z.: The internet of things (IOT) and cloud computing (CC) based tailings dam monitoring and pre-alarm system in mines. Saf. Sci. **50**, 811–815 (2012)

12. Sendra, S., Parra, L., Lloret, J., Llario, F.: Smart wireless sensor network to detect and protect sheep and goats to wolf attacks. Recent Adv. Commun. Netw. Technol. **2**, 91–101 (2013)
13. Wu, H., Aoki, A., Arimoto, T., Nakano, T., Ohnuki, H., Murata, M., Ren, H., Endo, H.: Fish stress become visible: a new attempt to use biosensor for real-time monitoring fish stress. Biosens. Bioelectron. **67**, 503–510 (2015)
14. Hibi, K., Hatanaka, K., Takase, M., Ren, H., Endo, H.: Wireless biosensor system for real-time l-lactic acid monitoring in fish. Sensors (Switzerland) **12**, 6269–6281 (2012)
15. Quality, W., Monitoring, I., Shrimp, F.O.R., Open, U., Hardware, S., Systems, F.I.: Camaronicultura por medio de un hardware de acceso. Biotecnia 45–49 (2016)
16. Cortez, G.D.: Design of an automated system for administration of food in culture tilapia. Investigatio **1**, 33–65 (2014)
17. Abdelsalam, M., Krishnan, R., Sandhu, R.: Clustering-based IaaS cloud monitoring. In: 2017 IEEE 10th International Conference on Cloud Computing (CLOUD), pp. 672–679. IEEE (2017)
18. Bhaskar, R.K., Anslow, C., Brosz, J., Maurer, F.: Developing usable APIs with XP and cognitive dimensions. In: 2016 IEEE Symposium on Visual Languages and Human-Centric Computing (VL/HCC), pp. 101–105. IEEE (2016)
19. Carbajal-Hernández, J.J., Sánchez-Fernández, L.P., Carrasco-Ochoa, J.A., Martínez-Trinidad, J.F.: Immediate water quality assessment in shrimp culture using fuzzy inference systems. Expert Syst. Appl. **39**, 10571–10582 (2012)
20. Urban, J.: Colormetric experiments on aquatic organisms. In: Rojas, I., Ortuño, F. (eds.) IWBBIO 2017. LNCS, vol. 10208, pp. 96–107. Springer, Cham (2017). https://doi.org/10.1007/978-3-319-56148-6_8
21. Xu, Z., Boyd, C.E.: Reducing the monitoring parameters of fish pond water quality. Aquaculture **465**, 359–366 (2016)
22. Costanzo, A.: An Arduino based system provided with GPS/GPRS shield for real time monitoring of traffic flows. In: AICT 2013 - 7th International Conference on Application of Information and Communication Technologies, Conference Proceedings (2013)
23. Szydlo, T., Nawrocki, P., Brzoza-Woch, R., Zielinski, K.: Power aware MOM for telemetry-oriented applications using GPRS-enabled embedded devices – levee monitoring use case. In: 2014 Federated Conference on Computer Science and Information Systems, FedCSIS 2014 (2014)
24. Al Harrasi, A., Onsy, A., Fragaki, K.: Remotely operated solar panel automated cleaning system. In: Joint Conference: MFPT 2015 and ISA's 61st International Instrumentation Symposium - Technology Evolution: Sensors to Systems for Failure Prevention (2015)

Blockchain in Agriculture: A Systematic Literature Review

Oscar Bermeo-Almeida$^{(\boxtimes)}$ (iD), Mario Cardenas-Rodriguez (iD),
Teresa Samaniego-Cobo (iD), Enrique Ferruzola-Gómez (iD),
Roberto Cabezas-Cabezas (iD), and William Bazán-Vera (iD)

Computer Science Department, Faculty of Agricultural Sciences,
Agrarian University of Ecuador,
Av. 25 de Julio y Pio Jaramillo, P.O. BOX 09-04-100, Guayaquil, Ecuador
{obermeo, mcardenas, tsamaniego, eferruzola, rcabezas,
wbazan}@uagraria.edu.ec

Abstract. Blockchain has been used to solve problems from different sectors. In agriculture, Blockchain is being applied for improving food safety, and transaction times. The increasing interest of Blockchain technology in agriculture calls for a clear, systematic overview. In this sense, we present a systematic literature review (SLR) whose objective is to collect all relevant research on Blockchain technology in agriculture to detect current research topics, main contributions, and benefits of applying Blockchain in agriculture. We have extracted 10 primary studies from scientific databases and web sources published between 2016 and 2018, which means that Blockchain is a recent research area in the agricultural sector. The results show that 60% of papers are focused on food supply chain. Also, 50% of the studies on Blockchain in Agriculture are dominated by Asian community researchers, especially from China. Similarly, the half of the studies addressed challenges related to privacy and security of the Internet of Things with Blockchain technology.

Keywords: Agriculture · Blockchain · Systematic literature review

1 Introduction

Agriculture is one of the most important sectors in the world. The agricultural productivity is important for a country's economy as well as the security, nutrition, and health of its population. In recent years, farmers have adopted different technologies such as IoT and Blockchain aiming to obtain greater yields in the agricultural process.

Blockchain technology has been used for responding to a wide range of challenges from different domains such as financial [1, 2], health [3, 4], and energy [5, 6], to mention but a few. In the agriculture sector, Blockchain is being applied in supply chain management systems to provide transparency, security, neutrality, and reliability of all the operations in a supply chain. Blockchain will also help in solving most of the Internet of things challenges related to security and reliability.

It is important to identify what topics related to the agriculture sector have been already studied and addressed in Blockchain and what are currently the biggest

© Springer Nature Switzerland AG 2018
R. Valencia-García et al. (Eds.): CITI 2018, CCIS 883, pp. 44–56, 2018.
https://doi.org/10.1007/978-3-030-00940-3_4

challenges and limitations that need further studies. To address these questions, we presented a Systematic Literature Review (SLR) to identify relevant papers related to Blockchain in agriculture. The systematic literature review presented was performed by following the methodology proposed by Brereton et al. [7]. This information could help other researchers in identifying possible research areas for future research as well as farmers to know technologies and approaches that are being used.

Although there are currently several works that present a systematic literature review of the Blockchain [8–12], there is still no proposal that presents a systematic literature review of Blockchain in agriculture.

The rest of this paper is organized as follows: Sect. 2 presents the research methodology which is divided into three parts: systematic review planning, systematic review execution, and results, while Sect. 3 presents a discussion of the obtained results. Finally, our conclusions are presented in Sect. 4.

2 Research Methodology

The main goal of a systematic literature review is to detect relevant literature in the subject area. This systematic literature review presented was performed by following the methodology proposed by Brereton et al. [7]. The process consists of three major phases: planning, execution, and result analysis. The first phase refers to planning the review, identifying its needs and defining its protocol which involves (a) research questions, (b) search strategy and (c) studies selection. The second phase consists of the execution of the established plan extracting relevant information. Finally, the third phase consists of providing results and conclusions.

2.1 Systematic Review Planning

This phase defines the way the systematic review will be performed and the research objectives. Hence, we define research questions to be addressed, and planned how the information sources and studies will be selected. This phase is composed of three steps: question formulation, search strategy, and studies selection.

Research Questions
This section presents the three research questions that guided us throughout the research and helped us meet the goals of the Systematic literature review. Table 1 presents the questions and the main motivations.

Search Strategy
The search strategy is at the core of a systematic review. The first stage of our search strategy was to identify the digital libraries and web sources wherein the search for primary studies would be carried out. We selected four digital libraries:

1. IEEE Xplore Digital Library,
2. ACM Digital Library,
3. ScienceDirect (Elsevier),
4. Springer

Table 1. Research questions

Research question (RQ)	Question	Motivation
RQ1	What research topics have been addressed in current research on Blockchain for agriculture?	To detect the main uses of the Blockchain in the agriculture
RQ2	Are there any use cases applicable to the IoT?	To identify cases where is combining IoT with Blockchain technology
RQ3	What are the main benefits of the Blockchain in the agriculture?	To identify the main benefits of the Blockchain in agricultural sector

Furthermore, we selected two Web sources to broaden or results:

5. Google Scholar,
6. Web of science.

The second stage consists of a keyword-based search. To this end, two tasks were performed: (1) we identified a set of keywords related to our research topic; and (2) we identified synonyms for the keywords and related concepts (see Table 2).

Table 2. Keywords used during the systematic review.

Area	Keywords	Related concepts
Agriculture	Agriculture, agricultural	e-Agriculture
		Agribusiness
		Farming
Blockchain	Blockchain	Blockchain

The search strings were built by combining the keywords presented in Table 2 with the connectors "AND" and "OR". Thus, the search chain that we use is the following:

(Agriculture OR e-agriculture OR Agribusiness OR Farming OR Agricultural) AND Blockchain.

Studies Selection

Regarding the studies selection, it began with the selection of only the studies that included at least one keyword referring to the Agricultural sector (e.g. Agriculture, farming, agricultural, e-agriculture), and the other one concerning to the Blockchain technology (Blockchain).

Secondly, we discarded those papers that were not directly related to the Blockchain technology and the agricultural sector.

Thirdly, the set of results obtained was reduced by applying the following exclusion criteria:

1. Papers written in other languages than English.
2. Master and doctoral dissertations.
3. Duplicated articles obtained from Google Scholar and Web of Science.

The objective of this step was to determine which piece of literature found by the search string provides important contributions to the agricultural sector. In cases where we were uncertain about the relevance of the paper, the full-paper was downloaded and sections such as introduction and conclusions were reading.

2.2 Systematic Review Execution

This phase consisted in executing the search in the digital libraries and web sources selected to evaluate the obtained studies considering the inclusion and exclusion criteria. The result of this process was a set of about 44 studies which were filtered by using the inclusion criteria established to give a set of about 18 relevant studies. This set of works was again filtered according to the exclusion criteria.

We obtained 10 primary studies in total (see Table 3). The inclusion and exclusion criteria help us to ensure that the studies were relevant for the research questions established at the planning phase.

Table 3. Total of primary studies.

Data source	Results
IEEE Xplore Digital Library	3
Springer	1
ScienceDirect (Elsevier)	1
Google Scholar	4
Web of Science	1

Information Extraction
Therefore, aiming to answer the research questions, we extracted from studies (1) basic information (publication title and authors), (2) information related to the study (main contribution, objective), and (3) results (topics that have been addressed, their benefits on agricultural sector, and cases applicable to the IoT).

Table 4 provides a general perspective of all studies selected.

Basic Information of the Studies
Figure 1 shows the publication year distribution of the selected primary studies. Most studies were published after the year 2016. This shows that Blockchain is a very recent research area in the agricultural sector. As can be seen, one paper (1%) was published in 2016, five papers (50%) were published in 2017 and four (40%) papers were published in 2018. This shows an increasing number of publications in recent years, which shows also a growing interest in Blockchain technology in the agricultural sector.

Table 4. General perspective of primary studies.

Work	Data source	Objective
Feng [13]	IEEE Xplore Digital Library	Provide an agri-food supply chain traceability system based on Radio-Frequency Identification and Blockchain to enhance food safety and quality of Chinese agri-food markets
Xie et al. [14]		Provide a secured data storage scheme based on Blockchain for agricultural products tracking
Tse et al. [15]		Improve the problem of agricultural food supply chain traceability
Patil et al. [16]	Springer	Provide security and privacy to smart greenhouse farms through a lightweight Blockchain based architecture
Leng et al. [17]	ScienceDirect (Elsevier)	Validate the hypothesis that the chain of agricultural supply chain based on double chain structure can obtain three advantages: (1) consider the openness and security of transaction information and the privacy of enterprise information, (2) self- adaptively complete rent-seeking and matching of resources, and (3) improve the credibility of the public service platform and the overall efficiency of the system
Lin et al. [18]	Google Scholar	Demonstrate that an Information and Communications Technology e-agriculture with a Blockchain infrastructure is the next step in the evolution of ICT e-agriculture
Lucena et al. [19]		Describe and highlight the gains obtained with the implementation of a Blockchain Business Network for Brazilian Agriculture exports
Carbone et al. [20]		Define a food-on-demand business model based on new Quality of Experience (QoE) food metrics to provide better performing value chains
Vinod Kumar [21]		Resolve the major issues in traditional rice supply chain management, logistics industry through of Blockchain technology
Papa [22]	Web of Science	Validate the hypothesis that agricultural sector has a great need for information that supports traceability

Figure 2 shows the geographical distribution of the selected papers. Most of them (30%) were published by universities or companies in China. Another common publication country was Singapore with 2 papers (20%). The rest of countries (USA, Australia, Malaysia, and Taiwan) had one paper published. The geographical distribution of the selected primary papers shows that Blockchain technology of agriculture sector has gathered research interest around the world.

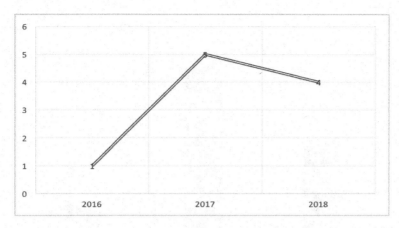

Fig. 1. Publication year of the selected primary studies.

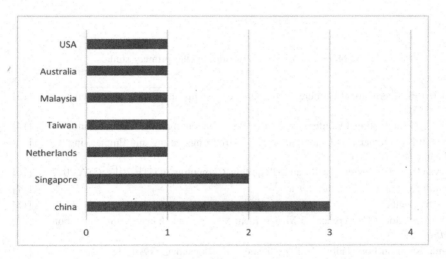

Fig. 2. Geographic distribution of the selected primary papers.

Figure 3 shows the publication type of the selected papers. Publication type means the channel where the paper was published. The publication types included in this study were conference, journal, and symposium. Most of the papers were published in conferences (6) (60%). The rest of the papers were published in journals (3) (30%), as a symposium (1) (10%). In addition, Table 2 shows the publication channel of each selected paper. As can be seen, each paper was published in different publication channels (Table 5).

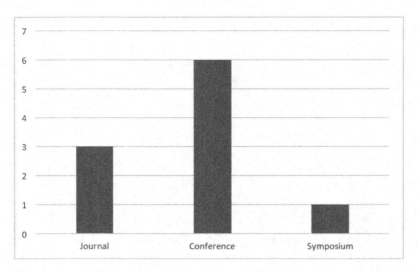

Fig. 3. Publication type.

Table 5. Chanel of publication of the primary studies.

Chanel	Paper
2016 13th International Conference on Service Systems and Service Management (ICSSSM)	[13]
2017 3rd International Conference on Big Data Computing and Communications	[14]
2017 IEEE International Conference on Industrial Engineering and Engineering Management (IEEM)	[15]
Advances in Computer Science and Ubiquitous Computing. CUTE 2017, CSA 2017	[16]
Future Generation Computer Systems	[17]
Environments	[18]
4th International Conference on Management Science and Management Innovation (MSMI 2017)	[22]
Symposium on Foundations and Applications of Blockchain (FAB '18)	[19]
Eighth International Conference on Advances in Computing, Electronics and Electrical Technology - CEET 2018	[20]
Advanced Science and Technology Letters	[21]

2.3   Results

Table 6 shows the studies selected in this systematic literature review, as well as a comparison of them regarding the relevant information established in the previous section. The order of the studies does not determine its importance regarding the goals of this study.

Table 6. Relevant information of the primary studies.

	Topics	Main contribution	IoT	Benefits in agricultural sector
Tian [13]	Agri-food supply chain traceability	An agri-food supply chain traceability system based on Radio-Frequency IDentification and Blockchain technology	No	All the information of the agri-food in the supply chain is transparent and open. In this sense, (1) logistics enterprise can implement real-time tracking for the agri-food products, (2) supervision regulator can execute traceability management and responsibility investigation for a defective product, and (3) the consumer can obtain the full information of the products in the entire agri-food supply chain. These points are important to establish a healthy market environment
Xie et al. [14]	Secured Data Storage	(1) An overall scheme of agricultural tracking data storage based on Blockchain. (2) A double-chain storage structure	Yes	The tracking data is written into the block unchangeably. Thus, the safety of the data and the safety of the food is also guaranteed
Tse et al. [15]	Food supply chain's processing	A supply chain system platform for production processors, brokers, and consumers	No	(1) A complete and smooth information chain which allows all the transaction information transparent among the distributors, suppliers or other relevant parts in the supply chain. The mistakes or errors coming from any part of the supply chain can be found easily. The participants can find out

(continued)

Table 6. (*continued*)

	Topics	Main contribution	IoT	Benefits in agricultural sector
				the solution in a short time and improve the efficiency of the supply chain. (2) Once fake or perishable food flow into the market causing the food safety incidents, it can be much easier to find the original source of the food or material for accountability
Patil et al. [16]	Remote monitoring and automation	A framework for Smart Greenhouse farming based on Blockchain, which provides lightweight and decentralized security and privacy	Yes	(1) Addressed challenges on the Internet of Things such as decentralization, anonymity, and security. (2) Improved reliability, faster and efficient operations and scalability
Leng et al. [17]	Agricultural supply chain	An agricultural supply chain system based on double chain architecture, considering dual chain structure and its storage mode, resource rent-seeking and matching mechanism and consensus algorithm	No	(1) Transparency and security of transaction information and privacy of enterprise information. (2) Improve the credibility of the public service platform and the overall efficiency of the system
Lin et al. [18]	Storage of agricultural and environmental monitoring data	An information and communications technology e-agricultural system based on a Blockchain which includes water quality monitoring data	Yes	Increase the probability of export to international markets since compliance with international standards becomes a transparent and undisputed matter
Lucena et al. [19]	Grain supply chain	A case study for grain quality assurance tracking based on a Blockchain Business Network	Yes	All the members of the Grain Exporters Business Network can share the same business rules and transaction data in their nodes reducing disputes among

(*continued*)

Table 6. (*continued*)

	Topics	Main contribution	IoT	Benefits in agricultural sector
				business partners, information asymmetries and consequently improving governance
Carbone et al. [20]	IoT Supply Chain Management	A distributed (decentralized) hyperledger platform based on Blockchain technology	Yes	Provide transparent and secure supply chain system as well as trust in the origin and entire process of production, transport, and distribution of the food on the market
Vinod Kumar [21]	Rice Supply Chain Management	A supply chain system based on Blockchain technology that assures the safety of rice during supply chain management processes	No	Integral traceability, fight fraud and minimize the system errors because all the events that occur in the supply chain are registering
Papa [22]	Transparency and Monitoring in Agricultural Trade	Apply Blockchain Technology in Agribusiness	No	(1) Manage the agricultural trade while providing guarantees in the certification procedures. (2) Manage trade while providing guarantees in procedures for certification of their quality or origin. (3) Simplify the work of all actors in the "Agri-chain" and make transactions more transparent

3   Result Analysis: Discussion

Taking into account the results obtained from the systematic literature review presented in this work, nowadays, several researchers are focusing their efforts in the supply chain for the agricultural sector. For instance, Tian [13] studied Agri-food supply chains including production (planting/feeding), picking/slaughter, processing, warehousing, distribution and sales. In [15], authors proposed a system to improve the efficiency of food supply chain. Lin et al. [18] presented an agricultural supply chain system based on double chain architecture that considers the security of the data and the privacy of enterprise data. Lucena et al. [19] presented a case of study to measure the quality throughout the transportation of grains along its supply chain. In [20], authors proposed a supply chain platform which is used in the fresh food area where agriculture sustainability is an important issue to address. Finally, Vinod Kumar [21] proposed a supply chain system which allows monitor security and quality of warehouse and transportation of rice from farmers to companies. Meanwhile, secured data storage, remote monitoring, and automation are the least studied.

The Internet of Things technology has been widely applied in agriculture, however, there are some challenges related to privacy and security that need to be addressed. To overcome these challenges, several authors use Blockchain which allows the creation of a distributed digital ledger of transactions that is shared among the nodes on IoT network.

With regards to the effects of Blockchain in agriculture, Blockchain technology has been applied with positive results. To name a few, some of its benefits are: (1) all the information in the supply chain is transparent and open, (2) it addresses challenges on the Internet of Things such as decentralization, anonymity, and security, (3) it improve reliability, faster and efficient operations and scalability.

4 Conclusions

The goal of this study was to identify research topics, main contributions, and benefits of the Blockchain technology in agriculture. We obtained and analyzed 10 primary studies from scientific databases and web sources.

The review papers on Blockchain in agriculture is very dominated by Asian research community, especially from China. Only 3 of the 10 reviewed papers are from non-Asian countries. We attribute this to the fact that agriculture is an important sector in China. In other continents, the concept of Blockchain was up to recently adopted. The most frequently addresses research topic is food supply chains. The dominance of studies dealing with food supply chains can be attributed to the importance management for food safety and food quality. Furthermore, 5 of 10 studies present the combination the IoT and Blockchain in order to addressed challenges related to privacy and security of the IoT.

As future work, we plan to extend this work by including a wider set of digital libraries such as the Wiley Online Library. Furthermore, we expect this systematic literature review to include more issues and proposed solutions to overcome challenges and limitations of Blockchain technology. Finally, we plan to evaluate the effectiveness of the proposed solutions in an objective way.

References

1. Treleaven, P., Gendal Brown, R., Yang, D.: Blockchain technology in finance. Computer (Long Beach, Calif.) **50**, 14–17 (2017)
2. Guo, Y., Liang, C.: Blockchain application and outlook in the banking industry. Financ. Innov. **2**, 24 (2016)
3. Angraal, S., Krumholz, H.M., Schulz, W.L.: Blockchain technology: applications in health care. Circ. Cardiovasc. Qual. Outcomes **10**, e003800 (2017)
4. Mettler, M.: Blockchain technology in healthcare: the revolution starts here. In: 2016 IEEE 18th International Conference on e-Health Networking, Applications and Services (Healthcom), pp. 1–3. IEEE (2016)
5. Mengelkamp, E., Notheisen, B., Beer, C., Dauer, D., Weinhardt, C.: A Blockchain-based smart grid: towards sustainable local energy markets. Comput. Sci. Res. Dev. **33**, 207–214 (2018)
6. Mannaro, K., Pinna, A., Marchesi, M.: Crypto-trading: Blockchain-oriented energy market. In: 2017 AEIT International Annual Conference, pp. 1–5. IEEE (2017)
7. Brereton, P., Kitchenham, B.A., Budgen, D., Turner, M., Khalil, M.: Lessons from applying the systematic literature review process within the software engineering domain. J. Syst. Softw. **80**, 571–583 (2007)
8. Conoscenti, M., Vetro, A., De Martin, J.C.: Blockchain for the internet of things: a systematic literature review. In: 2016 IEEE/ACS 13th International Conference of Computer Systems and Applications (AICCSA), pp. 1–6. IEEE (2016)
9. Yli-Huumo, J., Ko, D., Choi, S., Park, S., Smolander, K.: Where is current research on Blockchain technology?—A systematic review. PLoS ONE **11**, e0163477 (2016)
10. Hawlitschek, F., Notheisen, B., Teubner, T.: The limits of trust-free systems: a literature review on Blockchain technology and trust in the sharing economy. Electron. Commer. Res. Appl. **29**, 50–63 (2018)
11. Seebacher, S., Schüritz, R.: Blockchain technology as an enabler of service systems: a structured literature review. In: Za, S., Drăgoicea, M., Cavallari, M. (eds.) IESS 2017. LNBIP, vol. 279, pp. 12–23. Springer, Cham (2017). https://doi.org/10.1007/978-3-319-56925-3_2
12. Chitchyan, R., Murkin, J.: Review of Blockchain technology and its expectations: case of the energy sector (2018)
13. Tian, F.: An agri-food supply chain traceability system for China based on RFID & Blockchain technology. In: 2016 13th International Conference on Service Systems and Service Management (ICSSSM), pp. 1–6. IEEE (2016)
14. Xie, C., Sun, Y., Luo, H.: Secured data storage scheme based on block chain for agricultural products tracking. In: 2017 3rd International Conference on Big Data Computing and Communications (BIGCOM), pp. 45–50. IEEE (2017)
15. Tse, D., Zhang, B., Yang, Y., Cheng, C., Mu, H.: Blockchain application in food supply information security. In: 2017 IEEE International Conference on Industrial Engineering and Engineering Management (IEEM), pp. 1357–1361. IEEE (2017)
16. Patil, A.S., Tama, B.A., Park, Y., Rhee, K.-H.: A framework for Blockchain based secure smart green house farming. In: Park, J.J., Loia, V., Yi, G., Sung, Y. (eds.) CUTE/CSA - 2017. LNEE, vol. 474, pp. 1162–1167. Springer, Singapore (2018). https://doi.org/10.1007/978-981-10-7605-3_185
17. Leng, K., Bi, Y., Jing, L., Fu, H.-C., Van Nieuwenhuyse, I.: Research on agricultural supply chain system with double chain architecture based on Blockchain technology. Future Gener. Comput. Syst. (2018)

18. Lin, Y.-P., et al.: Blockchain: the evolutionary next step for ICT E-agriculture. Environments **4**, 50 (2017)
19. Lucena, P., Binotto, A.P.D., Momo, F.S., Kim, H.: A case study for grain quality assurance tracking based on a Blockchain business network. In: Symposium on Foundations and Applications of Blockchain (FAB 2018), pp. 1–6 (2018)
20. Carbone, A., Davcev, D., Mitreski, K., Kocarev, L., Stankovski, V.: Blockchain based distributed cloud fog platform for IoT supply chain management. In: Eighth International Conference on Advances in Computing, Electronics and Electrical Technology - CEET 2018, pp. 51–58. Institute of Research Engineers and Doctors (2018)
21. Vinod Kumar, M., Iyengar, N.C.S.N.: A framework for Blockchain technology in rice supply chain management. Adv. Sci. Technol. Lett. **146**, 125–130 (2017)
22. Papa, S.F.: Use of Blockchain technology in agribusiness: transparency and monitoring in agricultural trade. In: Proceedings of the 2017 International Conference on Management Science and Management Innovation (MSMI 2017). Atlantis Press, Paris (2017)

Mobile Applications for Crops Management

Katty Lagos-Ortiz[1]([email]) [ID], José Medina-Moreira[1,3],
Andrea Sinche-Guzmán[1], Mayra Garzón-Goya[1],
Vanessa Vergara-Lozano[1] [ID], and Rafael Valencia-García[2] [ID]

[1] Facultad de Ciencias Agrarias, Universidad Agraria del Ecuador,
Avenida 25 de julio, Guayaquil, Ecuador
`{klagos,jmedina,asinche,mgarzon,`
`vvergara}@uagraria.edu.ec`
[2] Facultad de Informática, Universidad de Murcia,
Campus de Espinardo, 30100 Murcia, Spain
`valencia@um.es`
[3] Facultad de Ciencias Matemáticas y Físicas, Universidad de Guayaquil. Cdla.
Universitaria "Salvador Allende", Guayaquil, Ecuador
`{katty.lagoso,jose.medinamo}@ug.edu.ec`

Abstract. Information and Communications Technology play an important role in the agricultural sector due to it helps to perform activities such as agricultural re-sources management. The efficiency in the crop production, i.e. produce more with less, is a challenge that must be addressed. Therefore, it is necessary to develop computer applications that help farmers and/or students of agronomy to perform activities such as treatment of plant diseases and pests, precision agriculture, and quality of production, among others. Smartphones and mobile applications have become part of the daily lives of people. Nowadays, mobile technologies offer optimal and integral solutions for agriculture. Hence, it is important to adopt these technologies for performing daily agriculture tasks. This work presents an evaluation and comparison of mobile applications for agriculture. This comparison considers the applications hosted in both Play Store for Android devices and App Store for IOS devices. Furthermore, this study considers the main characteristics required by farmers for performing crop control and monitoring such as pests and insects' management, meteorological aspects, machinery, working hours, geolocation, harvest time, tasks management, areas of cultivation, among others.

Keywords: Mobile applications · Mobile technology · Agriculture
Crop management

1 Introduction

ICT (Information and Communications Technology) play an important role in the agricultural sector due to it helps to perform activities such as agricultural resources management [1]. Considering that the demand for food by 2050 will be 900 billion, it will be necessary to increase food production by 60% to meet the feeding needs of the population [2]. The efficiency in the crop production, i.e. produce more with less, is a

R. Valencia-García et al. (Eds.): CITI 2018, CCIS 883, pp. 57–69, 2018.
https://doi.org/10.1007/978-3-030-00940-3_5

challenge that must be addressed. Therefore, it is necessary to develop computer applications that help small, medium, and large farmers and/or students of agronomy to perform activities such as treatment of plant diseases and pests, precision agriculture, and quality of production, among others.

The SPS (Sanitary and Phytosanitary) measures establish standards to protect animal and plant health as well as food safety [3]. These standards are important to minimize crop losses caused by pests, which remains a major challenge of productivity of farms from LAC (Latin America and the Caribbean) [4]. As was previous mentioned, TICs are important for the development and growth of the agricultural sector since they provide a wide variety of cost-effective solutions that can improve productivity and sustainability of small producers. Furthermore, they provide farmers a better access to financial services, agricultural data, weather forecasting and market-related information [5].

The evaluation of the effects of access to agricultural information in LAC shows that reducing information asymmetries can have a positive and significant impact on producers. This impact refers to the fact that they will be able to negotiate better prices or more attractive terms of sale. However, constraints on infrastructure, education or investment in complementary services throughout the region will limit producers to be part of these networks and value chains [6].

Smartphones and mobile applications have become part of the daily lives of people. On the one hand, mobile applications have evolved from only basic applications to applications with advanced multiplatform functions [7]. On the other hand, the use of mobile devices with access to the Internet has increased significantly, indeed, it is estimated that by 2020 two billion of people will have a smartphone [8]. There are different studies about the use of mobile applications in many areas, such as medicine and agriculture. For instance, in the medicine domain, they are used to help diseases management [9]. Meanwhile, in the agriculture domain, they are used for managing agricultural crops.

The development of technologies oriented to agricultural research can be improved through a greater involvement of IT specialists. Some tasks of agriculture that must be addressed are: (1) management of crops, including the diseases and pests management and the obtaining of higher yields; (2) insufficient labor, which can be addressed by considering the plant to be harvest in seasons of low labor demand; (3) pests management, which can reduces the need for more labor and the use of pesticides, as well as farmers' exposure to dangerous chemicals; (4) conservation agriculture, which reduces the work required for land preparation because the field is covered with protective crops and the planting does not require the preparation of the nursery.

In the countries of Latin America and the Caribbean, the agriculture has a great impact on the GDP (Gross Domestic Product). However, these countries invest on research for agriculture only $1.10 for every $100 generated by the agriculture sector. Meanwhile, in countries with better economies, the investment is typically three times greater than in LAC region [10].

Mobile technologies offer optimal and integral solutions for agriculture. Hence, it is important to adopt these technologies for performing daily agriculture tasks. In this work, a comparison of mobile applications for agriculture is presented.

The use of agricultural applications is not only a reality in developed countries where, according to several studies, it has been possible to integrate technological solutions to several areas. This phenomenon also allows obtaining evidence of the techniques used and knowledge about soils and pests. This information allows the agricultural community to understand the trends and measures to be considered for achieving a development both at scientifically and political levels [8].

The use of mobile applications in the agricultural area represents a tool capable of promoting different tasks which gone from basic education to the monitoring and reduction of deforestation and forest degradation. Finally, according to the World Bank mobile applications represent a pillar of the strategy for participatory rural development. Furthermore, the information generated by these applications can contribute to decision-making in times of crisis in this productive sector [11].

This work presents an evaluation and comparison of mobile applications for agriculture. This comparison considered the applications hosted in both Play Store for Android devices and App Store for IOS devices. This comparison considers the main characteristics required by farmers such as pests and insects' management, meteorological aspects, machinery, working hours, geolocation, harvest time, tasks management, cultivation areas, among others.

Additionally, and as future work, the authors intend to analyze the characteristics of each of the applications in order to create an efficient and intelligent application that covers all the functionalities required by farmers.

2 Classification of Mobile Applications

The processes of agroindustry require a better automation. In this sense, the TICs are very important for automating tasks such as crop monitoring and management [12]. The concept of precision agriculture refers to the management of agricultural parcels based on observation, measurement, and action against inter and intra-crop variability. The automated control and management of crops have also become priorities in this area.

The present study aims to classify the mobile applications according to the area they are focused. Next sections describe the main categories that were established for the purposes of this work.

2.1 Mobile Applications for Precision Agriculture

This category groups all those mobile applications that are focused on automating tasks related to precision agriculture. In other words, the mobile applications that allow managing spatial and temporal variability associated with all aspects of agricultural production. These applications aim to improve the crop yield and environmental quality [13].

One of the most outstanding mobile applications for precision agriculture is Agriprecision, which includes GPS functionalities to show farmers routes to collect samples from the field. Furthermore, this application calculates the glebe area, the generation of the sampling network, and the exportation of sampling and border grid points to generate sampled and recommended maps.

2.2   Mobile Applications for Crop Monitoring and Control

Most mobile applications for agriculture aims to control and manage crops. Despite these applications do not cover all aspects related to the crop management, all they try to meet all requirements of farmers. It is very important for farmers to control all processes related to the crop such as sowing, obtain a history of the crops and collect information about their state.

Agroptima is a mobile application that allows performing different tasks related to the control of crops. Some of these tasks are the generation of reports about the agricultural tasks, complying with the field notebook and increase the profitability through cost control [14]. Other applications that allow performing above tasks are Agrivi and Cutivapp.

2.3   Informative Applications - Reference Databases

This category groups all those mobile applications that allow obtaining information about agricultural products such as herbicides, pesticides, fertilizers, and vademecums. The applications PlantCarePro and "Soy de campo" belong to this because they were designed to provide all above-mentioned information to farmers.

2.4   Mobile Applications for Social Networks

There are mobile applications that aim to provide a database of professionals and farmers. AgroContactos is an application that allows keeping the updated information of people expert on agriculture such as farmers, sellers, specialists, suppliers, among others.

2.5   Mobile Applications for Pests and Nutrients Control

This category groups the applications focused on the control of pests that affect crops and the nutrients of plants. This kind of applications provide information about the optimal quantities of nutrients plant should have. Also, these applications help to instruct farmers in the control of crops including activities such as planting, harvesting and post-harvesting, nutrients control and herbicide control for pest control. Some of the most outstanding applications of this group are AgriApp and AgroIn.

3   Analysis of the Mobile Applications

3.1   Method

The present study attempts to find and analyze current mobile applications focused on agriculture. The search for applications was performed by using the terms agriculture, crop, and pests. To reinforce this study, a search for similar studies was performed [11] the authors presented the state of the art of the research literature in how smartphone have been used in agriculture using internal sensors. Therefore, based on the work presented in [8], exhaustive searches for applications focused on agriculture were performed.

From the App Store (IOS) 86 applications were obtained. From this group of applications, 2 were not considered in the study because they were oriented to home gardens and they do not meet all functionalities established in this study. Also, these applications received low rating from users who downloaded these applications. Regarding Play Store (Android), 104 applications were obtained, from which 6 do not meet all requirements established in this study.

A total of 190 applications focused on agriculture were analyzed. However, to reduce such group, the application must meet some of next features: crop monitoring, pests control, field notebooks, land measurement, use of pesticides, meteorological data, phytosanitary measures, crop care, crop productivity as well as magazines and information about agroindustry.

3.2   Results

There are a lot of applications that address tasks related to the agriculture. The search process considered the effectiveness of the applications, as well as their usability and popularity among users. The result of the search process is a set of 190 mobile applications. From this group of applications, 188 are free, i.e. users could download and use them freely. Regarding Android applications, there are 2 applications whose prices are \$2.07 and \$4.67. Regarding the rating provided by users to Android applications, all they were rated with 4.0 to 5.0 stars. About the IOS applications, 84 are free applications. The final set of applications to be analyzed in detail consists of 20 mobile applications (10 IOS applications and 10 Android Applications). The selection process of these mobile applications considered the popularity of them (most popular were selected) and the functionalities provided by them. A clear description of the search process is presented in Fig. 1.

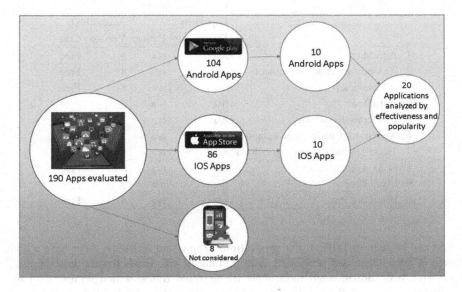

Fig. 1. Mobile applications evaluated in this work.

The study presented in this work is based on the analysis of the functionalities provided by the applications. However, other features were considered, namely input and output data, number of downloads, popularity, rating, functionality and effectiveness.

Tables 1 and 2 present a comparison of the 20 applications selected from Play Store (Android) and App Store (IOS) according to the features above-mentioned.

Table 1. Android applications.

	Application	General evaluation			
		Popularity		Accessibility	
		Downloads	Rating	Version	Cost
1	Agroptima	10 k	4.4	4.0.3	Free
2	ADAMA Alvo	50 k	4.6	4.1	Free
3	IZagro	10 k	4.6	4.0.3	Free
4	Syngenta Soluciones	50 k	4.3	4.0	Free
5	AgroMapp	10 k	4.5	2.3.3	Free
6	Agrosolución	1 k	4.4	4.2	Free
7	Appgro::Monitoreo agrícola	5 k	3.7	2.1	Free
8	Agrofarm	10 k	4.5	4.0	Free
9	Mi cultivo con Bayer	10 k	4.4	4.1	Free
10	Agri App	100 k	4.2	4.0.3	Free

Table 2. IOS applications.

	Application	General evaluation			
		Popularity		Accessibility	
		Downloads	Rating	Version	Cost
1	AgroMapp	n/a	n/a	5.1	Free
2	Agroptima - cuaderno agricola	n/a	n/a	8	Free
3	Agrosolución	n/a	n/a	8	Free
4	AgroDash	n/a	n/a	5	Free
5	Cuaderno de Campo	n/a	n/a	5.1	Free
6	Agricolum Cuaderno de campo	n/a	n/a	8	Free
7	Tierra Digital Adama Agricultura	n/a	n/a	9	Free
8	PLM Agroquímicos	n/a	n/a	6	Free
9	iAgricultor	n/a	n/a	9	Free
10	PlantCare Pro	n/a	n/a	8	Free

As can be seen in Table 1, the applications IZagro and ADAMA Alvo have a high degree of acceptance and popularity with a rating of 4.6. Furthermore, these applications have been downloaded more than 10 thousand times, which represents a big number compared to other applications that have been downloaded 1 thousand times.

Regarding accessibility, these applications are free and can be downloaded from any Android device (version 4.0 or higher). All mobile applications presented in Table 1 have been downloaded more than 256 thousand times. The most downloaded application is Agri App with more than 100 thousand times.

On the other hand, as can be seen in Table 2, the IOS applications analyzed are free, and the devices where they can be installed must have the operating system version 5.1 or higher (App Store does not provide more information).

The mobile applications selected were analyzed and a set of input (requested by the application) and output parameters (provided by the application) were obtained. On the one hand, input parameters refer to the information that must be provided by the user such as username, password, costs, geolocation, dates of cultivation, among others. Furthermore, these parameters include those that allows performing tasks such as the search for crops, pests, phytosanitary information, goods and financing. On the other hand, out parameters refer to the information provided based on the input parameters. This information is related to the crops, crop monitoring, meteorological data, and even alerts on pest control, among others. Next sections provide a description of the input and output parameters.

Input Parameters

The parameter requested by the applications are:

1. User and password. The application requests users to register to allow them to use the application.
2. Project's name, gleba, and area. This feature allows the application to obtain the name of the project as well as the area to cultivate, to determine the crop spaces (output parameter).
3. Start and end dates of the activity. It refers to the start and end dates of the activity to determine the harvest time (output parameter).
4. Distance, perimeter and surface of the crop. It allows providing the distance of crops, the perimeter and surface of the crop to be treated.
5. Phytosanitary products, fertilizers, seeds. It allows providing information about phytosanitary products, fertilizers and seeds to determine if these products are appropriate for the selected crops.
6. Insect, disease, pest. It refers to the insect, disease or pest that is affecting the crop to recommend the pesticide or herbicide to be used.
7. Number of people that help to control the crop. It refers to the number of people that control the crop to know its performance.
8. Meteorological data and geolocation. It allows providing meteorological information such as weather, humidity, among others, as well as the location of the area to be cultivated.
9. Costs of each cultivation. It refers to the costs of crops per hectare to calculate total costs.
10. Access from a personal computer. It allows accessing to the application from a personal computer and from the mobile device.

Tables 3 and 4 present the comparison of the Android and IOS mobile applications analyzed in this study. This comparison considers the input parameters above presented.

Table 3. Input parameters of the Android applications analyzed.

	Application	Input parameter									
		1	2	3	4	5	6	7	8	9	10
1	Agroptima	x	x		x	x				x	x
2	ADAMA Alvo					x	x		x		
3	IZagro	x				x	x				
4	Syngenta Soluciones		x			x			x	x	
5	AgroMapp		x			x	x				
6	Agrosolución					x				x	
7	Appgro::Monitoreo agrícola	x		x	x			x	x	x	x
8	Agrofarm		x	x		x				x	
9	Mi cultivo con Bayer	x		x		x		x			
10	Agri App	x				x					

Table 4. Input parameters of the IOS applications analyzed.

	Application	Input parameter									
		1	2	3	4	5	6	7	8	9	10
1	AgroMapp	x	x		x	x				x	x
2	Agroptima - cuaderno agricola		x			x	x				
3	Agrosolución					x				x	
4	AgroDash		x	x					x		
5	Cuaderno de Campo	x		x					x		
6	Agricolum Cuaderno de campo		x		x	x	x	x	x	x	
7	Tierra Digital Adama Agricultura	x				x	x		x		
8	PLM Agroquímicos					x			x		
9	iAgricultor	x	x			x	x		x		x
10	PlantCare Pro			x		x	x	x			

As can be seen in Table 3, some applications provide more features than other ones. For instance, the application "Appgro::Monitoreo agrícola" provides 7 out of 10 features, which makes this application the most complete. Meanwhile, the applications "Agrosolución" and "Agri app" provides support for only two input parameters, including phytosanitary products, costs of cultivation and user and password.

From Table 3, it can be noted that most applications (9 out of 10) provide support for phytosanitary products, fertilizer, and seeds (input parameter 5). Furthermore, the input parameters 1 (user and password) and 9 (cost of each cultivation) are presented in half of the applications. On the other hand, Ap-pgro::Monitoreo agrícola is the only application that provides support for register the number of people that control the crop (input parameter 7).

Regarding IOS mobile applications, Table 4 presents the comparison of these ones. As can be observed, the application that provides more functionalities is "Agricolum Cuaderno de campo" which provides support for 7 out of 10 features. Some features that it does not support are the start and end dates of the activity and access from a personal computer. The application that provides less functionalities is "Agrosolución", which deals with information about phytosanitary products, fertilizers and seeds and costs of each cultivation.

Like Android applications, the input parameter 5 (Phytosanitary products, fertilizers, seeds) is present in most IOS applications (8 out of 10). The second input parameter to which most IOS applications provide support is the number 8 (6 out of 10), which refers to the meteorological data and location. Finally, 5 out of the 10 applications analyzed in this work provide support for the input parameters 2 and 6 which refer to the project's name, gleba and area and insect, disease and pest, respectively.

Output Parameters
The output parameters comprised those data provided by the system in response to the parameters provided by the users. The output parameters considered in this study are:

1. Information about the use, application and dosage of the product to be used to deal with the pest. The application provides information about the pesticides and fungicides depending on the crop and disease.
2. Sampling and performance of the agricultural production. The application show information about the yield of agricultural productions by means of graphics.
3. Information related to the agriculture, goods and financing. It refers to the up-to-date information about agricultural products.
4. Alerts, control, planning and monitoring of agricultural activities and supplies. Considering the input parameters, the application generates alerts for the monitoring and control of crops, including reminders for supplies.
5. Alerts for the detection of a pest. It allows generating alerts when a pest is detected in the crop.
6. Phytosanitary products, studies of the field, field notebook. The application provides information concerning phytosanitary products used in crops. Furthermore, the application serves as field notebook thus allowing farmers to register the tasks of the agricultural process.
7. Offer and add information about control, register and monitoring of the crop. The application provides farmers information about the control and monitoring of the crop.
8. Sampling grid and calculation of the area of gleba. The application generates a sampling grid based on geolocation data. Furthermore, it computes the area of gleba.
9. Information about climate in greenhouse. In places where there are greenhouses, this option offers information about the weather of the day.
10. Information about deficiencies in crops. The application provides information concerning deficiencies that crops could have.

Table 5 presents the comparison results of the Android applications for agriculture. As can be seen, the best application is "Mi cultivo con Bayer", which provides information concerning 6 out of 10 aspects of agricultural processes. This application does not provide information about (2) sampling and performance of the agricultural production, (5) alerts for the detection of a pest, (8) sampling grid and calculation of the area of gleba, and (9) information about climate in the greenhouse. Meanwhile, the application that provides less information is "Agroptima", which only provides alerts for the detection of a pest.

Table 5. Output parameters of the Android applications analyzed.

	Application	Output parameter									
		1	2	3	4	5	6	7	8	9	10
1	Agroptima					x					
2	ADAMA Alvo	x									x
3	IZagro	x					x	x			
4	Syngenta Soluciones			x			x	x		x	x
5	AgroMapp	x			x			x		x	x
6	Agrosolución	x	x				x	x			x
7	Appgro::Monitoreo agrícola	x		x				x			x
8	Agrofarm			x			x	x			x
9	Mi cultivo con Bayer	x		x	x		x	x			x
10	Agri App	x		x			x	x			

The output parameter 7 (Information about control, register and monitoring of the crop) is supported by most Android applications (8 out of 10). Output parameters 1 (information about the use, application and dosage of the product to be used to deal with the pest) and 10 (information about deficiencies in crops) are present in 7 out of the 10 Android applications. Finally, the output parameter 6 (Phytosanitary products, studies of the field, field notebook) is present in 6 out of the 10 applications analyzed.

Finally, Table 6 presents the comparison of IOS mobile applications regarding output parameters. As can be observed, there are three application that provide a greater number of functionalities (5) namely "Agroptima - cuaderno Agricola", "Agrosolución" and "iAgricultor". All these applications provide information about the use, application and dosage of the product to be used to deal with the pest. Meanwhile, the application "AgroMapp" only provides alerts for the detection of a pest. Also, it can be observed that the application "AgroDash" is the only one that provides information about sampling and performance of the agricultural production.

Most IOS applications (7 out of 10) provides support for the out parameter 1 (information about the use, application and dosage of the product to be used to deal with the pest). Also, 5 out of the 10 analyzed applications provide support for the output parameters 7 (offer and add information about control, register and monitoring of the crop) and 10 (information about deficiencies in crops).

Table 6. Output parameters of the IOS applications analyzed.

	Application	Output parameter									
		1	2	3	4	5	6	7	8	9	10
1	AgroMapp				x						
2	Agroptima - cuaderno agricola	x		x			x		x	x	
3	Agrosolución	x	x			x	x			x	
4	AgroDash		x				x				
5	Cuaderno de Campo								x	x	
6	Agricolum Cuaderno de campo	x		x		x	x			x	
7	Tierra Digital Adama Agricultura	x					x		x		
8	PLM Agroquímicos	x	x	x						x	
9	iAgricultor	x				x	x		x	x	
10	PlantCare Pro	x					x				

Considering the analysis of the Android and IOS applications regarding input and output parameters that can be managed through them, the features that must be integrated into an optimal mobile application for crop management are:

- Input parameters. (a) Registration of phytosanitary products, fertilizers and seeds; (b) Meteorological data and geolocation; (c) Users and password management; and (d) registration of the project's name, gleba, and area.
- Output parameters. (a) information about the use, application and dosage of the product to be used to deal with the pest; (b) sampling and performance of the agricultural production; (c) alerts, control, planning and monitoring of agricultural activities and supplies; and (d) phytosanitary products, studies of the field, field notebook.

4   Conclusions and Future Works

This work presents an analysis of Android and IOS applications for agriculture. This analysis considered 20 applications (10 for Android and 10 for IOS), which were compared against 10 input parameters and 10 output parameters. The results indicate that the 85% of these applications allows providing information concerning phytosanitary products, fertilizers, and seeds. It should be mentioned that this information could have been registered in the database of the application. Also, the 70% of these applications provides information about agrochemical products, the application, and dosage of the product to be used to deal with the pest. Another data to be remarked is that 65% of the applications offer and add information about control, registration, and monitoring of the crop. Regarding possible crop deficiencies, 60% of the applications provide information about it.

The features above described are presented in most applications. However, it is also important to mention that the 50% of the applications allows the input of meteorological data, as well as the location of both crops and suppliers of agricultural products such as pesticides and herbicides. Also, 50% of the applications allow registering phytosanitary products, field studies and act as a field notebook. Only the 45% of the applications allows creating user profiles, as well as to provide information related to the project such as name, gleba, sowing, and area to cultivate. Finally, only the 20% of the applications allow access to the application through a personal computer, including support for the synchronization of data by means of a Web application.

Finally, it must be mentioned that the use of mobile technologies helps to improve and automate several agricultural tasks. Also, they help to address the gap between technologies and agriculture since many farmers use these tool for performing many tasks such as crop control and monitoring. Nowadays, the agricultural sector in Ecuador has been influenced by this technology, which has facilitated several agricultural processes, thus allowing to reduce the costs as well as to increase the yield of the them.

The future work is oriented to establish based on the analysis carried out, the implementation of a web and mobile application that allows covering all the expectations of the users regarding the control and monitoring of crops.

References

1. Salazar, L., Aramburu, J., González, M., et al.: Food Security and Productivity: Impacts of Technology Adoption in Small Subsistence Farmers in Bolivia (2016)
2. Zeigler, M., Truitt Nakata, G., Zeigler, M., et al.: O próximo celeiro global: Como a América Latina pode alimentar o mundo: Um chamado à ação para o enfrentamento dos desafios e a busca de soluções (2016)
3. Melgar-Quiñonez, H., Zubieta, A.C., Valdez, E., et al.: Validación de un instrumento para vigilar la inseguridad alimentaria en la Sierra de Manantlán, Jalisco. Salud Publica Mex. **47**, 413–422 (2005). https://doi.org/10.1590/S0036-36342005000600005
4. David, M.B.D.A., Dirven, M., Vogelgesang, F.: The impact of the new economic model on Latin America's agriculture. World Dev. **28**, 1673–1688 (2000). https://doi.org/10.1016/S0305-750X(00)00047-4
5. Ali, J., Kumar, S.: Information and communication technologies (ICTs) and farmers' decision-making across the agricultural supply chain. Int. J. Inf. Manag. **31**, 149–159 (2011). https://doi.org/10.1016/j.ijinfomgt.2010.07.008
6. López, C.A., Salazar, L., De Salvo, C.P.: Public Expenditures, Impact Evaluations and Agricultural Productivity: Summary of the Evidence from Latin America and the Caribbean (2017). https://doi.org/10.18235/0000627
7. Meyer, G., Shaheen, S. (eds.): Disrupting Mobility. LNM. Springer, Cham (2017). https://doi.org/10.1007/978-3-319-51602-8
8. Dehnen-Schmutz, K., Foster, G.L., Owen, L., Persello, S.: Exploring the role of smartphone technology for citizen science in agriculture. Agron. Sustain. Dev. **36**, 25 (2016). https://doi.org/10.1007/s13593-016-0359-9
9. Medina-Moreira, J., Lagos-Ortiz, K., Luna-Aveiga, H., Paredes, R., Valencia-García, R.: Usage of diabetes self-management mobile technology: options for ecuador. In: Valencia-García, R., Lagos-Ortiz, K., Alcaraz-Mármol, G., del Cioppo, J., Vera-Lucio, N. (eds.) CITI 2016. CCIS, vol. 658, pp. 79–89. Springer, Cham (2016). https://doi.org/10.1007/978-3-319-48024-4_7

10. Alston, J., Wyatt, T.J., Pardey, P., et al.: A Meta-analysis of Rates of Return to Agricultural R&D. IFPRI, Washington (2000)
11. Pongnumkul, S., Chaovalit, P., Surasvadi, N.: Applications of smartphone-based sensors in agriculture: a systematic review of research. J. Sens. **2015**, 1–18 (2015). https://doi.org/10.1155/2015/195308
12. Auernhammer, H.: Precision farming—the environmental challenge. Comput. Electron. Agric. **30**, 31–43 (2001). https://doi.org/10.1016/S0168-1699(00)00153-8
13. Pierce, F.J., Nowak, P. Aspects of Precision Agriculture, pp. 1–85 (1999)
14. Agroptima. https://www.agroptima.com/. Accessed 20 July 2018

SE-DiagEnf: An Ontology-Based Expert System for Cattle Disease Diagnosis

Abel Alarcón-Salvatierra[1](✉), William Bazán-Vera[1] (iD),
Teresa Samaniego-Cobo[1] (iD), Silvia Medina Anchundia[2] (iD),
and Pablo Alarcón-Salvatierra[2] (iD)

[1] Computer Science Department, Faculty of Agricultural Sciences,
Agrarian University of Ecuador, Av. 25 de Julio y Pio Jaramillo,
P.O. BOX 09-04-100, Guayaquil, Ecuador
{jalarcon, wbazan, tsamaniego}@uagraria.edu.ec
[2] Engineering in Networking and Telecommunications,
Faculty of Mathematical and Physical Sciences, State University of Guayaquil,
Av. Delta y Av. Kennedy, 471 Guayaquil, Ecuador
{silvia.medinaa, pablo.alarcons}@ug.edu.ec

Abstract. Cattle husbandry industry is an important development sector in many countries around the world. One of the main problems in this sector concerns cattle diseases which result in low productivity. A rapid diagnosis of the disease is particularly important for its prevention, control, and treatment. However, the main players on cattle husbandry industry highly depend on veterinarians to cope with this problem. Unfortunately, the number of veterinarians in some cities is very limited or they live far away from the farm. In this sense, it is necessary to provide farmers tools that help them to correctly diagnose the cattle diseases. Nowadays, there are technologies that can help to address this issue. On the one hand, expert systems are an active research area for medical diagnosis and recommending treatments. On the other hand, ontologies can be used for modeling the domain of cattle diseases diagnosis and for generating the knowledge base that is required by the expert system to perform its corresponding tasks. In this work, we present SE-DiagEnf, an ontology-based expert system that diagnoses cattle diseases based on a set of symptoms and provides recommendations for tackling the disease diagnosed. The main goal of this system is to decrease the dependency of farmers on veterinarians to cope with cattle diseases diagnosis and treatment. SE-DiagEnf was evaluated by farmers from Ecuador. In this evaluation, farmers had to provide a set of symptoms to allows the system to diagnose the cattle disease. The evaluation results seem promising based on the F-measure metric.

Keywords: Ontology · Cattle · Disease diagnosis

1 Introduction

Cattle husbandry industry is an important development sector in many countries around the world, in fact, cattle is one of the main sources of meat, milk, and labor [1]. One of the main problems in this area concerns the diagnosis and treatment of the diseases,

© Springer Nature Switzerland AG 2018
R. Valencia-García et al. (Eds.): CITI 2018, CCIS 883, pp. 70–81, 2018.
https://doi.org/10.1007/978-3-030-00940-3_6

indeed, cattle diseases result in low productivity in cattle husbandry sector. Therefore, a rapid diagnosis of cattle diseases is particularly important for their prevention, control, and treatment. However, the main players on cattle husbandry industry highly depend on veterinarians to cope with this problem. Unfortunately, the number of veterinarians in some cities is very limited or they live far away from the farm. Furthermore, since the disease cannot be accurately diagnosed by farmers, they use medicines or antibiotics that are not prescribed by experts. This situation can result in a significant impact on the ecological environment and food safety [2, 3]. In this sense, it is necessary to provide support to the cattle husbandry industry, particularly for the cattle diseases diagnosing. Indeed, the research of diagnostic, prevention and treatment methods and technologies for cattle diseases has become a priority among various research institutions.

Nowadays, there are a lot of technologies that can help to deal with the problem above mentioned. For instance, expert systems are an active research area as a mean for medical diagnosis and recommending treatment [4]. According to Darlington [5], an expert system is a program that attempts to mimic human expertise by applying inference methods to a specific body of knowledge. Hence, an expert system could help farmers to analyze the cattle health status and diagnose the disease without needing a veterinarian. On the other hand, ontologies are the main semantic web technology that allows computers to automate, integrate, and reuse high-quality information from distributed data sources [6]. Studer et al. [7] define an ontology as a formal and explicit specification of a shared conceptualization. Ontologies have been successfully applied in a variety of domains such as question-answering systems for Semantic knowledge bases [8], finances [9], and human resources management [10], to mention but a few. In this context, ontologies can be used for modeling the domain of cattle diseases diagnosis and for generating the knowledge base that is required by the expert system to perform its corresponding tasks.

Based on the fact described above, in this work, we propose the use of Information Technology (IT) to develop an intelligent system for cattle diseases diagnosis as well as for providing recommendations for tackling the diseases. The system determines the disease based on a set of symptoms provided by the farmer. The main goal of this system is to decrease the dependency of farmers on veterinarians to cope with cattle diseases diagnosis and treatment. In this way, the number of death cattle can be reduced.

The remainder of this paper is structured as follows: Sect. 2 discusses a set of systems for cattle diseases diagnosis that use multiple technologies such as fuzzy neural networks. Then, Sect. 3 details the components of the SE-DiagEnf architecture, whereas Sect. 4 addresses the evaluation performed to test the effectiveness of SE-DiagEnf in terms of efficacy regarding cattle disease diagnosis. Finally, Sect. 5 discusses the research conclusions and future directions.

2 Related Work

Because of the advances in hardware and software as well as processing capabilities, many researchers have proposed expert systems to improve animals' disease diagnosis. For instance, Jampour et al. [11] presented a Fuzzy-based system for diagnosing domestic animal diseases. This system uses neurological signs to reduce natural uncertainty regarding the diagnosis of the disease. On the other hand, Munirah et al. [12] proposed a Web-based expert system for dog's diseases diagnosis. This system aims to detect disease in an early stage and assist owners by providing them treatment suggestion. The system has a knowledge base with rules of symptoms and diseases. These rules use an IF/THEN structure where the information contained in the IF clause is related to the information contained in the THEN clause. Finally, it should be mentioned that all knowledge used by this system is obtained from a set of interviews performed to veterinarians.

There are research efforts focused on cow disease diagnosis, for instance, Zamsuri et al. [1] presented a Web-based expert system to determine the cow disease based on a set of symptoms experienced by animals. These symptoms are obtained through a set of questions that farmers must answer. To deal with uncertainty, this system conducts the diagnostic process using Certainty Factor. Furthermore, a set of rules for disease diagnoses have been made in accordance with the experts' knowledge. Nusai et al. [13] presented a cow diseases diagnosis method that consists in two phases namely: disease screening and disease diagnosis. Also, they proposed a knowledge model to infer the disease through variables such as gender, age range, and a weight of symptom to deal with uncertainty. In this way, the method uses the significant weight of symptom and the certainty factor of symptom to perform disease diagnosis. On the other hand, Lian et al. [14] consider that animal disease diagnosis is a pattern classification and identification problem. Therefore, they proposed a model for cow disease diagnosis that uses SVM (Support Vector Machine) and HSMC (Hyper Sphere Multiclass SVM) technologies. This model consists of three main modules namely preprocessing module, HSMC-SVM training module, and HSMC-SVM classification module. More specifically, this model implements the SMO (Sequential Minimal Optimization) training algorithm to train to classify types of animal diseases. Zhang et al. [15] established an evidence-weighted uncertainty illation model able to deal with uncertainty in the cow disease diagnosis process. Firstly, this model reasons out a hypothetical conclusion based on the initial symptoms. Then, it performs a backward inference to reason out the final diagnosis by validating the hypothetical conclusion. Wan et al. [16] designed an SVM (Support Vector Machine) based model for cow disease diagnosis. The model consists in a data preprocessing module, a training module, and a classification of a multi-value module. Furthermore, this model defines a separate SVM for each disease according to its category, then all classified SVM are integrated and combined into an SVM classification group. Finally, Rong et al. [17] proposed a Web-based expert system for cow disease diagnosis. This system implements an inference engine for disease diagnosis that is based on three algorithms namely: case-based reasoning, Bayesian theory, and D-S evidential theory. Furthermore, sometimes the user can choose one of these algorithms to get a reliable diagnostic result.

Regarding goat diseases diagnosis, Wenxeu et al. [18] proposed a goat diseases diagnosing mechanism based on two algorithms namely weighted uncertainty reason algorithm and the improved Bayesian method. This mechanism uses clinical models, disease templates and cases of sampled diseases to extract knowledge rules which are used by reasoning-components for the diagnosis process. Xiao et al. [19] proposed an animal diagnosis system composed of three main elements namely: a disease case management system, a knowledge management system, and an expert system. This system uses an augmented knowledge representation based on production rules to perform the diagnosis process. Finally, Babu et al. [20] presented an expert system to diagnose sheep and goat diseases. This system uses a sheep and goat diseases database implemented by means of rule-based techniques and machine-learning algorithms, more specifically ABC (Artificial Bee Colony) and PSO (Particle Swarm Optimization). When the system cannot diagnose the disease, it displays a message saying that knowledge is not enough to perform such task.

On the other hand, there are some works focused on aquatic animals' diseases diagnosis. For instance, Sun et al. [21] present an Android-based application for diagnosing aquatic animal diseases. This application diagnoses an animal disease by using a case-based inference engine in conjunction with an expert symptom scoring method. Both methods are used at the same time. However, when the diagnostic results of these methods are different, the system asks the farmer for feedback until he/she is satisfied with the result. Deng et al. [22] proposed a fish disease diagnosis expert system based on a three layers neural network. This system uses old cases of fish diseases to train the neural network i.e., it uses diagnostic instances provided by fish disease experts. In this way, when a new diagnostic instance is provided to the system, it infers the disease. Fish disease diagnosis is based on the fish symptoms and the anomaly of the water environment. Finally, Ma et al. [23] presented a Multi-agent based expert system for distributed fish diseases diagnosis. This system implements a module known as Computing Agent that allows the distributed diagnosis and management of fish diseases and decrease the flow of raw data on the network, thus reducing the network load.

Finally, with regards to cattle and swine diseases diagnosis, Anggraeni et al. [24] presented an Android-based mobile intelligent system for diagnosing cattle diseases as well as suggesting first aid actions. The intelligent engine of this application relies on Fuzzy Neural Network (FNN) as well as rule-based and frame-based techniques for representing the knowledge. In rule-based approach, the knowledge is represented as a set of rules. Meanwhile, in frame-based approach, knowledge is represented as a set of objects. On the other hand, Nusai et al. [25] presented an expert system for swine disease diagnosis. This system uses a weight-based method that assigns a weight to each symptom, which is defined by a veterinarian. Furthermore, the system provides a set of pictures and a description of each symptom to allow the user to specify the certainty factor correctly.

The works described in this section are focused on the development of expert systems for animals' diseases diagnosis. The authors of these works proposed solutions based on a variety of technologies such as machine learning, fuzzy neural networks, among others. Note that most of the examined methods or systems don't focus on cattle disease diagnosis. Also, disease diagnosis using ontologies is not specially reported in these works. SE-DiagEnf addresses these drawbacks by means of a modular expert system, whose main goal is to provide farmers support for cattle diseases diagnosis. To achieve this goal, SE-DiagEnf uses veterinarians' knowledge and experience to establish a set of rules that help to diagnose the cattle disease based on a set of symptoms provided by the farmer. The experts' knowledge is represented by means of Semantic Web technologies, more specifically ontologies. In the following section, the components of SE-DiagEnf and their interactions are thoroughly explained and described.

3 SE-DiagEnf: Architecture and Functionality

SE-DiagEnf is an expert system that relies on Semantic Web technologies for cattle diseases diagnosis. Furthermore, this expert system provides farmers with treatments for tackling the diagnosed disease. The development process of SE-DiagEnf followed the knowledge engineering methodology proposed in [26]. This methodology consists of six phases namely: problem assessment, data and knowledge acquisition, prototype development, complete system development, system evaluation, and integration and maintenance of the system. For the purposes of this work, only first five phases were performed, since integration and maintenance phase will depend on the organization that adopts our proposal.

3.1 SE-DiagEnf Architecture

The SE-DiagEnf's architecture is illustrated in Fig. 1. Note that this architecture has next three main components:

1. Ontology. It models the cattle diseases diagnosis domain through concepts such as disease, symptom, body system, treatment, among others.
2. Rule-based engine. It contains a set of rules for cattle diseases diagnosis. These rules are defined by using knowledge and information obtained from several sources such as books about cattle diseases and treatments, as well as from veterinarians with a wide expertise on the diagnosis and treatment of cattle diseases.
3. Cattle disease treatments database. It stores cattle disease treatments that will be provided by the system once the disease has been diagnosed.

It must be mentioned that each component of SE-DiagEnf has tasks and responsibilities clearly defined and distributed in order to allow easy maintenance and scalability. Furthermore, the workflow of SE-DiagEnf is defined by a set of interrelationships between such components. This workflow is briefly described below:

1. The first task of the workflow is performed by the farmer who collects all symptoms that perceives in the cattle and provides them to the system.
2. SE-DiagEnf receives the set of symptoms and diagnoses the cattle disease by using the experts' knowledge that is already available in the system in the form of rules. More specifically, this process is performed through the rule-based engine.

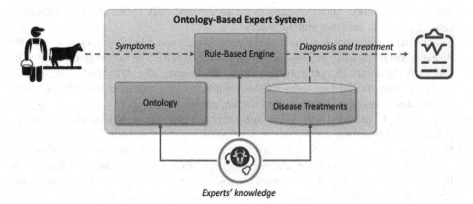

Fig. 1. Architecture of the ontology-based expert system for cattle diseases diagnosis.

3. If the symptoms provided by the farmer matches to the rules available in the knowledge base, the system displays the disease that cattle are suffering. However, when the set of symptoms does not match a rule, the system asks the user for more information.
4. Once the disease has been diagnosed by the system, it provides a treatment that can be followed by farmers to deal with the diagnosed disease.

Next subsections provide a more detailed description of the ontology for cattle disease diagnosis and the rule-based engine.

3.2 Ontology

The development of SE-DiagEnf required a knowledge acquisition process to gather experiences and knowledge from several domain experts, in this case, from veterinarians with a wide experience on cattle diseases diagnosing and treatment. Aiming to formally represent all gathered knowledge, an ontology was designed and implemented by using the OWL 2 Web Ontology Language [27]. The goal of this ontology is to provide a controlled vocabulary for cattle disease diagnosing as well as diseases treatments. This vocabulary allows experts to establish the set of rules that enables SE-DiagEnf to diagnose the correct cattle disease based on a set of symptoms provided by the farmer. The ontology presented un this work defines five main classes, namely: Disease, Symptom, Age range, Body System, and Treatment. All these classes were defined as disjoint classes, i.e. there is no instance belonging to all these classes. The classes defined by this ontology are described below.

- Disease. A disease is a disorder of structure or function in an animal that produces specific signs or symptoms or that affects a specific location. In this ontology, animal diseases are divided into infectious and noninfectious. Furthermore, noninfectious diseases can be further divided into nervous system disease, respiratory system, digestive system, to mention but a few. The first version of the ontology collects information about diseases such as ketosis, milk fever, mastitis, anaemia, food and mouth disease, among others.

- Symptom. A symptom is a phenome accompanying something, in this case, a cattle disease, and is regarded as evidence of its existence [28]. The ontology developed in this work describes 76 symptoms related to the diseases also described by it, such as watery yellowish diarrhea, dehydration, tremor, edema, vomiting, mucohemorrhagic, depressed appetite, reduced feed intake, among others.
- Age range. It includes five main age ranges: born, pre-weaning, post-weaning, puberty, and breeding.
- Body system. A body system is a collective functional unit made by several organs in which the organs work in complete coordination with one another. This class includes different body systems where symptoms occur such as digestive, nervous, respiratory, reproductive, urinary, circulatory, endocrine and muscular.
- Treatment. A treatment is an effort to cure or improve a disease or other health problem. In the medical domain, therapy is synonymous with the word treatment.

Despite the ontology proposed in this work describes relatively few cattle diseases and symptoms, it could be extended by veterinarians aiming to cover a wider range of diseases, including disease of other animals.

3.3 Rule-Based Engine

Animal diseases can be diagnosed by identifying a set of symptoms, thus allowing to control and treat the disease. However, there are symptoms that are related to more than one disease, thus making this process a complex task that cannot be performed by non-expert people. Considering this fact, in this work, we propose a rule-based engine that takes advantage of domain experts knowledge represented by means of semantic technologies, more specifically, ontologies. In other words, the ontology proposed in this work is the main source of computable knowledge that is exploited by the expert system to diagnose the cattle disease.

In the area of Artificial Intelligence, knowledge rule is the prime form to represent human knowledge [18]. Therefore, SE-DiagEnf adopts this approach to represent the relation between symptoms and cattle diseases i.e., we transfer the knowledge that experts have (which is represented by the ontology) into a set of rules that allows diagnosing cattle diseases based on a set of symptoms experienced by the animal which are provided by the farmer. In other words, the main task of the rule-based engine is to simulate experts' reasoning process based on a set of rules.

As was previously mentioned, there are symptoms that are related to more than one disease. However, there are symptoms that are more important than other ones i.e. a symptom can help more than any other symptom in diagnosing a disease. In an attempt to address this situation, we asked veterinarians to assign a significant weight to each symptom. In this way, when a symptom helps more than any other symptom, it has a greater weight. Furthermore, it should be noted that the weight assigned to each symptom varies from one disease to another one.

The rules established in this work were defined by using the SWRL language [29]. These rules are represented according to the format presented in Eq. 1:

$$R_1, R_2, R_3, \ldots, R_n \rightarrow D \tag{1}$$

Where R represents a condition that must be met to diagnose a disease. Meanwhile, D represents the disease that is diagnosed when all conditions are met. To be more specific, the disease diagnosing process performed by the rule-based engine works as follows. First, the user must provide specific information about the animal, for instance, the age and gender of the animal, the animal body temperature, salivary secretion, among others. Then, the user must provide the system all animal's symptoms as well as the body system where they occur. It is important to mention that each of the afore-mentioned data (age, gender, body temperature, symptom, among others) represent a condition (R in Eq. 1) that must be met to infer the disease. Having said that, once all information is provided by the farmer, SE-DiagEnf infers the disease based on the set of rules previously defined. There are different rules that can be applied to the set of symptoms provided by the user. However, the weight associated with each symptom plays an important role in the final diagnosis. Once disease diagnosis process finishes, the system provides farmers information about the cattle disease such as symptoms, prevention guides, animal care guides, as well as disease treatments. Next section provides a description of the evaluation process performed in this work to measure the effectiveness of SE-DiagEnf regarding cattle disease diagnosis.

4   Evaluation

The evaluation described in this section aims to measure the efficacy of SE-DiagEnf regarding cattle disease diagnosing. In other words, we assess how effective our pro-posal is in diagnosing a cattle disease based on a set of symptoms and animal's information provided by the farmer. The following sections describe the evaluation design and discuss the obtained results.

4.1   Evaluation Design

To evaluate SE-DiagEnf, we conducted an experiment that required 100 medical records with information regarding the animal (such as age and gender, among others), as well as the symptoms perceived by the veterinarian during disease diagnosis process. These medical records were provided by a group of veterinarians with a wide expe-rience in the diagnosis and treatment of cattle diseases. The data used in this evaluation process covers five different cattle diseases (20 medical records by each disease) namely:

1. Ketosis. It is a common disease of adult cattle. It is a metabolic disease that occurs when the cow is in a severe state of negative energy balance.
2. Milk fever. It is a disorder mainly of dairy cows close to calving. It is a metabolic disease caused by a low blood calcium level.

3. Mastitis. It is a persistent, inflammatory reaction of the udder tissue due to physical trauma or microorganisms' infections.
4. Anaemia. It is often caused by bush ticks that attach themselves to the livestock. This disease is common among young calves 8–12 weeks old but can affect cattle of all ages.
5. Foot and mouth disease. It is a highly contagious disease in livestock that causes lesions similar to blisters on the tongue, nose, mouth and toes of the animals.

Once the set of medical reports were collected and classified, we extract the information about the animal (such as age and gender, among others), as well as the symptoms described in the medical records. The extracted information was provided to SE-DiagEnf as input. Then, SE-DiagEnf performed the disease diagnosis process based on the rules established. Finally, the SE-DiagEnf efficiency regarding disease diagnosis was measured through accuracy metric whose formula is shown in Eq. 2.

$$Accuracy = C/A * 100 \tag{2}$$

Where C refers to the correctly diseases diagnosed. Meanwhile, A refers to the total of diseases diagnosed. Next section presents and discusses the evaluation results.

4.2 Evaluation Results

Table 1 depicts the evaluation results obtained by SE-DiagEnf. As can be observed, our proposal got an average accuracy score of 77%. The cattle disease that got the highest accuracy score was the ketosis, with a score of 85%. Meanwhile, the cattle disease with lowest accuracy score was Anaemia, with a score of 70%.

Table 1. Evaluation results

Heading level	Accuracy
Ketosis	85%
Milk fever	75%
Mastitis	80%
Anaemia	70%
Food and mouth disease	75%
Avg.	77%

The evaluation results demonstrating a good effectiveness of SE-DiagEnf regarding cattle disease diagnosis. However, based on a detailed analysis of all medical records used in the evaluation process we ascribe the variations among the accuracy scores obtained by each disease to next facts:

1. The known set of symptoms cannot match with any rule in the semantic knowledge base. In this case, the system cannot diagnose a disease because of the lack of rules in the knowledge base.

2. The known set of symptoms match with many rules, or there were many known symptoms which can match with one rule. In this case, because there are several rules that use the same symptoms, the system cannot determine which rule should be used, i.e. which disease must be provided to the farmer as result.

Finally, we observed that the diagnosis process performed by SE-DiagEnf is more precise when the set of symptoms provided to the system is bigger. However, there were different symptoms described in the medical records are not contained in the ontology. In this sense, it is necessary that the ontology proposed in this work describe more disease and symptoms, as well as to include their synonyms and jargon, i.e. special words used by veterinarians in the disease diagnosis process. In this sense, it would be desirable to extend the ontology regarding the set of diseases and symptoms. This, in turn, will allow us to generate a bigger set of rules that improve the effectiveness of our proposal.

5   Conclusions

This work presented SE-DiagEnf, an ontology-based expert system for cattle diseases diagnosis. The core engine of this system was implemented by using Semantic Web technologies, more specifically ontologies and SWRL language. Our proposal takes advantage of experts' knowledge collected from several sources such as books about cattle diseases and treatments, as well as from veterinarians. This knowledge was model by means of an ontology from which a set a set of rules for cattle disease diagnosis were generated. The main goal of SE-DiagEnf is to decrease the dependency of farmers on veterinarians to cope with cattle diseases diagnosis and treatment. The expert system proposed in this work was evaluated obtaining encouraging results with an accuracy score of 77% for five common cattle diseases. The contribution of this work is twofold. First, we propose an ontology for describing the cattle diseases diagnosis domain through concepts such as symptoms, diseases, body system, treatment, among others. Second, a set of rules for cattle disease diagnosis has been developed.

Further development of the expert system proposed in this work will focus on the following scopes. The first version of SE-DiagEnf can diagnose only five cattle diseases. As future work, we are planning to enhance the system to deal with other diseases whose symptoms are rarer. Furthermore, in order to improve the accuracy of cattle disease diagnosing we are planning to add new rules that consider a bigger set of symptoms as well as animal's features such as weight, breathing, pulse, among others. Furthermore, we are planning to integrate images with the experts' knowledge to help farmers describing the symptoms, thus making SE-DiagEnf more user-friendly. Finally, we plan to include living environment information to the disease diagnosis process such as weather, water, grass, among others. This information could help to determine the cause of the disease and to select the right medicine, thus improving the effectiveness of the treatment.

References

1. Zamsuri, A., Syafitri, W., Sadar, M.: Web based cattle disease expert system diagnosis with forward chaining method. IOP Conf. Ser. Earth Environ. Sci. **97**, 12046 (2017)
2. Li, D., Zhu, W., Duan, Y., Fu, Z.: Toward developing a tele-diagnosis system on fish disease. In: Bramer, M. (ed.) IFIP AI 2006. IIFIP, vol. 217, pp. 445–454. Springer, Boston (2006). https://doi.org/10.1007/978-0-387-34747-9_46
3. Zhang, J., Li, D.: A call center oriented consultant system for fish disease diagnosis in China. In: Li, D. (ed.) CCTA 2007. TIFIP, vol. 259, pp. 1447–1451. Springer, Boston (2008). https://doi.org/10.1007/978-0-387-77253-0_96
4. Kabari, L.G., Bakpo, F.S.: Diagnosing skin diseases using an artificial neural network. In: 2009 2nd International Conference on Adaptation Science and Technology, pp. 187–191 (2009)
5. Darlington, K.: The Essence of Expert Systems. Prentice Hall, Upper Saddle River (2000)
6. Berners-Lee, T., Hendler, J., Lassila, O.: The semantic web. Sci. Am. **284**, 34–43 (2001)
7. Studer, R., Benjamins, V.R., Fensel, D.: Knowledge engineering: principles and methods. Data Knowl. Eng. **25**, 161–197 (1998)
8. Paredes-Valverde, M.A., Rodríguez-García, M.Á., Ruiz-Martínez, A., Valencia-García, R., Alor-Hernández, G.: ONLI: an ontology-based system for querying DBpedia using natural language paradigm. Expert Syst. Appl. **42**, 5163–5176 (2015)
9. Salas-Zárate, M.P., Valencia-García, R., Ruiz-Martínez, A., Colomo-Palacios, R.: Feature-based opinion mining in financial news: an ontology-driven approach. J. Inf. Sci. **43**, 458–479 (2017)
10. Paredes-Valverde, M.A., del Pilar Salas-Zárate, M., Colomo-Palacios, R., Gómez-Berbís, J.M., Valencia-García, R.: An ontology-based approach with which to assign human resources to software projects. Sci. Comput. Program. **156**, 90–103 (2018)
11. Jampour, M., Jampour, M., Ashourzadeh, M., Yaghoobi, M.: A fuzzy expert system to diagnose diseases with neurological signs in domestic animal. In: 2011 Eighth International Conference on Information Technology: New Generations, pp. 1021–1024. IEEE (2011)
12. Munirah, M.Y., Suriawati, S., Teresa, P.P.: Design and development of online dog diseases diagnosing system. Int. J. Inf. Educ. Technol. **6**, 913–916 (2016)
13. Nusai, C., Chankeaw, W., Sangkaew, B.: Dairy cow-vet: a mobile expert system for disease diagnosis of dairy cow. In: 2015 IEEE/SICE International Symposium on System Integration (SII), pp. 690–695. IEEE (2015)
14. Lian, H.H., Bao, W.X., Wang, Y.H.: Animal diseases diagnosis expert system based on HSMC-SVM. Appl. Mech. Mater. **198–199**, 1036–1041 (2012)
15. Zhang, Y., Xiao, J., Fan, F., Wang, H.: The expert system of cow disease diagnosis basing on the uncertainty evidence illation. In: 2010 4th International Conference on Bioinformatics and Biomedical Engineering, pp. 1–4. IEEE (2010)
16. Wan, L., Bao, W.: Animal disease diagnoses expert system based on SVM. In: Li, D., Zhao, C. (eds.) CCTA 2009. IAICT, vol. 317, pp. 539–545. Springer, Heidelberg (2010). https://doi.org/10.1007/978-3-642-12220-0_78
17. Rong, L., Li, D.: A web based expert system for milch cow disease diagnosis system in China. In: Li, D. (ed.) CCTA 2007. TIFIP, vol. 259, pp. 1441–1445. Springer, Boston (2008). https://doi.org/10.1007/978-0-387-77253-0_95
18. Tan, W., Wang, X., Xi, J.: An animal disease diagnosis system based on the architecture of binary-inference-core. In: 2010 IEEE Fifth International Conference on Bio-Inspired Computing: Theories and Applications (BIC-TA), pp. 851–855. IEEE (2010)

19. Xiao, J., Wang, H., Zhang, R., Luan, P., Li, L., Xu, D.: The development of a general auxiliary diagnosis system for common disease of animal. In: Li, D., Zhao, C. (eds.) CCTA 2008. IAICT, vol. 294, pp. 953–958. Springer, Boston (2009). https://doi.org/10.1007/978-1-4419-0211-5_19

20. Babu, M.S.P., Ramjee, M., Narayana, S.V.N.L., Murty, N.V.R.: Sheep and goat expert system using artificial bee colony (ABC) algorithm and particle swarm optimization (PSO) algorithm. In: 2011 IEEE 2nd International Conference on Software Engineering and Service Science, pp. 51–54. IEEE (2011)

21. Sun, M., Li, D.: Aquatic animal disease diagnosis system based on android. In: Li, D., Li, Z. (eds.) CCTA 2015. IAICT, vol. 478, pp. 115–124. Springer, Cham (2016). https://doi.org/10.1007/978-3-319-48357-3_12

22. Deng, C., Wang, W., Gu, J., Cao, X., Ye, C.: Research of fish disease diagnosis expert system based on artificial neural networks. In: Proceedings of 2013 IEEE International Conference on Service Operations and Logistics, and Informatics, pp. 591–595. IEEE (2013)

23. Ma, D., Chen, M.: Building of an architecture for the fish disease diagnosis expert system based on multi-agent. In: 2012 Third Global Congress on Intelligent Systems, pp. 15–18. IEEE (2012)

24. Anggraeni, W., Muklason, A., Ashari, A.F., Wahyu, A., Darminto: Developing mobile intelligent system for cattle disease diagnosis and first aid action suggestion. In: Proceedings-2013 7th International Conference on Complex, Intelligent, and Software Intensive Systems, CISIS 2013, pp. 117–121. IEEE (2013)

25. Nusai, C., Cheechang, S.: Uncertain knowledge representation and inferential strategy in the expert system of swine disease diagnosis. In: 2014 International Conference on Information Science, Electronics and Electrical Engineering, pp. 1872–1876. IEEE (2014)

26. Negnevitsky, M.: Artificial Intelligence: A Guide to Intelligent Systems. Addison-Wesley, Boston (2005)

27. Grau, B.C., Horrocks, I., Motik, B., Parsia, B., Patel-Schneider, P., Sattler, U.: OWL 2: the next step for OWL. Web Semant. Sci. Serv. Agents World Wide Web **6**, 309–322 (2008)

28. Patil, J.K., Kumar, R.: Advances in image processing for detection of plant diseases. J. Adv. Bioinform. Appl. Res. **2**, 135–141 (2011)

29. Horrocks, I., et al.: SWRL: a semantic web rule language combining OWL and RuleML. W3C Member Submission 21, p. 79 (2004)

Architecture of a Meteorological Data Management System Based on the Analysis of Webmapping Tools

Maritza Aguirre-Munizaga[1]([⊠]) [iD], Vanessa Vergara-Lozano[1] [iD],
Andrea Sinche-Guzmán[1] [iD], Katty Lagos-Ortiz[1] [iD],
Karina Real-Avilés[1] [iD], Mitchell Vásquez-Bermudez[1] [iD],
and José Hernández-Rosas[2,3] [iD]

[1] School of Computer Engineering, Faculty of Agricultural Science,
Universidad Agraria del Ecuador,
Av. 25 de Julio y Pio Jaramillo, P.O. BOX 09-04-100, Guayaquil, Ecuador
{maguirre,vvergara,asinche,klagos,kreal,
mvasquez}@uagraria.edu.ec
[2] School of Environmental Engineering, Faculty of Agricultural Science,
Universidad Agraria del Ecuador,
Av. 25 de Julio y Pio Jaramillo, P.O. BOX 09-04-100, Guayaquil, Ecuador
jhernandez@uagraria.edu.ec
[3] Escuela de Biología, Facultad de Ciencias, Universidad Central de Venezuela,
Caracas, Venezuela

Abstract. The meteorological records represent atmospheric variables, which capture by means of sensors parameters such as: air temperature, humidity, direction and wind speed among others. Having a system that allows to monitor, visualize and analyze these variables contributes fundamentally to the decision-making of governmental entities, scientists and researchers. This article presents the architecture used in a meteorological data management system based on the analysis of webmapping tools that allow the monitoring and visualization of geospatial data, based on the results obtained by the project executed by researchers from the Agrarian University of Ecuador called "Platform for the monitoring of real-time atmospheric data of the network of meteorological stations of the Agrarian University of Ecuador, Guayaquil and Milagro."

Keywords: Webmapping · Meteorological data · Monitoring · Sensors

1 Introduction

In Ecuador there are data from conventional stations approximately since 1990 as recorded on the page of the Meteorological Service of Ecuador [1]. These can be taken by meteorological observers who take the information to the nearest offices to each station or send the notebooks by postal service. A conventional station is a mechanical device used to take measurements of meteorological variables based on the instruments used to perform the measurements. As mentioned in the literature [2] there are three types of stations: the main ones that perform 5 daily observations with a minimum of

© Springer Nature Switzerland AG 2018
R. Valencia-García et al. (Eds.): CITI 2018, CCIS 883, pp. 82–96, 2018.
https://doi.org/10.1007/978-3-030-00940-3_7

9 variables; the secondary ones that realize 3 daily observations with a minimum of 3 variables and the pluviometric ones that make observations once a day. Additional data records are observed at a national level and are monitored by automatic stations.

A meteorological record is an observation of an atmospheric variable, which plays a key role in many applications of flood, drought, environment and water resources. Although rainfall observations are the most used, other parameters of interest include air temperature, humidity and wind speed [3].

The Agrarian University of Ecuador maintains to date two meteorological stations, in Guayaquil and in Milagro. Each station measures values of temperature, humidity, rain, wind speed and direction as well as barometric pressure. The stations are kept within the premises of the University and transmit the records automatically on the basis that it is much more economical and sustainable to maintain an automatic station and obtain remote data from it considering that hiring staff who perform meteorological observations daily in conventional stations leads to higher costs as well as different types of obligations on the part of employers [4].

Ecuador, given its geographical position, is located in the intertropical zone, where the presence of the Andes mountains, the influence of the Pacific Ocean and the Amazonian forest, have formed diverse climatic floors and a great variety of subclimates, microclimates and topoclimates that go from the tropical to the naval [5].

With these climatic characteristics, it is important to have a system that allows in real time, to know parameters that help the common citizen to make quick decisions regarding the most suitable activities that can be done at a particular time and location, or historical information of what has happened to the comfort level of the environment, which can be known with the service explained in this document.

Guayaquil is the largest city in Ecuador with approximately 2.6 million inhabitants in the metropolitan area. The city is located at the sea level (2° 12' S and 79° 54' W). Due to the marshes in the west and the river in the east, the city has grown mainly towards the north and towards the south [6]. The aforementioned station is located in the south of the City in the University area.

Guayaquil has a warm and humid climate because it is part of the coastal zone of Ecuador. There are two distinct seasons: the rainy season from December to April and the dry season from May to November. The precipitation is limited to 4–5 months, the humidity remains high all year due to the proximity to the Pacific Ocean. The weather is very stable during the year despite the high temperatures. The wind speed is low, while the solar radiation is quite strong during the whole year. The rainy season has the worst thermal conditions, since both the air temperature and the vapor pressure are higher and the wind speed is lower.

With a great pre-Hispanic culture, the city of Milagro, where the Ciudad Universitaria Milagro (CUM) is located and has the second meteorological station, is placed further northwest (2° 8' S and 79° 35' O), further away from the sea on alluvial banks of the Milagro River at an average height of 11 m asl. The city is surrounded by a large agro-industrial activity of old date, conforming the sugar center of Ecuador [7].

The Tropical climate is thermal and humid. It characterizes the Canton Milagro, including the city Milagro, with a range of average daily temperatures of 25 to 27 °C and average annual rainfall of 1100 to 1800 mm, with a rainy period of 120 days to the west and 150 to the east, between the months of January to May, which favors agriculture. Likewise, other crops are favored in areas with hydric deficit of 400 to 600 mm and potential evapotranspiration of 1400 to 1500 mm [8].

According to different studies, Open Geospatial Consortium [9] information management services standards (WCS- Web Coverage Service, WFS- Web Feature Service and WMS- Web Map Service) are managed, which provide customizable visualization and access to both geospatial coverage and data of the features in a standard and simple way.

The purpose of this article is to review different tools for WMS services, taking into account that geospatial data are valuable for research in many areas.

The development of an approach based on sensors that are monitored through the web to derive typical information offered by a dynamic web mapping service (WMS) is described. The system allows easy and convenient synergistic research in a virtual platform for professionals from different areas and the general public, which greatly encourages the exchange of global data and collaboration to scientific research.

This study is based on web technology, generating a distributed architecture, which allows to easily add new nodes, computing and data to the storage system, providing a solid computing infrastructure for regional climate change.

2 Related Studies

Currently, scientists, researchers and developers have integrated efforts for the creation of information systems that allow the integration of meteorological stations with sensors installed in them. They also obtain access to geospatial data using different tools and models that allow decision-making based on the presented results. Webmapping technology is a widely used concept. It refers to the interactive process of designing, applying and generating geospatial data through the WWW, using a GML format (Geo-graphic Markup Language) [10] based on the specifications of OpenGIS Con- sortium [11].

In this context several efforts are made for the creation of such applications that allow the generation and diffusion of different types of geospatial data and the generation of maps on the web. So in [12] an interoperable framework is presented which generates images that can be accessed through the GIS software for different applications based on Earth science and the Web. The access is possible by the compliance of the Web Map Service (WMS) of OpenGeospatial Consortium for interoperability in such a way that any WMS viewer can access the service. Its main function is to use a series of interoperable services to support analysis of natural hazards, such as flood forecasts, real-time routing and support for other environmental decision-making applications, as well as disseminate various types of spatio-temporal data of Earth science.

On the other hand, [13] proposes an independent system to monitor the climate based on the IoT (Internet in things), which considers the use of the minicomputer with a low-cost ARM structure such as Raspberry Pi, in addition to using an external Wi-Fi module, for data processing. The system has been developed in Python. The information can be monitored from terminals such as laptops, smartphones and tablets that have easy access to the Internet. The information is provided in real time and includes parameters such as temperature, humidity, pressure, CO and harmful air pollutants. The system helps the sustainable growth of the city and improves the lives of citizens. The ubiquitous availability of dynamic datasheets in the dashboard and timely graphical representation can help plan control measures against rising pollution levels and raise people's awareness.

Also in [14] a WebGIS observatory platform is presented. It is designed for risk evaluation, preparation and response to emergencies in coastal areas. This tool combines a sophisticated prognostic modeling system for water map analysis including wave prediction, hydrodynamics and oil spills, with real-time monitoring networks with continuous validation. This system has been customized for the assessment of the risk of oil spills and the rapid response to an oil spill emergency. The authors seek to assess risks through georeferenced maps and layers of GIS information, in order to visualize predictions through georeferences.

There is an approach based on web sensors created by [15], which developed a prototype that provides daily maps of the productivity of the vegetation of the Netherlands with a spatial resolution of 250 m. The MODIS (Moderate Resolution Imaging Spectroradiometer) [16] surface reflectance products are daily available and the meteorological parameters obtained through a Sensor Observation Service (SOS) were used as input for a vegetation productivity model and they implement the automated processing facility.

In the literature there is also the development of systems for the analysis of geospatial data, such as the one presented in the article "Web-based Visualization Platform for Geospatial Data" [17], whose main objective is to explore new ways of visualizing and interacting with multidimensional satellite data and computed models of several Earth observations. This new V-MANIP platform facilitates a multidimensional exploration approach that allows to see the same data set in multiple viewers at the same time to search and explore efficient interesting features within the displayed data.

In general, the scheme of systems architectures based on geospatial web services has been presented in several investigations as an integral part of a virtual research environment (VRE) for statistical processing and the visualization of meteorological data and climate data. Thus, [18] presents an architecture consisting of a set of independent SDI nodes interconnected with corresponding data storage systems. Each node runs specialized software such as a geoportal, cartographic web services (WMS/WFS), a catalog of metadata and a MySQL database of technical metadata that describe geospatial datasets available for the node. It also contains geospatial data processing (WPS) services based on a modular compute backend perform statistical in order to process functionality and, therefore, provide analysis of large data sets with visualization, exporting results in standard format files (XML, binary, etc.). Some of the cartographic web services have been developed in a prototype system to provide capabilities to work with raster geospatial data and vectors based on OGC web services.

3   Evaluation of Tools to Enable WMS Service

3.1   Assessment of the Evaluation Criteria for WMS Tools

The project "Platform for monitoring real-time atmospheric data of the network of meteorological stations of the Agrarian University of Ecuador, Guayaquil and Milagro headquarters", suggests to incorporate different ways of representing monitored meteorological variables. One of the proposed ways is the implementation of the WMS service with an interface that helps with the spatial referencing of the results or analysis of meteorological data.

Through an evaluation of the tools for application of WMS services that currently exist, different criteria were established that are considered important within the implementation process and the presentation of results. For this purpose, 22 tools were analyzed, identifying 3 Factors of Analysis: (1) Form of Access, (2) Functional Requirements, (3) Presentation of Results [19].

Within the first factor analyzed -tool access- it was assessed how to acquire the 22 tools, whether they are free access with the value of 1, or through a license with the value of 0; finally we had 16 free access tools and 5 licensed tools. To evaluate each of the two remaining factors a survey was conducted with 30 users. The users indicated indicating whether the service is provided by the tool using the Likert scale where 0 means the absence of the service in the tool and 1 represents the presence of the service in the tool.

The second factor that was analyzed is the functional requirements, that is, the easiest and most intuitive way to use each of the tools described above. Four important criteria for the geospatial information survey process were specified at the time of monitoring environmental variables. The 22 tools were evaluated according to the four criteria on a scale of 0 to 1 where zero is the absence of the characteristic in the tool and 1 is the highest score of the characteristic. Within the third factor analyzed, three important criteria were identified for our project at the time of verifying the presentation of the meteorological data analysis. As we did in the functional requirements phase, we valued each tool under the three criteria in a scale from 0 to 1. These ratings are described in Table 1.

3.2   Identifying the Best WMS Tool

Once the different factors and criteria have been assessed to identify the tool that best fits within the project "Platform for the monitoring of atmospheric data in real time of the network of meteorological stations of the Agrarian University of Ecuador, Guayaquil and Milagro headquarters", two analysis were carried out. In the first instance, we proceeded with a Cluster analysis of the criteria evaluated in the three factors, since this multivariate statistical technique allows us to group the tools that have the criteria and/or characteristics with the maximum homogeneity and the greatest difference between the groups, with which we obtained a total of 4 groups (cluster) described in Table 2.

Table 1. Evaluation of WMS tools.

No	Factors Tools	Access Free	Functional Requirements			Results			
			Performance	Usability	Intuitiveness	Consistency	Accuracy	Integrity	Stability
1	Leaflet	1	1	0.8	1	0.7	0.7	1	0.8
2	Django-wms framework	1	0.8	0.9	0.7	0.8	0.9	1	0.9
3	Mapserver	1	1	0.8	0.8	0.9	1	1	0.9
4	Geozilla - geoforce	1	0.7	0.9	0.85	0.8	1	0.7	0.7
5	Arcmap	0	1	1	0.9	0.9	0.9	0.8	1
6	Mathworks-wmsread	0	1	1	1	1	1	1	1
7	Python-Based Web Mapping Service	1	0.8	0.9	0.7	0.9	0.9	1	0.9
8	QGIS server	1	1	0.5	0.5	0.9	0.9	1	0.9
9	GeoCommons	0	1	0.7	0.5	0.7	0.8	0.9	0.8
10	Tableau	0	1	1	1	1	1	1	1
11	Geoserver	1	1	1	0.8	0.9	1	1	1
12	Api-Google	1	1	0.8	1	0.7	1	0.5	1
13	TileStache	1	0.8	0.8	0.7	0.8	0.8	0.9	0.8
14	TileCache	1	0.8	0.8	0.8	0.9	0.8	0.7	0.9
15	Mapnik (python, c ++ y java script)	1	1	1	1	0.8	0.8	0.8	1
16	A Custom Server Built on GeoTools	1	0.7	0.6	0.6	0.7	0.7	0.7	0.6
17	MapZoom	1	0.3	0.3	0.3	0.3	0.3	0.3	0.3
18	Deegree	1	0.9	0.9	0.9	0.8	0.9	0.9	0.9
19	Geomajas	1	1	0.8	0.7	0.95	1	1	1
20	Mapguide Open Source	1	0.8	0.6	0.7	1	1	1	1
21	GeoMedia Map Publisher	0	0.9	0.9	0.9	1	1	1	1
22	MapViewer	0	1	1	1	1	1	1	1
	Maximum	**1**	**1**	**1**	**1**	**1**	**1**	**1**	**1**
	Minimum	**0**	**0.3**	**0.3**	**0.3**	**0.3**	**0.3**	**0.3**	**0.3**

Table 2. Analysis of evaluated factors

Tool	Normalized data								Cluster
	Free	Performance	Usability	Intuitiveness	Consistency	Accuracy	Integrity	Stability	
17	1.0000	1.0000	0.7143	1.0000	0.5714	0.5714	1.0000	0.7143	1
1	1.0000	0.7143	0.8571	0.5714	0.7143	0.8571	1.0000	0.8571	2
2	1.0000	1.0000	0.7143	0.7143	0.8571	1.0000	1.0000	0.8571	2
3	1.0000	0.5714	0.8571	0.7857	0.7143	1.0000	0.5714	0.5714	2
7	0.0000	1.0000	1.0000	0.8571	0.8571	0.8571	0.7143	1.0000	2
11	0.0000	1.0000	1.0000	1.0000	1.0000	1.0000	1.0000	1.0000	2
13	1.0000	0.7143	0.8571	0.5714	0.8571	0.8571	1.0000	0.8571	2
14	1.0000	1.0000	0.2857	0.2857	0.8571	0.8571	1.0000	0.8571	2
15	0.0000	1.0000	0.5714	0.2857	0.5714	0.7143	0.8571	0.7143	2
18	0.0000	1.0000	1.0000	1.0000	1.0000	1.0000	1.0000	1.0000	2
19	1.0000	1.0000	1.0000	0.7143	0.8571	1.0000	1.0000	1.0000	2
20	1.0000	1.0000	0.7143	1.0000	0.5714	1.0000	0.2857	1.0000	2
5	1.0000	0.7143	0.7143	0.5714	0.7143	0.7143	0.8571	0.7143	3
6	1.0000	0.7143	0.7143	0.7143	0.8571	0.7143	0.5714	0.8571	3
9	1.0000	1.0000	1.0000	1.0000	0.7143	0.7143	0.7143	1.0000	3
10	1.0000	0.5714	0.4286	0.4286	0.5714	0.5714	0.5714	0.4286	3
21	1.0000	0.0000	0.0000	0.0000	0.0000	0.0000	0.0000	0.0000	3
22	1.0000	0.8571	0.8571	0.8571	0.7143	0.8571	0.8571	0.8571	3
4	1.0000	1.0000	0.7143	0.5714	0.9286	1.0000	1.0000	1.0000	4
8	1.0000	0.7143	0.4286	0.5714	1.0000	1.0000	1.0000	1.0000	4
12	0.0000	0.8571	0.8571	0.8571	1.0000	1.0000	1.0000	1.0000	4
16	0.0000	1.0000	1.0000	1.0000	1.0000	1.0000	1.0000	1.0000	4

Verifying the centroids of each of the clusters, we identify that cluster 2 complies with the required characteristics. All the tools in this group are freely accessible and the average of the criteria for the data presentation factor is the highest of the other 3 groups that meet the first condition. This is described in Table 3.

Table 3. Centroids analysis

Cluster	Centroids							
	Free	Performance	Usability	Intuitiveness	Consistency	Accuracy	Integrity	Stability
1	1.00	0.30	0.30	0.30	0.30	0.30	0.30	0.30
2	1.00	0.90	0.85	0.80	0.86	0.89	0.94	0.92
3	0	0.98	0.93	0.88	0.93	0.95	0.95	0.97
4	1.00	0.85	0.70	0.74	0.78	0.90	0.73	0.80

Secondly, with the tools already grouped and the most appropriate group chosen, we gave weight to each factor according to the need and characteristics of our project, leaving 40% of the weight for the Acceptance Form factor, 25% for the functional requirements factor and 35% presentation of results. As we can see in Table 4, when obtaining the final score by applying the weights selected in the factors to each tool, we can identify that the tool that most adjusts to the characteristics of the Project is "Geoserver", since it is a free access tool and the percentage in the factor of presentation of results fulfills in 97% the weight of this factor. The aforementioned tool would be used in the implementation of the WMS service within the platform that is maintained.

Table 4. Tool analysis by weight

No	Tool	Access 40%	Functional requirements 25%	Results 35%	Final score
1	Leaflet	0.40	0.23	0.28	0.91
2	Django-wms framework	0.40	0.20	0.32	0.92
3	Mapserver	0.40	0.22	0.33	0.95
7	Python-Based Web Mapping Service	0.40	0.20	0.32	0.92
11	Geoserver	0.40	0.23	0.34	0.97
13	TileStache	0.40	0.19	0.29	0.88
14	TileCache	0.40	0.20	0.29	0.89
15	Mapnik (python, c ++ y java script)	0.40	0.25	0.30	0.95
18	Deegree	0.40	0.23	0.31	0.93
19	Geomajas	0.40	0.21	0.35	0.95
20	Mapguide Open Source	0.40	0.18	0.35	0.93

4 Methodology

This section shows the data monitoring model implemented on the project website. The installed sensors can obtain, access, manage and process environmental data in real time [20]. Therefore, a sensor web service platform is adopted that integrates the technology to provide the interfaces in GSW (Web Services Management) to record, plan and present relevant geostatistical information that supports the realization of the GIS data model in real time, which will be implemented in the future.

4.1 Monitoring Architecture

In general, the monitoring platform maintains a three-level architecture, with a structure designed in such a way that it allows to add meteorological stations to the network. This is shown in Fig. 1.

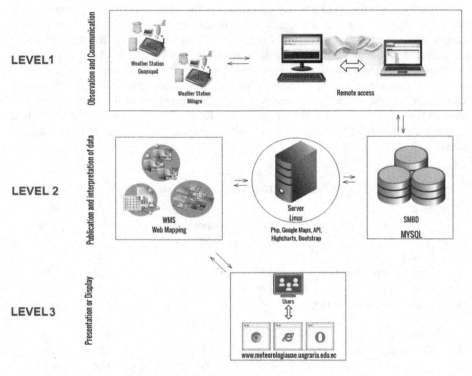

Fig. 1. Computational structure of the system

It can be seen in Fig. 1 that with the stations in operation there are currently three levels in the architecture: first level of observation, second level for data interpretation and the third level that involves presentation through the web. The level of observation supports the installed sensors, which measure different environmental parameters in real time (temperature, humidity, precipitation, wind speed and direction), maintaining communication with the web server through remote access, which is a limiting factor to obtain the measurements recorded by the stations currently installed and in operation.

The service of publication and interpretation of data allows the integration of third-party services such as WMS services commonly used within web geoprocessing [21]. This service is currently implemented through the Google maps APIs and encoded in php using Bootstrap.

Within the data interpretation process, Google Earth is used to generate a kml file that is a markup language based on XML to represent geographic data in three dimensions, since this language allows polygons to be added to mark specific sites of geographical areas within of a map.

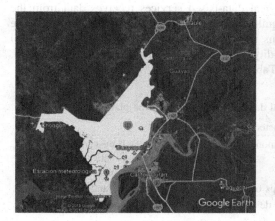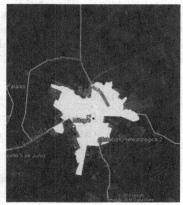

Fig. 2. Graphic representation of polygons

Figure 2 shows how the polygons were added in shapefile format to represent the Miracle area and the Guayaquil area. Then each polygon was downloaded in KML (Keyhole Markup Language) format.

Having the KML file with the marked areas, we proceeded to use Google "my maps", generating a main layer of the map. The pertinent permissions were released for publication and a KMZ (Keyhole Markup Zip) file was downloaded.

With the KMZ file generated, the Api Google circle was used and through Java script the Api is called with the kmz file previously generated to get a map with a marked area of Guayaquil and Milagro. In the coding the circle represents the heat index [22] previously calculated with the following formula:

$$IC = -8,78469476 + 1,61139411 \cdot T + 2,338548839 \cdot HR - 0,14611605 \cdot T \cdot HR$$
$$- 0,012308094 \cdot T2 - 0,016424828 \cdot HR2 + +0,002211732 \cdot T2 \cdot R$$
$$+ 0,00072546 \cdot T \cdot HR2 - 0,000003582 \cdot T2 \cdot HR2$$

Where IC equals the heat index, T is the air temperature and HR is the relative humidity.

The level of presentation of the information uses a protocol of access to resources and a standard service protocol, respectively, depending on the service that will be used, so in Sect. 5 all the information represented at this level is explained.

5 Environment of the Current Platform of Services Based on Meteorological Data

In the service platform currently implemented, an adaptive design has been used that allows users who visualize the platform to achieve a user experience based on usability.

The web platform of meteorological data-based services receives data from the stations located in the city of Guayaquil and Milagro, which are registered through the datalogger on the server that contains the web application that allows the statistical information about temperature, humidity, pressure, dew point, wind and precipitation. The services offered are detailed in Table 5.

Table 5. Meteorological data services offered by the platform

Service	Options	Parameters	Result
Statistics	Guayaquil	Day, month, year	Comparative graph by variable
	Milagro		Comparative graph between variables
			Dominant wind graph
WMS Service	Referenced data maps of the heat index of Guayaquil and Milagro		
Station data	Temperature	Fecha de inicio	Archivos de datos en formato *.cvs
	Humidity	Fecha de fin	
	Pressure		
	Dew point		
	Wind		
	Precipitation		

The option statistics allows you to select the city (Guayaquil or Milagro) and present the information by day, month or year, as can be seen in Fig. 3. It shows the data of February 12, 2018, corresponding to temperature and humidity.

The statistical graphs that the application generates -according to the data recorded by each sensor of the meteorological station- calculate the maximum and minimum measurement of the different variables, which are represented by colors.

Within this statistic the information about the speed distributions and frequency of variation of the wind directions is represented, through the graph of the rose of the winds, based on the observations captured by the weather stations of Guayaquil and Miracle. This is observed in Fig. 4.

The option of WMS services generates through different colors the graphic representation of the "Thermal Sensation", which is just the sensation of greater heat or cold that a person feels on their skin when exposed to an environment with certain special conditions of wind or humidity associated with the existing air temperature.

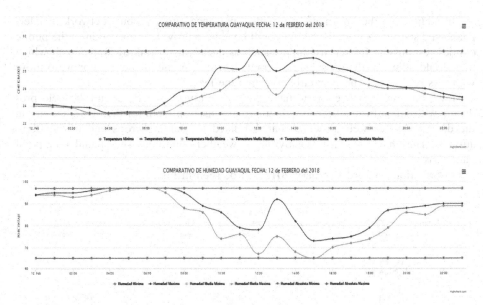

Fig. 3. Comparative of captured data of sensors of temperature and humidity

Fig. 4. Speed distributions and variation frequency of the wind directions

Likewise, through this information, we can manage the systems of climate conditioning of homes, offices and other areas of human activity, which need to be permanently adjusted, generating energy savings and satisfactory comfort indices. On the other hand, the compilation of this type of information can be used by architects and landscapers in the design of buildings, green areas, avenues, etc., providing better characteristics to those spaces for the use and enjoyment of its occupants.

In addition to the information provided and once a more robust network of interconnected stations is established, they will be able to provide information to the public entities responsible for service supply such as energy and drinking water, with which they could adjust tariffs on subsidies granted, with a social vision of support to those with less resources, who generally consume the least.

Last, but not least, we would have the possibility to directly attend the field producers with this information about the thermal sensation, both for their own activity in the daily work, as well as with what is related to planting crops and raising farm animals. They have different sensitivities to weather conditions and spatial - temporal variations.

Information on 23rd February 2018 can be seen in Fig. 5.

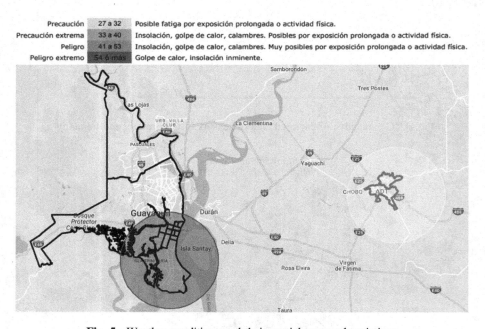

Fig. 5. Weather conditions and their spatial-temporal variations

In the future it is expected to present this information in real time. The platform in turn allows to obtain the data recorded in * cvs file format, entering the range of dates to obtain them. This is done with the option "station data".

6 Conclusions and Future Research

The main objective of this study was to suggest an evaluation that integrates a data representation model and a sensor web services platform within a geospatial services web framework for the management of environmental data. As a experiment it was carried out a monitoring of different environmental parameters in a range of 1 min, for approximately seven months in two different locations. The preliminary results show that the use of this method to administer environmental data in real time is feasible and effective. The objective of the experiment is to show the proposed model and platform under a GSW framework and its applications for environmental data management.

The future work will focus on analyzing the scientific problems associated with the experimental results, such as margin of error of the stations and implementation of visualization models based on other monitored variables using the GeoServer tool chosen in this work, under a cluster analysis. At the same time, the integration of other sensors such as solar radiation and UV index is suggested.

References

1. Instituto Nacional de Meteorología e Hidrologia: Anuario meteorológico 1990 № 30, Quito (2013)
2. Jácome, H.: Introducción a la Meteorología, Quininde (2014)
3. Sene, K.: Meteorological observations. In: Sene, K. (ed.) Hydrometeorology: Forecasting and Applications, pp. 37–70. Springer, Cham (2016). https://doi.org/10.1007/978-3-319-23546-2_2
4. Aguirre-Munizaga, M., Gomez, R., Aviles, M., Vasquez, M., Recalde-Coronel, G.C.: A cloud computing based framework for storage and processing of meteorological data. In: Valencia-García, R., Lagos-Ortiz, K., Alcaraz-Mármol, G., del Cioppo, J., Vera-Lucio, N. (eds.) CITI 2016. CCIS, vol. 658, pp. 90–101. Springer, Cham (2016). https://doi.org/10.1007/978-3-319-48024-4_8
5. Guillén, V.: Metodologia de evaluación de confort termico exterior para diferentes pisos climáticos en Ecuador. www.conama2014.org
6. Johansson, E., Yahia, M.W., Arroyo, I., Bengs, C.: Outdoor thermal comfort in public space in warm-humid Guayaquil. Ecuad. Int. J. Biometeorol. **62**, 387–399 (2018)
7. Vicuña, P.V.: Historia del ingenio valdez|Historia del cantón milagro. https://historiacantonmilagro.wordpress.com/9-historia-del-ingenio-valdez/
8. Sistema Nacional de Información-Ecuador: Plan de desarrollo y ordenamiento territorial. http://app.sni.gob.ec/sni-link/sni/PORTAL_SNI/data_sigad_plus/sigadplusdocumentofinal/0760027030001_PDOT/MILAGRO_30-10-2015_20-51-47.pdf
9. Wei, Y., Santhana-Vannan, S.K., Cook, R.B.: Discover, visualize, and deliver geospatial data through OGC standards-based WebGIS system. In: 2009 17th International Conference on Geoinformatics, pp. 1–6 (2009)
10. Geography Markup Language|OGC
11. Consortium, O.G.: OpenGIS Web Map Service version 1.3.0. (2006)
12. Cao, Y., Yang, C., Wong, D.W.: An interoperable spatiotemporal weather radar data dissemination system. Int. J. Remote Sens. **30**, 1313–1326 (2009)
13. Shete, R., Agrawal, S.: IoT based urban climate monitoring using Raspberry Pi. In: International Conference on Communication and Signal Process, 6–8 April 2016, India IoT, 2008–2012 (2016)
14. Oliveira, A., et al.: An interactive WebGIS observatory platform for enhanced support of integrated coastal management. J. Coast. Res. **70**, 507–512 (2014)
15. Kooistra, L., Bergsma, A., Chuma, B., De Bruin, S.: Development of a dynamic web mapping service for vegetation productivity using earth observation and in situ sensors in a sensor web based approach. Sensors **9**, 2371–2388 (2009)

16. Pagano, T.S., Durham, R.M.: Moderate Resolution Imaging Spectroradiometer (MODIS). Presented at the August 25 (1993)
17. Hecher, M., Traxler, C., Hesina, G., Fuhrmann, A.: Web-based visualization platform for geospatial data. In: Proceedings of the 6th International Conference on Information Visualization Theory and Applications, pp. 311–316 (2015)
18. Titov, A.G., Okladnikov, I.G., Gordov, E.P.: Architecture of a spatial data service system for statistical analysis and visualization of regional climate changes. IOP Conf. Ser. Earth Environ. Sci. **96**, 1–10 (2017)
19. Wu, H., Li, Z., Zhang, H., Yang, C., Shen, S.: Monitoring and evaluating the quality of Web Map Service resources for optimizing map composition over the internet to support decision making. Comput. Geosci. **37**, 485–494 (2011)
20. Chen, N., Chen, Z., Di, L., Gong, J.: An efficient method for near-real-time on-demand retrieval of remote sensing observations. J. IEEE J. Sel. Top. Appl. Earth Obs. Remote Sens **4**, 615–625 (2011)
21. Chen, N., Di, L., Yu, G., Gong, J.: Geo-processing workflow driven wildfire hot pixel detection under sensor web environment. Comput. Geosci. **36**, 362–372 (2010)
22. Aemet: Sensación térmica de frío y calor - Agencia Estatal de Meteorología - AEMET. Gobierno de España

Software Engineering

Study of the Maturity of Information Security in Public Organizations of Ecuador

Susana Patiño[1] and Sang Guun Yoo[2,3]

[1] Escuela de Sistemas y Computación, Pontificia Universidad Católica del Ecuador Sede Esmeraldas, Esmeraldas, Ecuador
susana.patino@pucese.edu.ec
[2] Departamento de Informática y Ciencias de la Computación, Escuela Politécnica Nacional, Quito, Ecuador
sang.yoo@epn.edu.ec
[3] Departamento de Ciencias de la Computación, Universidad de las Fuerzas Armadas ESPE, Sangolquí, Ecuador
yysang@espe.edu.ec

Abstract. The present paper makes a study of the maturity of Information Security Management Systems of the Public Sector of Ecuador. Through a theoretical study, 5 factors were determined that make up an effective Information Security Management System: internal organizational control, information security policy, information security culture, and technical activities for the security of information and new technologies. The five factors were evaluated through a scale to determine the level of maturity of the process of information security from the perception of ICT (Information Technology and Communication) managers of public sector entities. Findings of the analysis showed that technical activities for information security was the factor with a higher level of maturity due to the implementation of technological tools by the personnel of ICT area. On the other hand, internal organizational control was the least mature factor, indicating that this area needs more attention. Despite the requirement of the international standards of information security in most public entities, the process is still at a level of maturity between repeatable and defined.

Keywords: Information security · Information security policy
Information security culture · Internal control

1 Introduction

The National Secretariat of Public Administration (SNAP) of Ecuador is a public entity endowed with budgetary, financial, economic and administrative autonomy, in charge of establishing policies, management methodologies, institutional innovation and necessary tools for the improvement of efficiency and quality of management in the entities and bodies of the Executive Function. On the other hand, SNAP created the Commission for Information Security and Information Technology (CSITIC) which has the authority to establish computer security guidelines, as well as the protection of Information and Communication Technology (ICT) infrastructure [1].

© Springer Nature Switzerland AG 2018
R. Valencia-García et al. (Eds.): CITI 2018, CCIS 883, pp. 99–109, 2018.
https://doi.org/10.1007/978-3-030-00940-3_8

CSITIC, in its final report, describes that the governmental entities were under many threats in the last years, due to the fact that the computer systems or web portals do not comply with computer security standards. Likewise, crimes caused by misuse of passwords by certain officials have led to fraud and embezzlement of public funds, evidencing the lack of controls in some government systems [2].

In response to this situation, CSITIC proposed the adoption and adaptation of an international standard to safeguard information in the governmental organizations. For this, SNAP, through Ministerial Agreement N°166, determined the implementation of an Information Security Management System (ISMS) based on ISO/IEC 27001: 2005 as mandatory for entities of the Central Public Administration and those that depend on the Executive Function [3].

With the above background, this paper studies the level of maturity of the Information Security Management System of public organizations of Ecuador, with the aim of contributing to the efforts of public entities such as SNAP and CSITIC to improve security of the information of the Ecuadorian Entities.

The rest of the paper is structured as follows. Section 2 details basic information on key factors for a mature Information Security Management System by reviewing a selection of works related to the topic. Section 3 describes the case study including the research methodology, data collection, methods of analysis and results. Finally, the conclusion and future works are presented in Sect. 4.

2   Theoretical Concepts

In this section, several background concepts related to the development of the present study are explained.

2.1   Internal Organizational Control

Public sector companies, unlike the commercial sector, focus on the delivery of services for the general public with a social interest, seeking a beneficial result for the community. However, in the course of their activities, they must face different types of threats, both internally and externally. Therefore, it is necessary that public companies can anticipate and manage risks adequately, as do private companies.

Among different risk management control tools, one of the most important could be the internal audit, which is used to manage risks related to the operational, financial, legal and regulatory activities which add value to the organization [4].

The effectiveness of internal auditing in the public sector is related to the experience of audit staff, since effective internal audit professionals must have the ability to align the structure of audit knowledge with the dynamics of the operation of organization. Therefore, the experience has a significant impact within the efficient internal audit in public sector organizations [5].

2.2   Information Security Management

A primary objective of internal control is to achieve a correct culture of information security in the personnel of the organization. To create it, it is necessary to provide a guide for the personnel of the organization in order to avoid actions that may cause risks related to information technology and communication [6]. The lack of consideration of the information security management causes discoordination with the organization [7]. Therefore, the implementation of an effective Information Security Management System (ISMS) is required for the establishment of an adequate organizational culture oriented to information security [8]. In this sense, ISO 27001 establishes tangible guide for the implementation of an ISMS and provides a global tool for the establishment of a high quality system, indispensable and useful for any institution [9–11].

An important requirement of the ISO 27001 standard is the application of an Information Security Risk Management (ISRM) methodology. An ISRM allows identifying the level of risk in organizations by analyzing vulnerabilities of critical assets in order to establish plans to address the identified risks [12–15]. To achieve a mature ISRM within the organization, it is necessary to select effective preventive measures and combat threats actively [16]; and to achieve this, the quality of the information must be guaranteed since it is the key to decision-making in the treatment of risk [17]. Therefore, it is necessary to integrate the quality of information in an ISRM [18].

An effective ISMS needs the interaction of several factors, which when measured, will allow knowing the state of the ISMS implemented. Three types of factors have been used to measure an effective ISMS: organizational factor, factor based on technology and hybrid factors [8, 19, 20].

2.3   Information Security Policy

Information Security Policy (ISP) creates appropriate behavior among employees by providing clear instructions of the responsibilities to be followed in accordance with the terms and conditions described in those policies [20]. In this process, senior management has an important role since it must act as the main motivator and influencer in the application of the information security policy [21]. A clear and practical IPS can help improve the security of information in organizations. However, a constant review and update is necessary because the continuous changes in the organization may affect the effectiveness of the IPS [22].

In the same way, employees must know the existing threats and the danger they represent. This is important because careless employees who do not comply with the ISP are the biggest threat to information security. Therefore, it should be emphasized not only in the seriousness of information security infractions, but also to minimize information security violations. The sanctions applied for the execution of security infractions have a significant impact on the actual compliance of the IPS. In addition, professionals must establish sanctions for the breach of the IPS in a visible manner and make employees believe that their non-compliance will be detected quickly and will result in severe legal sanctions [23].

2.4   Technical Activities for the Information Security

Another important factor in the process of managing information security is the use of technology to safeguard information. It is important to have the knowledge and expertise in technical aspects, as well as in administrative ones. The administration has to deal with the non-technical aspects of information security, such as the development of security policies, training, the acquisition of security hardware and software, control and decisions on data processing; and, the ICT professionals must provide the technical support for information security [27]. In addition to the administrative and technical capacities, it is necessary to acquire Information Technology (IT) resources; therefore, proper management of IT resources is essential, as well as their integration, reconfiguration, acquisition and disposal [7].

2.5   New Technologies

With the emergence of new technologies, new security risks in organizations are also born; therefore, it is important to understand the details of those new technologies being used in organizations. Three of the most important new technologies which are being used widely for organizations are the cloud computing, mobile devices and social networks.

Cloud computing includes service-oriented architecture (SOA) and virtual hardware and software applications; it provides a scalable service platform in which resources are shared among service consumers, partners and suppliers [25]. In this sense, cloud-based computing presents new challenges related to the appropriate management of security [24]. On the other hand, mobile devices are very useful for organizational staff sin it allows the communication and storage of relevant information without dependence of place or time. However, their usage rises new risks and new security requirements [26]. Finally, another technology that has influenced to the organizational culture change is the social network since it has generated a new way to communicate between people and organizations, and share ideas.

3   Case Study

3.1   General Description

The present work analyzes the level of maturity of the Information Security Management System of public organizations in Ecuador. The study is based on 5 key factors, which are rated based on the perception of the ICT manager of different public organizations located in Esmeraldas city using a maturity level scale based on the Cobit's Framework. The obtained data was analyzed using SSPS system by means of descriptive statistical tests to generate frequencies, median, mean and standard deviation, to then, perform a correlation analysis between the factors with the objective of identifying the strength of association between them.

3.2   Research Methodology

This research measures the level of maturity of information security from the perception of the ICT managers. The perception of ICT managers was collected using a series of questions which had the objective to measure the level of maturity in five key factors, which are detailed in Table 1.

Table 1. Factors of an effective ISMS

Factor type	Factors
Organizational	Internal organizational control
	Information security policy
	Information security culture
Based on technology	Technical activities for the information security
Hybrids	New technologies

As mentioned before, a questionnaire that included closed questions based on a scale was used. In order to determine the level of maturity of the information security process in the organization, it was necessary to use a maturity model starting from level 0 (nonexistent) to level 5 (optimized) [26].

For the present work, the Cobit's Framework was considered, since it is used to measure the level of maturity of information technology processes in order to measure the alignment of IT with the organization.

The questionnaire is organized according to the defined factors and contains 25 questions. The factors with the elements are detailed in Table 2.

3.3   Data Collection

Questions indicated in [27] were adapted to the context of public entities, since they were created to be applied in the private sector. Questions were delivered through personal interviews; directions and purpose of the research were explained to the participants before executing interviews.

To evaluate the instrument, a pilot test was conducted. For the execution of the pilot test, 24 public sector organizations were contacted, of which 18 accepted their participation. From the participating organizations, information of the period between April and May 2017 was collected.

The questions of the questionnaire had a scale of 1 to 5 points and the reliability of the questionnaire was established by calculating the internal consistency of the questionnaire using the Cronbach alpha coefficient, which generated a coefficient of 0.929 for all the combined constructs. The calculated reliability can be considered adequate for current research since Cronbach alpha coefficient is the mostly used statistical test to determine the reliability of scale questions in questionnaire surveys [28].

Table 3 shows the characteristics of the contacted public entities, of which the majority (44.44%) are oriented to provide a social type of service such as: social insurance, inclusion, civil registry, among others. On the other hand, the majority have a low budget (of less than $ 50,000) for the technological area (44%).

Table 2. Elements of the questionnaire

Factor	Elements	Number of questions
1. Internal organizational control	Framework Audit area Risk management process Risk map	7
2. Information security policy	Establishment of information security policies Communication of information security policies Knowledge of policies noncompliance by staff	6
3. New technologies	Resources to identify changing threats Change in risk level due to the use of social networks, cloud computing and personal devices Risk management program for new technologies	3
4. Technical activities for the information security	Technology for the risk management process Virtualization technology Access management control	3
5. Information security management	Information security management system Information security committee Response plan Technological risk assessment Contingency plan	6

Table 3. Profiles of participants

Item	Variable	Frequency	Percentage (%)
Organization Type	Oil	2	11.11%
	Electricity	2	11.11%
	Telecommunications	1	5.56%
	Social	8	44.44%
	Health	2	11.11%
	Water Supply	1	5.56%
	Security	1	5.56%
	Education	1	5.56%
Annual ICT Budget	<50.000 dollars	8	44%
	50.000–100.000 dollars	4	22%
	>100.000 dollars	6	33%

3.4   Results

Once the data was entered into the SPSS system, several statistical tests were performed. Descriptive statistical tests were used to generate frequencies, median, mean and standard deviation. Table 4 presents the descriptive statistic values of factors.

Table 4. Factors and their descriptive statistics

Factors	Mean	Std dev	Min	Max
Internal Organizational Control	3.2778	1.33606	1.00	4.86
Information Security Policy	3.7315	1.28483	1.00	5.00
New technologies	3.5556	1.24722	1.00	5.00
Technical activities for the information security	4.3333	0.76696	2.33	5.00
Information security management	3.3611	1.12641	0.83	4.83

As shown in Table 4, the average of all the factors was greater than 3, that is, they have a defined level of maturity, which indicates that the process is documented and communicated.

Consequently, the results of the descriptive statistics revealed that, the *technical activities for the information security* is the factor with a higher level of maturity. This result is not surprising given that the personnel responsible for the ICT area focuses on acquiring technology to automate processes and thus mitigate the various security risks that organizations face.

The second most mature factor was the *information security policy*, due to the need to have a document that establishes guidelines for the personnel despite not having a fully implemented Information Security process in the organization. Therefore, ICT managers consider the execution, revision and dissemination, as well as the ISP update in case of changes in the technological infrastructure.

The results also revealed that the respondents consider the internal control with a lower level of maturity compared to the others, because the aspect imply a greater effort due to the importance of the support of top management in hiring specialists for the creation and implementation of an Efficient ISMS. In general, large companies or companies with resources create the internal control unit or continually hire specialized personnel in the area of information security; therefore, organizations with an internal audit function are more prepared to detect fraud than those that do not have one.

Figure 1 shows the box diagrams of the five analyzed factors. The Technical activities for the information security factor is evaluated with a value higher than 4.5 for more than 50% of the people. Likewise, all the factors have a measure higher than 3.5, which means that ICT manager perceives a level of maturity between defined but not completely administered in their organizations.

On the other hand, the answers provided for the Internal Organizational Control, Information Security Policy and New Technologies factors have greater variability than Technical Activity for the information security and information security management factors.

As shown in Table 5, the Pearson correlation indicates the strength of association between the factors. It is considered a positive correlation between the factors since the value is greater than 0.7. All factors correlated more strongly with their own measures than with any of the other factors. This indicates convergent and discriminant validity. Therefore, the results show that the different factors are reliable and consistent.

According to Table 5, the correlation of 0.766 between the *Information Security Policy* and *Internal Organizational Control* factors demonstrates that the maturity of

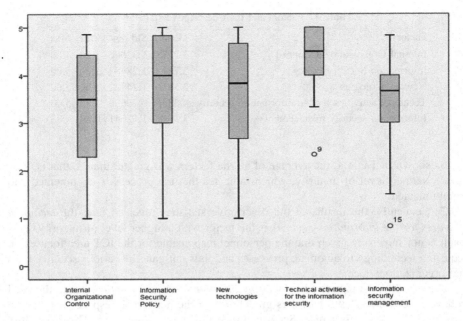

Fig. 1. Box diagram of factors

Table 5. Correlation between the different factors

Factors	1	2	3	4	5
1. Internal organizational control	1				
2. Information security policy	.766**	1			
3. New technologies	.534*	.480*	1		
4. Technical activities for the information security	.232	.053	.731**	1	
5. Information security management	.779**	.698**	.719**	.393	1

** means Correlation is significant at the 0.05 level (bilateral)
* means Correlation is significant at the 0.01 level (bilateral)

the internal audit facilitates the formulation of strategic security policies to achieve the company's objectives.

In the same way, the *Information Security Policy* and *Information Security Management* factors have a correlation of 0.698. Therefore, an adequate management of information security generates a mature ISP because it is considered as an influential organizational factor in the correct creation and execution of an Information Security Culture in an effective ISMS.

New technologies and *Information security management* are related due to their value of 0.719. The greater the level of maturity of the information security administration, the greater the awareness of the risks of using new technology within the organization. It is important to manage a mature ISRM through the effective selection of preventive measures capable of combating threats actively.

Likewise, new technologies and technical activities for information security have a positive correlation of 0.731, determining that a greater knowledge of new technologies achieves an adequate implementation of technological tools. However, a low investment in new technology training has a negative effect on the impossibility of carrying out technical activities to safeguard the information. Additionally, in the following, some important facts about key factors are presented.

Internal Organizational Control Factor: 44% of organizations have an automated risk management process and an updated risk map with identification and prioritization of risks. 22% of them perform risk management through the hiring of expert personnel on the subject, 11% contract only in certain processes and the remaining 11% consider that the personnel hired occasionally does not count with experience. From all the companies, only 33% have an internal audit area and another 33% hire audit and consulting services with independent companies.

Information Security Policy Factor: 67% of ICT managers said that their organization has a comprehensive ISP, evaluated and constantly updated. Slightly more than half i.e. 56% perceive the dissemination and strict compliance of ISP by the personnel. Likewise, 61% consider the personnel of the organization are trained and informed of the consequences of non-compliance of security standards.

New Technologies Factor: The majority of ICT managers (44%) do not perceive the emergence of new risks due to the use of social networks and mobile devices by the staff of the organization. 22% identify no changes in risks levels; however, 28% perceive changes in the control environment of their organization, and a minimum percentage (6%) considers an increase in risk levels. 56% have financial support from top management to acquire new resources for the identification of risks. 66% have an IT risk management program established, automated and comprehensive, considering the risks derived from the use of social networks, cloud computing and mobile personal devices.

Technical Activities for the Information Security Factor: Just over half of the respondents (56%) have the right technology to automate risk management. On the other hand, 94% have specific software for identity and access management that mitigates the risks associated with unauthorized access to systems and data.

Information Security Management Factor: 44.4% have a formal ISMS certification and have a fully optimized response plan. 5.6% have implemented an ISMS without a certification. 38.9% is in process of implementing an ISMS, and 11.1% has not considered the implementation of ISMS. In addition, 56% have a contingency and business continuity plan fully optimized and evaluated.

4   Conclusions

The implementation of an effective Information Security System depends on three types of factors: organizational, technological and hybrid. The factors considered in this study (internal organizational control, information security policy, information security culture, technical activities for information security and new technologies) allowed us to identify the level of maturity of the ISMS from the perspective of the ICT managers.

The findings of the analysis of statistical data showed a positive correlation between *information security policy* and *information security management* factors. The analysis indicated that as the level of maturity of the Information Security management increases/decreases, an increase/decrease in the level of maturity of the Information Security Policy is expected. For example, a high degree of support in the allocation of resources by top management in the Information Security risk assessment stage would result in a greater probability of success in the process of building the information security policy [29].

Regarding the experience in this work, future studies can be proposed, such as the application of the questionnaire to ICT managers in public entities of cities with a medium or greater population, focusing on the most relevant factors, developing an in-depth analysis of them in certified organizations.

References

1. Secretaria Nacional de Administración Pública: Acuerdo Interministerial 804
2. Comisión para la Seguridad Informática y de las Tecnologías de la Información: Informe Final
3. Secretaria Nacional de Administración Pública: Acuerdo ministerial 166
4. Coram, P., Ferguson, C., Moroney, R.: The value of internal audit in fraud detection. J. Account. Financ. **48**(4), 543–559 (2006)
5. Badara, M.S., Saidin, S.Z.: The Relationship between audit experience and internal audit effectiveness in the public sector organizations. Int. J. Acad. Res. Account. Financ. Manag. Sci. **3**(3), 329–339 (2013)
6. Chen, R.S., Sun, C.M., Helms, M.M., Jih, W.J.K.: Aligning information technology and business strategy with a dynamic capabilities perspective: a longitudinal study of a Taiwanese Semiconductor Company. Int. J. Inf. Manag. **28**(5), 366–378 (2008)
7. AlHogail, A.: Design and validation of information security culture framework. Comput. Hum. Behav. **49**, 567–575 (2015)
8. Hwang, K., Choi, M.: Effects of innovation-supportive culture and organizational citizenship behavior on e-government information system security stemming from mimetic isomorphism. Gov. Inf. Q. **34**(2), 183–198 (2017)
9. Patiño, S., Mosquera, C., Suárez, F., Nevarez, R.: Evaluación de seguridad informática basada en ICREA e ISO27001. Universidad Ciencia y Tecnología **21**(85), 129–139 (2017)
10. Candra, J., Brillyant, O., Tamba, S.: ISMS planning based on ISO/IEC 27001:2013 using analytical hierarchy process at gap analysis phase (case study: XYZ institute). In: Proceedings of 11th International Conference on Telecommunication Systems Services and Applications (TSSA). IEEE, Lombok (2017)
11. Rukth, L., Afzal, A.: Swiss army knife of software processes generic framework of ISO 27001 and its mapping on resource management. In: Proceedings of 2017 International Conference on Communication Technologies (ComTech). IEEE, Rawalpindi (2017)
12. Lichtenstein, S.: Factors in the selection of a risk assessment method. Inf. Manag. Comput. Secur. **4**(4), 20–25 (1996)
13. Shedden, P., Scheepers, R., Smith, W., Ahmad, A.: Incorporating a knowledge perspective into security risk assessments. Vine **41**(2), 152–166 (2011)

14. Patiño, S., Solís, E., Yoo, S.G., Arroyo, R.: ICT risk management methodology proposal for governmental entities based on ISO/IEC 27005. In: 2018 Fifth International Conference on eDemocracy and eGovernment (ICEDEG). IEEE (2018)
15. Vega, R.G., Arroyo, R., Yoo, S.G.: Experience in applying the analysis and risk management methodology called MAGERIT to identify threats and vulnerabilities in an Agro-Industrial Company. Int. J. Appl. Eng. Res. **12**(17), 6741–6750 (2017)
16. Chen, J., Pedrycz, W., Ma, L., Wang, C.: A new information security risk analysis method based on membership degree. Kybernetes **43**(5), 686–698 (2014)
17. Stvilia, B., Gasser, L., Twidale, M.B., Smith, L.C.: A framework for information quality assessment. J. Assoc. Inf. Sci. Technol. **58**(12), 1720–1733 (2007)
18. Shamala, P., Ahmad, R., Zolait, A., Sedek, M.: Integrating information quality dimensions into information security risk management (ISRM). J. Inf. Secur. Appl. **36**, 1–10 (2017)
19. Moon, Y.J., Choi, M., Armstrong, D.J.: The impact of relational leadership and social alignment on information security system effectiveness in Korean governmental organizations. Int. J. Inf. Manag. **40**, 54–66 (2018)
20. Siponen, M., Pahnila, S., Mahmood, A.: Employees' adherence to information security policies: an empirical study. In: Venter, H., Eloff, M., Labuschagne, L., Eloff, J., von Solms, R. (eds.) SEC 2007. IIFIP, vol. 232, pp. 133–144. Springer, Boston (2007). https://doi.org/10.1007/978-0-387-72367-9_12
21. Knapp, K.J., Marshall, T.E., Kelly Rainer, R., Nelson Ford, F.: Information security: management's effect on culture and policy. Inf. Manag. Comput. Secur. **14**(1), 24–36 (2006)
22. Alqahtani, F.H.: Developing an information security policy: a case study approach. Procedia Comput. Sci. **124**, 691–697 (2017)
23. Zakaria, O.: Employee security perception in cultivating information security culture. In: Security Management, Integrity, and Internal Control in Information Systems, pp. 83–92. Kluwer Academic Publishers, Boston (2006)
24. Soomro, Z.A., Shah, M.H., Ahmed, J.: Information security management needs more holistic approach: a literature review. Int. J. Inf. Manag. **36**(2), 215–225 (2016)
25. Kaufman, L.M.: Data security in the world of cloud computing. IEEE Secur. Priv. **7**(4), 61–64 (2009)
26. Grembergen, W.V.: Strategies for information technology governance. IGI Publishing, Hershey (2003)
27. Fernández, R., Montero, N.: Propuesta Metodológica para la Gestión de Riesgos Tecnológicos en Empresas Proveedoras de Servicios de Telecomunicaciones (2014)
28. Yi, M.Y., Davis, F.D.: Developing and validating an observational learning model of computer software training and skill acquisition. Inf. Syst. Res. **14**(2), 146–169 (2003)
29. Flowerday, S.V., Tuyikeze, T.: Information security policy development and implementation: the what, how and who. Comput. Secur. **61**, 169–183 (2016)

Evaluation of the Computation Times for Direct and Iterative Resolution Methods of MTJ Library Matrices Applied in a Thermal Simulation System

Christian Roberto Antón Cedeño[1]([⊠]) [iD],
Mitchell Vásquez-Bermúdez[1,2] [iD],
Juan Luis Foncubierta Blázquez[3] [iD], Ismael Rodríguez Maestre[3] [iD],
Jorge Hidalgo[2] [iD], María del Pilar Avilés-Vera[2] [iD],
and Néstor Vera-Lucio[2] [iD]

[1] Faculty of Mathematical and Physical Sciences, University of Guayaquil,
Cdla. Salvador Allende, Guayaquil, Ecuador
{christian.antonc,mitchell.vasquezb}@ug.edu.ec
[2] School Computer Engineering and Information Science,
Agrarian Sciences Faculty, Agrarian University of Ecuador,
Avenue 25 de Julio and Pio Jaramillo, Guayaquil, Ecuador
{mvasquez,Jhidalgo,maviles,nvera}@uagraria.edu.ec
[3] Polytechnic School of Algeciras, University of Cádiz,
Av. Ramón Puyol, 11202 Algeciras, Cádiz, Spain
{juanluis.foncubierta,ismael.rodriguez}@uca.es

Abstract. Thermal simulation systems in buildings, contribute to the design of energy-efficient structures; however, a significant amount of computational time is required in order to obtain the results of the simulation process. The main focus of this paper is examining the possibility of reducing time required for thermal simulation systems calculations. More specifically, the paper focuses on one of the major processes that requires computing resources at solving the system of equations obtained as a result of the thermal modeling of a building. This research was undertaken in order to determine the performance of Java library methods: Matrix Tool for Java (MTJ) for solving systems of linear equations, and identifying which of these was the optimum in terms of computation time. For this purpose, tests for the iterative methods combined with pre-conditioners were conducted. The tests of the direct method were done through the development of a software implemented in two case studies of buildings, and that was modeled with the parameters of the thermal simulation software called JEner, from the Thermal Engineering Research Group from the University of Cadiz in Spain.

Keywords: Thermal simulation · Iterative methods · MTJ

© Springer Nature Switzerland AG 2018
R. Valencia-García et al. (Eds.): CITI 2018, CCIS 883, pp. 110–123, 2018.
https://doi.org/10.1007/978-3-030-00940-3_9

1   Introduction

Nowadays, simulation systems are one of the most valuable tools used in science. Implementation of these systems provides data that can be examined to aid effective decision-making to predict the best possible scenarios and conditions of life for society.

There are different mathematical techniques employed for building models that allow performing simulations, however, it is very common for these mathematical processes to propose a system of nonlinear equations whose resolution results represents the expected reality. Researchers have found in the mathematical modeling and computing, two powerful tools that together have allowed the realization of high-performance simulations that can be used to solve extremely complex scenarios. For example, the thermal simulation of buildings and air conditioning systems, can predict the efficiency of energy usage under different scenarios, conditions, and timings.

However, the resolution of these systems of nonlinear equations is a task that demands a lot of computer resources, mainly the time required to compute solutions because is quite significant. This work was supported by the Research Group in Thermal Engineering (IITER) of the University of Cádiz, who developed a software tool that performs thermal simulations based on mathematical models [1], however, the construction of such models is based on extensive systems of equations and the outcome or resolution takes a large amount of time to return results. With this background, the present study was based on the models that build the software of IITER group and the assessment of methods of the MTJ library in the resolution of these.

It is important to emphasize that this work does not cover the construction of models for thermal simulation, but instead, lightens the mathematical resolution of the equation systems obtained from the model, using computer tools. However, it is necessary to explain certain elements of the IITER software for a better contextualization.

JEner is the name of the software created by IITER, this application implements the method of Newton-Raphson multivariable to solve the system of nonlinear equations by transforming it into a linear system which will then be solved by the direct method, incorporated in JAMA library. The present work proposes a study of the performance of the various methods of solving linear equations, in order to identify the optimum in terms of computation time, for this purpose alternatives libraries that incorporate other numerical methods were studied, being selected Matrix Toolkit for Java which presents a significant growth within the scientific community. For results and further analysis, two real case studies were determined by thermal simulation based on the parameters of JEner software.

Both JAMA and MTJ are libraries written in Java programming language. These are widely used in the international scientific community for solving problems based on matrices. The software that was developed with this work, was introduced to undergo the performance and testing methods offered by the MTJ library, in terms of balancing stability, convergence and computational times that have been written in Java, which is also one of the languages most widely used in the world [2, 3] and is widely used in the development of thermal simulation and thermal certification applications; software such as HEED 1.2 [4], GEC, HULC are written in this language.

2 Related Jobs

In [5] Frenkel made a comparative study concerning computation times on the algorithms of Pothen and Fan [6] and graph-based methods proposed by Tarjan [7], Ford, Jr [8], where the algorithm Pothen and Fan was highlighted in most of the case studies, although you can notice the dependence of the methods with the type of system to solve.

There is research on alternatives other than the traditional numerical methods for optimizing computing time in thermal simulation, such as Magnier and Haghighat [9] that propose a model based on genetic algorithms and neural networks for the optimization in construction and design of houses, the work is presented with the GAINN approach to present the RNA and multi-object genetic algorithm NSGA-II for optimization.

According to work carried out by [1] Foncubierta, it indicates that currently, the estimation of consumption in buildings through implemented models has become an essential way for the design, implementation of energy legislation and integration of energy management systems, it emphasizes that there is countless computer software that incorporates generation control algorithms.

In other investigations, such as the one proposed by [10] Bolivar, a library is developed in Java to solve computational and matrix algebra problems by using two-dimensional matrices that serve the users of the University of Carabobo. In addition, the JAMA library was used for matrix manipulation which consists of six classes that are: matrices, Cholesky decomposition, LU, QR, singular value, and Eigenvalues. In García's work [11] the solving of linear equations matrix was studied by means of iterative methods based on subspaces of Krylov.

Another area of study is [12] Guerrero, where a flow simulator was modified, using Saint-Venant equations based on the method of Preissmann which has allowed it to have a dynamic analysis tool that allows studying how liquid separation is produced. On the other hand, [13] Maestre indicates that computers of the last generation have drastically reduced computational costs. In addition, it presents how to evaluate errors in the radiation of incidents, for this practice, it is used a method for reducing time of calculations in BEPS that are commonly used in ray and cut paths. In general terms, it can be stated that the search for improvements in computational times aims to develop optimal methods of solving systems of equations, either by improving current ones or based on them.

In general, all the aforementioned works are directed towards the optimization of resolution times of the equation systems, in some cases the study concentrates on mathematical algorithms, however, this research studies the behavior with respect to computational times of the numerical methods incorporated in the MTJ library in a scenario composed by two cases of study with matrices of different dimensions.

3 Iterative Schemes

It exists different numerical methods for solving a system of nonlinear equations, how-ever, generally classical methods such as Newton-Raphson and its derivatives have the solving strategy of linearizing the system by calculating the Jacobian calculation [15]:

$$[J]_k[\delta X] = [F]_k$$

Where $[\delta X] = [X]_k - [X]_{k+1}$; $[X]_{k+1}$ is the vector of n unknowns for the next iteration k + 1; $[X]_k$ is the vector of n unknowns for the current iteration k; $[J]_k$ is the inverse of the Jacobian of the system of dimension n; y$[F]_k$ is the vector of each function eval-uation system for $[X]_k$. It is possible for the Jacobian calculation to be costly [16] but there are alternatives such as free derivative methods [17, 18] or Jacobian-Free methods [19] that approximate the product Jv, where J is the Jacobian and v is the vector resulting from the application of the decomposition methods of Krylov subspace, by Taylor series expansion.

3.1 Resolution of the Linear System

There are two types of solving methods for a system of linear equations: solutions that apply the direct method and solutions that apply iterative numerical methods. Those that employ the direct method, perform the inversion of the matrix using techniques such as LU factorization [20], QR [16], Cholesky [17], among others. The iterative ones employ numerical methods to solve linear problems, these methods are mostly based on the Krylov subspace, the best known are BiConjugate Gradient Methods (BCGD) [21], Conjugate Gradient Methods (CG) [21], Generalized Minimal Residual Method (GMRES) [23] among others. Iterative processes can become faster if they are combined with pre-conditioners and that is to transform the matrix system into a more advantageous one by using methods like Incomplete LU factorization [24], Incomplete Cholesky factorization [25], Multigrid Methods [26].

4 Java Libraries for Matrix Operations

There are projects that are being developed and enjoy good acceptance among developers of applications where there is involved the use of matrices, among the most well-known projects, exist JAMA [27], LA4J [28], COLT [29], MTJ [30], Commons Math [31] Efficient Java Matrix Library [32], jBlasj [33], jScience [34], OjAlgo [35], Parallel COLT [36] Universal Java Matrix Package [37]. There are tools like [38] which allows comparative performance tests among all the libraries mentioned. However, these tests are general, the tests carried out in this paper are intended to subject the library to a stress based on real scenarios, such as the thermal stress modeling. In this context, the MTJ library was selected for its characteristics and references [39], and additionally, it was contemplated to test the direct method of JAMA library for being the one currently used by JEner. According to [14], the JAMA library produced by the National Institute of Standards and Technology, is a library of objects which is based on different attributes since it is quite complex and includes most of the operations in matrices. JAMA provides user-level classes to build and manipulate real, and dense matrices. MTJ is a library written in Java and has a complete set of tools for linear algebra operations with dense matrices and a partial set of tools for sparse matrices. Originally developed by Bjorn-Ove Heimsund, among its main features there is that it allows handling dense and sparse, tridiagonal and symmetric, and sparse unstructured matrices. It also allows performing intrinsic operations such as matrix-vector multiplication, matrix-matrix multiplication, using methods such as direct resolution, LU and Cholesky decomposition, BiConjugate Gradient Methods (BCGD), Conjugate Gradient Methods (CG), among others.

5   Analysis of Initial Resolution System

Considering that this work was based on the solution proposed by JEner, the design of the test application obeys its resolution scheme to the system of nonlinear equations, which diagram of classes in UML is shown in Fig. 1. In which it shows that the Newton-Raphson method is developed in the NewtonRaphson class, which implements the Solver interface and generates instances of the GestorEcuaciones class that is in charge of modeling the system to solve. The Newton-class sets the workspace of this research, this class contains several methods, but there is one which contains the main programmatic logic of the class, this method is public double [] resolver (). Within this method there are three sections where control variables were placed to measure the computational times, these sections were: Creation of the function vector, resolution of the Jacobian and resolution of the linear system of equations. At the beginning and end of Solver, control variables were also placed to measure the total times.

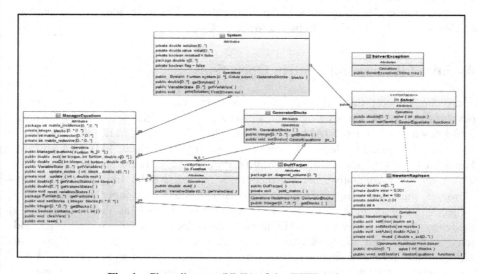

Fig. 1. Class diagram (UML) of the IITER solver [1].

5.1 Design of the Tool to Perform the Tests and Studies

The tool design presents an interface that allows the determination of the method to be assessed in various combinations with different preconditioners and present results through a grid, as shown in Fig. 2. In the mentioned figure, it can be seen how the application allows the researcher to select the method to be evaluated, and through a grid, they can observe the table of data or results obtained in the three sections and in the general method where the control variables were located. It was added to the screen an element for controlling the number of times that the solver was invoked, that could be between 1 and 105120 times, this number obeys the calculation of an effective simulation of every 5 min for a period of one year, which would allow to obtain the performance or annual energy efficiency of a structure.

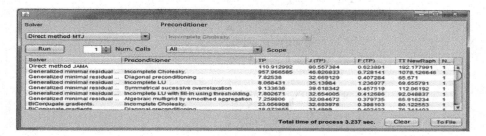

Fig. 2. Class diagram (UML) of the IITER solver [1].

The application logic is to invoke the solver and relate it to a system of nonlinear equations (case study) that is encoded in a class, then run the solution the number of times requested, and present the results.

For the results, it is considered as a unit of time the milliseconds and it is controlled: The average time it takes the solver execution, construction of the Jacobian, building the function; and the total time of Newton-Raphson with each method. The computer on which the test case studies were carried out has the following technical features: Intel Core 2 Quad Q8200 2.34 GHz, 8 GB RAM, 64 bits.

6 Case Studies

6.1 Case Study 1

It corresponds to the design of an air conditioning system in a pipes network with five elements that alter the load as shown in Fig. 3. The modeling of this small system yielded a total of 13 equations that can be seen in Fig. 4 and that form the system of linear equations of the case study 1, to be solved by the methods that were evaluated.

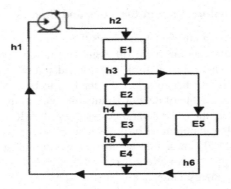

Fig. 3. Piping system design, Case Study 1

$$f_1 : 0 = h_1 - h_2 + 15q_1^{-0.5}$$
$$f_2 : 0 = h_2 - h_3 - 1.5q_2^{1.84}$$
$$f_3 : 0 = h_3 - h_4 - 0.6q_3^{1.84}$$
$$f_4 : 0 = h_4 - h_5 - q_4^{1.84}$$
$$f_5 : 0 = h_5 - h_6 - 1.2q_5^{1.84}$$
$$f_6 : 0 = h_1 - h_6 - 0.5q_6^{1.84}$$
$$f_7 : 0 = h_3 - h_6 - 2q_7^{1.84}$$
$$f_8 : 0 = q_6 + q_1$$
$$f_9 : 0 = q_1 - q_2$$
$$f_{10} : 0 = q_3 - q_4$$
$$f_{11} : 0 = q_4 - q_5$$
$$f_{12} : 0 = q_5 + q_6 + q_7$$
$$f_{13} : 0 = h_1$$

Fig. 4. System of equations, Case Study 1

6.2   Case Study 2

Figure 5 shows the design of a cooling system composed of a chiller and two elements of Thermal Units (U.T) and whose modeling derives on 15 equations that can be observed in Fig. 6. This system is allocated in each of the floors of a 10-floor building so that 10 similar systems are obtained, which generates a total of 150 linear equations (Case Study 2) to be solved by the methods that will be evaluated.

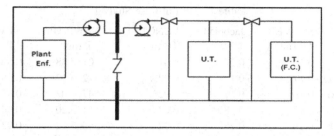

Fig. 5. Cooling system design, Case Study 2

$$f_1 : \Delta p_{PE} = K_{PE} m_{PE}{}^n$$

$$f_2 : \Delta p_{PE} = A - B \cdot m_{PE} - C \cdot m_{PE}{}^2$$

$$f_3 : P_{PE} = P_{PE,N} \cdot f(T_{PE,S}, T_{ext}, m_{PE})$$

$$f_4 : P_{PE} = m_{PE} \cdot C_p (T_{PE,E} - T_{PE,S})$$

$$f_5 : T_{PE,E} = T_D$$

$$f_6 : \Delta p_{FC} = K_{FC} \dot{m}_{FC}{}^n$$

$$f_7 : \Delta p_{FC} = A - B \cdot m_{FC} - C \cdot m_{FC}{}^2$$

$$f_8 : P_{FC} = P_{FC,N} \cdot f(T_{FC,S}, T_{ext}, m_{FC})$$

$$f_9 : P_{FC} = m_{FC} \cdot C_p (T_{FC,S} - T_{FC,E})$$

$$f_{10} : T_{FC,E} = T_D$$

$$f_{11} : m_{PE} C_p T_{PE,S} - m_{PE} C_p T_D + m_{FC} C_p T_{FC,S} - m_{FC} C_p T_D - UA \cdot (T_D - T_{ext}) = \rho V C_p \frac{T_D - T_D^{i-1}}{\Delta t}$$

$$f_{12} : \Delta p_{FC} = K_{FC2} m_{FC2}$$

$$f_{13} : T_{FC2,E} = T_D$$

$$f_{14} : P_{FC,2} = m_{FC,2} C_p (T_{FC2,S} - T_{FC2,E})$$

$$f_{15} : P_{FC,2} = P_{FC,2NDm} f(T_{FC2,E}, T_A, m_{FC2})$$

Fig. 6. System of equations, Case Study 2

7   Evaluation and Results

7.1   Case Study 1

In this first case study, the obtained results shown in Table 1, indicate that the construction of the Jacobian and the function vector remain constant in the JAMA library as for MTJ and any of its methods. Similarly, it is observed that the construction of the Jacobian in a system of 13 equations takes practically the same time as the resolution of the linear system of equations, while the construction of the vector function in this case study shows insignificant values within the total time that it takes for the Newton-Raphson to run.

Table 1. Data of Case Study 1

SOLVER	SOLVER TP (ms)	Jacobian TP (ms)	FUNCTION TP (ms)	NEWRAPH TT (ms)	NEWRAPH TT (min)
MD-JAMA	0.10	0.17	0.01	30157.88	0.50
GMRES-ICHO	0.17	0.17	0.02	57246.12	0.95
GMRES-PERD	0.16	0.17	0.02	54707.02	0.91
GMRES-ILU	0.16	0.18	0.02	56445.20	0.94
GMRES-SSO	0.16	0.17	0.02	56065.12	0.93
GMRES-Ilut	0.18	0.19	0.02	66869.34	1.11
GMRES-AMSA	0.17	0.20	0.02	61208.34	1.02
BCG-ICHO	0.15	0.18	0.02	55896.25	0.93
BCG-PERD	0.15	0.18	0.03	55543.48	0.93
BCG-ILU	0.15	0.18	0.02	55596.41	0.93
BCG-SSO	0.15	0.18	0.02	55969.94	0.93
BCG-Ilut	0.16	0.19	0.02	61530.34	1.03
BCG-AMSA	0.16	0.19	0.02	58607.09	0.98
BCGs-ICHO	0.21	0.18	0.02	63858.16	1.06
BCGs-PERD	0.21	0.19	0.02	63398.37	1.06
BCGs-ILU	0.22	0.18	0.02	62652.72	1.04
BCGs-SSO	0.21	0.18	0.02	62337.99	1.04
BCGs-Ilut	0.21	0.18	0.02	66645.35	1.11
BCGs-AMSA	0.21	0.18	0.02	61391.17	1.02
CGS-ICHO	0.14	0.18	0.02	53315.64	0.89
CGS-PERD	0.14	0.18	0.02	53185.74	0.89
CGS-ILU	0.14	0.18	0.02	52520.54	0.88
CGS-SSO	0.14	0.18	0.02	53376.58	0.89
CGS-Ilut	0.14	0.18	0.02	56805.48	0.95
CGS-AMSA	0.14	0.18	0.02	52297.20	0.87
QMR-ICHO	0.17	0.18	0.02	55787.45	0.93
QMR-PERD	0.17	0.18	0.02	55289.46	0.92
QMR-ILU	0.17	0.18	0.02	55764.97	0.93
QMR-SSO	0.17	0.17	0.02	55602.41	0.93
QMR-Ilut	0.17	0.18	0.02	59782.02	1.00
QMR-AMSA	0.17	0.17	0.02	55245.08	0.92
MD-MTJ	0.02	0.18	0.02	24816.52	0.41

In Fig. 7 the analysis focuses exclusively on the time of the solver (column SOLVER TP) where the values are given in milliseconds and although in this case, the direct methods were faster, the average of the iterative methods exceeds by 663% the time employed by the Direct Method MTJ (MD-MTJ) and Direct Method JAMA (MD-JAMA) exceeds the MD-MTJ by 348%, that is, to solve this case, MD-JAMA employed 3.5 times the time it took the MD-MTJ, while the MTJ iterations exceed the

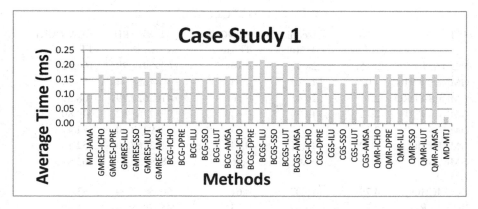

Fig. 7. Graph of results of case 1

MD-JAMA by 70%. For this case, the MD-MTJ was much faster than others and the total execution time of the Newton-Raphson reflects the superiority of this method over the others. For this system of equations, all the solver converged.

From the iterative methods, it shows that the Conjugate Squared Gradients method (CGS) that was combined with Incomplete Cholesky Preconditioners (ICHO), Diagonal preconditioning (PERD), Incomplete LU (ILU), Symmetrical Successive Overrelaxation (SSO), Incomplete LU with fill-in using thresholding (ILUT) and Algebraic Multigrid by Smoothed Aggregation (AMSA) proved to be the fastest in this system of 13 equations, the small variation of the values attribute the efficient of the method over the preconditioners with which it can be inferred about the adaptability of this method to the use of any preconditioner. This feature, in this case, is also seen in the Quasi-Minimal Residual method (QMR).

7.2   Case Study 2

In this second case study a system of 150 linear equations was solved, the results obtained shown in Table 2 indicate that the construction of the Jacobian and the vector function remain constant between JAMA library and MTJ, the Jacobian in a system of more than 100 equations, far exceeds the time of resolution of the linear system of equations with the exception of the direct method of JAMA library. In contrast, the construction of the function vector in this case study shows little significant values within the total time it takes for the Newton-Raphson run.

In Fig. 8 the analysis focuses exclusively on the time of the solver (column SOLVER TP) where values are given in milliseconds and allows to note that iterative methods in systems of more than 100 equations become much more efficient in terms of computational time, the average of the iterative methods exceeds by 454% the time spent by the direct method of MTJ and the direct method JAMA exceeds by 2696% the direct method MTJ, in other words, to solve this case JAMA's direct method spent 27 times the time it took for the MTJ direct method, while the MTJ iterative method

Table 2. Data of Case Study 1

SOLVER	SOLVER TP (ms)	Jacobian TP (ms)	FUNCTION TP (ms)	NEWRAPH TT (ms)	NEWRAPH TT (min)
MD-JAMA	32.15	28.47	0.16	6390914.29	106.52
GMRES-ICHO	4.07	13.96	0.63	3044658.94	50.74
GMRES-PERD	2.11	26.41	0.56	4103627.79	68.39
GMRES-ILU	2.12	13.99	0.63	2987752.62	49.80
GMRES-SSO	2.12	29.17	0.63	4469352.40	74.49
GMRES-Ilut	2.12	15.11	0.64	3153767.80	52.56
GMRES-AMSA	2.10	14.01	0.56	3829235.05	63.82
BCG-ICHO	4.79	15.07	0.61	5005002.90	83.42
BCG-PERD	4.78	13.79	0.53	4307915.36	71.80
BCG-ILU	4.79	13.80	0.61	3320055.19	55.33
BCG-SSO	4.78	13.80	0.61	4776950.76	79.62
BCG-Ilut	4.79	13.80	0.62	3408617.81	56.81
BCG-AMSA	4.78	13.80	0.53	4074151.67	67.90
BCGs-ICHO	5.64	31.55	0.62	5117517.23	85.29
BCGs-PERD	5.63	14.00	0.54	4303245.45	71.72
BCGs-ILU	5.63	14.00	0.62	3268518.68	54.48
BCGs-SSO	5.62	13.99	0.62	3266176.93	54.44
BCGs-Ilut	5.63	14.00	0.63	3392528.86	56.54
BCGs-AMSA	5.62	14.14	0.54	3206014.22	53.43
QMR-ICHO	5.06	17.24	0.62	3515877.15	58.60
QMR-PERD	5.05	27.15	0.54	4483241.29	74.72
QMR-ILU	5.05	13.92	0.62	3294685.60	54.91
QMR-SSO	5.06	15.23	0.62	3431416.06	57.19
QMR-Ilut	13.18	13.93	0.63	4150257.27	69.17
QMR-AMSA	19.36	13.93	0.54	4597636.80	76.63
MD-MTJ	1.19	13.84	0.14	1797484.42	29.96

employed only 17% of the time of the JAMA's direct method. The execution of Newton-Raphson reflects the superiority of the MTJ direct method over the other methods. For this system of equations, the CGS solver did not converge. In this case study, it could be noted that the Generalized Minimal Residual method (GMRES) combined with 6 preconditioners had better performance than the other iterative methods, however, combined with ICHO it did not have the same performance as presented with other preconditioners. For both case studies, the BiConjugate Gradients (BCG) and BiConjugate Gradients Stabilized (BCGs) methods, despite converging, they have been the iterative methods of lowest performance.

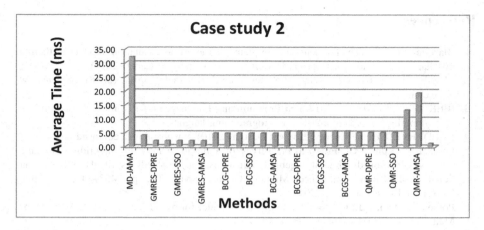

Fig. 8. Results graph case 2

8   Conclusions and Future Work

There are several libraries for the operation with matrices and numerical methods in Java, however, the two most commonly used libraries are JAMA and MTJ, being the latter the biggest boom at present within the developer community. The direct method of MTJ library proved to be much more efficient in terms of computational time than the JAMA library, mainly when the workload was increased because its performance grew exponentially. For iterative methods, the greater the dimension of the system of equations, the greater their efficiency. The direct method of JAMA library is more efficient in small systems. Whereas in the resolution of the two cases, the average of the iterative methods increased its time by 3240%, the direct method MTJ by 5450% and the direct method JAMA by 32783%, this suggests that in even larger systems, the efficiency of the iterative methods would exceed the direct method of MTJ. Performance of the iterative method can be affected negatively or positively using preconditioners as seen in the results of case 2 in the combination of GMRES method with ICHO preconditioner.

Although mathematical algorithms make evident that iterative methods tend to solve linear equations systems in better times than the application of direct methods, in the execution of these algorithms in a computer, the direct method of MTJ presented a better time than the iterative methods, which would justify an expanded work in the future about the behavior, stability and convergence of mathematical algorithms of iterative methods that are applied to diverse programming languages.

References

1. Blázquez, J.L.F.: Development and implementation of a simulation model of thermal installations in buildings. Doctoral Dissertation, University of Cadiz (2014)
2. TIOBE: TIOBE Index for May 2018 Headline: Scala cracks top 20 (2018). https://www.tiobe.com/tiobe-index/
3. IEEE SPECTRUM: The 2017 Top Programming Languages (2017). https://spectrum.ieee.org/computing/software/the-2017-top-programming-languages
4. HEED: HEED Home Energy Efficient Design (2010). www.aud.ucla.edu/heed
5. Frenkel, J., Kunze, G., Fritzson, P.: Survey of appropriate matching algorithms for large scale systems of differential algebraic equations. In: Proceedings of the 9th International MODELICA Conference, Munich, Germany, vol. 076, pp. 433–442. Linköping University Electronic Press (2012)
6. Pothen, A., Fan, C.J.: Computing the block triangular form of a sparse matrix. ACM Trans. Math. Softw. (TOMS) 16(4), 303–324 (1990)
7. Tarjan, R.: Depth-first search and linear graph algorithms. SIAM J. Comput. 1(2), 146–160 (1972)
8. Ford, L.R., Fulkerson, D.R.: Flows in Networks. Princeton University Press, Princeton (1962)
9. Magnier, L., Haghighat, F.: Multiobjective optimization of building design using TRNSYS simulations, genetic algorithm, and Artificial Neural Network. Build. Environ. 45(3), 739–746 (2010)
10. Bolívar, A.: Development of a Library of Java Classes to Solve Computation and Matrix Algebra Problems Using Two-Dimensional Arrays. University of Carabobo, Carabobo (2013)
11. García León, M.D.: Strategies for solving large systems of linear equations. Modified quasi-minimal waste methods. Doctoral Dissertation, University of Las Palmas de Gran Canaria (2003)
12. Guerrero, A.M., Gonzalo, N., Luque, J.S.: Simulator extension for operation as a liquid manifold-distributor using two free surface equations. Ciencia e Ingeniería 28(2), 103–109 (2007)
13. Maestre, I.R., Blázquez, J.L.F., Gallero, F.J.G., Cubillas, P.R.: Influence of selected solar positions for shading device calculations in building energy performance simulations. Energy Build. 101, 144–152 (2015)
14. Di Mare, A.: Introduction to the use of algebra libraries for engineering students. In: Eighth LACCEI Latin American and Caribbean Conference for Engineering and Technology (LACCEI) (2010)
15. Javadoc.IO: Matrix Toolkits for Java 1.0.4 API. http://www.javadoc.io/doc/com.googlecode.matrix-toolkits-java/mtj/1.0.4
16. swMATH: MTJ. https://www.swmath.org/software/22708
17. Knoll, D.A., Keyes, D.E.: Jacobian-free Newton-Krylov methods: a survey of approaches and applications. J. Comput. Phys. 193(2), 357–397 (2004)
18. Stanimirović, P.S., Pappas, D., Katsikis, V.N., Stanimirović, I.P.: Full-rank representations of outer inverses based on the QR decomposition. Appl. Math. Comput. 218(20), 10321–10333 (2012)
19. Sharma, J.R., Arora, H., Petković, M.S.: An efficient derivative free family of fourth order methods for solving systems of nonlinear equations. Appl. Math. Comput. 235, 383–393 (2014)

20. Jain, P.: Steffensen type methods for solving non-linear equations. Appl. Math. Comput. **194** (2), 527–533 (2007)

21. Dewilde, P.: On the LU factorization of infinite systems of semi-separable equations. Indagationes Mathematicae **23**(4), 1028–1052 (2012)

22. Wright, S.J.: Modified Cholesky factorizations in interior-point algorithms for linear programming. SIAM J. Optim. **9**(4), 1159–1191 (1999)

23. Joly, P., Eymard, R.: Preconditioned biconjugate gradient methods for numerical reservoir simulation. J. Comput. Phys. **91**(2), 298–309 (1990)

24. Hestenes, M.R. and Stiefel, E.: Methods of conjugate gradients for solving linear systems, vol. 49, n° 1. NBS, Washington, DC (1952)

25. Saad, Y., Schultz, M.H.: GMRES: a generalized minimal residual algorithm for solving nonsymmetric linear systems. SIAM J. Sci. Stat. Comput. **7**(3), 856–869 (1986)

26. Monga Made, M.M., Van der Vorst, H.A.: A generalized domain decomposition paradigm for parallel incomplete LU factorization preconditionings. Future Gener. Comput. Syst. **17**(8), 925–932 (2001)

27. Li, D., Zhang, C.: Split Newton iterative algorithm and its application. Appl. Math. Comput. **217**(5), 2260–2265 (2010)

28. Slaybaugh, R.N., Evans, T.M., Davidson, G.G., Wilson, P.P.: Multigrid in energy preconditioner for Krylov solvers. J. Comput. Phys. **242**, 405–419 (2013)

29. National Institute of Standards and Technology: JAMA: A Java Matrix Package (2012). https://math.nist.gov/javanumerics/jama/#Authors

30. Kostrokov, V.: Linear Algebra for Java (la4j) (2012). https://code.google.com/archive/p/la4j/

31. CERN: The Colt Project, European Organization for Nuclear Research (2004). http://dst.lbl.gov/ACSSoftware/colt/

32. GitHub: Matrix Toolkit for Java, GitHub, Inc. (2016). https://github.com/fommil/matrix-toolkits-java

33. Apache Commons: Linear Algebra, Apache Commons Math (2016). http://commons.apache.org/proper/commons-math/userguide/linear.html

34. Abeles, P.: Efficient Java Matrix Library, Google Código (2015). https://code.google.com/p/efficient-java-matrix-library/

35. Braun, M.L., Schaback, J., Jugel, M.L., Oury, N.: JBLAS Linear Algebra for Java, Mikiobraun (2010). http://mikiobraun.github.io/jblas/

36. Dautelle, J.M.: Java Tools and Libraries for the Advancement of Sciences, JScience (2014). http://jscience.org/

37. Optimatika: oj! Algoritmos 2017. http://ojalgo.org/

38. Wendykier, P.: Parallel Colt (2010). https://sites.google.com/site/piotrwendykier/software/parallelcolt

39. Arndt, H., Bundschus, M., Nägele, A., Huso, R., Carlsen, F.: Universal Java Matrix Package, Holger Arndt (2018). https://ujmp.org/

40. Abeles, P.: Java Matrix Bench-mark, Google Código (2010). https://code.google.com/archive/p/java-matrix-benchmark/

41. McMahan, H.B., Gordon, G.J.: Fast exact planning in Markov decision processes. In: ICAPS, pp. 151–160 (2005)

Revenue Assurance Model for Project Management Organizations Using Outlier Mining

Gilberto F. Castro[1,2(✉)] ⓘ, Anié Bermudez-Peña[3] ⓘ,
Francisco G. Palacios[2], Mitchell Vásquez-Bermúdez[2,4] ⓘ,
Diana J. Espinoza[2], Fausto R. Orozco[2], and Inelda A. Martillo[1,2]

[1] Facultad de Ingeniería, Universidad Católica Santiago de Guayaquil,
Guayaquil, Ecuador
{gilberto.castro,inelda.martilloa}@cu.ucsg.edu.ec
[2] Facultad de Ciencias Matemáticas y Físicas,
Universidad de Guayaquil, Guayaquil, Ecuador
{francisco.palacioso,mitchell.vasquezb,
diana.espinozavi,fausto.orozcol}@ug.edu.ec
[3] Departamento de Gestión de Proyectos,
Universidad de Ciencias Informáticas, Habana, Cuba
abp@uci.cu
[4] Facultad de Ciencias Agrarias,
Universidad Agraria del Ecuador, Guayaquil, Ecuador

Abstract. The increase of competitiveness in global markets has led to the need for improvements in project management organizations aimed at stimulating financial health and revenue. Revenue assurance combines statistical techniques, scope, time and risk management with the goal of reducing costs and maximizing revenue in organizations that apply it. The objective of this paper is to present a revenue assurance model for project management organizations that allows the detection of planning errors and revenues maximization during the projects development. As part of the research novelty, the proposed model combines risk management, outlier mining and soft computing techniques. Risk management is developed with a proactive approach, based on the application of computing with words for qualitative risk assessment. In the research, cross validation tests are carried out comparing different techniques for the detection of anomalous situations. In the comparison, project management databases are used for the development of computer solutions. The model is introduced in a platform for integrated project management and the results of its application are also presented.

Keywords: Revenue assurance · Project management · Outlier mining

© Springer Nature Switzerland AG 2018
R. Valencia-García et al. (Eds.): CITI 2018, CCIS 883, pp. 124–139, 2018.
https://doi.org/10.1007/978-3-030-00940-3_10

1 Introduction

One of the forms of organization that has gained strength due to its applicability in different scenarios is Integrated Project Management, which has led to the growth of a number of project management organizations. These organizations develop new products or services, establishing their resources in the form of projects with well-determined start and end dates, as suggested in the PMBOK guide [1]. Project management must be supported by the use of information systems that help decision-making.

In this type of organization, despite efforts to improve management efficiency, there are still many difficulties that generate income losses. A study carried out by Standish Group International, showed that historically, the numbers of projects satisfactorily managed, renegotiated and canceled, have moved by around 29%, 52% and 19% respectively [2]. An important element that must be analyzed beyond the number of renegotiated or failed projects is the economic and social impact of the same ones.

In this context, shortcomings in the planning, control and monitoring processes, as well as insufficient mechanisms for risk management and human resources management, are identified among the fundamental causes of project failure [3]. During the development of plans, defects that can significantly affect the costs foreseen for the project execution are introduced, caused by human errors or masking processes of corruption and fraud. Some of these causes can be mitigated if the outliers contained in the information systems of the organizations themselves are analyzed [4, 5].

Revenue assurance as a knowledge area arises since the end of 1970s in telecommunications sector, as a discipline oriented to the protection and recovery of the financial resources of organizations [6, 7]. We adopt the concept of revenue assurance as: set of techniques, policies and models, applied with the objectives of increasing revenues and reducing the costs of the organizations that apply those following reactive, active and proactive approaches. There are a set of errors in project management that have a high impact on its success and therefore in revenue assurance of the organizations [4–16]:

- Little attention to the project's risks, which frequently causes a slight override in project costs, affecting revenue and profits.
- They depend on human resources for their application, which in turn are also subject to possible operation errors.
- In project management organizations, phenomena that traditional revenue assurance techniques do not manage properly are presented, such as heterogeneity in data, imprecision, and uncertainty.
- Frequently, the proposed solutions are only based on reactive approaches and do not adequately use active or proactive strategies for revenue assurance.
- Often, the implemented solutions constitute black boxes supported by proprietary tools that affect the technological sovereignty of the organizations. The full impact of the information management with these external tools is not known for sure.

It has been identified that many of these problems affect the efficiency and effectiveness of revenue assurance processes from the perspective of the ability to detect anomalous situations. Within data mining, a particular area known as outlier mining is dedicated to the detection of outliers in data samples, with applications in different areas such as telecommunications and health [17]. As a strategy to help solving some of these problems, this research aims to improve the detection and prevention processes of situations that affect revenue in project management organizations.

This paper presents a revenue assurance model for project management organizations. As part of the novelty of the research, the proposed model combines risk management techniques, outlier mining and soft computing techniques; as well as the identification of situations that generate outliers in project management organizations.

The rest of this paper is structured as follows. Section 2 provides a description of the most relevant works related to: revenue assurance, project management schools, outlier mining, and soft computing techniques. Section 3 presents the revenue assurance model for project management organizations. Evaluation and results are described in Sect. 4. Finally, conclusions and feature work are presented.

2   Related Works

2.1   Revenue Assurance

Revenue assurance is an interdisciplinary field that combines statistical techniques, risk management, scope, time and outlier mining, among other techniques. In this context, definitions have emerged to describe the subject matter of this discipline. Among them, Khan emphasizes that "revenue assurance is the set of activities that are applied to ensure that business processes, organizational structure, control, and information systems, related to revenue cycle of organizations, work together effectively" [14].

With the development of revenue assurance discipline, spaces for the training of specialists and the creation of standards emerged: TM Forum [6] and the Global Association of Revenue Assurance Professionals GRAPA [5, 15] are two of them. GRAPA is founded with the objective of defining, standardizing and professionalizing the work related to revenue assurance; in addition to provide support throughout the world to professionals in this knowledge area [16]. According to GRAPA, among the most used techniques in revenue assurance are: risk analysis, exchange analysis, process analysis, systems analysis and statistical analysis. TM Forum argues that among the main factors that influence the maturity of the revenue assurance processes are the level of experience of insurance teams and technologies; both with a 23% relevance [6].

After a study carried out, it was possible to confirm that techniques proposed for revenue assurance worldwide are still insufficient both for telecommunications companies, where they arose, and for project management organizations. In this scenario, the need for techniques to deal with the imprecision and uncertainty of the data is identified. It is also identified the need to combine the statistical techniques traditionally used with other data analysis techniques such as those found in the outlier mining discipline.

To combine reactive and active strategies, that reduce the time of detection of income leaks, with proactive strategies that aim at preventing failures, fraud among other anomalous situations is identified as a trend. Most authors report that there is a need for the development of novel tools that adapt to the dynamism of new technologies to ensure the successful application of revenue assurance techniques.

2.2 Influence of Project Management Schools on Revenue Assurance

The discipline of Project Management is instituted by schools or institutions dedicated to the formalization of organization methods. These institutions include the Project Management Institute (PMI) with the PMBOK standard [1], the Software Engineering Institute (SEI) with the Capability Maturity Model Integration (CMMI) [18], the International Project Management Association (IPMA) and the ISO with its standards 10006 and 21500 [19]. These standards include activities and techniques that can influence revenue assurance from the point of view of different areas of processes: scope, integration, time, cost, quality, human resources and others. These are mostly based on manual analysis with a strong influence of experts. The greatest contribution of these methodologies to revenue assurance can be found in the area of risk management that does constitute proactive analysis techniques.

The main project management standards do not sufficiently address the issue of revenue assurance; it is in PMBOK version 6 (September 2017) that they begin to talk about the importance of data analysis in projects [1]. As a strategy to solve these problems in project management organizations, the authors developed research associated with the application of data mining and soft computing techniques [20].

2.3 Outlier Mining and Soft Computing Techniques

An outlier can be defined as an observation that deviates a lot from the rest, appearing as a suspicious observation that could be generated by mechanisms different from the rest of the data [21]. Outlier mining contributes significantly in revenue assurance process, particularly in reactive and active approaches for the detection of possible records that reflect money leakage due to concepts of fraud, system failures among others.

Some techniques that have been implemented in this knowledge area are based on: clustering techniques [22], density-based models, statistical models based on distribution and models based on artificial neural networks [21]. There are several approaches for characterization of application scenarios of outlier mining [4, 21–24], among which stand out: heterogeneity; dimensionality; volume of information; uncertainty and inaccuracy; outlier types (punctual, contextual or collective) and the way of data presentation (punctuation or labeling). For the application of outlier mining in revenue assurance, the specificities of each scenario and the nature of its data must be considered.

A strategy to treat the imprecision, inconsistency and uncertainty of the data during revenue assurance, combine outlier mining, soft computing and good practices in project management. Soft computing techniques provide tools to approximate human reasoning through the use of accumulated experience. Under this principle, fuzzy systems, neural networks, evolutionary computing, probabilistic reasoning, as well as combinations thereof, are considered soft computing techniques [25]. These techniques allows gaining in robustness, efficiency, adaptability, and proper balance between power prediction and interpretation, which are integrated to support decision-making.

It can be concluded that there are no deterministic solutions for revenue assurance applicable to all organizations. This occurs because in each scenario there are specific internal and external factors, with a high impact on decisions for their management.

3   Revenue Assurance Model

In this section, a revenue assurance model for project management organizations is presented [20]. The model is divided into the following sections: conceptualization of the proposed model and description of the processes for the application of the model.

3.1   Conceptualization of the Model

The proposed model is structured by three components which interact under a systemic approach with a close relationship:

1. Understanding the organizations: includes techniques and diagrams that allow guiding the process of understanding the business of the organizations under analysis. This component generates as output, a diagnostic document, a taxonomy with the main problems that can generate revenue losses, and the data model that characterizes the data collected in the information systems of the organization.
2. Analysis and data processing: this component includes groups of algorithms and techniques for data analysis that reflect the activity of the analyzed organizations. It generates as output: results analysis report, list of prioritized risks and list of outliers.
3. Decision-making: component associated with the evaluation of the results obtained in the second component and the implementation of the solutions. It generates as outputs, the decisions taken and the lessons learned. All outputs of this component are inputted to the first component, which allows to adjust and improve the model behavior in the real application scenario.

The model can be adapted according to the specificities of each real application scenario. For the instrumentation of the model, the processes in Fig. 1 are followed.

3.2   Instrumentation Processes of the Model

Process 1. Understanding of the Organization
Initially, an understanding of organization and diagnosis of its projects is made. This first stage focuses on understanding the organization processes to define a taxonomy that helps identify anomalous situations that affect revenue, as possible causes of failure, bad planning, fraud, and errors in projects execution or simply leaks revenue.

A set of experts builds the sequence of primary and support activities that make up the value chain of the organization. Based on the analysis of the value chain, a SWOT matrix is constructed, identifying elements that influence each primary activity both in the reduction of costs and in the improvement of revenues. In this identification and

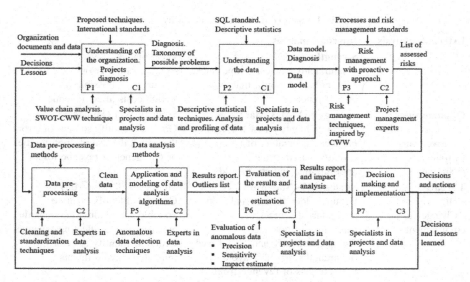

Fig. 1. Instrumentation of revenue assurance model. Where C1, C2 and C3 correspond to the components model, and P1–P7 are the process.

evaluation of elements that influence revenue of the organization, six groups are identified, see Table 1. These six groups allow experts to evaluate each element that influences revenue, grouped by their nature. Following the 2-tuples model of computing with words [26], the evaluations of the experts are added, consolidating the same for each element to be evaluated. To mitigate, avoid or enhance each element based on its impact on revenue, the experts propose a set of actions to be executed. Generally, actions of different groups can be executed in parallel.

Groups 2, 3 and 5 concentrate the internal or external factors, the possible sources of errors and other anomalous situations that affect the revenue. Groups 4 and 6 have recommended actions and will be used following a proactive approach in process 3 of the model. Group 1 are aimed at exploiting the opportunities and will be considered following a proactive approach in process 3 of the model.

Process 2. Understanding the Data
In this process, the data model collected from the organization information systems is characterized and constructed. The nature of the data, the existence of missing values and the most frequent errors in them are analyzed. To do this, descriptive statistics techniques combined with the facilities of the information systems are used:

- Information gathering: analysis of documents and databases, personal or group interviews with specialists with more experience working with the organization data.
- Data profiling techniques: they allow to understand the data structure, its characteristics and quality.
- Identification of generating situations of outliers reflected in the databases of the organization.

Table 1. SWOT matrix constructed by experts

External analysis	Internal analysis	
	Strengths - Natural advantages, competences - Strengths in control that avoid loss of revenue	**Weaknesses** - Organization errors - Sources of possible fraud - High costs affect revenue
Opportunities - Technological improvements - Strategic positioning	Strategy SO (Max-Max) Group 1: Identify new services or products, generators of new revenue, based in the opportunities and strongholds	Strategy WO (Min-Max) Group 2: Identify sources of errors that affect the use of opportunities or that generate revenue losses
Threats - High risks - Changes in the environment	Strategy ST (Max-Min) Group 5: Identify external risks and external sources that can cause loss of revenue Group 6: Identify activities based on strengths that help avoid or mitigate loss of revenue from external threats	Strategy WT (Min-Min) Group 3: Identify errors or possible anomalous situations that enhance threats affecting revenue Group 4: Identify activities to mitigate or avoid threats

Process 3. Risk Management

It is based on the application of risk management techniques combined with soft computing for the planning and qualitative evaluation of risks, generating a list of prioritized risks. The techniques and processes of the PMBOK are applied (Risk-PMBOK). In addition, a new technique is introduced in the risk qualitative analysis (Risk-CWW), it is based on the 2-tuples model of computing with words [26]. The algorithm/steps used for the evaluation of risks using Risk-CWW technique are:

1. Select the set of experts.
2. Identify the risks with impact on revenue assurance.
3. Establish the risk assessment criteria. In this case, the following criteria are taken: probability of occurrence, impact and ease of detection.
4. Evaluate each of the identified risks using computing with words techniques.
5. Following the 2-tuples model of computing with words, the evaluations of the experts are added, consolidating the same for each element to be evaluated.
6. Upon completion, the identified risks and their impact on revenue assurance processes are taken into account.

Process 4. Data Pre-processing

In this process, data cleaning techniques are applied for the elimination of possible noises that affect the detection of the true outliers. Cleaning activities, standardization and the selection of attributes are carried out. The steps used for data cleaning are:

1. Identification of errors and definition of a taxonomy to classify the different types of errors found. The taxonomy or a checklist for the classification of errors is applied. This may include the types of data: incomplete, incorrect and inconsistent.

2. Measurement of the volume of errors in the data, based on a metric for the data quality evaluation.
3. Application of data cleaning techniques based on three strategies: errors elimination, strings replacement for standardization problems and data imputation for specific cases of missing values.
4. Analysis of the obtained results: once the cleaning is finished, the obtained results are analyzed, the amount of many errors eradicated and the data quality level that the modified databases present.
5. Proposals for improvements to computer tools, in order to maintain the quality level obtained with the cleaning.

Process 5. Application and Modeling of Data Analysis Algorithms

Its objective is the design and application of algorithms for the detection of outliers that reflect income losses, supporting active and reactive approaches. Different techniques and algorithms are applied to project management databases, discovering causal relationships and effective and efficient combinations to detect anomalous situations that generate income losses. Among the algorithms used are: based on Mahalanobis distance, hybrids that combine clustering, based on distances, heuristics, pattern recognition, and based on spatial analysis of data through angles. Below is the Meta algorithm designed to combine the results of multiple algorithms. For more details see [20].

Meta algorithm based on the combination of different techniques

```
1. AlgorithmBasedCombinationMethods (D, A)
   Inputs:
      D: represents the data set to be analyzed
      A: represents the set of algorithms, where A_i is an
      algorithm and denotes A_i ∈ A
      A_active: represents an active learning algorithm with
      intervention of experts
2. Start
   3. i =1
   4. D_1 = D
   5. Until remain algorithm without doing, if not go to step 11
      6. Select the A_i algorithm
      7. Select the data set from the original set Di = D
      8. P_i = A_i(D_i) // Detection of possible anomalous data
      9. i ++
   10. Go back to step 5
   11. O_i = A_active(P_i)∀i // Application of active learning to
   verify anomalous data
   12. O = ∪ O_i // combination of anomalous data detected in
   each iteration
   13. Return anomalous data contained in O and mark them for
   learning
14. End
```

A summary of the algorithms used in data analysis is presented below. They are all applied in order to find those that report best results for each specific problem.

Angle Algorithm. It is based on spatial analysis of data, in particular an angles based method. It performs the detection of anomalous values based on angles in a specified data frame. This algorithm is recommended for high dimensionality scenarios [27].

Crossclustering Algorithm. It is based on partial grouping with automatic estimation of clusters number and identification of outliers, combined with evolutionary algorithms [28].

Kmodr Algorithm. It is based on the use of simultaneous grouping methods. It is an implementation of K-means algorithm with a unified approach to group and detect outliers. It is useful to create potentially tighter groups than K-means standard and simultaneously find anomalous data at low cost in a multidimensional space [29].

Distance_mahalanobis Algorithm. It is based on Mahalanobis distance. It has as inputs nearest number of neighbors and data set. It uses a maximum distance function, concept of neighbor and allows working with dynamic thresholds refining the search, by default it is the identity function. It returns anomalous data ordered downwards according to the distance to its nearest neighbors.

Kmeans_euclidean Algorithm. It is a hybrid algorithm, based on K-means grouping combined with Euclidean distance. It has as inputs the number of expected centers and the data set. It uses Euclidean distance function and a cut threshold. It calculates the centers of found groupings and returns anomalous data found.

Kmeans_norm_euclidean Algorithm. It is a hybrid algorithm, similar to the Kmeans_euclidean Algorithm, but works with normalized input data.

Kmeans_stats Algorithm. This is a hybrid algorithm that combines grouping techniques with distance-based methods and pattern recognition techniques. It returns the set of anomalous data for which distance is greater than the threshold. To improve the efficiency of this algorithm, it is used as a strategy to plant the centers initially according to the types of tasks, taking into account the information of problem in question.

Combine_outlier Algorithm. It is a hybrid algorithm that combines grouping techniques based on heuristics and descriptive statistics techniques. The algorithm calculates a list of attributes ordered by degree of dispersion for each group. It applies active learning to determine clusters with anomalous data. To improve the efficiency of this algorithm, knowledge of the application scenario is used to know in advance the number of groups expected, knowledge that is used for the search by subspaces.

Process 6. Evaluation of the Results and Impact Estimation
The results are evaluated and the impact for the organization's revenue is estimated. The quality of the applied algorithms is measured to detect the outliers, according to the specific scenario. Accuracy and recall metrics are adapted, considering that outliers by

definition are rare and exceptional. Accuracy is defined as the percentage of outliers reported, see Eq. (1); Recall is the percentage of the true outliers, see Eq. (2).

$$Accuracy_{(\rho)} = 100 \frac{|S(\rho) \cap T|}{S(\rho)} \tag{1}$$

$$Recall_{(\rho)} = 100 \frac{|S(\rho) \cap T|}{T} \tag{2}$$

Where ρ is the recovery threshold of outliers on the ordered list of possible anomalous data, $S(\rho)$ denotes the set of outliers retrieved, while T represents the set of true outliers. As part of this step, the Accuracy and Recall metrics are combined based on the application of an OWA operator [30].

In the proposed model, the results are finally evaluated, the impact for the organization of the detected risks is estimated and a detailed analysis is carried out. When you reach this step you have three groups of situations aimed at recovering revenue:

- Set of risks that are avoided or mitigated, allowing to reduce the flight of revenue.
- Set of measures taken proactively to mitigate or eliminate risks, but which have an implementation cost that should also be considered in revenue assurance.
- List of anomalous situations detected that reflect situations of revenue leakage due to fraud, operating errors or other causes.

To estimate the economic impact of these situations, a set of techniques is proposed: estimation by three values (most probable amount, optimistic and pessimistic recovery amount), ascending estimation and network based analysis.

Process 7. Decision-Making
Decisions are made and the results are collected in the form of lessons learned, which allows sustainability in the application of the techniques of revenue assurance in the organization. To do the decision-making, the use of information systems combined with expert judgment is proposed. In each evaluation section, the results of the anomalous situations identified and their evolution are analyzed. The causes of the difficulties for each project or knowledge area are analyzed. Anomalous situations are prioritized according to their economic impact. And decision-making is made considering the evolution from one section to the next. Agreements and lessons learned are documented.

4 Evaluation and Results

To validate the proposed model, methodological triangulation techniques are used combining techniques for data triangulation, expert triangulation and methodological triangulation. Next, the databases used for the experimentation and the comparison of the applied algorithms are described. Finally, the results of validation of the model and their application in a case study are presented. For more details see [20].

4.1   Description of the Databases and Comparison of the Algorithms

For the experimentation, information about fourteen real software development projects was used. That projects are already concluded and we know how they behaved. This information about what actually happened with the projects is considered as the desired response in a supervised learning and represents a comparison pattern for the results of the algorithms applied in the data analysis.

The algorithms are compared by analyzing their performance in five databases: alone_rate, col_mix, mul_plan, mul_rate, mul_mix from the Research Laboratory in Project Management repository, at University of Informatics Sciences. Databases are composed by 23 attributes, more than 9400 records, 5% of records with outliers and twenty partitions for the application of cross-validation techniques.

For the comparison of the algorithms results with the five databases and their partitions, the populations formed by the results of the algorithms are compared using non-parametric Wilcoxon test for two samples related to a 95% confidence interval [31]. Wilcoxon is used because the Shapiro Wills test of normality, showed that the samples do not comply with the normal distribution with a p-value = 0.00032.

Several experiments are carried out with the five databases and different configurations for eight data analysis algorithms: Angle, Crossclustering, Distance_mahalanobis, Kmeans_euclidean, Kmeans_norm_euclidean, Kmeans_stats, Kmodr, Combine_outlier. Then, the best combinations of the algorithms that were detected in the experiments are compared with respect to the variables effectiveness and efficiency, in the detection of outliers for revenue assurance.

Figure 2 shows effectiveness considering accuracy and recall simultaneously; a larger area corresponds to better results. The effectiveness reflects the ability for the correct detection of anomalous situations in the data. It is appreciated that the Kmeans_stats and Combine_outlier algorithms have very similar results in all databases except for the collective outliers (Col_mix), where the Combine_outlier algorithm is slightly higher. The worst result was Kmeans_euclidean_9_0.92. The numbers after the algorithm means the training parameters; in this case, 9 is the number of expected centers, and 0.92 is the percentile value to determine the distance threshold.

Once the Wilcoxon test is applied, significant differences were found among the algorithms. Figure 3 shows the efficiency of the different algorithms with respect to the databases used. The efficiency evaluates the time used by the algorithm, for the outlier detection. The algorithms with the best results were Distance_mahalanobis_3_473_0.92, Kmeans_euclidean_9_0.92 and Kmeans_stats_3. Meanwhile, the worst results were presented by Angle_5_473_0.95 and Crossclustering_5_3.

4.2   Application of the Model in a Case Study

The proposal model was implemented on the GESPRO platform due to its versatility and large number of functionalities for revenue assurance [32, 33], among which are:

- Data analysis and revenue assurance module, which integrates libraries in R for the outlier detection.
- Risk management module, appropriate for proactive analysis.

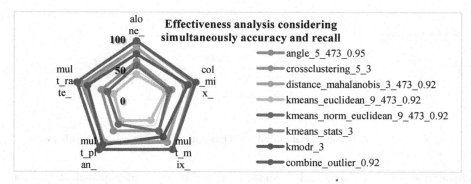

Fig. 2. Effectiveness considering accuracy and recall simultaneously (a larger area corresponds to better results)

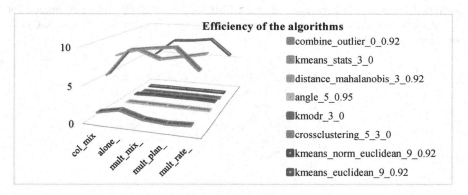

Fig. 3. Stability in the efficiency of the algorithms

- Scorecard with indicators and early warnings, aimed at detecting shortcomings in the planning and projects execution.
- Reach and quality management regarding the coverage of the requirements in the schedule and quality control.
- Project costs management and project costs prediction based on the data behavior.

Figure 4 shows a view of the risk management module as part of revenue assurance subsystem in the GESPRO tool.

For validation, methodological triangulation of methods and experts are applied in the comparison of the proposed proactive approach for risk management against the PMBOK technique. An experiment is carried out to validate the risk management proposal proactively associated with revenue losses. The traditional technique proposed in the PMBOK (Risk-PMBOK) is compared with the technique based on the 2-tuples model of computing with words (Risk-CWW).

A group of six project management experts who did not participate in the selected projects were designated for validation. The experts consulted for risk assessment are

#	Nombre	Categoría	Estado	Prob.	Impacto	Detec	Exposición	Evaluaciones		
2	Pérdida de recursos humanos	Human resource management	Identify	(Bajo; 0.0)	(Alto; 0.0)	(Muy alto; 0.0)	(Medio; 0.0)	1 Ver	Modificar	Borrar
1	Planificación sobre costos	Financial management	Identify	(Medio; 0)	(Medio; 0)	(Medio; 0)	(Medio; 0.0)	0	Modificar	Borrar
3	Pérdida de Recursos Humanos	Human resource management	Identify	(Alto; 0.0)	(Alto; 0.0)	(Medio; 0.0)	(Medio; 0.0)	2 Ver	Modificar	Borrar
4	Dificultades con fenómenos ...	Natural Disasters	Analizad	(Bajo; 0.0)	(Alto; 0.0)	(Bajo; 0.0)	(Medio; 0.0)	1 Ver	Modificar	Borrar

Riesgos del Centro — Nuevo riesgo · Ayuda

Filtros

(1-4-4)   Exportar a: CSV

Fig. 4. View of risk management in GESPRO as part of revenue assurance subsystem

characterized by: 4 PhD's and 2 Masters; regarding years of experience: 18.8 on average, 9.8 standard deviation, 14 minimum years and 37 maximum years dedicated.

Eighteen of the most common risks in this scenario were taken into account, covering all knowledge areas of project management. Finally, the mean squared errors calculated according to each method (Risk-PMBOK, Risk-CWW) were compared for each project. As shown in Fig. 5, the best results are obtained with the Risk-CWW assessment method.

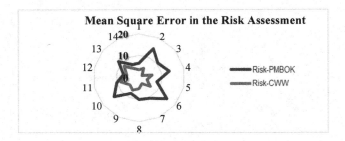

Fig. 5. Radial graph that represents the mean square error in the risk assessment (a smaller area indicates better algorithm)

Among advantages of the proposed model, there is the ease of interpretation of the results when both evaluations of experts and final results are expressed in words. The proposed model also allows the simultaneous assessment of multiple experts.

Some of the anomalous situations detected are shown below:

- Situation 1: the records of tasks that do not have assigned resources with the required competences or that due to their volume, require more human resources than those assigned.
- Situation 2: the records of tasks whose time or cost estimate is above or well below the predicted values.
- Situation 3: the records of tasks that do not respect in the chronogram the logical precedence or that have an excessively high waiting clearance with respect to other tasks.
- Situation 4: the requirements records in the Work Breakdown Structure of the project for which there are no tasks recorded in the project schedule, dedicated to the development of the same.

- Situation 5: project records that, although similar to others because of their scope, may have estimated costs well above average.
- Situation 6: the recorded schedules that show an overload of human or non-human resources in multiple project development scenarios simultaneously.

With the application of the proposal in GESPRO, a total of fourteen information technology development centers have benefited, in which more than two hundred Cuban projects are managed and where more than five hundred tool users converge. In addition, the model was implemented in the Ecuadorian company QuitusServices, dedicated to the provision of information technology and communication services [34]. In this company, with the application of the proposed model, an amount of 500 USD were recovered in one month. This amount is obtained from the analysis of the income behavior, costs and income leakage of the company during the six months of application.

5 Conclusions and Future Work

The main project management standards do not sufficiently address the issue of revenue assurance. The need to combine reactive strategies with active and proactive strategies was identified as a trend in revenue assurance strategies, in order to reduce the time of detection of income leaks and prevent possible failures or fraud actions. The proposal combines project management, outlier mining, risk analysis and computing with word techniques to apply revenue assurance following reactive, active and proactive approaches. In addition, it requires the presence of multiple experts for its application. Regarding the qualitative risk assessment methods, it is concluded that the method based on computing with word reports better results than the traditional technique proposed by the PMBOK. The proposed model is integrated into the GESPRO platform. The use of this platform is proposed for its application in decision-making due to the versatility and functionalities for revenue assurance.

In the instrumentation of the proposed model, for decision-making, recommendations systems can be used, among other emerging computing techniques. It is recommended that this subject continue to be researched in future works. We must also continue working on the application of the proposed model in real-time scenarios using strategies for high performance computation and enhancing the application of the model in an active approach to revenue assurance.

References

1. PMI: A Guide to the Project Management Body of Knowledge, PMBOK® Guide, 6th edn. Project Management Institute, Pennsylvania, EE.UU (2017)
2. The Standish Group International: Standish Group 2015 Chaos Report. The Standish Group International, Inc., New York (2015)
3. Mossalam, A., Arafa, M.: The role of project manager in benefits realization management as a project constraint/driver. Housing and Building National Research Center, HBRC J. 56–67 (2014). https://doi.org/10.1016/j.hbrcj.2014.12.008

4. Aggarwal, Ch.C.: Outlier Analysis. IBM T.J. Watson Research Center Yorktown Heights, New York, Springer Science, Business Media, Heidelberg, Dordrecht, London (2013). https://doi.org/10.1007/978-4614-6396-2
5. Mattison, R.: The Telco Revenue Assurance Handbook. XiT Press, Oakwood Hills, Illinois (2005). http://www.grapatel.com/A-GRAPA/07-Library/RABook.asp#top
6. TM Forum: Revenue Assurance a survey pre-result blog: lack of cross-functional mandate holds back change, say Revenue Assurance professionals (2015)
7. Acosta, K.: Aseguramiento de ingresos: una actividad fundamental en las empresas de telecomunicaciones. Revista de Ingeniería Industrial 29(2), 1–6 (2008)
8. Burke, R.: Project Management: Planning and Control Techniques, 5th edn. Wiley, Hoboken (2013). 428 pages
9. Schwalbe, K.: Information Technology Project Management, 7th edn. Cengage Learning, Boston (2015). 656 pages
10. Phillips, J.: PMP, Project Management Professional (Certification Study Guides), Sybex 7th edn. McGraw-Hill Osborne Media (2013). 696 pages
11. Leach, L.P.: Critical Chain Project Management, 1st edn. The North River Press, Artech House (2014). 246 pages
12. Verzuh, E.: The Fast Forward MBA in Project Management, 5th edn. Wiley, New York (2015)
13. Wojnar, K.: Comparison between ISO 21500 and PMBOK® Guide, 5th edn. Theoretical background and practical usage of ISO 21500 in IT projects (2013)
14. Khan, N.: Internship Report on Revenue Assurance and Fraud Management. ID: 10104009. BRAC Business School (2014)
15. Mattison, R.: The Revenue Assurance Standards. Release 2009, GRAPA. XiT Press, Oakwood Hills, Illinois (2009)
16. GRAPA: The Global Revenue Assurance Professional Association (GRAPA) Professionalizing the Information, Communications and Technology Industry (2016)
17. Bansal, R., Gaur, N., Singh, S. N.: Outlier detection: applications and techniques in data mining. In: 6th International Conference—Cloud System and Big Data Engineering (Confluence), Noida, pp. 373–377 (2016). https://doi.org/10.1109/confluence.2016.7508146
18. CMMI Product Team: CMMI for Development, Version 1.3. Software Engineering Institute, Carnegie Mellon University, Pittsburgh, Pennsylvania, Technical Report CMU/SEI-2010-TR-033 (2010). http://resources.sei.cmu.edu/library/asset-view.cfm?AssetID=9661
19. ISO: ISO 21500:2012 Guidance on Project Management. International Organization for Standardization (2012)
20. Castro, G.F.: Modelo para el aseguramiento de ingresos en organizaciones orientadas a proyectos basado en minería de datos anómalos. Tesis de Doctorado en Ciencias Técnicas, Universidad de las Ciencias Informáticas, La Habana, Cuba (2017)
21. Hawkins, S., He, H., Williams, G., Baxter, R.: Outlier detection using replicator neural networks. In: Kambayashi, Y., Winiwarter, W., Arikawa, M. (eds.) DaWaK 2002. LNCS, vol. 2454, pp. 170–180. Springer, Heidelberg (2002). https://doi.org/10.1007/3-540-46145-0_17
22. Sathishkumar, E.N., Thangavel, K.: A novel approach for outlier detection using rough entropy. WSEAS Trans. Comput. 14, 296–306 (2015)
23. Souza, A.M., Amazonas, J.R.: An outlier detect algorithm using big data processing and Internet of Things architecture. Procedia Comput. Sci. 52, 1010–1015 (2015). https://doi.org/10.1016/j.procs.2015.05.095
24. Whyte, J., Stasis, A., Lindkvist, C.: Managing change in the delivery of complex projects: configuration management, asset information and 'big data'. Int. J. Proj. Manag. 34(2), 339–351 (2016). https://doi.org/10.1016/j.ijproman.2015.02.006

25. Zadeh, L.A.: Fuzzy logic, neural networks and soft computing. Commun. ACM **37**(3), 77–84 (1994). https://doi.org/10.1145/175247.175255
26. Herrera, F., Martinez, L.: A 2-tuple fuzzy linguistic representation model for computing with words. IEEE Trans. Fuzzy Syst. **8**(6), 746–752 (2000). https://doi.org/10.1109/91.890332
27. Kriegel, H.-P., Schubert, M. et al.: Angle-based outlier detection in highdimensional data. In: KDD 2008, Las Vegas, Nevada (2008). 978-1-60558-193-4/08/08
28. Tellaroli, P., et al.: Cross-clustering: a partial clustering algorithm with automatic estimation of the number of clusters. PLoS ONE **11**(3), e0152333 (2016). https://doi.org/10.1371/journal.pone.0152333
29. Chawla, S., Gionis, A.: k-means: a unified approach to clustering and outlier detection. In: Proceedings of the 2013 SIAM International Conference on Data Mining, Texas, pp. 189–197 (2013). https://doi.org/10.1137/1.9781611972832.21
30. Merigó, J.M., Yager, R.R.: Norm aggregations and OWA operators. In: Bustince, H., Fernandez, J., Mesiar, R., Calvo, T. (eds.) Aggregation Functions in Theory and in Practise. AISC, vol. 228, pp. 141–151. Springer, Heidelberg (2013). https://doi.org/10.1007/978-3-642-39165-1_17
31. Wilcoxon, F., Katti, S.K., Wilcox, R.A.: Critical values and probability levels for the Wilcoxon rank sum test and the Wilcoxon signed rank test. Institute of Mathematical Statistics, Selected Tables in Mathematical Statistics, vol. 1, pp. 171–259 (1973)
32. Castro, G.F., et al.: Platform for project evaluation based on soft-computing techniques. In: Valencia-García, R., Lagos-Ortiz, K., Alcaraz-Mármol, G., del Cioppo, J., Vera-Lucio, N. (eds.) CITI 2016. CCIS, vol. 658, pp. 226–240. Springer, Cham (2016). https://doi.org/10.1007/978-3-319-48024-4_18
33. Piñero, P., Lugo, J.A., Menéndez, J., et al.: Solución de software Xedro-GESPRO v13.05. Centro Nacional de Registro de Derecho de Autor de Cuba, No Registro CENDA: 2336-06-2015, La Habana, Cuba. DCN-002/2016 (2015)
34. QuitusServices, Portal corporativo compañía de servicios informáticos. Guayaquil-Ecuador (2018). https://businessredmine.herokuapp.com/portal/quitusservices

Intelligent and Knowledge-Based Systems

An Intelligent Information System Prototype to Facilitate Healthy Alimentation

Alexander José Mackenzie Rivero[1(✉)], Teddy G. Miranda-Mena[2,3],
and Rodrigo Martínez-Béjar[2,3]

[1] Faculty of Technical Sciences,
State University of Southern Manabí, Jipijapa, Ecuador
mackenzie.alexander@unesum.edu.ec
[2] Faculty of Informatics, University of Murcia, Murcia, Spain
teddymirandamena@gmail.com,
rodrigo.alternativa@gmail.com
[3] Fundación para la Investigación y el Desarrollo
Tecnológico de la Sociedad del Conocimiento, Murcia, Spain

Abstract. The amount of information available on the Internet today makes it difficult to obtain efficient and accurate knowledge. The information obtained by users from the Internet is often not entirely satisfactory. Therefore, it is necessary to design systems that enhance performance and improve the information retrieval process in an intelligent way. The ontologies are useful for knowledge representation. To achieve the goal of enhancing knowledge retrieval in the Nutrition and Food domain, a recommended intelligent system prototype has been developed that can respond and fill gaps in users information about maintenance of a balanced diet, focusing in Mediterranean diets. According to individual characteristics such as age, weight, height, or sex, individuals can see what to eat in order to meet their nutritional needs and maintain a balanced diet. Individuals can also request information to suit health related problems, which foods are recommended and which ones should be avoided.

Keywords: Semantic web · OWL ontologies · Diet

1 Introduction

In the last 10 years, with the penetration of the internet it has become evident a growing number of consumers with a concern for a healthy and balanced diet and a better quality of life. The fact is that nowadays consumers are looking for food which fits their lifestyle and improves health, prevents disease and helps them feel better physically and emotionally.

When doing internet searches a large amount of data and inconsistent information can be obtained including false myths and home remedies not recommended by nutrition experts what can increase user confusion. At the same time, competing interests of companies can contribute to searches confusion. Thus, companies in this sector are benefiting from the boom of increasingly healthy and balanced food, modifying their products to artificially enrich their nutritional values. This is causing

© Springer Nature Switzerland AG 2018
R. Valencia-García et al. (Eds.): CITI 2018, CCIS 883, pp. 143–157, 2018.
https://doi.org/10.1007/978-3-030-00940-3_11

concern among nutrition experts who about the danger that many people, in their intention to lead a healthy lifestyle, opt blindly for such products despite the fact artificial food will never be healthier than natural fresh food.

The arduous task of searching for specific information objects can be supported by intelligent systems, which can interpret meta-information. Such systems can improve the information retrieval process by structuring plans for internal algorithms on the web. Underpinned by automatic logical deductions, these systems can interpret the meaning of the web information and all process content, as required. This paper aims to promote the creation and use of ontologies which structure and organize existing information in the field of nutrition. Specifically, an ontology has been created that focuses on information relating to the diet which has been described as ideal for its combination of balance and complete set of food types based on fresh, local seasonal food namely, the Mediterranean Diet.

The paper is organized as follows: Sect. 2 describes the main Semantic Web characteristics highlighting one of its fundamental components, namely, ontologies. In Sect. 3, the methodology used is described. In Sect. 4, the main processes and features of the system developed are point out. Section 5 information about of the system is given. Finally in Sect. 6, the main conclusion are put forward.

2 Semantic Web

The Semantic Web is a Tim Berners-Lee innovative vision of the Web, where the main objective is to provide the Web with embedded knowledge that can be accessed by applications to improve information retrieval. For instance, a browser should be able to understand the information and return a result providing meaning generated from knowledge webpages store. According to Berners-Lee, the Semantic Web is an extension of the current Web in which information is provided with well-defined meaning, where information may be read by both computer agents and by people [1]. Enabling advanced applications and functionality on the Web will enable computers to be able to consult, process, integrate and present the web contents of these in a more intelligible way. As Antoniou and Harmelem (2004) pointed out, one of the goals of the Semantic Web is, to allow for the advancement of knowledge management systems.

The Semantic Web has been progressing with a significant market reach [2], although progress is slower than expected since the Semantic Web requires for the use and development of a significant number of technologies. The key components of the architecture of the Semantic Web have been structured by levels, establishing a hierarchy of abstraction and dependencies between different levels.

The Unicode and URI (Uniform Resource Identifier) elements provide for a common syntax. URI provides a standard to refer to entities allowing for an unambiguous access to any resource on the Web. Unicode is a universal standard for text encoding that allows for the use of international characters and alphabets. This allows the information on the Semantic Web to be expressed in any language.

The meta-language XML (Extensible Markup Language) is the technical layer of the Semantic Web. The XML has known since its beginnings an undeniable success.

Defined since its origins as a meta-language facilitating the development of specialized tags Languages, nowadays many documents benefit from the XML frame.

XML groups the different technologies that enable understanding among agents, it establishing a common format for exchanging documents. XML Schema allows for the definition of valid grammars as well as describing the structure and constraining the contents of XML documents. The relationship between XML and XML Schema is a syntactic control relationship. Currently, standardization of both layers is widely accepted and implemented. However, this language has a limited semantic expression, as the XML data model consists of a tree that does not distinguish between objects and relationships, apart from having no notion of class hierarchy [3].

RDF (Resource Description Framework) is the first level where the information is some how intelligible to the machine. This layer defines the universal language that can express different ideas on the Semantic Web. It also provides interoperability between applications that exchange intelligible information in the Web [4].

The expressions described by RDF are called resources. A resource can be a page (such as HTML documents), part (HTML or XML element within the document source) or collection of Web pages (an entire Web site), as well as an object that is not directly accessible via web, for example a book, a person or concept. RDF resources are always designated by URI's, which their extensibility allow for the introduction of identifiers for any entity. A property is a specific quality, characteristic, attribute, or relation used to describe resources. Each property has a specific meaning, where the allowed values are defined the types of resources that it is able to describe and its relationships with other properties.

A specific resource together with a named property plus the value of that particular property for this particular resource is an RDF statement. In other word, a sentence consists of three individual parts called subject, predicate and object. Where, the subject and object represent the resources and the predicate properties respectively.

RDF Schema is an RDF vocabulary that allows definition of class hierarchies through object orientation. It not only offers a description of the data, but also some semantic information.

The next layer is Ontology Vocabulary. Currently, the standard language for developing ontologies is Web Ontology Language (OWL), which is considered an extension of RDF, including all its expressive capacity and allowing for the use of logical expressions. The ontology concepts is analyzed next.

2.1 The Ontology Concept

Ontology can be thought as a main constituent of the Semantic Web that allows for explicit, well-defined understanding of concepts among agents [6]. Also, a detected rising trend in the Software Engineering community has been noticed that consists in exploiting ontologies to exchange and interconnect Software Engineering knowledge across the Web [7]. The Semantic Web project has been useful in recent years to establish what we might call the current term of ontology [5]. However, this concept had already been developed (in different ways) in the philosophical field.

Ontology can also be defined differently. Thus, it can be viewed as the science of something and nothing, of being and not-being, of the thing and the mode of the thing, of substance and accident [8]. Another popular definition is the one seeing an ontology as a doctrine of pure element of all our complete cognition, that is, it contains the sum of all our pure concepts that we can have a priori about things [9]. One of the broadest and most recognized definitions in different fields, especially in the field of artificial intelligence and more recently in the Semantic Web, within the context of knowledge reuse has been proposed by Gruber [10] defines ontology as an explicit specification of a conceptualization. A definition very close to the one provided in [10] is to view ontology as a formal specification of a shared conceptualization [11].

By considering the last two above definitions, we can obtain the following: one a explicit formal specification of a shared conceptualization, where the conceptualization represents the abstract model of a phenomenon. A formal specification comprises a theoretical organization of terms and relationships used as tools for the analysis of the concepts of a domain. A shared specification is referred to as the capture of consensual knowledge that is approved by a community, and finally, explicitly my refer to the specification of the concepts and restrictions on them [12]. Therefore, an ontology is a description of concepts and relationships that allow for the existence of an agent or a community of agents.

2.2   Ontology Components and Types

"Ontology mainly consists of two parts, concepts and relations. How to extract the concept from the data source is the first step in the construction of the domain ontology. Before extracting the concept of ontology, it is needed to determine the source of data to obtain the concept" [13]. Ontologies and standard languages such as Resource Description Framework (RDF), Simple Protocol, RDF Query Language (SPARQL) and Web Ontology Language (OWL) are considered to add several semantic value to a dataset [14]. The knowledge in an ontology is formalized using component types, namely classes, relations, properties, axioms and instances [10]. A class or a type is a set of objects (physical, functions, tasks, reasoning processes, etc. A class is usually organized into a taxonomy. Classes are based on the representation of knowledge by means of ontologies, because they describe the domain concepts. A class where its members are classes are called superclasses or metaclasses.

Relationships represent the interactions between the established concepts of an ontology. They are formally defined as any subset of a product of n sets: $R: C_1 \times C_2 \times \ldots \times C_n$, where C_i represents the sets with $i = 1 \ldots n$. Some of the more used relationships are:

- Instance: associating objects to classes.
- Temporal relationships: they imply precedence in time.
- Topological relationships: to establish spatial connections between concepts.
- Taxonomic relations.

Axioms are elements used to model sentences that are always true. The axioms can be structural or nonstructural.

Structural axioms constitute conditions related to hierarchies of ontology concepts and defined attributes, while a structural axiom is the relationship between attributes of a concept, and are specific to a domain.

Instances or individuals are object members of a class which are used to represent elements and can be grouped into classes.

Properties or slots. The objects are described by a set of characteristics or attributes that are stored in slots. These slots store different kinds of values. Specifications, ranges and restrictions on these values or characteristics are called facets.

There are different types of ontologies depending on the perspective one applies. Mainly, two criteria are followed for these classifications, namely, the kind of knowledge they contain and the motivation to, the ontology.

The criteria where there is greater diversity is in the classification by the knowledge they contain. In [15], ontologies are classified according to the amount and type of structure of the conceptualization, distinguishing three types of ontologies:

- Terminology and linguistic ontologies. These specify the terms that are used to represent knowledge in the universe of discourse. An example of this is the UMLS semantic network (Unified Medical Language System) [16]. They are usually used for the unification of the vocabulary in a given field. One of the most used language ontologies is WordNet [17, 18], which is a large lexical database in which different types of relationships are contemplated.
- Information Ontology. They specify the storage structure databases providing a framework for storing standardized information. The database scheme is one example.
- Ontology modeling knowledge. They specify conceptualizations of knowledge. These ontologies contain a rich internal structure and are the ontologies that are more specifically suited to the knowledge they describe.
- An alternative classification is that which can be found in [19], where three categories are also suggested:
- Task Ontologies. They describe the vocabulary related to a generic task or activity providing a systematic vocabulary of terms used to solve problems related to the tasks that don't belong to the same domain. These ontologies use the domain knowledge to search for information while another could manage the allocation of free memory blocks.
- Domain ontologies. They contain all the concepts associated with a particular domain.
- General ontologies. Common or general ontologies are used to expose common reusable knowledge through the domain, containing vocabulary related to objects, events, temporal relationships, causal relationships, role models and functionalities.

2.3 OWL

In the last few years, a variety of ontology languages have been developed, so that these have been adopted in the context of the Semantic Web [20].

According to Zhang et al. [21], "the World Wide Web Consortium has contributed much towards standardizing the specification necessary for Semantic Web technology" by introducing the Resource Description Framework (RDF) and the RDF Schema [22].

OWL (Web Ontology Language) is a proposal for standardization of ontological language specified by a working group of the W3C Web Ontology [23], which would help solve the current impediments to the cooperative construction of ontologies between different ontological construction platforms, as well as empowering the Semantic Web. OWL provides a language that uses the connection provided by RDF to add the following capabilities to ontologies:

- Ability to be distributed across multiple systems.
- Scalable to Web needs.
- Compatible with Web standards and accessibility internationalization.
- Open and extensible.

The first draft specification of the language (OWL 1.0) appeared in July 2002 and formally presented by the W3C in February 2004 [23]. In October 2009, the latest, robust OWL version so far, the 2.0, was released.

In OWL 1.0, the following three sub-incremental expression languages are defined:

OWL Lite is the least expressive sub-language. It provides a quick migration path for thesaurus and other taxonomies. It is intended primarily for users who require for a hierarchical classification and simple restrictions.

OWL DL provides maximum expressiveness of computation that includes all OWL language constructs, but it can only be used through certain restrictions. Its name is well known due to its correspondence with description logics (DL), because of the fact of ensuring the completeness and finiteness of the arguments for the formal foundation of OWL.

OWL Full is intended for users who require maximum expressiveness and syntactic freedom by RDF but without computational guarantees. It allows the ontology to increase the meaning of predefined vocabulary, RDF or OWL. In OWL 2.0, three new sub-languages with useful processing properties are defined. Furthermore, the nomenclature of the sub-languages has been modified to the profile concept, these being orientated to the particular characteristics. These depend mainly on the expressivity required by the application, the priority given by reasoning about classes or data, the size of the datasets and the importance of scalability, among other things.

OWL 2 EL is intended for applications employing ontologies that contain a large number of properties and/or classes. The acronym EL reflects the origin of the sub-language in the EL family of descriptive logics. It is simple to implement and allows for great scalability for complex expressions. However the expressiveness it provides is rather limited thus it. It doesn't allow for negation and disjunction of classes, universal quantification of properties nor inverse properties.

OWL 2 QL. This profile is recommended for applications with a large volume of instance data, and where query performance is very important [24]. It is designed for applications that prioritize interoperability of OWL with databases. It is a variant of OWL-Lite, which is very common in database integration tasks. It is suitable for applications with lightweight ontologies which have a large number of individuals requiring access to data. It is easy to extend the usual relational languages (such as SQL), incorporating consultations with axioms defined by sub-sets. The reasoning can be implemented efficiently by rewriting techniques for queries. Finally, it facilitates the mapping between UML and Entity-Relationship diagrams giving an immediate schematic representation of data. Regarding expressiveness, it is still quite a limited one (for example, it does not allow existential quantifiers or chained properties).

OWL 2 RL is suitable for applications that require scalable reasoning without sacrificing too much expressivity. It is aimed primarily at applications that prioritize interoperability of OWL with rules machines, defining a syntactic subset of rules for their implementation through rules-based technologies, so facilitating reasoning. Such implementations allow for the direct operation on RDF triples and can be applied arbitrarily to RDF graphs.

3   Methodology

There are currently many methodologies for developing information systems focused mainly on the control of each process, carefully setting each task, resources and performance actions. Such methods have proven to be effective and necessary for the development of projects whose size and complexity required a more rigorous approach. However, they have shown problems in other projects. The process of achieving the methodology is difficult to follow and even limits the ability of the team itself to solve the project.

Another possibility is to focus on other factors, such as to give greater importance to the individual, in collaboration with the client or the incremental development of software with very short iterations. This is the philosophy of agile methodologies, which are proving effective in projects with varying requirements and when one needs to dramatically reduce development time while maintaining management and quality.

Scrum is an Agile project management software development, based on a process of constant, iterative and incremental work [25]. It is particularly suitable for projects which produce a change of requirements and needs to be applied quickly. It is mainly characterized by the way in which it establishes patterns of development of the project, in which raw defining tasks through iterations, called sprints, typically last 30 days. The result of each sprint is a phase that the tutor tests for validation and on which to apply corrections, additions or change of requirements based on current needs.

As discussed above, the domain the ontology aims to cover is that of food and nutrition. The ontology created consists of the representation of food, nutritional components and the recommended daily amount for an individual to meet their nutritional needs. A software application has been implemented that takes information from the ontology and is aimed at any person interested in knowing the food to eat to get the recommended daily nutrients. In order to pursue healthy eating based on a Mediterranean diet, most foods include fresh, low fat foods.

They have also contemplated cases of unhealthy foods, such as alcoholic beverages or bakery products, in order to deal with them in the recommendations section, in which, for certain problems or circumstances it is not recommended to take this kind of food.

The ontology contains a number of recipes and menus related to their food and associated with a particular group of people, depending on gender and the recommended daily calorific intake. The latter is calculated from the formula of total energy expenditure of the individual according to their basal metabolic rate and intensity of the regular physical activities he does.

Subsequent maintenance and enrichment of ontology could be entrusted to a person with more knowledge in the field of food, as it could to a nutritionist. To carry out this work enrichment, it would be necessary to create a role with permissions to insert new data into the ontology. These users could add new recipes or expand the number of foods, thereby achieving greater nutritional knowledge.

These nutrition-relevant terms were grouped to achieve a hierarchical structure in which all items were related to each other and from which there would be a semi-structured knowledge base.

In this first idea only three main concepts were covered: Food, Nutrients and people, so that, after calculating the total energy expenditure (TEE) of a person (depending on gender and age), we could get the complete nutritional needs of that person from the number of calories each food contains. However, having defined these concepts, it was realized that a complete menu could not be created by only using the food and its nutrients, so it was decided to group foods into recipes.

Thus, a recipe would consist of various foods in which it would be taken into account the overall calorific content of food, favoring the most appropriate menu search for the individual. Refining a little more, we include these recipes in menus for each hour of the day and in daily menus to form our weekly menu. So, to get to our final solution, we use an increasingly refined iterative process.

To reach this end result, Methontology [12] has been used, namely method that includes the identification of the ontology development process (a life cycle based on evolving prototypes), where one should specify the set of activities to be incorporated into product development.

This method proposes beginning with planning activities to identify tasks, corrections, time and resources for each prototype. After specifying the prototype, a conceptual model is constructed which is mainly supported by the activity of acquiring knowledge.

After the conceptualization, the formalization and implementation activities can be achieved, which allows us to return to previous activities if we detect any detail that would need modifying or refining.

Thus, we can distinguish the following phases according to Methontology [12]:

Initial specification. This step describes the scope of the ontology and its granularity. It usually specifies who the developers are, what the purpose is or what the sources of knowledge are. These steps have already been discussed in the introduction to this paragraph.

Conceptualization. Having defined the concepts that would form part of the ontology, they must then be organized and converted into a casual perception of a domain in a semi-formal specification using a set of intermediate representations such as tables or diagrams that can be understood by experts in the field and developers of ontologies.

Implementation. After defining the organizational structure of the ontology, we conceptualized it using a formal language. Using the Protégé tool allows us to formalize the previous model.

Evaluation. In this last phase we will check the performance of the ontology. In this way we discover that our initial idea was not entirely feasible to arrive at the final solution, so it was necessary to repeat these increasingly refined steps until we arrive at the final structure.

In our case, the most important points are the stages of conceptualization and implementation, whose development is detailed below. In the ontology conceptualization phase, a more defined view of the scope is obtained. Methontology provides the steps to follow to carry out the determination of each element that the ontology will consist of. Each stage is designed to facilitate the organization of knowledge acquired in a more or less formal way.

4   System Development

To develop the ontology, Protégé Ontology Editor has been used. It is a free framework for the development of ontologies and knowledge-based systems which implements a comprehensive area for designing, modeling, implementation, visualization and manipulation of ontologies in various formats such as RDF, DAML+OIL and OWL. It is developed in Java and can run perfectly under Windows [12].

Another tool for the construction of our project has been Jena, namely an open-source framework for building Java applications related to the Semantic Web. It provides a programming environment for working with ontologies in different languages such as RDF, RDFS and OWL and includes an Rules based inference engine.

Thanks to the Jena API, we are able to automate the process of building our application model, creating a variable from OntModel the hierarchy of classes, properties, and restrictions. In addition, using ARQ, a Jena component that interprets the SPARQL queries, RDF statements can be retrieved on the ontology query results [25].

To define the ontology, we have used a combined method, which first finds outs all possible terms that one wants to cover and then distinguishes between general and specific concepts.

To create the final classification scheme, a top-down method has been used which takes higher levels as a starting point until the final branches are reached and that which are examples of the more specific and detailed concepts of the ontology.

27 basic concepts have been classified which form the general outline of the ontology. The main purpose of this ontology being to get a weekly menu associated with the characteristics of each person. Thus, the objective was to build and establish recipes in order to create menus, which divided among three meals a day, were to provide the calories required by the individual.

There is a hierarchy and transitive relationship between the elements, since a concept can be achieved from one to another through the connection established between them.

In these first levels we can find the general concepts to form the basis of knowledge. 10 main classes can be distinguished, which will be used to create the necessary individuals along with the existing relationships between them to form the full menu.

The main concept is at level 1 and reflects what will be the subject of this ontology, namely diets, and the other relevant items. It has been established in this particular way, instead of the default class (Thing), with the propose of organizing the concepts and gain a higher level of abstraction.

At the second level we find the generic classes; Problem, Property, Nutrient, Food, Recipe, Menu, Daily Menu, Weekly Menu and Person to be combined strategically in order to achieve the objective. In general, in this ontology properties related to certain individuals of certain classes have been used. Most of the relationships used in this ontology are functional (and inverse to this). For each individual, there is at least some on other individual connected through some of these properties. The relationships between the first level classes have been established more generically to avoid inconsistencies in the ontology by linking individuals of different subclasses. Transitive relations among certain classes to link three concepts using a single property have also been used.

The cardinality defines how many values a relationship can have. One can distinguish between single or multiple cardinality. Cardinality is exemplified as follows to indicate that a weekly menu has exactly 7 daily menus (multiple cardinality) and a daily menu has exactly one breakfast, lunch, afternoon tea and dinner (single cardinality). The user can also set minimum and maximum cardinality to indicate that a relationship must have at least or at most a number of values. For example, a menu is contemplated in the ontology that should contain at least one recipe (see Fig. 1 below).

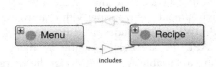

Fig. 1. Relationship between Recipe and Menu

We can harness the knowledge to connect all the concepts of ontology and obtain better results in every search through the use of binary relations. This allows us to be able to answer any questions of competence [9] to determine the scope of the ontology, which also serves as proof of quality control and to know if the ontology is real sufficiently complete in order to answer these questions. A tool implementation has been carried out that supplies a personalized response to questions in the field of nutrition and food.

The tool aims to act in the same way as a professional would do it, analyzing and interpreting physical and personal data of a healthy user, to provide a balanced diet based on the healthy and culinary aspects of the Mediterranean diet. Besides, by taking into account the continued increase in sales of smartphones and the high demand for mobile applications today, mobile devices can be seen as dynamic systems having a high capacity of communication and processing that enable information retrieval to billions of users anywhere and anytime about any domain. Moreover, mobile native apps can also supply information about healthcare, whose authors decided to create a small application that summarizes the main functionality of the web, so that the user could consult it at any time anywhere, and what menu would be the most advisable when a choice is offered in a restaurant. Thanks to this application these decisions would be taken extremely quickly and easily.

After analyzing several free applications on the Android Market (now Play Store) it is clear that there is no application which gives users a personalized diet according to their personal characteristics. In general, most applications of this type only show a set of predefined and static diets that do not provide the user with any value for it to meet their needs. The activity diagram of the Android application framework is a simplification of the web application. In the case of the mobile platform, it does not require a registration process in the system since the application requests enter the user's physical data beforehand which is then registered on the device. Therefore, to access the application there are two scenarios: to display the data entry form or go directly to the main menu if they already exist.

Having accessed the application, the user can access his/her daily menu, nutritional consultations for certain problems, check the nutritional value in the section of the calculator or edit your physical data.

Having identified the user, the Initial tool interface is displayed. They are the following:

Languages Box: It is available in English and Spanish languages.

Login Box: The user can sign in and login in for the application system. The information captured here is only to register the personal information of the user.

In addition to the specific content of the home page, the browse menu is highlighted from any page, which shows the following options: Home, Diet, Food Guide, Recommendations, Calculator, Downloads and Help.

The weekly diet menu displays the necessary fields needed to calculate our body mass index (BMI) or total energy expenditure (TEE). These, together with others factors, interact with the ontology in order to obtain the best diet to adapt these parameters (Figs. 2 and 3).

Fig. 2. Data request Form for working out diet

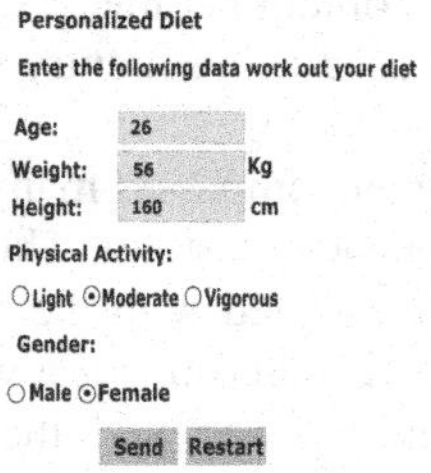

Personalized Diet

Enter the following data work out your diet

Age: 26

Weight: 56   Kg

Height: 160   cm

Physical Activity:

○ Light ⊙ Moderate ○ Vigorous

Gender:

○ Male ⊙ Female

Send Restart

Fig. 3. Calculator of values

5 Software Prototype Preliminary Evaluation

The prototype evaluation was performed by means of 10 cases studies for personalized diet and validated by a nutritionist, so that the results of such evaluation are shown in Table 1.

Table 1. Case studies summary

Case	Age	Sex	Weight	Height	Physical Activity	Nutritionist Evaluation
1	26	Female	56 kg	160 cm	Moderate	Positive
2	40	Male	80 kg	175 cm	Moderate	Positive
3	37	Male	82 kg	178 cm	Moderate	Positive
4	25	Female	46 kg	158 cm	High	Positive
5	54	Male	112 kg	181 cm	Low	Positive
6	24	Female	48 kg	160 cm	Moderate	Positive
7	39	Male	87 kg	178 cm	Moderate	Positive
8	41	Female	61 kg	163 cm	Low	Positive
9	38	Female	56 kg	162 cm	High	Positive
10	43	Male	90 kg	165 cm	Low	Positive

6 Discussion and Conclusion

The work presented here aims to promote the creation and use of ontologies to structure and organize existing information in the field of nutrition. Specifically, the ontology has focused on information relating to the Mediterranean diet, namely, one that combines a complete and balanced based on fresh, local and seasonal products. The Mediterranean Diet.

Our approach aims do implement an intelligent system that can respond and meet the information needs of users for maintaining a balanced diet based on the attributes of a Mediterranean diet. The implemented system acts in the same way as one would find with a nutrition professional, that is the analysis and interpretation of the user's personal data.

For this requirement, an ontology has been developed to structure and organize information related to nutrition and to obtain a personalized and balanced diet. The user must provide information about age, sex, values weight, height and physical activity to allow for a series of calculations to obtain parameters such as body mass index or total energy expenditure which will be used as a set entry criteria to match the attributes of ontology concepts.

Obviously, the field of nutrition encompasses many aspects to consider because it is a very broad topic with many branches of study. Thus, the ontology concentrated on basic concepts and relationships associated with the food intake of healthy users.

Once the ontological scheme was determined, a web application that provides the communication interface between the user and the ontology was developed. The application requests the data for the user and obtains the required results through the use of ontology query languages. The application displays a weekly diet complete with menus which are suitable for any time of day/seven days a week. In addition to this utility, one can also check for the nutritional value of each food, its nutritional properties and a section for tips on which foods to eat in order to prevent or palliate a particular problem.

On the other hand, we know how difficult it is for a user to maintain a diet today, so creating a mobile application that allows access to the ontology at any time and place, greatly simplifies monitoring. For example, if a user is away from home and is forced to eat at a restaurant, the mobile application can give the possibility of consulting the menu to decide which menu would correspond to the current time and day, providing the choice of an à la carte menu in the restaurant.

With all, the end result of our work is a nutritional recommendation for Mediterranean diets consisting of two applications, one for web access and an additional one for mobile devices. However, the bulk of the project has focused on the organization and structuring of nutritional information for the creation of an ontology.

The nutritional study and gathering of information in the area of food has resulted in an ontology with the following characteristics (Table 2):

Table 2. Ontology composition summary

Number of concepts	388
Number of defined attributes	31
Average concept attributes	2,53
Number of relations	17
Number of instances	256
Levels of hierarchy	7

This first version of both the Web application and the adapted version for Android devices has focused largely on the exploitation of knowledge through ontologies in the field of nutrition. This means that other functional pathways to complete the usability of both applications remain to be contemplated and expanded.

In the web application we can find, among other things, the calculation section and the personalized diet recommendations, as well as highlighting another feature called 'Food Guide'. This paragraph acts as a starting point for developing a new way of consulting the ontology, a way of obtaining interesting information through OWL. The purpose is to collect the output interface for consultations aimed at obtaining nutritional information on various foods as well as their nutritional properties and the variety of recipes that cover them.

Another pathway which will be of particular interest is in customizing of user management. Currently, the web version of the application has the option of user registry which also stores personal data at the same time in Liferay. But this content also offers a host of other interesting management system utilities, such as rights management or customization of the site based on each user's role. However, a function which would really be useful and necessary is to include physical data for each user in the records. This data is essential for the calculation of the diet, so if it is left stored in the database it would avoid the user having to introduce the data in each new access of the application.

If this situation in the Android application is taken into account, we realize that the main reason for its implementation in this platform is none other than to facilitate frequent and immediate consultation of the diet. Having a mobile application is synonymous with comfort and speed of access to information anywhere. To facilitate this speed it was necessary to include the storing of the user data, so that a procedure is implemented for registration of the same, at least in the mobile device.

For the latter, we consider one way of future development based on this line: the unification of user management to keep information accessible from a single database that would connect the two applications.

An ontology can be a complement as the context requires or permits, so its expansion with new rules would be interesting. Implementing a centralized user management would add a restricted access section for nutrition experts, encouraging the provision of advanced knowledge on food when there are certain health problems that require the interaction of nutrition experts because of the sensitivity of the subject.

These users would be assigned a specific role to give them permission to insert new information in the ontology, providing dynamism and promoting their enrichment with new concepts, relations, instances and/or rules.

Acknowledgements. We thank Laura María García Delgado and Eva María Brocal Hernández for their involvement and dedication in the implementation tasks of the approach presented here.

References

1. Berners-Lee, T., Hendler, J., Lassila, O.: The Semantic Web. Scientific American Magazine, vol. 284 (2001)
2. Cardoso, J.: The Semantic Web Vision: Where are we? Intell. Syst. **22** (2007)
3. Castells, P.: The Semantic Web Interactive and Collaborative Systems in the Web. Universidad of Castilla-La Mancha editions (2003)
4. Lassila, O., Swick, R.R.: Resource description framework (RDF) model and syntax. World Wide Web Consortium. http://www.w3.org/TR/WD-Rdf-Syntax. Accessed 23 Aug 2017
5. Pedraza-Jiménez, R., Codina, L., Rovira, C.: Semantic Web and Ontologies about the documental information processing. Inf. Prof. **16**, 569–578 (2007)
6. Yadav, U., Narula, G.S., Duhan, N., et al.: Development and visualization of domain specific ontology using Protégé. Indian J. Sci. Technol. **9**(16) (2016)
7. Bhatia, M.P.S., et al.: Ontologies for software engineering: past, present and future. Indian J. Sci. Technol. **9**(9) (2016)
8. Couturat, L.: Opuscules et fragments inédits de Leibniz. Extraits des manuscrits de la Bibliothèque royale de Hanovre. Paris, France (1903)
9. Kant, I.: Lectures on Metaphysics—Part III Metaphysik L2. Cambridge University Press, Cambridge (2001)
10. Gruber, T.R.: A translation approach to portable ontology specifications. Knowl. Acquis. **5**, 199–200 (1993)

11. Schwaber, K.: Agile Project Management with Scrum. SCRUM Development Process (2009)
12. Corcho, O., Fernández López, M., Gómez Pérez, A., López Cima, A.: Construction of legal ontologies using METHONTOLOGY methodology and the webODE tool. Faculty of Informatics. Polytechnic University of Madrid
13. Lima, V.C., Lopez, R.P., et al.: From guidelines to decision-making: using mobile applications and semantic web in the practical case of guides to support patients. Procedia Comput. Sci. **121**, 803–808 (2017)
14. Liu, Y., Shi, M., Li, C.: Domain ontology concept extraction method based on text. In: IEEE ICIS 2016 (2016). http://ieeexplore.ieee.org/abstract/document/7550933/. Accessed 30 Jan 2018
15. Van Heijst, G., Schreiber, A.T., Wielinga, B.J.: Using explicit ontologies in KBS development. Int. J. Hum. Comput. Stud. **46**, 183–292 (1997)
16. Lindberg, D.A., Humphreys, B.L., McCray, A.T.: The unified medical language system. Methods Inf. Med. **32**, 281–291 (1993)
17. Miller, G.A.: WordNet: a lexical database for English. Commun. ACM **38**, 39–41 (1995)
18. Fellbaum, C.: WordNet: An Electronic Lexical Database. The MIT Press, Cambridge (1998)
19. Mizoguchi, R., Vanwelkenhuysen, J., Ikeda, M.: Task ontology for reuse of problem solving knowledge. In: Towards Very Large Knowledge Bases. Knowledge Building and Knowledge Sharing, pp. 46–59 (1995)
20. Slimani, T.: Ontology development: a comparing study on tools, languages and formalisms. IJST **8**(24), 1–12 (2015)
21. Zhang, Y., Luo, X., Li, J., et al.: A semantic representation model for design rationale of products. Adv. Eng. Inf. **27**(1), 13–26 (2013)
22. McBride, B.: The Resource Description Framework (RDF) and its vocabulary description language RDFS. In: Staab, S., Studer, R. (eds.) Handbook on Ontologies, pp. 51–65. Springer, Heidelberg (2004). https://doi.org/10.1007/978-3-540-24750-0_3
23. McGuinness, D.L., Van Harmelen, F.: OWL web ontology language. http://www.w3.org/TR/owl-features/. Accessed 31 Aug 2017
24. Zhang, S., Boukamp, F., Teizer, J.: Ontology-based semantic modeling of construction safety knowledge: towards automated safety planning for job hazard analysis (JHA). Autom. Constr. **52**, 29–41 (2015)
25. Pani, S., Mishra, J.: Modeling the requirements based on contexts in mobile native apps. Indian J. Sci. Technol. **10**(10) (2017)
26. Preuveneers, D., Berbers, Y., Joosen, W.: The future of mobile e-health application development: exploring HTML5 for context-aware diabetes monitoring. Procedia Comput. Sci. J. **21**, 351–359 (2013)
27. Dodds, L.: Introducing SPARQL: querying the semantic web (2005). http://www.xml.com/pub/a/2005/11/16/introducing-sparql-querying-semantic-web-tutorial.html

Concept Identification from Single-Documents

José Luis Ochoa-Hernández[(✉)] [iD], Mario Barcelo-Valenzuela[iD],
Gerardo Sanchez-Smitz[iD], and Raquel Torres-Peralta[iD]

Department of Industrial Engineering, Universidad de Sonora,
Blvd. Rosales y Transversal, 83000 Hermosillo, Sonora, Mexico
{joseluis.ochoa,mbarcelo,gsanchez,
rtorres}@industrial.uson.mx

Abstract. This article presents a method that extracts relevant concepts automatically, consisting of one or several words, whose main contribution is that it does so from a single document of any domain, regardless of its length; however, documents of short length are used (which are the most frequent to obtain on the web) to perform the work. This research was conducted for documents written in Spanish and was tested in multiple randomized domains to compare their results. For this, an algorithm was used to automatically identify syntactic patterns in the document. This work uses the previous work of [1] to obtain its results. This algorithm is based on statistical approximations and on the length of the identifiable patterns contained in the document, applies certain heuristic that can enhance or decrease the patterns' choice according to the selection of one of the 5 methods that are processed (M1 to M5), with these patterns the candidate concepts are obtained, which go through another evaluation process that will obtain the final concepts. This proposal presents at least four advantages: (1) It is multi-domain, (2) It is independent of the text length, (3) It can work with one or more documents and (4) It allows the discarding of garbage or undesirable patterns from the beginning. The method was implemented in 11 different domains and its results range varies between 58%–70% of precision and 25%–46% of recall.

Keywords: Concept extraction · Syntactic patterns · Text analysis
Single-documents

1 Introduction

The concepts extraction, despite the fact that it emerged in 1954 based on Harris' distributional hypothesis [2] is an activity that still presents important advances. This activity is applied to a large number of tasks that are being used daily, especially in those tasks that use natural language as a source of information for their development, some very common examples of these are: translations of texts, phrases or words from one language to another as [3] which translates from English to Arabic for sentiment analysis purposes, or [4] which translates from Polish to English with human judgment; the detection of plagiarism in articles, research or books [5–7] which presents a work using syntactic-semantic based Natural Language Processing (NLP) techniques for Unmasking text plagiarism; generation of summaries from large corpus of concrete

© Springer Nature Switzerland AG 2018
R. Valencia-García et al. (Eds.): CITI 2018, CCIS 883, pp. 158–173, 2018.
https://doi.org/10.1007/978-3-030-00940-3_12

domain such as Biomedicine [8] or for single-documents of any domain [9]; in fact, there are a great variety of methods as exposed [10] in this review, as well as the creation of domain glossaries in very common languages such as English where [11] create one based on the text acronyms or in less frequent languages such as Islam [12] who creates an unsupervised concept hierarchy.

Another field in which concept extraction has been applied fairly recently is for the creation, extension or integration of ontologies in different domains. As is the case of [13–15]. Transforming the common web into semantic web [16, 17] is another application because with the current web, too much time is lost in knowing which pages are relevant and which are not [10, 18].

In the most recent area where concept extraction is applied is in decision support tools for doctors in different domains, as is the case of [19] who integrate NLP and Machine Learning Algorithms to categorize Oncologic Response in Radiology Reports or [20] which generate structured reports for cancer from free-text (non-structured) pathology reports.

The concept extraction is therefore a process that continues in development. Both in the latest research and in the initial ones, these are mainly based on having a large number of texts from the same domain in order to identify the principal concepts in a "more precise" or "more efficient" way, either by a model, for other or by combining these as in [19].

The initial problem that arises in almost all investigations is to form a sufficiently robust corpus [21] to be able to apply the different algorithms that exist today to extract the concepts, some examples of this are the NLP techniques that use lexical and syntactic analysis [22], lexical and syntactic patterns [23], the C value/NC Value of [24–26].

1.1 Related Works and Distribution

To know if these extracted concepts are relevant, is necessary to use metrics to measure the importance of the concept usually in the CORPUS. One of the most common methods used in this type is the Term Frequency – Inverse Document Frequency (TF-IDF) proposed by [27] and it is used in works like [28]. There are others like Domain Relevance and Domain Consensus, which are measures to know how much a concept is used in a domain CORPUS and to measure the distribution of use from a term in a domain; co-occurrence and others more mentioned in [29] also require a large number of texts to work and provide better results, without generating too much "garbage". However, in the case of a single document these metrics do not work by their own nature, the metrics of Precision, Recall and F-score are those that can be adapted as commented in [30].

There are multiple studies that refer to work with single-documents. Here we mention three similar works, including one that would be great to try with the single-document methodology. It's shown because he says he worked hard to get his corpus from a lot of places and the research is very interesting, however this work could have been avoided using this proposal.

The mentioned work is from [31] who presents a work for the extraction of concepts, they discover concepts based on a CORPUS that was "extracted from many places", his proposal includes semantic extraction, a statistical filtering and a semantic analysis. It uses manual elements in several parts of its proposal that make it dependent on an expert. The main difference with our work is the CORPUS and the methods that it applies, since this research is based on linguistic patterns and statistical analysis to a single-document.

The majority of the investigations related to single documents are those that work with text summaries, there are very few that only extract concepts, the work of [30] that identifies key concepts using a method similar to ours was found, instead of applying the identification of key patterns, use the concept of k-core on the graph-of-words representation of text for single-document keyword extraction, retaining only the nodes from the main core as representative terms. This approach that takes better into account proximity between keywords and variability in the number of extracted keywords through the selection of more cohesive subsets of vertices. Within the process of Graph-of-words perform a pre-process similar to ours: (1) tokenization; (2) part-of-speech, annotation and selection; (3) stop-words removal; and (4) stemming. And for validate the results they use the metrics of precision and recall with very good values.

In [32] it is proposed a novel approach for extraction of key phrases from single-document without usage of external information. To achieve this extraction, it is necessary to identify a list of hierarchical key concepts (activity of our interest), his analysis is based on the method contained in the area of Formal Concept Analysis (FCA), known as concept lattice, where combination of sentences or paragraphs are used as objects and the presence of terms are attributes. This form hierarchically organized groups of sentences that share the same or similar set of attributes/terms, evaluate their results with various metrics like Term Frequency, TF-IDF, Chi-Square and Information Gain function. Quality of methods is compared with precision and recall metrics.

[33] is another investigation that requires identifying key concepts to create a summary from a single document, however, to achieve it, its methodology is divided into 4 phases, the one that is of our interest is "text pre-processing", which is divided into 5 stages: segmentation, tokenization, elimination of stop-words, stemming, and building document words stems list. The difference in this stage is that they use any punctuation mark to divide into sentences the text and we do not, they also have a limited stop-word list, which we eliminate with syntactic patterns, therefore, a predefined list will never be required, finally, they generate a list of keywords that do not specify how they got it, which use to evaluate the extracted sentences and then measure them by an adaptation of the TF-IDF metrics in vectors similarly called IDF, TF and TF-IDF, which count the times a term occurs in a sentence.

So "being able to identify concepts from a single document" was what motivated the development of this research. The work was done and shows that the result is promising, since they manage to identify between 58%–72% of the concepts with precision and a 25%–47% of recall, low percentage because there are big differences when working with a single document vs multiple documents [30].

The article is structured as follows, Sect. 2 briefly discusses the tools used to understand this research, Sect. 3 presents the methodology followed in this research and Sect. 4 presents a practical case with 11 different domains, Sect. 5 presents the results obtained and in the last section the conclusions are shown.

2 Tools Used in This Investigation

In this research, two tools were used and modified during the development of the project: (1) Freeling for the process of language analysis (unmodified) and (2) Pattern learning, which will obtain a first approximation of the relevant morpho-syntactic patterns and thus obtain the domain concepts (modified).

2.1 Freeling

The Freeling tool is a library that provides language analysis functionalities (morphological analysis, named entity detection, PoS-tagging, parsing, Word Sense Disambiguation, Semantic Role Labelling, etc.) for a variety of languages (English, Spanish, Portuguese, Italian, among others) [34].

This tool uses the labels proposed by the EAGLES group to achieve the morphosyntactic annotation of lexicons (linguistic analysis). This annotation provides a lot of information, an example can be seen in Table 1, which shows the category Adjectives, Adverbs, Articles, Determinants, Nouns, Verbs, Pronouns and some more, can be seen in full on the Eagles Tags website[1].

Table 1. Attributes and values of Eagles tags.

Position	Attribute	Value
1	Category	Adjective
2	Type	Qualifying
3	Grade	Appreciative
4	Gender	Male
		Female
		Common
5	Num	Singular
		Plural
		Invariable
6	Case	-
7	Function	Participle

Table 1 contains in the first column a position which is used to identify the meaning of the letter on the label, the attribute is used to know what type of information is being read and the value provides the meaning that this attribute has.

2.2 Automatic Pattern Learning

Automatic pattern learning is a tool proposed by [1] which shows a set of multi-word morpho-syntactic patterns suggested as a result of the textual analysis that is made to a corpus of any domain, based on a set of guiding patterns to do the work.

The article comments that the only thing that needs to be specified is the length and specialization of the pattern (understanding as length, the size of words that will contain

---

[1] http://www.lsi.upc.es/ ∼ nlp/tools/parole-sp.html.

a term to be considered in the selection of candidates). For example, a term of length 3 would be "diseñadores de moda"/"fashion designers", one of length 2 would be "estrella michelin"/"Michelin Star". And specialization, refers to the use of Eagles tags. So a specialization degree 2 would be something like "NC – Common Noun" o "VM – Main verb", a specialization degree 3 would be "NCM – Common Male Noun", "NCF – Common Female Noun", etc. and a specialization degree 1 would be "N – Noun", "A – Adjective", "R – Adverb", etc.

So to obtain a list of patterns like those presented in Table 4, it is necessary to specify these two elements in the tool, for example: we want terms of length 2 with grade 2, the pattern guide would be XX·XX, terms of length 3, grade 2, the pattern guide would be XX·XX·XX, activity that in [21] was considered difficult to recognize and extract (multi-word terms).

The code was adapted in order to test how the tool works with a single document instead of a large corpus. In the same way, the code was adapted in a way that it could identify single length patterns, and these could be processed in a better way, since the concepts of length 1 represent the majority.

Five methods are also proposed in [1] (M1, M2, M3, M4 and M5) which obtain different patterns according to their procedure, in this case the methods M1 to M5 were not modified, because they were studied and the decision was made to leave them without any alteration.

2.3 Evaluation Method

To evaluate this research we used a typical method that is used in information retrieval, commonly called Precision and Recall, some jobs that have implemented these evaluation forms are [30, 35]. Similarly, F-score was used as an integrating measure, which is considered as a harmonic mean that combines the values of precision and recall [36], his equations are the following:

$$\text{Precision} = \frac{terms\ correctly\ identified\ by\ the\ tool}{correct\ terms\ of\ the\ expert} \tag{1}$$

$$\text{Recall} = \frac{terms\ correctly\ identified\ by\ the\ tool}{candidate\ terms\ of\ the\ tool} \tag{2}$$

$$\text{F - Score} = 2 * \frac{prcision * recall}{precision + recall} \tag{3}$$

It is necessary to clarify that these equations were adapted to be able to compare the achievement level of concept identification. It was done because these metrics are recognized and are easily comparable, in addition to the other metrics such as those mentioned in [29] are applicable to multiple-Documents. In the work done by [33] something similar happened, the TF-IDF metrics were adapted to be able to measure their results.

3   Concept Extraction Process from a Single Document

3.1   The Proposal

In this section we explain the elements of the proposal that is made to extract concepts from a single document, it is formed by 4 main components: the Text, the morphological labeling, the pattern learning and the concepts selection. In Fig. 1 it is possible to see this proposal.

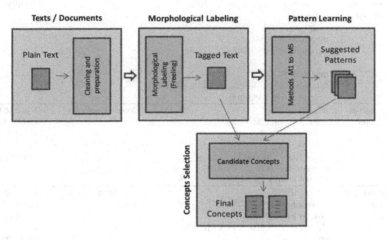

Fig. 1. Proposal of concept extraction process from a single document.

3.2   The Text/Documents

Free text is the source of most research involving NLP. For this purpose, any text of the domain of interest is selected, normally constituted by documents, which can be short in length [32]. The document is transformed into plain text and pre-processed to "*clean the text*" of characters that may cause errors or bad results in the following stages. This is a process that is done manually, in this case, Freeling for example, does not process certain *single or double quotes* which cause errors when tagged. For this, the quotes are replaced by the same ones using another type of character coding, the dashes or long dashes are other elements to review. Likewise, punctuation marks are verified so that sentences, quantities, dates, etc., are well identified.

3.3   Morphological Labeling

Morphological labeling is a key process for this research, Freeling tool is used which performs a text language analysis; it is proven that it does a good job in the labeling process [37, 38]. The result of this process is a list of words morphologically labeled, which during this testing process are reviewed in detail to verify that they have been tagged without errors, in case any word has been mislabeled, given the circumstances discussed in Sect. 3.1. The source text is modified and re-labeled (see Table 2). In this table it can be seen that the gray marked text, is the text that presented an error when it was labeled.

Table 2. Common mistakes in morphological labeling

Text	Labeled	Error type	Solution
'Social Media': menos gurús, más formaciónSílvia Sivera	'·'·Fe Social_Media·social_media·NP00000 '·'·Fe :·:·Fd menos·menos·RG gurús·gurús·NP00000 ,·,·Fc más·más·RG formaciónSílvia·formaciónsílvia·AQ0FS0 Sivera·sivera·NP00000	Text without separation	Separate words manually
… la intención es que "leáis" con interés …	la·el·DA0FS0 intención·intención·NCFS000 es·ser·VSIP3S0 que·que·CS ?leái·?leái·VMN0000 con·con·SPS00 interés·interés·NCMS000	Double quotes in "leáis"	Change the quotes for them in another encoding
En septiembre nos "tomaremos" en Barcelona…	En·en·SPS00 septiembre·[??:??/9/??:??.??:??]·W nos·yo·PP1CP000 ?tomaremo·?tomaremo·VMIC3S0 en·en·SPS00 Barcelona·barcelona·NP00000	Double quotes in "tomaremos"	Change the quotes for them in another encoding

3.4   Identification of Key Patterns

Based on the proposed methods (M1 to M5) of [1], this research developed a complete study to know which method provided the best results. The original patterns were obtained and compared with the patterns recommended by the tool, these patterns were analyzed and the method that provided the best results in all cases was the M1 method.

The automatic patterns learning was modified to eliminate those patterns that were useless or unproductive from the beginning, a series of elements that help to configure this method were defined, which improves the accuracy of the results, an example of these are the following (see Table 3):

Table 3. Example of unseen patterns of different lengths with an example of concepts.

Length 1		Length 2		Length 3		Length 4
DI	Un	SP DA	De las	DI AQ NC	Una nueva manera	DI AQ NC SP
CC	Y	PR DA	Donde el	P0 VM VM	Se está haciendo	P0 VM VM DI
RG	más	CC NC	Y restautrantes	SP VS AQ	De ser fijo	PR DA NC
SP	De	SP VM	De comprar	PR DA NC	Donde el espacio	VM
P0	Se	DI AQ	Una única	CC AQ SP	Y temporal para	SP DA NC PR
DA	Las	RG RG	Casi siempre	RG DI SP	Solo algunas de	DA PR P0 VA
						CS DA NC SP

3.5   Selection of Candidate Concepts

With the chosen M1 method (which may vary for other documents) and applied to each document, the results are presented in a list (see Table 4), this list is organized by grammatical categories i.e.: names, verbs, adjectives, etc. in which all the patterns found and suggested by the tool are included.

The tool uses these patterns to identify the candidate concepts of the text. Under normal circumstances of large corpora, it is possible to work with different proposals such as [21]. However, in this new context, identifying the elements in a very precise way is more complicated, the statistical approximation and the heuristic of methods Ml to M5 are the key elements that define the candidate patterns of each document.

3.6   Final Concepts Selection

The process of selecting the final concepts includes a cut level according to the method proposed (M1 to M5), which is the minimum level to accept concepts according to their process and the number of times they have appeared in the text, to the list of concepts obtained based on the suggested patterns, the cut level is applied and a final list of concepts is obtained (see Table 4).

Table 4.   Example of patterns contemplated with their concepts in a document.

Length 1 (AQ)	Length 1 (NC)	Length 1 (NP)	Length 2 (NC AQ)
8·nuevo	7·espacio	6·pop-up	2·casa particular
2·fijo	5·tienda	2·nueva_york	1·experiencia irrepetible
2·itinerante	4·restaurante	2·londres	1·prestigio internacional
2·sorprendente	4·marca	2·nike	1·entorno sorprendente
2·particular	3·concepto	2·barcelona	1·vía alternativo
2·social	3·chefs	1·elisenda_estanyol	1·coste fijo
.....	....	.....	....

4   Case Study - Concept Extraction for 11 Different Domains from a Single Document

This study took as reference the article published by [39] in the journal "Studies of Information and Communication Sciences of the Open University of Catalonia (UOC), COMeIN", which is entitled "Dissection contents from concepts". In the article, key concepts are extracted to draw a knowledge map and several examples of different thematic areas/domains are shown, for example: restaurants, online courses, advertising, nostalgia, etc. These domains where randomly selected by the author and they had already identified some concepts and they are related in some way.

4.1   The Text/Documents

For this case the 11 articles that are handled in the article [39], were converted to plain text. They were manually pre-processed, eliminating those characters that could cause errors and were left ready to be labeled. An example of this text is shown in Fig. 2.

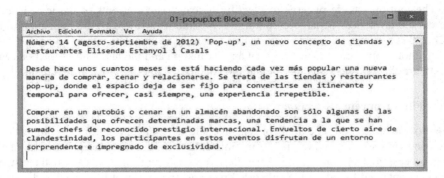

Fig. 2. Plain text of the article – 'Pop-up', a new concept of shops and restaurants (http://comein.uoc.edu/divulgacio/comein/es/numero14/articles/Article-Elisenda-Estanyol.html).

4.2   Morphological Labeling

The Freeling tool was applied to the texts and the result obtained are labeled and lemmatized text, this is shown in the "Labeling" column. For example, given the line "tiendas·tienda·NCFP000" the word "tiendas" is the original text, "tienda" is the lemmatized text and "NCFP000" is the label. A more extensive example can be seen in Table 5, where Text 1 is part of document 01- Creativity and Text 2, is part of document 02-Social media:

Table 5. Table with some texts labeled.

Text 1	Labeling	Text 2	Labeling
'Pop-up', un nuevo concepto de tiendas....	'·'·Fe	Hubo un tiempo en que para aprender acudíamos a clases...	Hubo·haber·VAIS3S0
	Pop-up·pop-up·NP00000		un·uno·DI0MS0
	'·'·Fe		tiempo·tiempo·NCMS000
	,·,·Fc		en·en·SPS00
	un·uno·DI0MS0		que·que·CS
	nuevo·nuevo·AQ0MS0		para·para·SPS00
	concepto·concepto·NCMS000		aprender·aprender·VMN0000
	de·de·SPS00		acudíamos·acudir·VMII1P0
	tiendas·tienda·NCFP000		a·a·SPS00
			clases·clase·NCFP000

Table 5 show how the labels provide great value to each word, which facilitates the "creation" of knowledge. For example, in Table 6 we see the scope and specialization of labels:

Table 6. Meaning of some labels.

Term	Labeling	Description of the label
Tiendas	NCFP000	It is a Name, Common, in Feminine, in Plural.
Hubo	VAIS3S0	It is a Verb, Auxiliary, Indicative, in the past, in the third person and in the singular.
Un	DI0MS0	It is an undefined determinant, masculine and singular.

4.3   Identifying Key Patterns

With the labeled texts, the chosen pattern learning method M1 is applied, to find the patterns. A complete example for the document 01-Creativity of the results obtained can be seen in Table 8, the rest of the suggested patterns for each document are shown in Table 7, omitting the non-suggested ones. It is appreciated that the amount of patterns found in single-documents is smaller compared to large corpora; this is precisely due for the documents size.

Table 7. Suggested patterns for the 11 documents analyzed.

02- Social Media	03-Media Planning	04-Advertising	05-Journalism	06-Political Communication
NC	AQ	AQ	NC	NP
NP	NC	NC	NP	NC AQ
NC AQ	NP	NP		NC SP NC
NC SP NC	NC AQ	NC AQ		
	NC SP NC	NC SP NC		
		NP NP NP		

07-Digital Communication	08-Crisis Communication	09-Television	10-Cinema	11-Audiovisual design
NC	AQ	AQ	NC	NC
NP	NC	NC	NP	NP
	NP	NP	NC AQ	NC AQ
	NC AQ	NC AQ	NC SP NC	NC SP NC
	NC SP NC	NC SP NC		

4.4   Candidate Concepts Selection

Once the best method has been identified, the patterns found in it are applied separately to each of the texts to obtain the candidate concepts. The result is a list of concepts. At this point, it was proposed to show only the concepts that were best positioned in the study document. However, these concepts were not sufficient to identify all the valid concepts of the document; instead, they were used to identify the most representative concepts of the domain, which are used in other studies as seed concepts [22] (see Table 9).

Table 8. Example of suggested and not suggested patterns of the 01-Creativity document.

Method	Suggested patterns		Non Suggested patterns		
M1	AQ·50·*		AO·1	NC·NP·14·*	NC·SP·NC·14·*
	NC·135·*		AQ·NC·22·*	NC·NC·13·*	NC·SP·NP·7·*
	NP·42·*		AQ·NP·5	NP·NC·5·*	NC·NC·NC·5
	NC·AQ·29·*		AO·NC·1	NP·NP·3·*	NC·AQ·NC·4
			AQ·SP·NP·2	NP·AQ·1	NP·DI·AQ·2
			AQ·DI·AQ·1		NP·NC·NP·2
M2	NC·135·*		AQ·50·*	NP·42·*	NC·AQ·NC·4
	NC·SP·NC·14·*		AO·1	NC·AQ·29·*	NP·DI·AQ·2
			AQ·NC·22·*	NC·NP·14·*	NP·NC·NP·2
			AQ·NP·5	NC·NC·13·*	NC·DI·NC·2
			AO·NC·1	NP·NC·5·*	NP·DI·NC·2
			AQ·SP·NP·2	NP·NP·3·*	NC·AQ·NP·2
M3	AO·1	NP·42·*	AQ·50·*	NC·135·*	
	AQ·NP·5	NP·NC·5·*	AQ·NC·22·*	NC·AQ·29·*	
	AO·NC·1	NP·NP·3·*		NC·NP·14·*	
	AQ·SP·NP·2	NP·AQ·1		NC·NC·13·*	
	AQ·DI·AQ·1	NC·NC·NC·5		NC·SP·NC·14·*	
	AQ·NP·NC·1	NC·AQ·NC·4		NC·SP·NP·7·*	
M4	AQ·50·*	NC·NP·14·*	AO·1	NC·135·*	NP·NC·NP·2
		NC·NC·13·*	AQ·NC·22·*	NP·42·*	NC·DI·NC·2
		NC·SP·NP·7·*	AQ·NP·5	NC·AQ·29·*	NP·DI·NC·2
		NC·NC·NC·5	AO·NC·1	NP·NC·5·*	NC·AQ·NP·2
			AQ·SP·NP·2	NP·NP·3·*	NC·NC·AQ·2
			AQ·NP·NC·1	NC·SP·NC·14·*	NC·NP·AQ·1
M5	AQ·NC·22·*	NC·135·*	AQ·50·*	NP·42·*	NC·AQ·NC·4
		NC SP	AO·1	NC·AQ·29·*	NP·DI·AQ·2
		NC·14·*	AQ·NP·5	NC·NP·14·*	NP·NC·NP·2
			AO·NC·1	NC·NC·13·*	NC·DI·NC·2
			AQ·SP·NP·2	NP·NC·5·*	NP·DI·NC·2
			AQ·DI·AQ·1	NP·NP·3·*	NC·AQ·NP·2

Table 9. Sample of relevant terms obtained in five domains worked.

07-Digital Communication	08-Crisis Communication	09-Television	10-Cinema	11-Audiovisual design
amenaza	información	clase	cine	mapping
difusión	filtración	cultural	año	edificio
fotografía	caso	social	industria	proyección
gigapíxeles	documento	cultura	público	técnica
imagen	periodismo	actividad	innovación	contenido
internet	fuente	tipo	distribución	efecto
panorámica	secreto	consumo	exhibición	espacio
publicación	wikileaks	emoción	muerte	contexto
tecnología	vaticanleaks	fanático	tecnología	percepción
....	....	....	....	....

It should be noted that in the documents there are concepts of different lengths, one, two, three, four or more words; the tool removes some patterns that are rare and therefore are not taken into account, which diminishes the accuracy value, since these concepts, if they are not defined in the proposed patterns, will not be found.

4.5   Final Concepts Selection

To the list of candidate concepts, a parameter known as the "cut level" is applied, it is set at 70%, that is, we only keep the best 70% of the candidates, this level helps to discard some other concepts that may appear only once in the text, some of which may be relevant and others may not.

In addition to the original process, in this research was done a manually identification of each valid concept for the 11 documents of this study case, the results can be obtained by comparing those found by the expert and those found by the tool.

An example of the final concepts for each document can be seen in Table 10, in which it is possible to see that most are good patterns, however, patterns that are not very good are also included as in 04-Publicidad, where the pattern NP NP NP does not provide right concepts:

Table 10.   Sample of final concepts of some domains.

01- Creativity	02- Social Media	03-Media Planning	04-Advertising
	--NC--	--AQ--	--NC--
--AQ--	7·manera	9·publicitario	9·pasado
8·nuevo	6·clase	6·íntimo	7·nostalgia
2·fijo	5·aprendizaje	4·público	--NP--
2·itinerante	4·pared	3·líquido	3·polaroid
2·sorprendente	--NP--	--NC--	2·ray_ban
--NC--	3·mooc	10·medio	2·jameson
7·espacio	2·massive_open_on	4·lavabo	--AQ--
5·tienda	line_courses	4·publicidad	3·actual
4·restaurante	2·internet	4·espacio	2·propio
4·marca	2·web	--NC AQ--	--NC AQ--
--NP--	2· --NC AQ--	3·medio publicitario	1·vínculo emocional
6·pop-up	2·red social	2·mensaje publicitario	·público objetivo
2·nueva_york	1·mundo profesional	2·medio íntimo	1·foto antiguo
2·londres	1·aulas virtuales	2·papel higiénico	--NC SP NC--
2·barcelona	--NC SP NC--	--NC SP NC--	1·sensación de
--NC AQ--	1·aulas con pared	1·punto de vista	autenticidad
2·casa particular	1·espacio con pared	1·publicidad de guerra	1·estilo de vida
1·experiencia	1·clase sin pared	1·guerra en retretes	1·cantidad de dinero
irrepetible	1·educación a distancia	1·cuarto de baño	--NP NP NP--
1·prestigio	1·proceso de	1·muestra de perfume	1·ray_ban vinils mini
internacional	aprendizaje	--NP--	1·vinils mini polaroid
1·entorno	......	2·portugal	1·mini polaroid tetris
sorprendente		.....	......
.....			

5   Results

Table 11 shows the results obtained for this study case, the 11 different domains considered were processed.

In this table the name of the documents are shown in the first column, the words per document are in the second column, the number of concepts found in the document

Table 11. Results obtained after processing the 11 different domains documents.

Document Name	Words per document	Originals	Candidates	Founds	Precision %	Recall %	F-Score %
		#	#	#			
01- Creativity	609	103	178	70	67.96	39.33	49.82
02- Social Media	764	121	154	71	58.68	46.10	51.64
03-Media Planning	834	142	247	83	58.45	33.60	42.67
04-Advertising	977	152	244	94	61.84	38.52	47.47
05-Journalism	755	68	173	48	70.59	27.75	39.83
06-Political Communication	727	82	201	52	63.41	25.87	36.75
07-Digital Communication	683	88	171	52	59.09	30.41	40.15
08-Crisis Communication	1094	185	274	122	65.95	44.53	53.16
09-Television	894	144	276	99	68.75	35.87	47.14
10-Cinema	1095	167	296	103	61.68	34.80	44.49
11-Audiovisual Design	735	120	190	79	65.83	41.58	50.97
Average					63.84	36.21	45.83

manually (originals) are in the third column, the number of candidate concepts (found by the proposed method) are in the fourth, the number of candidate concepts equal to the originals are in the fifth and in the following 3 are the parameters of Precision, Recall and F-Score, which help us to compare these results in a standard way.

The cells that are above the general average of the 11 documents were marked in gray, for Precision and Recall 5 of 11 are above average and for the F-Score column, 6 of 11 elements are above the average, in bold the highest values of each column are found, it is highlighted that 8 of the 11 are above 60% of Precision.

6   Conclusions

The results of the research show that it is possible to extract good key concepts from a particular domain from a single document (in this case 11 different areas were studied) without the necessity of a large corpus, it is concluded that it is possible to identify up to 70% of the validated concepts in the documents with a maximum precision of 46%, improving the maximum 25% of [1]. The key elements for this investigation were: Freeling, the automatic pattern learning, the modification to filter out undesirable/unproductive patterns and the modification to detect single word patterns.

Consequently, these helped us to obtain the important concepts for each document. The adaptation that was made to be able to obtain the formed concepts by a single word, helped to conform 70% of our valid concepts, since without this adaptation, 82% of the original concepts of the document would be lost.

We also found potential to improve the automatic pattern learning process adding neural networks or genetic algorithms, which will be presented in a new publication.

References

1. Ochoa, J.L., Almela, A., Hernández-Alcaraz, M.L., Valencia-García, R.: Learning morphosyntactic patterns for multiword term extraction. Sci. Res. Essays **6**(26), 5563–5578 (2011)
2. Harris, Z.S.: Distributional structure. WORD **10**(2–3), 146–162 (1954). https://doi.org/10.1080/00437956.1954.11659520
3. Elnagar, A., Einea, O., Lulu, L.: Comparative study of sentiment classification for automated translated Latin reviews into Arabic. In: 2017 IEEE/ACS 14th International Conference on Computer Systems and Applications (AICCSA), Hammamet, Tunisia, pp. 443–448 (2018). https://doi.org/10.1109/aiccsa.2017.82
4. Wołk, K., Glinkowski, W., Żukowska, A.: Enhancing the assessment of (Polish) translation in PROMIS using statistical, semantic, and neural network metrics. In: Rocha, Á., Adeli, H., Reis, L.P., Costanzo, S. (eds.) WorldCIST'18 2018. AISC, vol. 746, pp. 351–366. Springer, Cham (2018). https://doi.org/10.1007/978-3-319-77712-2_34
5. Vani, K., Gupta, D.: Text plagiarism classification using syntax based linguistic features. Expert Syst. Appl. **88**, 448–464 (2017). https://doi.org/10.1016/j.eswa.2017.07.006
6. Vani, K., Gupta, D.: Detection of idea plagiarism using syntax–semantic concept extractions with genetic algorithm. Exp. Syst. Appl. **73**, 11–26 (2017). https://doi.org/10.1016/j.eswa.2016.12.022
7. Vani, K., Gupta, D.: Unmasking text plagiarism using syntactic-semantic based natural language processing techniques: comparisons, analysis and challenges. Inf. Process. Manag. **54**(3), 408–432 (2018). https://doi.org/10.1016/j.ipm.2018.01.008
8. Moradi, M., Ghadiri, N.: Different approaches for identifying important concepts in probabilistic biomedical text summarization. Artif. Intell. Med. **84**, 101–116 (2018)
9. Yousefi-Azar, M., Hamey, L.: Text summarization using unsupervised deep learning. Exp. Syst. Appl. **68**, 93–105 (2017). https://doi.org/10.1016/j.eswa.2016.10.017
10. Gambhir, M., Gupta, V.: Recent automatic text summarization techniques: a survey. Artif. Intell. Rev. **47**(1), 1–66 (2017). https://doi.org/10.1007/s10462-016-9475-9
11. Spasić, I.: Acronyms as an integral part of multi-word term recognition—a token of appreciation. IEEE Access **6**, 8351–8363 (2018). https://doi.org/10.1109/ACCESS.2018.2807122
12. Ali, A.A., Saad, S.: Unsupervised concept hierarchy induction based on Islamic glossary. ARPN J. Eng. Appl. Sci. **11**(13), 8505–8510 (2016)
13. Ochoa, J.L., Hernandez-Alcaraz, M.L., Almela, A., Valencia-Garcia, R.: Learning semantic relations from Spanish natural language documents in the financial domain. In: IEEE 3rd International Conference on Computer Modeling and Simulation (ICCMS 2011), Mumbai, India (2011)
14. Kuang, Z., Yu, J., Li, Z., Zhang, B., Fan, J.: Integrating multi-level deep learning and concept ontology for large-scale visual recognition. Pattern Recognit. **78**, 198–214 (2018). https://doi.org/10.1016/j.patcog.2018.01.027
15. Ochieng, P., Kyanda, S.: Ontologies' mappings validation and annotation enrichment through tagging. Artif. Intell. Rev. 1–28 (2018). https://doi.org/10.1007/s10462-018-9632-4
16. Berners-Lee, T., Hendler, J., Lassila, O.: The semantic web. Sci. Am. **284**(5), 34–43 (2001)
17. Maedche, A., Staab, S.: Ontology learning for the Semantic Web. IEEE Intell. Syst. **16**(2), 72–79 (2001). https://doi.org/10.1109/5254.920602
18. Unadkat, R.: Survey paper on semantic web. Int. J. Adv. Pervasive Ubiquit. Comput. (IJAPUC) **7**(4), 13–17 (2015). https://doi.org/10.4018/IJAPUC.2015100102

19. Chen, P.H., Zafar, H., Galperin-Aizenberg, M., Cook, T.: Integrating natural language processing and machine learning algorithms to categorize oncologic response in radiology reports. J. Digit. Imaging **31**(2), 178–184 (2018). https://doi.org/10.1007/s10278-017-0027-x

20. Nguyen, A., Lawley, M., Hansen, D., Colquist, S.: Structured pathology reporting for cancer from free text: Lung cancer case study. Electr. J. Health Inf. **7**(1) (2012). Art. No. e8

21. Wermter, J., Hahn, U.: Finding new terminology in very large corpora. In: Proceedings of the 3rd International Conference on Knowledge Capture (K-CAP 2005), pp. 137–144. ACM, New York (2005). http://dx.doi.org/10.1145/1088622.1088648

22. Zouaq, A., Nkambou, R.: Enhancing learning objects with an ontology-based memory. J. IEEE Trans. Knowl. Data Eng. **21**(6), 881–893 (2009)

23. Ochoa, J.L., Almela, A., Ruiz-Martínez, J.M., Valencia-García, R.: Efficient multiword term extraction in Spanish. Application to the financial domain. In: IEEE International Conference on Intelligence and Information Technology (ICIIT 2010), Lahore, Pakistan, vol. 1, pp. 426–430 (2010)

24. Frantzi, K.T., Ananiadou, S., Tsujii, J.: The *C-value/NC-value* method of automatic recognition for multi-word terms. In: Nikolaou, C., Stephanidis, C. (eds.) ECDL 1998. LNCS, vol. 1513, pp. 585–604. Springer, Heidelberg (1998). https://doi.org/10.1007/3-540-49653-X_35

25. Frantzi, K.T., Ananiadou, S.: The C-value/NC value domain independent method for multi-word term extraction. J. Nat. Lang. Process. **3**(6), 145–180 (1999)

26. Frantzi, K.T., Ananiadou, S., Mima, H.: Automatic recognition of multi-word terms: the C-value/NC-value method. Int. J. Digit. Libr. **3**(2), 115–130 (2000)

27. Salton, G., Buckley, C.: Term-weighting approaches in automatic text retrieval. Inf. Process. Manag. **24**(5), 513–523 (1988)

28. Hisamitsu, T., Tsujii, J.: Measuring term representativeness. In: Pazienza, M.T. (ed.) Information Extraction in the Web Era. LNCS (LNAI), vol. 2700, pp. 45–76. Springer, Heidelberg (2003). https://doi.org/10.1007/978-3-540-45092-4_3

29. Pazienza, M.T., Pennacchiotti, M., Zanzotto, F.M.: Terminology extraction: an analysis of linguistic and statistical approaches. In: Sirmakessis, S. (ed.) Knowledge Mining. Studies in Fuzziness and Soft Computing, vol. 185, pp. 255–279. Springer, Heidelberg (2005). https://doi.org/10.1007/3-540-32394-5_20

30. Rousseau, F., Vazirgiannis, M.: Main core retention on graph-of-words for single-document keyword extraction. In: Hanbury, A., Kazai, G., Rauber, A., Fuhr, N. (eds.) ECIR 2015. LNCS, vol. 9022, pp. 382–393. Springer, Cham (2015). https://doi.org/10.1007/978-3-319-16354-3_42

31. Yao, X., Gan, J., Xu, J.: Concept extraction based on hybrid approach combined with semantic analysis. In: 2017 International Conference on Applied Mechanics and Mechanical Automation (AMMA 2017)

32. Smatana, M., Butka, P.: Extraction of keyphrases from single document based on hierarchical concepts. In: IEEE 14th International Symposium on Applied Machine Intelligence and Informatics (SAMI), Herlany, pp. 93–98 (2016). https://doi.org/10.1109/sami.2016.7422988

33. Al-Abdallah, R.Z., Al-Taani, A.T.: Arabic single-document text summarization using particle swarm optimization algorithm. Proc. Comput. Sci. **117**, 30–37 (2017). https://doi.org/10.1016/j.procs.2017.10.091

34. Padró, L., Stanilovsky, E.: FreeLing 3.0: towards wider multilinguality. In: Proceedings of the Language Resources and Evaluation Conference (LREC 2012) ELRA. Istanbul, Turkey. (2012). UPCommons, http://hdl.handle.net/2117/15986. Accessed 08 June 2018

35. Ochoa, J.L., Hernández-Alcaraz, M.L., Valencia-García, R., Martínez-Béjar, R.: A semantic role-based methodology for knowledge acquisition from Spanish documents. Int. J. Phys. Sci. **6**(7), 1755–1765 (2011)
36. Subramaniam, T., Jalab, H.A., Taga, A.Y.: Overview of textual antispam filtering techniques. Int. J. Phys. Sci. **5**(12), 1869–1882 (2010)
37. Kotelnikov, E., Razova, E., Fishcheva, I.: A close look at russian morphological parsers: which one is the best? In: Filchenkov, A., Pivovarova, L., Žižka, J. (eds.) AINL 2017. CCIS, vol. 789, pp. 131–142. Springer, Cham (2018). https://doi.org/10.1007/978-3-319-71746-3_12
38. Ferrés, D., AbuRa'ed, A., Saggion, H.: Spanish morphological generation with wide-coverage lexicons and decision trees. Procesamiento del Lenguaje Natural, Sl, **58**, 109–116 (2017)
39. Vázquez-García, M.: (COMeIN) Disección de contenidos a partir de conceptos. http://comein.uoc.edu/divulgacio/comein/es/numero15/articles/Article-Merce-Vazquez.html. Accessed June 08 2018

Description and Analysis of Design Decisions: An Ontological Approach

Yordani Cruz Segura[1](✉), Nemury Silega Martínez[1],
Ailía Parra Fernández[1], and Oiner Gómez Baryolo[2]

[1] Universidad de las Ciencias Informáticas, Habana, Cuba
{ysegura,nsilega,ailiapf}@uci.cu
[2] Universidad Tecnológica ECOTEC, Guayaquil, Ecuador
ogomez@ecotec.edu.ec

Abstract. A success software development process requires a good design stage. During the design, a set of decisions is made in order to improve the productivity, reduce costs for reimplementation and obtain reliable systems, in special for critical domains, such as bank management systems or systems for aeronautics. Nevertheless, it is not easy to find documentation about design decisions or tools which support this process. To address this issue, this article describes a solution based on ontologies to describe design decisions. In order to identify the main elements a systematic literature review was carried out. This review also helped to identify some of the most common design decisions. These elements were used to develop the ontology which allows answering the problem raised. This ontology could be a useful tool for architects and designers during the design stage of a system.

Keywords: Ontology · Design decision · Software

1 Introduction

The software development has become one of the most prominent fields of the last times due to the application of continuous technological advances and a wide trend to the automation of tasks in every areas of society. A success software development process requires a good design stage. During the design, a set of decisions is made in order to improve the productivity, reduce costs for reimplementation and obtain reliable systems, in special for critical domains, such as bank management systems or systems for aeronautics.

In spite of the development of the software industry, it cannot be considered a success industry. For example, in 2015 only 29% of the projects were successful, while 52% and 19% of the projects were delayed and failed respectively [1]. Some of the main causes for these bad results are: problems with the specification, the insufficient participation of users and the lack of resources. The 10.7% of the consulted people considered that the adoption of little robust technologies to develop the systems is an important reason for the failure of such systems. Hence the selection of the technology is one of the most important design decisions in the beginning of a software development project [2].

R. Valencia-García et al. (Eds.): CITI 2018, CCIS 883, pp. 174–185, 2018.
https://doi.org/10.1007/978-3-030-00940-3_13

There are several factors that determine the number and quality of the design decisions, such as experience of the team that achieves this task as well as the adoption of good practices applied in success projects. The particular characteristics of the system and the adopted methodology are important factors too. Nevertheless, it is not easy to find information about design decisions and the impact of them. Therefore, a knowledge base with design decisions could be very useful. This knowledge base could be an instrument to assist to designers and architects in the process of making design decisions.

On the other hand, the ontologies are a suitable technology to represent knowledge. Hence, the objective of this article is to describe an ontology-based approach to describe design decisions. This approach could be useful to improve the quality of the design decision making process.

The structure of the paper is as follows. In the next section some related works are analyzed. In Sect. 3 basic concepts for the research are presented. Section 4 describes the approach to represent design decisions based on ontologies. In Sect. 5 the applicability of the approach is demonstrated through some examples. Finally, future work and conclusions are presented.

2   Related Works

In this section some researches that deal with representation of design decision are analyzed.

López et al. [3] created TREX, an approach composed by two ontologies (Toeska and NDR) which allows representing architecture design decisions. TREX allows loading information automatically about architecture which is represented in formal documents. This enables the automatic reasoning about this information. However, this proposal focuses on architecture decisions, so important design elements are out of scope, for example decisions about design patterns.

Gómez et al. [4] developed an ontology to represent the set of structural and behavioral diagrams as well as the GRASP and GoF patterns which are applied during the software design stage. The ontology represents basic concepts of design in order to be used by students enrolled in the career of Systems Engineering. This solution does not consider important design decisions, for example, the technologies to be adopted in the development of the software.

Ming et al. [5] created an ontology which represents the hierarchy of the design decisions. This approach is applied mainly in the design of complex systems which involve the design of main systems and dependent systems. This proposal is focused on addressing the design of systems developed following a hierarchical approach. Therefore, its scope is limited.

De Sousa et al. [6], propose to apply domain ontologies in agile software development to reduce the ambiguity caused by using natural language as ubiquitous language to report user stories. To demonstrate the applicability of the approach, they present a case study that combines Scrum and Behaviour-Driven Development (BDD) in the development of an educational support system. This approach is only based on user stories and does not consider design elements.

The approaches analyzed are usually dependent of the system characteristics and consider a low number of design decisions. These approaches are usually created to address a specific issue, for example the hierarchy among decisions.

3 Background

3.1 Software Design and Architecture

According to Somerville [7], the software design is a creative activity where components and their relations are identified considering the requirements of a client. The definition of the architecture is a crucial step during the software design stage. The community of software engineering has developed several definitions for architecture [8, 9]. However one the most interesting ones defines architecture as a set of design decisions [10]. This definition remarks the relevance of the design decisions. Architecture also deals with the concerns about the quality of the systems [11].

3.2 Ontology

The researchers in the Artificial Intelligence field, specially the researchers of the knowledge representation field understood the benefits of adopting the ontologies to describe the knowledge in order to be analyzed by intelligent systems [12]. An ontology is a formal explicit description of concepts in a domain of discourse (classes (sometimes called concepts), properties of each concept describing various features and attributes of the concept (slots (sometimes called roles or properties)), and restrictions on slots (facets (sometimes called role restrictions)) [13]. In the scientific literature it is possible to find a wide number of approaches which exploit ontologies to describe and analyze several elements of architecture [3–5, 14, 15] as well as other areas [16–18].

4 Ontology-Based Approach to Represent Design Decisions

4.1 Usual Design Decisions

The systematic review of the literature [19] allows identifying the characteristics of the approaches that deal with design decisions during the development of a software. The number of research works demonstrated the interest of the design decisions for the scientific community. The review yielded 79 publications, 15 of them are relevant for this research [2, 7, 11, 14, 20–30]. Eleven of these publications are journal articles, three classical books and two magister thesis. The authors of the publications belong to 13 countries. This fact evidences the international interest for this topic. Figure 1 depicts the distribution of countries per authors.

After the analysis of the 15 works, 14 design decisions were identified. Table 1 shows the representativeness of each design decision according to the number of works that consider it.

Among the design decisions with the highest percentage of representativeness are those related to the definition of design patterns, architectural patterns, components,

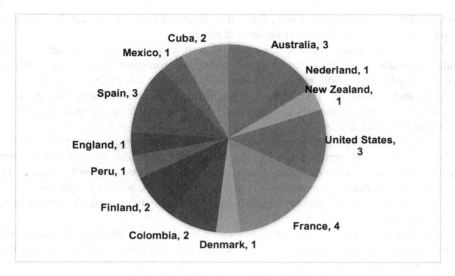

Fig. 1. Distribution of authors per country

Table 1. Most common design decisions

No.	Design decisions	Representativeness (%)
1	Define the design patterns	80.0
2	Define the architecture patterns	66.6
3	Define the design methodology	13.3
4	Define components and their relations	73.3
5	Define the navigation model	13.3
6	Define the graphical user interface design	73.3
7	Define structure of the data base and the information to be recorded	66.6
8	Select the CASE tools	6.6
9	Define the architectonic styles	53.3
10	Define the architectonic views	40.0
11	Define the development tools	40.0
12	Define the internal and external interface comunications	73.3
13	Define the codifications and modeling standards	20.0
14	Define the solution to distribute the system	13.3

subsystems, design classes and their relations. The definition of communication interfaces between the application components and external systems in the design stage is an issue widely discussed in the literature. This last issue has received the attention of the scientific community in recent times due to the increasing of the interoperability between the systems found on the market today and the need for them to communicate and to operate in an integrated way. Since the objects and subsystems can be designed in parallel, the interfaces have to be defined clearly.

On the other hand, a pattern is a description of a problem and the essence of its solution, so that the solution can be reused in different configurations. The patterns are not a detailed specification, rather, it can be considered as a description of accumulated wisdom and experience, a well-tested solution to a common problem. The patterns should include information about when and how it is suitable to use it as well as its strengths and weaknesses [7].

A good selection of both design and architecture patterns guarantees to have tested solutions and avoids spending time developing solutions that already exist and that are published by the national or international community. A good decision lies in linking more than one pattern in our solution. This depends on the characteristics of the system to be developed and the functional and non-functional requirements that the system must guarantee.

The design of the user interface is another of the most cited design decisions in the consulted bibliography. This demonstrates the importance of the user interfaces and the acceptance of end users.

The design of the user interface creates a means of communication between man and machine. During this design, the objects and actions of the interface are identified and a screen format that will form the basis of the user interface prototype is created [23].

Defining the information to be stored and the structure of the data is a fundamental issue within the data architecture. The structure of the data has always been an important part of software design. At the level of the components of the program, the design of the data structures and the associated algorithms required for their manipulation are the essential part in the creation of high quality applications [23].

On the other hand, the definition of architecture views is another of the decisions highlighted in the revised bibliography. The views are responsible for representing how a system is composed by modules, as well as the way that components of the system are distributed through a network. Furthermore, the views are useful at several stages of the software development process, for example to carry out the system design the definition of multiple views of the software architecture is required [7].

In order to complement the findings of the literature review and to know the opinion of software development specialists about this 14 design decisions, a focal group (FG) was applied. The focal group is a particular group discussion that helps to obtain different perspectives about the discussion object [30]. To apply the FG three groups were created. Each group is composed by researchers and specialists with experience in the discussion topic. Two meetings were held. In the first meeting the 14 design decisions already identified were presented and each group gave some ideas about these design decisions. In the second meeting, the three groups got together to discuss about the ideas that each group gave independently. The discussion yielded the follow conclusions:

- Discard the design decisions with low level of representativeness, such as the definition CASE tools, the design methodology, the standard definition and others with low level of representativeness.

- The definition of the architectonic style was remarked because several decisions depend on this one.

After the execution of the review and the FG, an ontology-based method to represent design decisions was elaborated.

4.2 Definition of the Method

Figure 2 depicts the six activities that the method includes: *analyze software requirements, analyze knowledge base, identify relevant concepts, identify concepts not considered in the ontology, update the ontology and describe design decisions.*

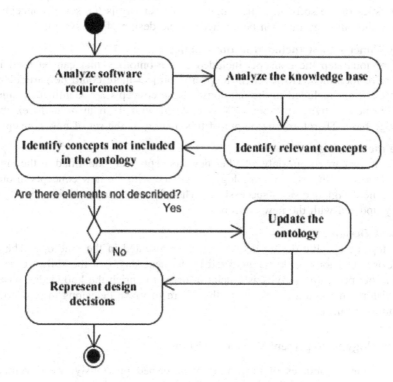

Fig. 2. Activities diagram of the method

The method is defined to be applied after the execution of the software requirement stage. Some details about the activities are described below:

Analyze Software Requirements
The descriptions of functional and non-functional requirements are the input for this activity. In this step the designers and architects make a deep study of requirements in order to make a proposal of system design and architectonic structure to guarantee their fulfillment.

Analyze the Knowledge Base
For the execution of this activity a knowledge base with descriptions of design decisions is required. This work considered as knowledge base the ontology which was developed with the results of the review and the application of the focal group. During the first execution of this step, only the structure of the ontology will be available because no design decisions have been made; therefore instances in the ontology will not exist. Once the ontology has data of design decisions, it will be consulted and analyzed in order to improve the design decisions making process.

Identify Relevant Concepts
After the analysis of the knowledge base, designers and architects must identify the concepts that can be adopted by their particular system regarding the requirements and characteristics of the software. The output of this activity is the set of concepts considered in the ontology that can be applied for the design of the system.

Identify Concepts not Included in the Ontology
In the previous step the concepts included in the ontology that can be used in the project were identified. However, in a specific project there could be particular concepts that are not included in the ontology. These concepts are identified in this step and in the next activity; the ontology is updated with them in order to extend the knowledge base. Therefore, the output of this activity is the set of new concepts.

Update the Ontology
This activity is carried out only whether new concepts were identified in the previous activity. Hence, in this step the ontology is updated with the new concepts in order to represent the design decisions successfully. Therefore, the output of this activity is the ontology updated with the new concepts.

Represent Design Decisions
In this step the specific design decisions are represented in the ontology. Therefore, these design decisions could be analyzed in the next stages of the software development. Furthermore, this activity is crucial in order to enrich the knowledge base with new decisions that could be useful in the future to make decisions in new software development projects.

4.3   Ontology to Represent Design Decisions

To exploit the advantages of the ontology described previously, we developed an ontology to represent design decisions. There are several languages to represent ontologies, i.e. On Ontolingua, XML Schema, RDF (Resource Description Framework), RDF Schema (o RDF-S) y OWL (Ontology Web Language). OWL is distinguished because of its set of operators: intersection, union and negation. It is based on a logical model which allows defining the concepts similar to their descriptions. Furthermore, the option of using reasoners allows checking the consistence of the models automatically [31]. Due to these advantages, we chose OWL as the language to represent the ontology. Furthermore, the tool Protégé was adopted to create and edit the ontology. Protégé is a free tool that is widely adopted for the manipulation of ontologies in OWL.

Classes, properties, restrictions and instances are the most important components of an ontology. Figure 3 depicts some of the 93 classes that were identified. The flexibility of the method allows updating the ontology if new concepts are identified during the design stage of a Project. The other key component of the ontologies are the properties which represent the relations of the classes. We defined several object properties to represent relations among classes as well as data properties to describe the classes with simple metadata.

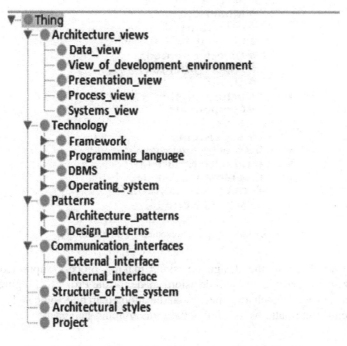

Fig. 3. Entity of the ontology to represent design decisions

5   Validation of the Approach

In order to demonstrate the applicability of the method we carried out the defined activities. Finally, we obtained an ontology to represent design decisions. For checking the quality of this ontology we applied a validation method [18], which evaluates the ontology through:

- Checking its properties as formal logical system.
- Testing that the ontologies fulfill its requirements.

The reasoners are widely used to check the logical-formal properties of the ontology [18]. In this case we used Pellet which demonstrated that the ontology achieves the requirements defined for an ontology in OWL 2.

On the other hand, to proof the applicability of the ontology to support the design decisions process, we represented the design decisions of a specific Project. Figure 4 shows instances of the classes specified in the ontology. In the ontology, seven of the most popular architecture patterns were represented. Likewise we considered the results of the literature review to represent the design decisions.

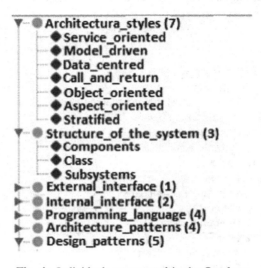

Fig. 4. Individuals represented in the Ontology

In order to illustrate the design decisions making process supported with the ontology, we described eight design decisions made for the Project X. Figure 5 depicts these design decisions which are related with the adopted architectonic style, the design patterns, architecture patterns as well as the programming language.

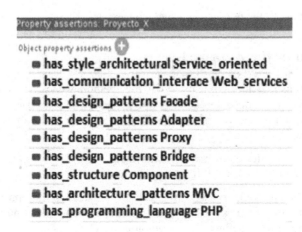

Fig. 5. Design decisions for the Project X

The adoption of ontologies to describe design decisions allows the use of reasoners to validate the descriptions as well as to make inferences that could be interesting to support de design decision process. For example, Fig. 6 shows that the reasoner inferred that PHP is the programming language of two projects and the basic language of the platform Symfony. This information could be very useful for the designers and architects to decide the programming language to be adopted because now they can know the programing languages adopted in other projects.

Fig. 6. Inferences of the reasoner

6 Conclusions

The literature review and the application of the focal group allow identifying usual design decisions. An ontology-based method to describe design decisions was developed. This method is composed by six activities and supports the work of designers and architects during the design decisions making process. An ontology in OWL is a formal language to represent knowledge. Hence the information represented about design decisions can be formally analyzed and validated. Specifically, the use of reasoners enable checking the consistence of the represented information. With the systematic application of this method the knowledge base will grow and will be a useful instrument for designers and architects during the development of software. The validation method used allowed to verify the logical-formal properties of the ontology and demonstrated that it meets the established requirements.

References

1. Standish Group 2015 Chaos Report: https://www.infoq.com/articles/standish-chaos-2015. Accessed 29 Mar 2018
2. Tibermacine, C., et al.: Software architecture constraint reuse-by-composition. Future Gener. Comput. Syst. **61**, 37–53 (2016)
3. López, C., et al.: Bridging the gap between software architecture rationale formalisms and actual architecture documents: an ontology-driven approach. Sci. Comput. Program. **77**(1), 66–80 (2012)
4. Gómez, G.L.G., Acevedo, J.F., Moreno, D.A.: Una ontología para la representación de conceptos de diseño de software. Avances en Sistemas e Informática **8**(3), 103–110 (2011)

5. Ming, Z., et al.: Ontology-based representation of design decision hierarchies. J. Comput. Inf. Sci. Eng. **18**(1), 0110011–01100112 (2018)
6. de Souza, P.L., do Prado, A.F., de Souza, W.L., dos SFP, S.M., Pires, L.F.: Improving Agile Software development with domain ontologies. In: Latifi, S. (ed.) Information Technology— New Generations. AISC, vol. 738, pp. 267–274. Springer, Cham (2018). https://doi.org/10. 1007/978-3-319-77028-4_37
7. Somerville, I.: Ingeniería de Software. PEARSON EDUCACIÓN, México (2011)
8. Perry, D.E., Wolf, A.L.: Foundations for the study of software architecture. ACM SIGSOFT Softw. Eng. Notes **17**(4), 40–52 (1992)
9. Bass, L., Clements, P., Kazman, R.: Software Architecture in Practice. Addison-Wesley Professional, Boston (2003)
10. Shaw, M.: Research toward an engineering discipline for software. In: Proceedings of the FSE/SDP Workshop on Future of Software Engineering Research, pp. 337–342. ACM (2010)
11. Galaster, M., Mirakhorli, M., Medvidovic, N.: Bringing architecture thinking into developers' daily activities. ACM SIGSOFT Softw. Eng. Notes **41**(6), 24–26 (2017)
12. Welty, C., Guarino, N.: Supporting ontological analysis of taxonomic relationships. Data Knowl. Eng. **39**(1), 51–74 (2001)
13. Noy, N.F., et al.: Ontology development 101: a guide to creating your first ontology (2001)
14. Chauhan, M.A., Babar, M.A., Sheng, Q.Z.: A reference architecture for provisioning of tools as a service: meta-model, ontologies and design elements. Future Gener. Comput. Syst. **69**, 41–65 (2017)
15. Silega, N., Nogera, M., Macias, D.: Ontology-based transformation from CIM to PIM. IEEE Latin Am. Trans. **14**(9), 4156–4416 (2016)
16. López, Y.A., Hidalgo, Y., Silega, N.: Método para la integración de ontologías en un sistema para la evaluación de créditos. Revista Cubana de Ciencias Informáticas **10**(4), 97–111 (2016)
17. Silega, N., Laureiro, T.T., Noguera, M.: Model-driven and ontology-based framework for semantic description and validation of business processes. IEEE Latin Am. Trans. **12**(2), 292–299 (2014)
18. Guerrero, R.S.: Ontología para la representación de las preferencias del estudiante en la actividad de aprendizaje en entornos virtuales. Tesis Doctoral, Cuba (2012)
19. Petersen, K., Ali, N.B.: Identifying strategies for study selection in systematic reviews and maps. In: International Symposium on Empirical Software Engineering and Measurement (ESEM), pp. 351–354. IEEE (2011)
20. Van Vliet, H., Tang, A.: Decision making in software architecture. J. Syst. Softw. **17**, 638–644 (2016)
21. Silva, D., Mercerat, B.: Construyendo aplicaciones web con una metodología de diseño orientada a objetos. Revista Colombiana de Computación–RCC **2**(2) (2001)
22. Leinonen, T., Durall, E.: Pensamiento de diseño y aprendizaje colaborativo. Comunicar **21** (42) (2014)
23. Jacobson, I., Booch, G., Rumbaugh, J.: El proceso unificado de desarrollo de software. Pearson Educación (2000)
24. Pressman, R.S.: Ingeniería del software. Un enfoque práctico. McGraw-Hill, México (2010)
25. Norma técnica peruana NTP ISO/IEC 12207: Tecnología de la información. Procesos del ciclo de vida del software. Comisión de Reglamentos Técnicos y Comerciales (2006)
26. Codorniú, C.L.: Solución arquitectónica de la configuración general del sistema para la parametrización de negocio de Cedrux. Tesis de Maestría, Cuba (2011)

27. León, A.R.S., Ramírez, M.D.H.: Modelo de descripción de arquitectura de almacenes de datos para ensayos clínicos del Centro de Inmunología Molecular. Revista Cubana de Ingeniería **3**(1), 15–20 (2012)
28. López, J.A., et al.: Ingeniería de software aplicada a la educación en el área de matemáticas. Pistas Educativas **36**(114) (2018)
29. Medina, I.I.S., Rojas, F.M., Medina, J.M.C.: Diseño de software para calcular la huella de carbono e hídrica durante la producción de café. J. Eng. Educ. **14**(24) (2018)
30. Jumbo, L.A., et al.: Desarrollo de Aplicación Web para la Gestión de Producción de Camarón. Revista ESPACIOS **39**(04) (2018)
31. Trujillo, Y.: Modelo para valorar las organizaciones desarrolladoras de software al iniciar la mejora de procesos. Tesis Doctoral, Cuba (2014)
32. Silega, N., et al.: Framework basado en ontología para la descripción y validación de procesos de negocio. Ingeniería Industrial **38**(3) (2017)

Analysis of Traditional Web Security Solutions and Proposal of a Web Attacks Cognitive Patterns Classifier Architecture

Carlos Martínez Santander[1,2] , Sang Guun Yoo[1,3(✉)] ,
and Hugo Oswaldo Moreno[4]

[1] Facultad de Ingeniería de Sistemas, Escuela Politécnica Nacional, Quito,
Ecuador
{carlos.martinez03, sang.yoo}@epn.edu.ec
[2] Carrera de Medicina, Universidad Católica de Cuenca, Cuenca, Ecuador
[3] Departamento de Ciencias de la Computación,
Universidad de las Fuerzas Armadas ESPE, Sangolquí, Ecuador
[4] Facultad de Informática y Electrónica, Escuela Superior Politécnica de
Chimborazo, Riobamba, Ecuador
h_moreno@espoch.edu.ec

Abstract. The present work proposes a security architecture for web servers called Web Attacks Cognitive Patterns Classifier, which makes use of cognitive security concepts to deliver a more complete solution than existing ones. The architecture proposes the development of an integrated software solution where existing tools such as Elasticsearch, Logstash and Kibana are incorporated. The proposed system will be nurtured using data of attacks obtained from honeypots implemented in hacker communities; such data will be analyzed by using machine learning algorithms and behavioral parameters to determinate attack patterns and classifications. The present work also makes a literature review of existing web security solutions, to understand their limitations and to explain the reasons why the creation of the proposed architecture was necessary. We can say that usage of different technologies oriented to a specific problem can generate better solutions; in the case of this work, different technologies such as ELK Stack, Cognitive Security, Machine Learning techniques and Honeypots have been combined for the assurance, prevention and proactive security of Web Servers.

Keywords: Cognitive security · Web attacks · Cybercriminals
Machine learning

1 Introduction

Security has been considered a very important issue in different areas of computer sciences such as electronic devices [1–3], network [4–6], software engineering [7], among others, and security in Internet applications is not the exception. Internet Security Threat Report published by Symantec Corporation reports that web attacks were one of the highest incidence caused in 2016 with around 229,000 attacks per day.

© Springer Nature Switzerland AG 2018
R. Valencia-García et al. (Eds.): CITI 2018, CCIS 883, pp. 186–198, 2018.
https://doi.org/10.1007/978-3-030-00940-3_14

A study carried out by the same company on vulnerability scanning in web servers resulted that more than three quarters of websites worldwide have vulnerabilities, of which 9% are critical [8]. The most sought-after sites by cybercriminals are those with technology and business content, since they generate more economic value. However, the economic reason is not the only one that motivates attackers to commit this type of crime. Nowadays, there is a large number of sites that are being hacked by hacktivist groups (being most of them from countries that are at war e.g. as Syria and Pakistan) or by groups sponsored by governments. One of the most used techniques by these groups is defacement which consists on making changes to the visual appearance of the site; list of servers hacked with this modality can be found at www.zone-h.org [9].

Given the growing threat in the cyber world, new security solutions are proposed continuously. Among them, cognitive security is considered one of the most important trend. Cognitive systems help to improve the security by monitoring threats on a global scale and preparing themselves for possible attacks. Cognitive systems also facilitate the work of security analysts, providing human-centered tools such as advanced visualizations, interactive vulnerability analysis, and risk assessment [10, 11]. The three main pillars of the cognitive security are: (1) organization and understanding of unstructured data and natural language text, (2) reasoning based on the ability to interpret and organize information, and (3) continuous learning from the accumulated data and knowledge extracted from the interactions [10].

Given these changes in security trends, this paper proposes a simple but useful security model for classifying cyberattacks in specific patterns which are created from a learning process based on previous attacks, which is called as Web-attacks Cognitive Patterns Classifier (WCPC). WCPC will use machine learning techniques to classify attacks according to detected cognitive patterns. For gathering attacks' data (which will be used for the generation of cognitive patterns), honeypots with intentional vulnerabilities will be published in different hacker communities.

The rest of the paper is organized as follows. First, Sect. 2 explains some of the concepts used in this work. Then, Sect. 3 develops a systematic literature review of current security solutions for web servers. Later, Sect. 4 details the proposed WCPC architecture. Finally, Sect. 5 concludes this paper and explains the future works.

2 Background

This section explains some concepts and technologies used in this paper.

2.1 Computer Security Solutions

Computer security solutions have evolved rapidly over time. Around the year 2000, computer security was focused on techniques based on detection, analysis and elimination of malicious codes using specialized software (antivirus), which objective was to ensure Endpoint Protection [10]. From 2005, the security solutions were focused on networking devices which detected anomalies in network traffic; they made it possible to alert security personnel when there was unusual traffic. In this period, a new term called Security Intelligence became popular [11]; this technology consisted in analytics of massive amount of real-time data to detect possible attacks. For 2010, technologies were more robust and they analyzed, in addition to network traffic, server logs and devices; in other words, reactive security is left aside and proactive security was born [12]. From 2015 until now, a new concept of security called Cognitive Security is being studied; this technology fixes its bases in security intelligence but with a further vision, where systems were able to understand, reason and learn. This kind of systems make use of artificial intelligence to simulate the human thought process with the ability to analyze structured and unstructured data, and understand their behaviors and meanings. Cognitive systems untangle vulnerabilities by connecting points, detecting divergences and searching millions of events to feed the knowledge database [13].

2.2   Cybercriminal

Cybercriminals are those people who access to computer systems without permission, generating fraud and/or computer abuse. Many researches focus on determining what motivates hackers to cause these disturbances. Results of such researches indicate that most of attackers are key employees of the same companies and they execute such activities to obtain professional and/or economic recognition, and in some cases, for fun or revenge [12].

2.3   Artificial Intelligence

The objective of Artificial Intelligence is to reproduce the reasoning of people in machines. This objective is achieved by executing two activities i.e. (1) by imitating the method of reasoning, which requires psychological experiments manipulating cognitive science, and (2) by replicating the functionality of the brain, which is supported by neurobiology [14].

2.4   Machine Learning

Machine learning belongs to the disciplines of Artificial Intelligence; it is responsible for information optimization and it is supported by information theory, statistics and cognitive science. This technique allows computers to learn to discover, recognize patterns, and make predictions automatically. Furthermore, it deepens underlying relationships that exist in the thousands of data that are handled. This field has evolved as the volume of data and its complexity have grown on a large scale [14–18].

Machine Learning has solved a variety of problems and it was used in different applications fields, such as search engines, automatic control systems, recognition systems, and data mining. This field is typically classified into two general categories: (1) supervised learning that learns from tagged data obtaining desired inputs and outputs, and (2) unsupervised learning that learns from the environment, providing only inputs without desired objectives and reinforcement [16].

2.5 Honeypots

Honeypot is a security instrument created to be explored, attacked and compromised; its goal is the detection and recognition of the malicious actions. This tool is very important since it helps to understand different kind of attacks and get answers of security problems from those incidents. This mechanism makes a hacker to spend his effort since he/she does think that the honeypot is a real server with important information [19].

3 Previous Works on Web Security

3.1 Existing Web Security Solutions

To have a holistic perspective of current web security solution, this work has executed a study of the state of the art on the subject. This section shows the advantages, disadvantages, and limitations found in previous works. In the following, several of efforts in delivering web securities are described. Additionally, the summary of the analysis is shown in Table 1.

SkyShield is an architecture developed to counteract against Distributed Denial of Service (DDoS) attacks [34]. This solution quickly reduces malicious requests, generating a limited impact on normal users. The problem of this architecture lies in its high rate of false positives. Another proposed solution is a vulnerability scanner called Black-Box Fuzzing [37]; this work delivers good results in detecting security flaws, however, its limitation lies in the fact that it is just an isolated security solution and in the fact that there is no studies that evaluate systematically the performance of this tool.

Another security alternative for protecting databases is Misery Digraphs [28]. It proposes the concealment of the route where the website's database is stored. This solution makes attackers take longer time to achieve his/her goal, reaching up to 1000 steps before discovering the route. Support Vector Machines (SVM) based solution [33] is an improved proposal in relation to the previous one. The idea is to integrate the already discovered attack patterns and train an SVM to improve detection rate; the limitation of the solution lies in the generation of a large number of alerts since the entire process is not completely automated.

The statistical analysis methods also have been used in web security solutions e.g. SAT [38]. SAT combines several methods to analyze information and to reduce false positives generated by IDSs.

Finally, there are also many studies such as references [31, 39–43] to stop DDoS, SQL injection, and Cross-site Script attacks. Furthermore, there are solutions based on cryptography [29], policy-based management of the distributed system, security in JavaScript [30], browser security, and semantic analysis of web protocols [31], among others.

As mentioned before, given the complexity of the web, research efforts in this area are scattered around many different issues and problems, and until now, a complete development of web security is not achieved. In this situation, the present work proposes a theoretical architecture that is capable of responding with proactive features based on cognitive security and patterns generated in the different known attacks.

Table 1. Literature review of different web security solutions

Attack	Solutions	Applications or Description	Limitation	Required Future works
Attacks to databases (SQL)	LogitBoost [27]	NSL KDD, UNSW-NB15	Limited capacity of the system to store the traffic of new entrances (benign and malicious) and to evaluate False Alarm Rate, Detection Rate and Accuracy	Algorithm improvement based on an enhanced database to store executed attacks for comparison and discarding
	Misery Digraphs [28]	Hides the network path of the asset	Limited storage capacity of the database	Algorithm improvement for its best concealment
	GroupSec [29]	Http, https, http-GS	Require additional loads when the cache is not in the network path. Sustainable load equivalent to regular http. Page load latency	Adapt Https to GroupSec by changing protocols and demonstrating resistance against attack vectors
	Model-based analysis of Java EE web security misconfigurations [30]	Applied to GitHub repositories of Java Web EE projects	Programmatic security restrictions, access security restriction of underlying data, concealment	Take advantage of results incorporated in the study and extract Java models using engineering techniques that explore the extraction of security limits from database systems
	ORE [31]	Ontology Rule Editor Editor. Security based on rules	It need to consider more features	Refine policies from the point of high-level security and low-level configuration

(continued)

Table 1. (*continued*)

Attack	Solutions	Applications or Description	Limitation	Required Future works
Attacks to IDS	Data mining based Approach [32]	Intrusion Detection Systems (IDSs) are one of the components of Defense-in-depth.	Data mining techniques are limited because it is difficult to deal with asymmetric class distribution, learn from data streams and label network connections	Develop a general framework to improve the problem of asymmetric distribution
	Support vector Machines (SVM) [33]	ANN	Applying this algorithm with vital and selected data decreases the accuracy of anomaly detection	Include sensitivity selector in the IDS
DDoS	SkyShield [34]	Bloom Filters (Black, White Lists) to filter requests	The processing time is affected by hash function calculations	Integrate CAPTCHA techniques, capability based mobile defense mechanisms and proxy nodes to obtain an effective network traffic monitor for DDoS attacks
	Model-based analysis of Java EE web security misconfigurations [30]	Applied to GitHub repositories of Java Web EE projects	Programmatic security restrictions, access security restriction of underlying data, concealment	Take advantage of results incorporated in the study and extract Java models using engineering techniques that explore the extraction of security limits from database systems

(*continued*)

Table 1. (*continued*)

Attack	Solutions	Applications or Description	Limitation	Required Future works
	GroupSec [29]	Http, https, http-GS	Incur additional loads when the cache is not in the network path Sustainable load equivalent to regular http Page load latency	Adapt Https to GroupSec by changing minimally protocols and demonstrating resistance against attack vectors
	SPRECON-E [35]	Encrypted network management protocol	Additional skills are needed in the field of IT security	Implementation of the proposed solution
Code related attacks (Cross-site-script)	Model-based analysis of Java EE web security misconfigurations [30]	Applied to GitHub repositories of Java Web EE projects	Programmatic security restrictions, access security restriction of underlying data, concealment	Take advantage of results incorporated in the study and extract Java models using engineering techniques that explore the extraction of security limits from database systems
	HOP [36]	Prevents attacks automatically reviewing the syntax of the program	The author does not provide information about the application	Improve Programming Level
	SQLCHECK [36]	Protection on Code injection Attacks for PHP and JSP applications	It does not generate queries with user inputs	Crear Place holder
	CANDID [36]	Transforms programs syntactically	The execution times in the input query can infer vulnerabilities and software errors	Improve the execution times in the input queries

(*continued*)

Table 1. (*continued*)

Attack	Solutions	Applications or Description	Limitation	Required Future works
Security Flaws	Black-box Fuzzing [37]	Web vulnerabilities Scanner	It is not a complete solution	Performance evaluation of this solution
	SAT [38]	Static Analysis Tools for Web Security	Not effective solution since it is generic and depends on other free tools. It does not always improve the performance of vulnerability detection	Combine with other tools to improve results

3.2 Fields Where Cognitive Security has Been Applied

Cognitive systems have been used in different technological environments such as Intelligent Transportation Systems where the cognitive algorithms have helped to optimize the safety of passengers [23]. Lately, this area is also beginning to flourish in the area of computer security. For example, K. Gale presents a cognitive architecture for the analysis of information stored in an information system [20]. On the other hand, J. Morris Chang proposes a cognitive security architecture focused on user authentication; the work uses machine-learning techniques to collect the keystrokes of users, classify them and create different profiles according to the cognitive patterns [21]. Additionally, Sumari proposes a model that, through artificial cognitive intelligence, tries to recreate the functionality of the human brain applied to computer security systems in a general way [22]. These researches are not the only ones. For B.A. Usha, the idea of cognitive cryptography has been adapted to give rise to cognitive steganography [24]. The purpose of the developed application is to decide the most suitable steganography approach to hide input data, considering its semantic meaning and the intended application. On the other hand, J. Park studies information management intelligence systems based on cognitive techniques that analyze processes and support strategic decision-making [11]. The cognitive analysis carried out by an Understanding Based Managing Support System (UBMLRSS) [25] includes not only the evaluation of the current company, but also the reasoning based on the analyzed data. Finally, L. Ogiela describes a new paradigm of cognitive cryptography [25, 26]. This new scientific area is marked by a new generation of information systems focused on the development of intelligent cryptographic protocols and procedures that use cognitive approaches to processing information. This work shows how the systems are designed to perform semantic analysis of encrypted data to select the most appropriate method of encryption.

In summary, cognitive security has been applied in several fields; however, such technology has not been widely used in a specific solution in the field of web security. Given this background, this paper aims to propose a simple but useful cognitive security architecture for the delivery of protection to web servers.

4   Web-Attacks Cognitive Patterns Classifier Architecture

This work proposes a theoretical architecture to protect web servers based on data gathered by honeypots. In the first instance, several honeypots with WCPC will be published on hacker communities for collecting information about the different attack techniques. Honeypots will gather the data that will be used for analysis of cognitive patterns left by the hackers. The data will be analyzed with different Machine Learning techniques to deduce the best one for patterns classification. The Machine Learning algorithm may be an unsupervised learning algorithm either clustering or principal Component analysis (PCA). For data analysis, several characteristics of attacks will be used such as time zone (even though, intermediary machines e.g. VPN and Botnet are used generally in attacks), attack technique, fingerprint erase techniques, and key-strokes [21].

- As shown in Fig. 1, WCPC is composed of the following elements:

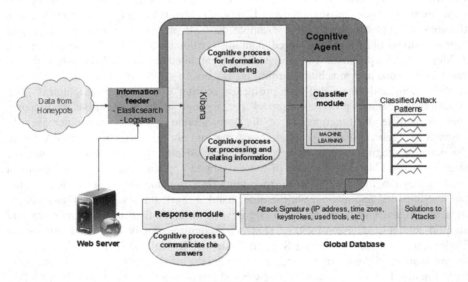

Fig. 1. WCPC architecture

- Information feeder: It is in charge of obtaining the information from the Internet using Elasticsearch. It allows to generate a search engine with multi-tendency capability. On the other hand, Logstash will be used to classify the information of the logs coming from the Honeypots [38–40].

- Cognitive Agent: This module consists of cognitive processes for gathering information, for processing and related information, and for communicating results. This component will use Machine Learning techniques supported by Kibana, which will be used for the analysis of the collected information by the Information Feeder. The processed information will contain the cognitive patterns of the attackers. After evaluation of the patterns, the information are stored in Global Database [44–46].
- Global Database: All the attack information, once classified, will be stored in this database according to their signatures i.e. attacker's IP address, time zone, keystrokes, used tools, and left traces. The Database also contains other important data such as URL of pages that have been hacked (extracted from pages where they publish this information e.g. http://www.zone-h.org) and answers/solutions to the attacks.
- Response Module: Response module will take an action to prevent or mitigate the attack by using the solutions already known for the type of the attack. The type of the attack is known thanks to the classification of the cognitive patterns. Each response will be stored within the Global Database to records system's activities.

The aforementioned elements interacts each other executing the following processes:

- Pre-classification: This process is executed by the Information Feeder and consists on collecting information of attacks from honeypots and Internet. In this process, two open source tools are incorporated: (1) Logstach collects logs of devices for subsequent searches; on the other hand, (2) Elasticsearch contributes to the cognitive process through searches in data that is being modified in real time.
- Cognitive process: In this process, the collected information are analyzed using a series of parameters. Kibana, a tool that allows to explore, visualize and Discover Elasticsearch data, supports this process by allowing the classification of the information according to given parameters. For example, if the attacker performs a port reading (using tools such as nmap, nbtscan, and metasploit) in the fingerprinting stage, this activity is stored in the logs; the classifier module will relate the extracted information to a classification pattern.
- Classification process: This process is executed by the Classifier Module, which will be in charge of the definitive evaluation of the information. The evaluated information will be stored in the corresponding database according to its classification.
- Response process: This process is executed once the Global Database is implemented. When a web servers with WCPC receives an attack already known by the system, the Response Module executes the different solutions included in the Global Database.

ELK Stack (Elasticsearch, Logstash and Kibana) was selected since they allow obtaining and analyzing data in real time. It means that this set of tools becomes very useful for the present project since it will allow to obtain and analyze data from the logs of honeypots. Another reason of using such tools is because they are open source which means that such tools could be modified with new features of adaptations if were required.

5   Conclusions and Future Works

In this article, a web server security architecture based on cognitive approach is proposed. We have proposed the usage of cognitive security since it advances day by day, and since the effectiveness of this technology has been proved in other fields with good results. The presented architecture provides a theoretical solution for detecting attacks through cognitive processes, where the pre-classification of information reveals the strategy of the attackers and machine learning algorithms allows learning from the threats that the systems face. The main advantages of the proposed system is the constant gathering of new data about attacks and solutions against them. We can say that usage of different technologies oriented to a specific problem can generate better solutions; in the case of this work, different technologies such as ELK Stack, Cognitive Security, Machine Learning techniques and Honeypots have been combined for the assurance, prevention and proactive security of Web Servers.

Since this paper only includes the initial part of the research, the implementation and experimentation of the proposed architecture is left for future works. Additionally, as future work, this research could be applied to the Digital Forensics field to apply the Cognitive Security technology to collect specific patterns of successfully perpetrated attacks.

References

1. Yoo, S.G., Park, K.Y., Kim, J.: Confidential information protection system for mobile devices. Secur. Commun. Netw. 5(12), 1452–1461 (2012)
2. Kim, D.J., Chung, K.W., Hong, K.S.: Person authentication using face, teeth and voice modalities for mobile device security. IEEE Trans. Consum. Electron. 56(4), 2678–2685 (2010)
3. Park, K.Y., Yoo, S.G., Kim, J.: Debug port protection mechanism for secure embedded devices. J. Semicond. Technol. Sci. 12(2), 240–253 (2012)
4. Yoo, S.G., Kang, S.H., Kim, J.: SERA: a secure energy and reliability aware data gathering for sensor networks. In: Proceedings of 2010 International Conference on Information Science and Applications, Seoul, South Korea. IEEE (2010)
5. Ren, Z., Liu, H.: Design and implementation of network security transmission system for intelligent home video surveillance. In: Proceedings of 2018 International Conference on Electronics Technology (ICET), pp. 398–402 (2018)
6. Yoo, S.G.: 5G-VRSec: secure video reporting service in 5G enabled vehicular networks. Wirel. Commun. Mob. Comput. (2017). Article number 7256307
7. Park, K.-Y., Yoo, S.-G., Kim, J.: Security requirements prioritization based on threat modeling and valuation graph. Commun. Comput. Inf. Sci. 206, 142–152 (2011)
8. Symantec: Internet Security Threat Report ISTR (2017)
9. Cybenko, G., Giani, A., Thompson, P.: Cognitive hacking. Adv. Comput. 60, 35–73 (2004)
10. IBM: Cognitive security. IBM Security, p. 11 (2016)
11. Ogiela, M.R., Ogiela, L.: Security of cognitive information systems. In: Park, J.J.(Jong Hyuk), Barolli, L., Xhafa, F., Jeong, H.Y. (eds.) Information Technology Convergence. LNEE, vol. 253, pp. 427–433. Springer, Dordrecht (2013). https://doi.org/10.1007/978-94-007-6996-0_44

12. Armstrong, H.L., Forde, P.J.: Internet anonymity practices in computer crime. Inf. Manag. Comput. Secur. **11**(5), 209–215 (2003)
13. Thill, S.: Considerations for a neuroscience-inspired approach to the design of artificial intelligent systems. In: Schmidhuber, J., Thórisson, K.R., Looks, M. (eds.) AGI 2011. LNCS (LNAI), vol. 6830, pp. 247–254. Springer, Heidelberg (2011). https://doi.org/10.1007/978-3-642-22887-2_26
14. Bailly, S., Meyfroidt, G., Timsit, J.F.: What's new in ICU in 2050: big data and machine learning. Intensiv. Care Med. **44**(9), 1–4 (2017)
15. Abadi, M., et al.: TensorFlow: Large-Scale Machine Learning on Heterogeneous Distributed Systems (2016)
16. Holzinger, A.: Interactive machine learning for health informatics: when do we need the human-in-the-loop? Brain Inform. **3**(2), 119–131 (2016)
17. Blum, A.L., Langley, P.: Selection of relevant features and examples in machine learning. Artif. Intell. **97**(1–2), 245–271 (1997)
18. Qiu, J., Wu, Q., Ding, G., Xu, Y., Feng, S.: A survey of machine learning for big data processing. EURASIP J. Adv. Signal Process. **2016**(1), 67 (2016)
19. Ogweno, K.L., Oteyo, O.E., Ochieng, H.D.: Honey pot intrusion detection system. Int. J. Eng. Invent. **4**(5), 2278–7461 (2014)
20. Kroeck, K.G., Kirs, P.J., Fiedler, A.M.: Cognitive biasing effects in information systems: implications for linking real world information with human judgment. In: Proceedings of the Twenty-Second Annual Hawaii International Conference on System Sciences, vol. 3, pp. 517–524 (1989)
21. Chang, J.M., et al.: Capturing cognitive fingerprints from keystroke dynamics. IT Prof. **15**(4), 24–28 (2013)
22. Sumari, A.D.W., Ahmad, A.S.: Cognitive artificial intelligence: the fusion of artificial Intelligence and information fusion. In: Proceedings of 2016 International Symposium on Electronics and Smart Devices (ISESD), pp. 1–6 (2016)
23. Muraleedharan, R., Osadciw, L.A.: Cognitive security protocol for sensor based VANET using swarm intelligence. In: Proceedings of 2009 Conference Record of the Forty-Third Asilomar Conference on Signals, Systems and Computers, pp. 288–290 (2009)
24. Usha, B.A., Ksrinath, N., Ravikumar, C.N., Vismayas, P.: Cognitive prediction of the most appropriate image steganography approach. Int. J. Comput. Appl. **121**(8) (2015)
25. Ogiela, L., Ogiela, M.R.: Advances in Cognitive Information Systems, vol. 17. Springer, Heidelberg (2012). https://doi.org/10.1007/978-3-642-25246-4
26. Ogiela, L., Ogiela, M.R.: Towards cognitive cryptography. J. Internet Serv. Inf. Secur. (JISIS) **4**(1), 58–63 (2014)
27. Kamarudin, M.H., Maple, C., Watson, T., Safa, N.S.: A LogitBoost-Based Algorithm for detecting known and unknown web attacks. IEEE Access **5**, 26190–26200 (2017)
28. Almohri, H.M.J., Watson, L.T., Evans, D.: Misery digraphs: delaying intrusion attacks in obscure clouds. IEEE Trans. Inf. Forensics Secur. **13**(6), 1361–1375 (2018)
29. Sevilla, S., Garcia-Luna-Aceves, J.J., Sadjadpour, H.: GroupSec: a new security model for the web. In: Proceedings of 2017 IEEE International Conference on Communications (ICC), pp. 1–6 (2017)
30. Martínez, S., Cosentino, V., Cabot, J.: Model-based analysis of Java EE web security misconfigurations. Comput. Lang. Syst. Struct. **49**, 36–61 (2017)
31. Garcia Clemente, F.J., Martinez Pérez, G., Muñoz Ortega, Botia, A.J.A., Gómez Skarmeta, A.F.: Towards semantic web-based management of security services. Ann. Telecommun. **63**(3–4), 183–193 (2008)

32. Baravati, H.B., Hosseinkhani, J., Keikhaee, S., Ostad, M., Khayat, H., Havasi, M.: A new data mining-based approach to improving the quality of alerts in intrusion detection systems. IJCSNS Int. J. Comput. Sci. Netw. Secur. **17**(8), 194–198 (2017)
33. Aljumah, A.: Securing modern web services from distributed denial of service using SVM. IJCSNS Int. J. Comput. Sci. Netw. Secur. **17**(10), 23–31 (2017)
34. Wang, C., Miu, T.T.N., Luo, X., Wang, J.: SkyShield: a sketch-based defense system against application layer DDoS attacks. IEEE Trans. Inf. Forensics Secur. **13**(3), 559–573 (2018)
35. Medved, A.: Auswirkungen der IT-Sicherheit auf die Bahnstromautomatisierung. e & Elektrotechnik und Informationstechnik **134**(1), 117–120 (2017)
36. Bugliesi, M., Calzavara, S., Focardi, R.: Formal methods for web security. J. Log. Algebr. Methods Program. **87**, 110–126 (2017)
37. Mago, V.K., et al.: Analyzing the impact of social factors on homelessness: a fuzzy cognitive map approach. BMC Med. Inform. Decis. Mak. **13**(1), 94 (2013)
38. Nunes, P., Medeiros, I., Fonseca, J., Neves, N., Correia, M., Vieira, M.: On combining diverse static analysis tools for web security: an empirical study. In: Proceedings of 2017 13th European Dependable Computing Conference (EDCC), pp. 121–128 (2017)
39. Odirichukwu, J.C., Asagba, P.O.: Security concept in web database development and administration—a review perspective. In: Proceedings of 2017 IEEE 3rd International Conference on Electro-Technology for National Development (NIGERCON), pp. 383–391 (2017)
40. Kearney, P., Chapman, J., Edwards, N., Gifford, M., He, L.: an overview of web services security. BT Technol. J. **22**(1), 27–42 (2004)
41. Hsiao, H., Chen, D. Wu, T.: Detecting hiding malicious website using network traffic mining approach. In: Proceedings of 2010 2nd International Conference on Education Technology and Computer (2010)
42. Yu, B., et al.: Rule-based security capabilities matching for web services. Wireless Pers. Commun. **73**(4), 1349–1367 (2013)
43. Debar, H., Tombini, E.: Web analyzer: accurate detection of HTTP attack traces in web server logs. Annales Des Télécommunications **61**(5–6), 682–704 (2006)
44. Bajer, M.: Building an IoT Data Hub with Elasticsearch, Logstash and Kibana. In: Proceedings of 2017 5th International Conference on Future Internet of Things and Cloud Workshops (FiCloudW), pp. 63–68 (2017)
45. Doan, D.N., Iuhasz, G.: Tuning Logstash Garbage collection for high throughput in a monitoring platform. In: Proceedings of 2016 18th International Symposium on Symbolic and Numeric Algorithms for Scientific Computing (SYNASC), pp. 359–365 (2016)
46. Hasani, Z., Fondaj, J.: Improvement of implemented infrastructure for streaming outlier detection in big data with ELK stack. Trends and Advances in Information Systems and Technologies, pp. 869–877 (2018)

SePoMa: Semantic-Based Data Analysis for Political Marketing

Héctor Hiram Guedea-Noriega[1]([⊠]) (iD)
and Francisco García-Sánchez[2] (iD)

[1] Escuela Internacional de Doctorado,
University of Murcia, 30100 Murcia, Spain
hector.guedea@um.es
[2] DIS, Faculty of Computer Science,
University of Murcia, 30100 Murcia, Spain
frgarcia@um.es

Abstract. Political marketing is a discipline concerned with the study of the right political communication strategies. Precise decision making in political marketing largely depends upon the thorough analysis of vast amounts of data from a variety of sources. Relevant information from mass media, social networks, Web pages, etc., should be gathered and scrutinized in order to provide the insights necessary to properly adjust the political parties' and politicians' messages to society. The main challenges in this context are, first of all, the integration of data from disparate sources, and hence its analysis to extract the relevant information to use in the decision-making process. Big data and Semantic Web technologies provide the means to face these challenges. In this paper, we propose SePoMa, a framework that applies semantic Big data analysis techniques to the political domain to assist in the definition of political marketing strategies for political entities. SePoMa explores the pertinent structured, semi-structured and unstructured data sources and automatically populates the political ontology, which is then examined to generate electorate knowledge. An exemplary use case scenario is described that illustrates the benefits of the framework for the automation of electoral research and the support of political marketing strategies.

Keywords: Semantic big data analysis · Political marketing · Ontology
Ontology population

1 Introduction

More than ever, modern political campaigns rest on strategies formulated based on what is known as political marketing. Political marketing consists on the application of market research techniques and advertising concepts to political communication [1]. It encompasses most of the political process, from the definition of the political product through a rigorous analysis of the citizen's needs, to the development of the political campaign and the management of the political communication [2]. The main aim of political marketing is to assist in tracking and forming public opinion [3] as well as persuading the electorate through both traditional media (e.g., radio, TV, etc.) and new digital media (e.g., social networks, apps, etc.). As part of the political marketing process, it becomes essential to collect as much information as possible about prospective voters. Electorate data gathering should be performed both before and during the political campaign to define the electoral strategy [4]. Certainly, the success of the political strategy is closely related to its alignment with the interests and concerns of society [5]. However, dealing with data about thousands, maybe millions, of voters is a very challenging endeavor.

Big data is a novel approach to data analysis mainly characterized by three properties of the data being processed, namely, volume (i.e., size in bytes), velocity (i.e., data growth rate), and variety (i.e., data format and data source heterogeneity), which are known as the 3Vs of Big data [6]. Other Vs or properties typically associated with Big data are value, veracity, volatility, validity and viability [7]. A more formal definition of Big data is provided in Gartner and describes Big data as *"information assets characterized by their high volume, high speed and high variety, which demand innovative and efficient processing solutions for the improvement of knowledge and decision-making in the organizations"* [8]. Given these properties, a number of challenges should be considered when dealing with Big data in data analysis implementations, from the extraction and linking of heterogeneous data coming from diverse sources, to the analysis, organization, modeling and visualization of the obtained knowledge [9, 10].

The technologies associated to the Semantic Web [11] and Linked Data [12] have proved effective for the automatic treatment of information in different contexts [13, 14]. The underlying ontological models, which are based on logical formalisms, enable computer systems to somehow interpret the information that is being managed [15]. They also allow to carry out advanced reasoning and inferencing processes [16]. The scientific community within these research fields have developed tools that make use of semantic technologies to both (i) integrate data from heterogeneous data sources [17, 18], and (ii) allow the analysis of large amounts of data at the knowledge level [19], with different degrees of success. In this paper, we propose SePoMa, a framework that integrates Big data analytics techniques with Semantic Web technologies to assist in the definition of political marketing strategies through the gathering and analysis of electorate data available all over the Internet. To the extent of our knowledge, there are no other works in the literature focused on the exploitation of semantic technologies in the political marketing domain.

The main aim of the framework described in this work is to improve the efficiency of political marketing processes thus obtaining better results, specifically in market research and data analysis. In order to do that, the proposed system incorporates a semantic layer that enables a more advanced data processing and inferences capabilities. With all, data coming from disparate, heterogeneous sources can be seamlessly integrated and processed at the knowledge level, providing more precise insights on the needs, concerns, and viewpoints of the electorate. The benefits of exploiting these insights in the political marketing context are manifold. First, SePoMa offers a broader and more precise knowledge about potential voters through a faster and cheaper mechanism than traditional methods (i.e., surveys and interviews). Second, the collected data can assist in predicting election results. Finally, the proposed approach promotes a new research area that supports the use of these new methodologies for the development of efficient digital political marketing campaigns.

The rest of the paper is organized as follows. In Sect. 2, background information on political marketing and the application of semantic technologies to enhance Big data analysis processes is provided. SePoMa, the framework proposed in this work to facilitate political marketing by leveraging semantically-enabled data analysis tools, is described in Sect. 3. In Sect. 4, an exemplary use case scenario that illustrates the benefits of the framework for the automation of electoral research and the support of political marketing strategies is described. Finally, conclusions and future work are put forward in Sect. 5.

2 Related Work

Today, most political parties carry out some kind of market analysis to acquire deep insights about society's main concerns, likes, dislikes, needs and preferences. Also, the reaction of citizens (positive or negative) to government performance, political proposals and news is checked with the aim of defining the right political strategies. The use of such insights with the purpose of improving political communication is referred to as political marketing. In this section, the field of political marketing will be characterized and the impact of Semantic Web technologies in the area of Big data analytics will be discussed.

2.1 Political Marketing

Political marketing began in the 1950s when for the first time an US president, Dwight Eisenhower, hired an advertising agency to take charge of his television campaign. This meant the incorporation of market research techniques and advertising to political communication. In [5] political marketing is defined as *"the discipline oriented to the creation and development of political concepts related to specific parties or candidates to satisfy certain groups of electors in exchange for their votes"*. According to these same authors, the key principle of political marketing is the application of marketing concepts to the overall behavior of the political institution. This leads to (i) the design of political products using marketing intelligence becoming voter-centric, (ii) the definition of behaviors for politicians and their parties, (iii) the development of open offers for the electorate, and (iv) the measurement of the degree of coverage of the needs of the electorate that reach those offers and products.

There are three fundamental aspects linked to political marketing [20]: (i) the political product, (ii) identification and segmentation of the voter market, and (iii) marketing intelligence applied to politics. The political product refers to the ideas to be transmitted by politicians and parties, which must be defined from the identification of the electorate needs. On the other hand, electorate segmentation consists of dividing the heterogeneous electoral mass into smaller sections that have something in common with the objective of detecting large enough groups to which the political product can be especially attractive. For this, different techniques can be used such as geographic (i.e., the place where people live according to regions and zones within those regions), behavioral (i.e., based on the actions of the individual), demographic (i.e., age, type of family, social class, income, etc.) or psychographic (i.e., characteristics of lifestyle, common values, beliefs, attitudes, activities, interests and opinions). Finally, marketing intelligence enables the understanding of what the political market, that is, the electorate, wants from political elites, that is, political parties and candidates, using quantitative and qualitative research techniques. The ultimate goal of marketing intelligence is to place the political product in an ideological niche that is unapproachable by competitors because of its competitive advantage, which is capable of attracting the sufficient number of votes to achieve the desired electoral goal.

In response to these principles of political marketing, it is increasingly common in modern political campaigns for parties to resort to the analysis of large data sets and its power to predict the future, enhancing their competitive advantage, and attributing much of their success to the speed and reliability of processing information transforming it into electoral knowledge. Nowadays, the Internet, and its hundreds of new collaborative and informative technologies, where the user is creator of information and opinion leader, generates a collective intelligence environment, but it is difficult to obtain, classify, sort and store in specific domains to be used for electoral purposes [3]. The technologies associated with the Semantic Web have proven useful in the integration of data from heterogeneous sources [17, 18] and in the analysis of data at the knowledge level [19]. In the last few years, ontologies specifically, and semantic technologies in general, have been used in the political domain for various purposes, but mainly focused on decision making [21–23]. In [24], the authors propose a methodology for building a political ontology by extracting knowledge from various data sources. The goal is to provide decision makers with an intelligent decision process in this domain. Finally, in [25] one of the most outstanding challenges in political marketing, that is, the administration and extraction of useful knowledge from the content publish in social sites, is partially overcome by means of an ontology-based approach and the semantic analysis of the data.

2.2 Semantic Technologies in (Big) Data Analysis

For many years, companies have exploited the data registered in their transactional systems concerned with their everyday operations in order to obtain useful information and assist in the decision-making process. To this end, different data analysis techniques and business intelligence strategies have been applied. Data analysis includes the processes associated to data inspection, cleansing, transformation and modelling, with the objective of producing useful information, leading to findings, and supporting decision making [26]. The technological architecture of most data analysis solutions is comprised by three main components [27]: (i) tools for data extraction, transformation and loading (ETL), (ii) a repository to store the integrated data, namely, data warehouse, and (iii) data processing and visualization systems, including report generators, multi-dimensional analysis techniques (OLAP), and statistics-, symbolic- or artificial intelligence-based data mining methods. In recent years, the increase in the volume of data, along with variety in data and the velocity at which data is being produced, has led to the conception of novel processing mechanisms capable of dealing with such huge amount of data, namely, Big data [6]. In general terms, the Big data and data analysis processes include three main stages, namely, data pre-processing, data processing, and data visualization.

The main difficulties associated with Big data management are linked to its collection and storage, search, sharing, analysis and visualization [10]. The Semantic Web provides the means to overcome some of these challenges. Certainly, the formal underpinnings of Semantic Web technologies enable the automated processing of data through sophisticated inference and reasoning techniques. RDF (Resource Description Framework) is a standard model for data interchange on the Web and is based on graphs, allowing the representation of data in the form of triples subject-predicate-object [28]. RDF triples can be used to create datasets and to establish explicit relationships among data; this collection of interrelated datasets on the Web is referred to as Linked Data [12]. One of the main aims of Linked (Open) Data is to add a semantic layer over the data, making it understandable by machines so that they can perform some data analysis operations on behalf of human users [29]. Thus, the Semantic Web can assist in the discovery, integration, representation and management of knowledge [30]. In particular, semantic technologies have been successfully applied in a number of scenarios for the integration of heterogeneous data [31], data analysis at the knowledge level [30], and visualization of Linked Data [32].

In the last few years, a large number of published research papers have explored the benefits in using semantic technologies in data analysis and Big data [19, 25, 31, 33–36]. The impact of semantics in this field covers the whole process, from preprocessing (data acquisition and organization) to visualization through data processing and analysis. Ontology models can be used to harmonize heterogeneous data from structured, semi-structured and unstructured sources, thus allowing its integrated storage in ontology repositories [31]. The formal grounding of the Semantic Web enables reasoning processes useful to infer new knowledge not explicitly stated in the source data [34]. Finally, many tools have been proposed that provide retrieval and visualization features for Linked Data and Big Linked Data [35, 36].

3   Knowledge Management for Political Marketing

Political marketing requires the use of market research techniques that perform a systematic and objective extraction and use of information in order to improve decision-making processes related to the identification of problems and opportunities, and the generation of their corresponding responses. In a political context, this can help to find unmet needs or demands within a segment, niche or sector of the population. In this section, we present SePoMa, a semantic-based political marketing framework that first generates a politics-related knowledge base by gathering information from multiple, heterogeneous sources, and then, analyses such knowledge base in order to understand the electoral market and assist political strategists in the definition of the communication objectives to improve the performance of the political campaign through the candidate-citizen communication. For this, qualitative and quantitative research on the target electorate is essential, applying geographic and time limits.

3.1   Proposed Framework

The functional architecture of the SePoMa framework is shown in Fig. 1. It is composed of four main elements: (i) an ontology population component, responsible for gathering knowledge from heterogeneous sources, (ii) a knowledge base built on top of a political ontology, where the gathered knowledge is stored, (iii) a semantic data analysis tool, which explores the knowledge base collecting relevant information items, and (iv) the electorate knowledge component, which include the knowledge items to be visualized by external users for assisting in the decision-making process.

In a nutshell, the SePoMa framework works as follows. First, relevant data sources are identified. These data sources could be either structured, such as databases with relevant information about the affiliates of political parties, semi-structured, such as XML or JSON files with citizen participation at different events[1], or unstructured, such as the content published by eligible voters in Web 2.0 sites. Different ontology population strategies are then employed to deal with those disparate and heterogenous sources, ant to create ontology instances in the knowledge base. The knowledge repository is based on a political ontology that covers the main concepts, insights and relationships within the political domain to respond to the questions and needs of political marketing. Once the knowledge base has been populated, semantic data analysis techniques are used to extract meaningful knowledge related with (i) the design of political products, (ii) the definition of behaviors for politicians and their parties, (iii) the development of open offers for the electorate, and (iv) the measurement of the degree of coverage of the needs of the electorate that reach those offers and products, as required in a political marketing scenario. All this knowledge is then exposed through the electorate knowledge component, which includes the tools to assist in the proper visualization of the analyzed data by end users.

Next, the components that comprise the SePoMa framework are described in detail.

3.2   Political Ontology

In the last few year, a large number of ontologies in the political domain have been developed [37–40]. They all focus on "government" and "government services", and none of these ontologies include some of the most relevant concepts required in a political marketing context for the definition of the correct political communication strategies. Under these circumstances, the political ontology to be used in the SePoMa framework was built from scratch, but has been linked, when possible, to well-known ontology models such as FOAF[2], the Organization Ontology[3] and DBpedia[4], among others. For the design of the ontology, three fundamental political marketing-related research questions were considered:

1. What opinions do citizens have about the candidates and the political parties?

---

[1] https://catalog.data.gov/dataset/citizen-participation.

[2] http://www.foaf-project.org/.

[3] https://www.w3.org/TR/vocab-org/.

[4] https://wiki.dbpedia.org/services-resources/ontology.

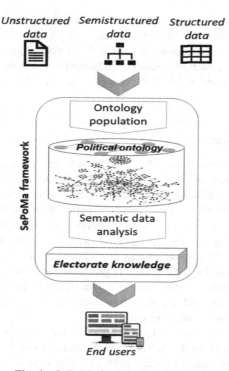

Fig. 1. SePoMa functional architecture

2. How are the candidates' and political parties' proposals in the core elements of political issues (i.e., health, education, economy, law and order, etc.) received by society?

3. How are candidates and political parties positioned in comparison to their opponents?

The ontology, which has been defined in OWL 2[5] using Protégé[6], contains five main concepts (see Fig. 2), namely, candidates, political parties, political proposals, electorate and opinion. These elements enable SePoMa to answer to the aforementioned questions and can be defined as follows:

- Candidate: person affiliated to a political party who has made known his or her intention to seek, or campaign for, local or state office in a general, primary or special election.
- PoliticalParty: organized group of people with common values and goals, who try to get their candidates elected to office.

---

[5] https://www.w3.org/TR/owl2-overview/.

[6] https://protege.stanford.edu/.

- **Politics**: proposals suggested by candidates or political parties as to how the country or jurisdiction should be governed.
- **EligibleVoter**: person who has the right to vote at an election.
- **Opinion**: the expression of a belief or judgment with respect to political proposals or news about the main political themes (i.e., health, education, economy, etc.).

3.3 Ontology Population

Ontology instantiation has to do with the extraction and classification of instances of the concepts and relations that have been defined in the ontology. Instantiating ontologies with new knowledge is a relevant step towards the provision of valuable ontology-based knowledge services. However, performing such task manually is time-consuming and error-prone. As a result, research has shifted attention to automating this process, introducing ontology population, which refers to a set of methodologies for automatically identifying and adding new instances of concepts from an external source into an ontology [41]. Ontology population does not affect the concept hierarchies and the relations in the ontology, leaving the structure of the ontology unmodified. What is affected are the individuals (a.k.a. concept instances) and the relationships between individuals in the domain.

The political ontology described in the previous section constitutes the backbone of the knowledge repository in the SePoMa framework. In order to populate the knowledge base with the relevant instances from the identified data sources, an ontology population component has been conceived. This component makes use of different strategies in order to cope with the challenges related to each of the different data source models considered, namely, structured, semi-structured and unstructured data sources. A rule-based approach as suggested in [42] has been used to deal with structured content. This module consists of a set of rules describing the transformation steps to gather the data from known relational databases and generate the ontology instances. Similarly, the ontology population from semi-structured data module follows the guidelines described in [43]. This module is comprised of a document parser, which transforms the input data into a common representation format in JSON, and a JSON2RDF algorithm, which produces the ontology instances by making use of an 'affinity' function that identifies the ontology classes each instance belongs to. As for unstructured content, a sentiment analysis (a.k.a., opinion mining) approach as shown in [44] has been considered. It involves the calculation of the polarity (i.e., positive or negative orientation) of the different features that can be found in free text documents (such as news or users' posts in social sites).

Finally, Linked Data sources have been also considered as a valuable input data source for the SePoMa knowledge base. For this purpose, a user-friendly graphical user interface application called PROPheT[7] is used. PROPheT enables instance extraction and ontology population from Linked Data by (i) gathering instances through searches via SPARQL endpoints, (ii) enriching those instances with data properties, and

---

[7] http://mklab.iti.gr/project/prophet-ontology-populator.

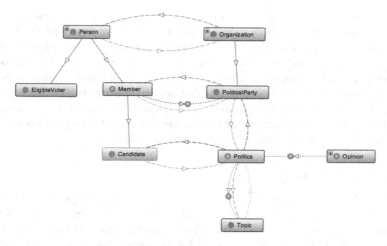

Fig. 2. Excerpt of the political ontology

(iii) mapping it all to a given ontology model. With all, the proposed ontology population component assists in the quick, easy and automatic collection and classification of large volumes of information.

3.4   Semantic Data Analysis

Ontologies facilitate the management of information at the knowledge level and enable an integrated access to heterogeneous sources, being able to use various inference and reasoning techniques to analyze the data [19]. However, it has been demonstrated that the analysis of large volumes of data has implications for knowledge management [45]. In order to handle such a huge amount of data, different solutions have been proposed [19, 33, 46–49]. One possibility is the use of the concepts and methods of Formal Concept Analysis, which is a method where data are structured into units that represent formal abstractions of concepts of human thought, allowing comprehensive interpretation, and facilitating the representation of knowledge and the management of information [19, 33]. Another relevant approach in this context is the generation of a multidimensional ontology layer to consolidate the analysis at different levels on the repository, so as to add more meaning to the data, eliminate redundancies and irrelevant information, and to obtain an enhanced analysis [19].

OLAP (Online analytical processing) systems can also benefit from the use of ontologies [46]. The ontological model, which provides an unambiguous definition of the domain terms associated to the specific needs of OLAP, strengthens the correlation and enrichment of the data automatically with grouping algorithms. It also provides the means to perform tasks of comparative analysis of highly heterogeneous data originating from different sources, platforms and technologies. In [47], the authors suggest the use of rules expressed in SWRL (Semantic Web Rule Language) along with the intrinsic inference mechanisms of ontologies to analyze knowledge bases thus producing new relevant knowledge.

The potential shortcomings that can arise from the application of ontology-based big data management have been explored in [49]. The complexity of the reasoning process and the related performance issues can be addressed by considering ontology languages that trade expressivity for reduced reasoning complexity. Yet, the benefits are massive. The integration of new data sources is facilitated, and usability is boosted. Both reusability of data and maintainability of applications can be also improved with the use of semantics. The visualization of knowledge is impacted too, since it is possible to represent information in different forms thus enhancing end users understanding of the insights derived from the knowledge base.

3.5 Electorate Knowledge

The outcome of the semantic data analysis component is specific pieces of knowledge that can respond to the needs of political marketing. That knowledge, which is related to the research questions set out in Sect. 3.2 to support decision making in this context, is represented in the SePoMa framework as the electorate knowledge component. That is, once the SePoMa framework has collected the data from the different sources, organized it, and effectively analyzed it, it produces the relevant electorate knowledge which is to be shown to the political marketing strategists.

The next logical step is to provide end users the means to explore and visualize the relevant knowledge. Vital requirements at this stage are scalability, functionality and response time [35]. However, it is necessary to take into consideration some challenges that might arise due to the large size and dynamic nature of the data, coupled with the problems related to performance. One of the most interesting proposals to face these issues is the so called 'Linked Data Visualization Model' [32], which is an adaptation of the 'Data State Reference Model' (DSRM) [50] conceived to visualize RDF and Linked Data. In addition, it extends DSRM with three reusable software components, namely, analyzers, which that generate the RDF representation of data sources, transformers, which produce an appropriate RDF structure according to the visualization technique to be used, and visualizers, which create the visualization for end users.

4   Use Case Scenario

In order to devise the potential benefits of the application of the SePoMa framework in a real environment, in this section an illustrative use case scenario is presented. The basic idea behind this sample scenario is to show the typical process flow in political marketing and describe the usual actors involved. SePoMa would be placed in the spotlight of the scenario to provide the electorate knowledge that supports decision-making processes for the definition of communication strategies in political marketing (see Fig. 3).

The exemplary scenario is depicted in Fig. 3. Candidates or political parties (1) define sensible political, economic and social proposals (2) which are then transmitted through mass media (3) to the citizens (4). The conveyed messages cause an

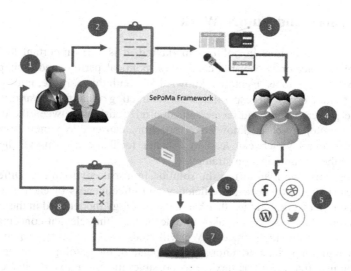

Fig. 3. The SePoMa framework in its context

impact on citizens, who share their feelings by posting text comments to different websites (5). Then, SePoMa collects the data from the different sources, organize it, and effectively analyze it, producing the relevant electorate knowledge (6). Political marketing strategists make use of the proper visualization tools to get access to the required knowledge (7) and take advantage of it to adjust the policy proposals (8). At that moment, the process starts over again, but this time the candidates' and political parties' communication strategy is better aligned to the changing needs of citizens.

During the recent Mexico's 2018 Election, social networks were the main means of interaction for the average citizen, where they not only participated critically, but used it as a form of communication and graphic reaction (e.g., Internet Meme[8]) to the different events, statements or incidents of the candidates' public activities. Quantitative analyses were performed[9], which shown that the winning candidate (Andrés Manuel López Obrador) had a greater impact on social media than his opponents. SePoMa could help enhance the insights derived from these analyses and assist in defining the best political marketing strategies prior and during the elections process. With SePoMa it would be possible to integrate data coming from heterogenous sources, analyze such data at the knowledge level, and show the most interesting elements to the political strategist.

---

[8] http://www.scielo.org.mx/scielo.php?pid=S0187-57952014000200005&script=sci_arttext [Accessed: 17-Jul-2018].

[9] http://www.eluniversal.com.mx/elecciones-2018/amlo-el-candidato-que-mas-crece-en-redes-sociales [Accessed: 17-Jul-2018].

5   Conclusions and Future Work

In order to make decisions in political marketing, it is very important to know the sentiment of the electorate towards candidates, political parties, and their proposals, which can be referred to as 'electorate knowledge'. With this purpose, in this paper we propose a framework with capabilities for extracting data from various sources, organize the gathered data, and create semantic relationships between the data items. The resulting ontology-based knowledge repository can enable a more sophisticated and precise analysis which can lead to a better feedback to improve the political message and the communication strategy.

As future work, we plan to test the solution in a real environment. Different tests should be carried out to check the efficiency and effectiveness of each distinct component of the framework. On the other hand, the ontology model used in the framework is in continuous change so that it takes into account all the relevant concepts to better support the decision-making process. We will study the possibility of integrating an ontology evolution approach to automate the update of the ontology scheme. With the aim of defining a framework as flexible as possible, making it even suitable for other domains beyond political marketing, a plugin set up will be considered. Once in place, anyone will be able to use the framework with their own built components for ontology population or semantic data analysis.

Acknowledgements. This work has been supported by the Spanish National Research Agency (AEI) and the European Regional Development Fund (FEDER/ERDF) through project KBS4FIA (TIN2016-76323-R).

References

1. Mendoza Bustamante, L.B.: Estrategia de comunicacion de mercadotecnia politica para una eleccion municipal. Universidad de las Américas Puebla (2004)
2. Juárez, J.: Hacia un estudio del marketing político: limitaciones teóricas y metodológicas. Espiral IX **27**, 60–95 (2003)
3. Costa, L.: Manual de Marketing Político (2012). http://www.costabonino.com/manual.htm. Accessed 10 June 2018
4. Valdez Zepeda, A.: Las campañas electorales en la nueva sociedad de la información y el conocimiento. Estudios Políticos **20**, 155–165 (2010)
5. Alonso Coto, M.A., Adell, Á.: Marketing político 2.0: lo que todo candidato necesita saber para ganar las elecciones. In: Gestión 2000, Barcelona (2011)
6. Laney, D.: 3D data management: controlling data volume, velocity, and variety. In: Application Delivery Strategies (2001). https://blogs.gartner.com/doug-laney/files/2012/01/ad949-3D-Data-Management-Controlling-Data-Volume-Velocity-and-Variety.pdf. Accessed 24 July 2018
7. Maté Jiménez, C.: Big data. Un nuevo paradigma de análisis de datos. Revista: Anales de Mecánica y Electricidad **41**(6), 10–16 (2014)
8. Beyer, M., Laney, D.: The Importance of "Big Data": A Definition. Gartner Publications, pp. 1–7, June 2012

9. Mayer-Schönberger, V., Cukier, K.: Big Data: A Revolution That Will Transform How We Live, Work, and Think. Houghton Mifflin Harcourt, Boston (2013)
10. Kale, S.A., Dandge, S.S.: Understanding the big data problems and their solutions using Hadoop and map-reduce. Int. J. Appl. Innov. Eng. Manag. (IJAIEM) 3(3), 439–445 (2014)
11. Shadbolt, N., Berners-Lee, T., Hall, W.: The semantic web revisited. IEEE Intell. Syst. 21 (3), 96–101 (2006)
12. Bizer, C., Heath, T., Berners-Lee, T.: Linked data—the story so far. Int. J. Semantic Web Inf. Syst. 5(3), 1–22 (2009)
13. Rahoman, M.-M., Ichise, R.: A proposal of a temporal semantics aware linked data information retrieval framework. J. Intell. Inf. Syst. 50(3), 573–595 (2018)
14. Di Iorio, A., Rossi, D.: Capturing and managing knowledge using social software and semantic web technologies. Inf. Sci. 432, 1–21 (2018)
15. Studer, R., Benjamins, V.R., Fensel, D.: Knowledge engineering: principles and methods. Data Knowl. Eng. 25(1–2), 161–197 (1998)
16. Rodríguez-García, M.Á., Hoehndorf, R.: Inferring ontology graph structures using OWL reasoning. BMC Bioinform. 19(1), 7 (2018)
17. García-Sánchez, F., Fernández-Breis, J.T., Valencia-García, R., Gómez, J.M., Martínez-Béjar, R.: Combining semantic web technologies with multi-agent systems for integrated access to biological resources. J. Biomed. Inform. 41(5), 848–859 (2008)
18. Santipantakis, G., Kotis, K., Vouros, G.A.: OBDAIR: ontology-based distributed framework for accessing, integrating and reasoning with data in disparate data sources. Expert Syst. Appl. 90, 464–483 (2017)
19. Neuböck, T., Neumayr, B., Schrefl, M., Schütz, C.: Ontology-driven business intelligence for comparative data analysis. In: Zimányi, E. (ed.) eBISS 2013. LNBIP, vol. 172, pp. 77–120. Springer, Cham (2014). https://doi.org/10.1007/978-3-319-05461-2_3
20. Zamudio, Y.: Etapas del plan de marketing, UVEG (2015). http://roa.uveg.edu.mx/repositorio/postgrado2015/37/Etapasdelplandemarketing.pdf. Accessed 10 June 2018
21. Al Shayji, S., El Kadhi, N.E.Z.: Building fuzzy-logic ontology for political decision-makers. Int. J. Math. Models Methods Appl. Sci. 5(5), 991–1001 (2011)
22. Andreasen, T., Christiansen, H., Eberholst, M.K.: Ontology-based roles association networks for visualizing trends in political debate. In: Christiansen, H., Stojanovic, I., Papadopoulos, G.A. (eds.) CONTEXT 2015. LNCS (LNAI), vol. 9405, pp. 477–482. Springer, Cham (2015). https://doi.org/10.1007/978-3-319-25591-0_35
23. Wu, Y., Wong, J., Deng, Y., Chang, K.: An exploration of social media in public opinion convergence: elaboration likelihood and semantic networks on political events. In: 2011 IEEE Ninth International Conference on Dependable, Autonomic and Secure Computing, Sydney, NSW, Australia, pp. 903–910. IEEE (2011)
24. Al Shayji, S., El, N., El, Z., Wong, P.Z.: Building ontology for the political domain. In: Arabnia, H.R., Marsh, A., Solo, A.M.G. (eds.) Proceedings of the 2011 International Conference on Semantic Web and Web Services, pp. 106–112. CSREA Press, Las Vegas (2011)
25. Wongthontham, P., Abu-Salih, B.: Ontology-based approach for identifying the credibility domain in social big data. Cornell University Library (arXiv) (2018). http://arxiv.org/abs/1801.01624. Accessed 24 July 2018
26. Bihani, P., Patil, S.: A comparative study of data analysis techniques. Int. J. Emerg. Trends Technol. Comput. Sci. (IJETTCS) 3(2), 95–101 (2014)
27. Gómez Vieites, A., Suárez Rey, C.: Sistemas de información : herramientas prácticas para la gestión empresarial. RA-MA (2011)
28. W3C: RDF—Semantic Web Standards (2014). https://www.w3.org/RDF/. Accessed 10 June 2018

29. Hu, B., Carvalho, N., Matsutsuka, T.: Towards big linked data: a large-scale, distributed semantic data storage. Int. J. Data Wareh. Min. **9**(4), 19–43 (2013)
30. Barceló Valenzuela, M., Sánchez Schmitz, G.G.A., Perez-Soltero, A.: La web semántica como apoyo a la gestión del conocimiento y al modelo organizacional. Revista Ingeniería Informática **12** (abril), 1–14 (2006)
31. Konys, A.: A framework for analysis of ontology-based data access. In: Nguyen, N.-T., Manolopoulos, Y., Iliadis, L., Trawiński, B. (eds.) ICCCI 2016. LNCS (LNAI), vol. 9876, pp. 397–408. Springer, Cham (2016). https://doi.org/10.1007/978-3-319-45246-3_38
32. Brunetti, J.M., Auer, S., García, R., Klímek, J., Nečaský, M.: Formal linked data visualization model. In: Proceedings of International Conference on Information Integration and Web-Based Applications and Services—IIWAS 2013, pp. 309–318. ACM Press, New York (2013)
33. Airinei, D., Berta, D.: Semantic business intelligence—a new generation of business intelligence. Inform. Econ. **16**(2), 72–80 (2012)
34. Kureychik, V., Semenova, A.: Combined method for integration of heterogeneous ontology models for big data processing and analysis. In: Silhavy, R., Senkerik, R., Kominkova Oplatkova, Z., Prokopova, Z., Silhavy, P. (eds.) CSOC 2017. AISC, vol. 573, pp. 302–311. Springer, Cham (2017). https://doi.org/10.1007/978-3-319-57261-1_30
35. Bikakis, N., Sellis, T.: Exploration and visualization in the web of big linked data: a survey of the state of the art. In: 6th International Workshop on Linked Web Data Management (LWDM 2016), Bordeaux, France, pp. 1–8 (2016)
36. Nuzzolese, A.G., Presutti, V., Gangemi, A., Peroni, S., Ciancarini, P.: Aemoo: linked data exploration based on knowledge patterns. Semantic Web **8**(1), 87–112 (2017)
37. Moreira, S., Batista, D., Carvalho, P., Couto, F.M., Silva, M.J.: POWER—politics ontology for web entity retrieval. In: Salinesi, Camille, Pastor, Oscar (eds.) CAiSE 2011. LNBIP, vol. 83, pp. 489–500. Springer, Heidelberg (2011). https://doi.org/10.1007/978-3-642-22056-2_51
38. Ortiz, A.: Polionto: ontology reuse with automatic text extraction from political documents. In: 6th Doctoral Symposium in Informatics Engineering, pp. 1–12. Universidade do Porto, Portugal (2011)
39. Daquino, M., Peroni, S., Tomasi, F., Vitali, F.: Political roles ontology (PRoles): enhancing archival authority records through semantic web technologies. Proc. Comput. Sci. **38**, 60–67 (2014)
40. Alcock, C., Oliver, S., Smethurst, M., Somerville, A., Woodhams, B.: UK Parliament Ontologies, Parliament of the United Kingdom (2018). https://ukparliament.github.io/ontologies/. Accessed 6 June 2018
41. Buitelaar, P., Cimiano, P.: Ontology Learning and Population: Bridging the Gap Between Text and Knowledge. IOS Press, Amsterdam (2008)
42. Boumlik, A., Bahaj, M.: Advanced set of rules to generate ontology from relational database. J. Softw. **11**(1), 27–43 (2016)
43. García-Sánchez, F., García-Díaz, J.A., Gómez-Berbís, J.M., Valencia-García, R.: Financial knowledge instantiation from semi-structured, heterogeneous data sources. In: Silhavy, R. (ed.) CSOC2018 2018. AISC, vol. 764, pp. 103–110. Springer, Cham (2019). https://doi.org/10.1007/978-3-319-91189-2_11
44. Salas-Zárate, M.P., Valencia-García, R., Ruiz-Martínez, A., Colomo-Palacios, R.: Feature-based opinion mining in financial news: an ontology-driven approach. J. Inf. Sci. **43**(4), 458–479 (2017)
45. Chan, J.O.: Big data customer knowledge management. Commun. IIMA **14**(3), 45–56 (2014)
46. Kupershmidt, I., et al.: Ontology-based meta-analysis of global collections of high-throughput public data. PLoS ONE **5**(9), e13066 (2010)

47. Bao, Q., Wang, J., Cheng, J.: Research on ontology modeling of steel manufacturing process based on big data analysis. In: MATEC Web of Conferences 45 04005 (2016)
48. Bennett, M., Baclawski, K.: The role of ontologies in linked data, big data and semantic web applications. Appl. Ontol. 12(3–4), 189–194 (2017)
49. Eine, B., Jurisch, M., Quint, W.: Ontology-based big data management. Systems 5(3), 45 (2017)
50. Chi, E.H.: A taxonomy of visualization techniques using the data state reference model. In: Proceedings of IEEE Symposium on Information Visualization, INFOVIS 2000, pp. 69–75. IEEE Comput. Soc., Salt Lake City (2000)

Neuromarketing and Facial Recognition: A Systematic Literature Review

Marcos Antonio Espinoza Mina[1,2](✉)
and Doris Del Pilar Gallegos Barzola[3]

[1] Universidad Ecotec, Samborondón, Ecuador
mespinoza@ecotec.edu.ec
[2] Universidad Agraria del Ecuador, Guayaquil, Ecuador
mespinoza@uagraria.edu.ec
[3] MADO S.A., Guayaquil, Ecuador
doris@ecuaportales.com

Abstract. Companies and marketing departments are devoting many resources to the implementation of neuromarketing with facial recognition. This document presents a systematic review of the literature whose main objective was to look for computer systems and technologies of facial recognition that are available to support neuromarketing. As a result, it was found that very few academic and scientific articles focus on this topic in a systematic way. None carry out an analysis for a complete solution and the studies are limited with databases that do not offer a group of images which are sufficiently broad to allow the performance of complete tests. Many works emphasize research on algorithms that increase the level of accuracy of the information analyzed at the time of facial recognition.

Keywords: Software · Neuromarketing facial recognition · Technology

1 Introduction

Marketing is a discipline that has been developed under this term for the last century. It responsible for analyzing the behavior of markets and consumers, always oriented to the satisfaction of the costumer. Companies want to increase their economic benefits, getting new clients and reinforcing the loyalty of the existing ones. That is why they make use of diverse techniques and tactics through equipment and tools that allow to detect the clients' needs in a more efficient way. They even create wishes for a specific product.

Avendaño Castro [1] considers that advances in the areas of psychology, neuroscience, the cognitive field and understanding of the functioning of the human brain have enabled other disciplines and areas of knowledge to formulate new theories. This is the case of marketing. It relies on the latest discoveries about the brain, and has incorporated strategies to attract clients. Neuromarketing considers the true essence of man's thought, uncovering more information about the consumer. This information is qualitatively richer and more truthful [2].

Neuromarketing applies neuroscience techniques to marketing stimuli in order to understand how the brain is activated and reacts to marketing actions. The use of facial

R. Valencia-García et al. (Eds.): CITI 2018, CCIS 883, pp. 214–228, 2018.
https://doi.org/10.1007/978-3-030-00940-3_16

recognition in neuromarketing pursues the collection of the face image with a camera; The main advantage over other techniques or equipment is that when using a camera, it is not necessary to physically connect any device to the person; that is, no cables will be placed or added. It is a very simple and non-invasive way for the consumers, which is very important when trying to know their tastes and preferences.

This review was made following the process described by Kitchenham [3], who points out that a systematic review synthesizes existing work in a way that is fair and seen as fair. For example, systematic reviews should be carried out according to a predefined search strategy, which explains how effective these studies have been when used for software engineering issues.

The main aim of this review is to compile the most complete list of software that allows facial recognition, to support neuromarketing and present these results as a visual summary (map) of classified characteristics. The classification of the tools will be based on characteristics which are common to all the studies (mainly related to the facial recognition due to its importance).

This work contains four more sections: the first one outlines the methodology used to carry out the systematic review of the mapping, including the formulation of questions, the selection of sources and studies, the extraction of information and the mapping process; in the second, the results obtained after carrying out the systematic mapping of the review are shown; the third one presents the interpretation of those results and finally the conclusions and the planning of future works are shown.

2 Systematic Review

2.1 Generality

The aim of this study consists of carrying out a systematic mapping of literature review of facial recognition tools that support neuromarketing, and obtain information on which computer systems are available and the characteristics they include.

2.2 Definition of the Research Question

The availability of computer systems for facial recognition was obtained by asking the following question: What facial recognition computer systems are available to support neuromarketing?

The list of keywords used to carry out the research were the following: software, neuromarketing, facial recognition and technology.

Once the systematic mapping review was completed, the research question was formulated and it provided the following results:

- Recognize the software or hardware tools that are used or available for facial recognition.
- Distinguish the main characteristics of computer systems and technologies related to facial recognition.
- List the areas supported by the facial recognition computer technology, especially neuromarketing.

2.3   Selection of Sources

The objective of this phase is to identify the sources used for searching; in order to do so, the selection criteria described below were defined: (1) search for digital versions of articles, journals and conferences on neuromarketing and facial recognition using the established key words; (2) bibliographic sources must have a search engine that allows executing advanced search queries; and (3) all the studies had to be written in English.

On the basis of the criteria above, searching was done in the following digital research libraries: Ebscohost.com, ACM Digital Library and IEEE Xplore.

Although the defined digital sources index the most relevant investigations, other sources of information were added in the present study, separately for their analysis, such as web pages of recognized commercial companies that offer software for facial recognition applied in the neuromarketing.

2.4   Search Strategies

A series of terms and key words were selected to answer the posed question and obtain the expected results. The search strategy was based on key words and/or synonyms, see Table 1.

Table 1. Key words and concepts used in the systematic review.

Area	Key words	Related concepts
Marketing	Neuromarketing	
Systems	Facial recognition software, technology	Facial recognition technology

The structured search chain was the following: facial recognition software or facial recognition technology and neuromarketing. The string was applied to: summary and full text. When the summary fit the subject of the investigation, the complete article was obtained and revised. The language or language of searching for the publications was English. The first year of the publications was 2013.

2.5   Inclusion and Exclusion Criteria

Inclusion criteria: (1) Articles published since 2013; all software has a certain support time, and then they stop receiving updates; for those who evolve, new studies are created quickly with the new functionalities; therefore, it is considered that any document that studies a tool before this year could be considered obsolete. (2) Software contents for facial recognition and neuromarketing. (3) Articles from conferences, magazines and international workshops. (4) When an article is repeated in several digital libraries as a result of the query, only one of them is selected.

Exclusion criteria: (1) Articles of which content is not related to neuromarketing, software for facial recognition or something similar. (2) Works on slides and books. (3) Works which are published outside the specified time range. (4) Gray literature.

2.6   Extraction of Information and Review of Works

This phase allowed to identify the relevant documents, with respect to the objectives of this systematic review and the scope of the research question. The main difficulty in achieving this goal was that the terms used in the question led to results that were too broad. For example, the word "software" is widely used in many types of publication, and therefore a large number of documents appeared in the results obtained, see Table 3.

In order to obtain the most valuable documents and do a deeper analysis in relation to the aim and the research question, the search chains and additional options applied were defined, see Table 2.

Table 2. Chain and additional options for search in sources.

Source	Chain of specific search	Included additional options
Ebscohost.com	facial recognition software **or** facial recognition technology **and** Neuromarketing	Software and technology of facial recognition, neuromarketing in the option "any field"
ACM Digital Library	facial recognition software facial recognition technology	In the option "any field", for each search
IEEE Xplore	facial recognition software **or** facial recognition technology **and** Neuromarketing	Software and technology of facial recognition, neuromarketing in the option "any field"

Table 3 contains the number of articles found, the chains of search and the different inclusion criteria.

Table 3. Selection of studies.

Phase	Inclusion criteria	Articles found		
		EBS	ACM	IEEE
Based on chain of search in any field	None	930	167	14
Based on chain of search in selected fields	Facial recognition software in field title	25	1	3
	Facial recognition technology in field title			
	Neuromarketing in field summary			
Based on chain of search in selected fields	All the search terms in field summary	29	19	3
	Additional filter in academic publications			

Ebscohost.com (EBS), ACM Digital Library (ACM), IEEE Xplore (IEEE)

Initially the most relevant documents were obtained through the realization based on search chain in "any field", see Table 3. In this first phase, a large number of results were obtained, but these results were not useful, since they consisted of comments, letters or repeated works that were not only limited to the search of software or technology for facial recognition, but all kinds of articles were visualized, in which software applied to different activities was analyzed. The second phase, based on search chain in fields selected by "titles", allowed to eliminate some unusable results and repeated works, making the search of software and facial recognition technology only in titles; search whose results were not yet adequate to satisfy the investigation. Finally, in order to obtain the definitive list of primary studies, a search based on the search chain is performed with fields selected by "summary" and from academic sources.

During the process of extracting information and reviewing works, it was assumed that the quality of the work obtained would be guaranteed by the evaluation made in the sources from which they were taken, since the studies are shown by their relevance. As regards the collection process, these documents are taken from those that were in line with the approach of the research question and the systematic review.

3 Results of the Review

Table 4 shows the studies selected for the present work, as well as a comparison between them, which is based on the relevant information that was found and established under the parameters described in the previous section. They are arranged alphabetically and their order does not determine their importance with respect to the objectives of this work. This table contains the following information for each analyzed work: (1) work, (2) ad hoc development, (3) software evaluated, (4) programming framework or tool, (5) integrated to software or technology, (6) test database, and (7) related devices.

There are several areas in which we work with facial recognition. Many researchers have opted for developing their own algorithms in order to be sure that they will provide reliable results for each area, while others have used available technology to verify and validate their data. As an attempt to give more validity to their research, some authors present the programming tools with which they have worked and the methods used in the analysis of facial expressions and recognition of emotions.

Many articles show that facial recognition algorithms will be integrated to other technologies and they pursue greater agility in the processing of the information they have. Opportune feedback is sought mainly by taking their emotions and data are collected through a webcam and a microphone [12]. There are several databases with photographs that are currently available to make facial recognition tests, but there are also many cases in which the authors are creating their own databases. Padrón-Rivera et al. [22] tested the accuracy of a tool with the Cohn-Kanade images and the results of the comparisons showed an accuracy of 70%.

As regards hardware related to facial recognition, it was found that there are several devices that currently serve to capture the images of the faces and facial expressions of the individuals being investigated. This is somehow uncomfortable because the person must stop doing their regular activities to lend themselves as models and support the studies. Others are simply recorded while doing their tasks.

Table 4. Summary of articles with the detail of the technology used, its characteristics and the area of application.

1	Software					Hardware
	2	3	4	5	6	7
[4]	Yes	Boosted Deep Belief Network (BDBN)			Extended CohnKanade (CK+), JAFFE	
[5]	No	FaceAPI	MHP (Multimedia Home Platform, version 1.1.3)	Moodle y T-EDUCO		Camera Ip
[6]	No	S/N		TTL signals		Eyetracking, EEG
[7]	No	S/N				
[8]	No	S/N		TTL Signals		3dMDface
[9]	No	Picasa				Photographs
[10]	No	Face2Gene				
[11]	Yes	FACSGen 2.0 animation software		Facial Action Coding System, FACS		
[12]	Yes	S/N	FILTWAM y C++	EMERGO Web Service Client	Cohn–Kanade (CK+)	Web cam and microphone
[13]	Yes	S/N	Visual Studio versión 2010			Ip Camera
[14]	No	Stimulus control, versión 2.0 Software				
[15]	Si	S/N			CFEE, DISFA and CK+	
[16]	No	FaceReader software				Web cam
[17]	Yes	S/N			CASIA, 3DMAD, UVAD	Kinect
[18]	Yes	S/N			Cohn-Kanade database, JAFFE and FEEDTUM datasets	
[19]	No	Attention Tool V5.3 de Computer Expression Recognition Toolbox (CERT)			Jerusalem Facial Expressions of Emotion (JeFEE)	

(*continued*)

Table 4. (*continued*)

1	Software					Hardware
	2	3	4	5	6	7
[20]	Yes	S/N			Image Database	Laptop
[21]						
[22]	Yes	S/N			Cohn-Kanade AU-Coded	Video camera
[23]	No	FaulhaberComp, MuecasJointComp, CamaraComp, IMUComp, RGBDComp, JoystickComp	RoboComp			Multi-sensor robotic head, Microsoft Kinect and sensor Xtion PRO LIVE
[24].	No	CSIRO Face analysis SDK			Audio-Visual Emotion Challenge (AVEC) dataset	Web cam
[25]	No	G8 commercial face recognition software				Monitoring solutions package provided by L1 systems
[26]	No	Matlab 7.0, Emotient FACET SDK v4.1 (iMotions, A/S, Copenhagen, Denmark)			KDEF	
[27]	No	AdaBoost			JAFFE	
[28]	No	FaceReader 5 Noldus		Rosie 2		Eye tracker technology Tobii T60XL

1 = Work, 2 = Ad hoc development, 3 = Software evaluated, 4 = Framework or programming tool,
5 = Integrated in software or technology, 6 = Test database, 7 = Related devices

The application of facial recognition and its advances in the areas of technology, medicine and education are those that are being studied the most. Some of the characteristics found in the selected articles are shown below.

3.1   Areas of Study in the Application of Facial Recognition

Area of Technology

The highest percentage of the articles evaluated and categorized corresponds to those researches related to improving or complementing facial recognition technology. In these articles we find methods that seek to fully satisfy facial recognition regardless the circumstances in which an image is taken, such as combining the average face in 3D and improved Ada-Boost (adaptive algorithm that combines weak classifiers to obhave a robust classifier), to recognize facial expressions in motion, under conditions of poor visibility of the face [27]. Wahab et al. [13], propose an automatic image acquisition system using multicamera to capture facial images from 50 different angular views, which extend horizontally 180° from left to right, and vertically from horizontal to 70° above the face; using 30 IP cameras that were mounted on two rigid steel arms. The technological contributions of the basic forms of emotional expression that appear on the faces of people are of vital importance for neuromarketing as well as for other areas that assist with facial recognition. Recio et al. [11], conducted a face classification study that shows facial expressions of six basic emotions in static and dynamic presentation modes and three different types of neutral movements. The stimuli were created with software that allows a detailed control of the action units and the dynamic characteristics. Those expressions are evaluated by computer vision algorithms for recognition and registration of databases of millions of images of emotion facial expressions, under different conditions and environments such as nature [15].

Facial recognition is combined with other technological methods to avoid transgression when used in private security. Studies that involve methods to detect attempts of impersonation in facial recognition systems are proposed, with the hypothesis that during the acquisition there will be re-captured biometric samples that allow to create a discriminatory signature of the video generated by the biometric sensor [17]. According to Wahab et al. [13], you can recognize facial expressions in 3D formats, get to identify body language and have accurate biometric control with facial recognition.

Facial recognition also allows to improve many processes such as digital security and it improves people's quality of life, as shown by Carter [20]. This author proposes a password system, which is easy to memorize, graphic, and specifically designed for older users, achieving a level of password entropy comparable to traditional PINs and text passwords. It highlights how through facial recognition you can obtain an adequate selection of proposed images as part of passwords for the elderly. In the field of robotics, there are studies of mechanisms that allow direct interaction between the robot and its human companion through the different modalities of natural language: speech, body language and facial expressions [23].

Area of Medicine

Degenerative diseases can be detected in a timely manner by performing simple scans and identifying the genes that cause them. There are studies that support this solution, such as the approach of a facial recognition medical software to achieve the highest precision in the prediction of the gene that causes a disease of physical deformation [10].

The depressive states can also be clearly identified with the facial expressions accurately identified by facial recognition. In this sense, it is important to remark a depression prediction system (mood disorder) that uses a feature selection approach based on audio, visual and linguistic signals to predict depression scores for each session [24].

Studies point out that the medical and forensic sciences are finding great support for their investigations through facial recognition. Whitelam and Bourlai [25] propose an algorithm that improves facial recognition performance in terms of range identification rates, with a practical value for forensic tool operators in the field of Biometrics, to avoid manual locating the eye centers of all the facial images available in a data set. Parks and Monson [7] conducted a study to examine the accuracy with which facial CT images were extracted and paired with available photographs for identification.

Guo et al. [8] present a non-rigid registration method for mapping 3D facial images, which uses seventeen facial references through recognition of functions. They use an independent software to help with the development of an antrophotometric analysis of high content and performance, very useful in anthropology, diagnosis and forensic studies of the human facial morphology.

Area of Education

Education is another area in which researchers are looking for improvement with the use of facial recognition. Many online courses allow you to see the faces of the students, which is being used to provide them with better assistance and support. Baldassarri et al. [5] indicate that this allows them to personalize the courses so that the students take better advantage of the content provided.

Computer systems allow the best detection of the student's emotional state and transmit it to the tutor so that he or she appropriately addresses the tutoring. The development of a tutorial platform for IDTV (Interactive Digital TeleVision) that uses the automatic recognition of facial emotions to improve the tutor-student relationship is studied. The system goes beyond simply transmitting an interactive educational application, and it allows the personalization of the course content thanks to the timely detection of emotions [5].

Nowadays, information is collected on the behavior of people before academic activities, allowing the synchronization of conductual, emotional and cognitive data. This is possible thanks to various applications with sensors that incorporate facial recognition techniques. Studies are being proposed to specifically improve adaptive assessment environments, such as those by Charland et al. [6], who propose a methodology to collect and synchronize data on multidimensional engagement in learning tasks, through the collection of electro-dermal electroencephalography, eye tracking and facial emotion recognition data in four different computers. The use of specialized integration software offers a better understanding of dynamics among the multiple dimensions of commitment.

The virtual training processes are assisted by multimodal recognition, so that teachers can identify students' emotions in real time for their feedback, improving online communication and learning performance. Bahreini et al. [12] propose multimodal emotion recognition software in real time to provide more adequate feedback to students through online communication skills training.

Facial recognition studies and their application in the academic areas generate offer results for predictive use. For example, there is the research carried out by Padrón-Rivera et al. [22] that reveals that through facial recognition, students with confusion during interaction with the mathematics tutoring system had better learning gains than students who had more instances of frustration on their faces [22].

Other Areas

The systematic review revealed that facial recognition computer techniques are applied to many areas, beyond the important impact they may have on neuromarketing.

Dalton et al. [16] contribute to the economic area, through a study in which they use facial recognition and show whether exposure to poverty can lead to affective states that decrease productivity.

As for business, the application of facial recognition in the area of administration, allows to verify the effect of different types of feedback on the performance of a task and achieve the best strategies of satisfaction of those involved [14].

In the area of human resources, software and technology are considered useful to examine the emotional responses shown by social workers and those in charge of health in a child protection center [28].

Facial recognition used by the police is oriented from different perspectives, for example, independent tools of the standard of suspicion are incorporated, which allow restricting the scope of criminal investigations and discard innocents, using facial recognition software and combining it with data mining [21].

In the area of neuromarketing there is few but important research, such as Lopes et al. [4], who present the evaluation of a simple solution for the recognition of facial expressions using a combination of standard methods, such as the convolutional neuronal network and the step of image preprocessing specific to convolutional networks, and machine learning methods [4]. Likewise, Mostafa et al. [18] offer a system that uses the facial action units of the face that identify a person recognized by CNN (Convolutional neural networks) first and incorporate the recognition of the seven basic emotional states.

An important contribution related to marketing is posed by Calvo et al. [26], who present the evaluation of a software that measures basic emotions through calculations. They show very low levels of intensity in order to know if they can be recognized, since they have considerable practical relevance for everyday life, where many emotional expressions are subtle due to social restrictions.

Results are not always favorable for the applications created. For example, Yitzhak et al. [19] present a study that reveals that a facial recognition software can identify the classic prototypical facial expressions of images recorded in the available databases, but unfortunately it could not analyze or capture the natural ones as a reaction to a pipeline, which contain the wealth of everyday emotional communication.

Facial recognition applications can be complex or simple but useful for different areas, for example when incorporating them to the Picasa software, used by the photographic archives personnel. It allowed to identify ways in which the creation of metadata could be automated, giving them time to focus on those areas where human judgment is most valuable [9].

3.2 Facial Recognition Software

Below there is a short detail of software for facial recognition that has specialized in supporting the area of neuromarketing at the commercial level, brought from outside the digital research libraries:

- Software iMotions Neuromarketing Startup Package is characterized by combining different biometric sensors. iMotions exactly reveals what a person is looking at (Attention), if he or she is having a positive or negative feeling (Valence), the intensity of that feeling (Arousal) and the emotions that are expressed at a specific point [29].

- Facial Action Coding System is an online platform to measure emotions and understand human behavior through face analysis. Together with emotional analysis and moods, they allow a much more accurate prediction of consumer behavior [30].
- Affdex allows facial coding and emotional analysis. Advertisers can measure unfiltered and unbiased consumer emotional responses to digital content [31].
- E-Prime is a more complete software available for behavioral research. It performs analysis of patterns of attention, behavior and visual search with the eye Tobii Pro [32].
- Face recognition made easy Kairo is used for collecting unique information in real time about people who interact with the company, brand or product, through face detection, face verification, emotional detection, etc. [33].

Most of the neuromarketing software found on commercial websites has online testing platforms. You must learn to manage them or cancel consulting to reach an adequate and correct interpretation of the obtained results.

4   Discussion

Having established that there was a need for this systematic review and that no other need had been published in this area and approach, the mapping study was carried out. After conducting the systematic mapping review one of the goals was to identify which software or hardware tools are used and available for facial recognition.

When reviewing the primary articles, it was found that in some of them the Noldus FaceReader software was used, which is the one that has been used the most for tests, since it analyzes data (live, video or still images) saving time in the tests. It can be downloaded from the web, but it can also be used as an online application on the Internet. This software is found in some articles because it has been used for more than a decade, in more than 600 universities, research institutes and market companies. According to Reeves et al. [28], FaceReader includes several user-selectable models that provide optimal performance for different groups of people and conditions; it serves as support for the areas of psychology, education, neuromarketing, etc.

Cohn-Kanade was the most used test database to obtain images, followed by the Jaffe database and in third place is the Casia database. Cohn-Kanade has become one of the most widely used test banks for the development and evaluation of algorithms with the purpose of promoting research to automatically detect individual facial expressions.

In the facial recognition article published in 2016 [34] it was already pointed out that improvement in this technology is constantly evolving due to the fact that we want to improve the detection of facial features, even if the person's face has shadows. It even detects faces in the dark. At the present time it allows to interact with different branches of science that facilitate the recognition of an individual through his physical features of his face and his gestures.

It was found in the review that there are several scientific articles in which there was an ad hoc development, that is, the application of algorithms created to improve the times and effectiveness of facial recognition was created and documented.

Among the articles in which new software and algorithms were found, it is evident that the characteristic they have in common is the search for ways to achieve greater speed when performing facial recognition, considering the six basic emotions, which allows a greater productivity and efficiency, and reaches more than 95% accuracy in the information analyzed. Most studies find the main weakness when performing facial recognition, that is, the angle in which the face to be recognized is found or the equipment malfunctions in low light situations, in addition to long hair, sunglasses or other objects that cover part of the face, which makes facial recognition very difficult to do.

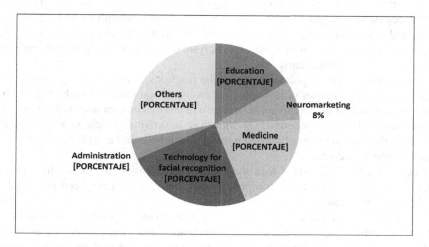

Fig. 1. Main areas supported by facial recognition studies

According to Fig. 1, the two areas in which the facial recognition studies have focused the most are: improvement of general facial recognition technologies and medicine. The percentage of the area called "neuromarketing" corresponds to two articles specifically related to this area. Both are similar in their goals and contain a similar scheme of presentation of the research. The two authors make it clear that they are aimed at supporting the activity of neuromarketing.

Leaving digital research libraries aside, neuromarketing gains commercial interest, for example in the big industry of Hollywood or in developed countries that have technology, market and distribution [35]; such is the case that Disney tracks the facial expressions of an audience when watching a movie in order to evaluate the emotional reactions to it, recognizing a series of facial expressions of the audience such as smiles and laughter.

Another very representative case in the use of neuromarketing is the corporation of Walmart stores, which are even patenting the use of video cameras in the register boxes or store exits, with which they will analyze the facial expressions and the movements of the clients in such a way that they will be able to identify unsatisfied customers. The goal is for as few dissatisfied customers as possible to leave a store without a Walmart employee coming to listen to their possible problems or dissatisfaction.

5 Conclusions and Further Research

This work presents a systematic literary review of neuromarketing mapping with facial recognition and was carried out following the Kitchenham guidelines [3]. In most of the articles reviewed, what is documented in the abstracts does not provide specific information about the potential of the tools, the programming language or framework used, which makes the literary systematic review process more complex.

After the review had been carried out, a first conclusion was reached that points out the existence of few published neuromarketing articles about facial recognition. Most research efforts are focused on finding algorithms that improve the effectiveness of facial recognition assisted by computer programs. It was difficult to find detailed and specialized information, but in any case several serious documents were found that make it possible to clarify terms and find analysis to technical solutions that have been in the market for several years.

It has become very important to know the reactions of human beings doing facial recognition through a series of technological tools and equipment, for which algorithms have been developed that try to solve or improve a series of events and situations such as: achieving greater productivity in industry, improving people's quality of life, facilitating the forensic work, improving teaching methods and expediting the decisions to buy finished products.

Cohn-Kanade, Jaffe and Casia databases are extensive databases that provide images of faces (faces) and the complete human body. They have been used to carry out the algorithms tests.

Although the comparative review shows that there are studies and analysis of software to perform facial recognition, no significant studies were found that emphasize its direct application in neuromarketing, so that gaps have been detected that must be filled. This shows that new lines of research are open to learn more about proposals that get deeper in neuromarketing with facial recognition, so that these gaps are filled. Yet, there is not scientifically documented a technique that provides a robust solution for all kinds of situations in which an image is captured in order to analyze and identify a face under any circumstance.

As future work, this systematic review of the literature is intended to include more innovative technologies when reviewing a broader set of digital libraries. Future work is expected to bring about more findings on the use of hardware and software that support facial recognition in neuromarketing as the main axis, based on continuous improvement.

References

1. Avendaño Castro, W.R.: A case study for the analysis of visual neuromarketing in Plaza Ventura (Cucuta-Colombia). Cuadernos de Administración (Universidad del Valle) **29**, 17–27 (2013). https://doi.org/10.1080/10447318.2016.1159799
2. Vera, C.: Generación de impacto en la publicidad exterior a través del uso de los principios del neuromarketing visual. Telos **12**(2), 155–174 (2010)

3. Kitchenham, B.: Procedures for performing systematic reviews. Keele University Technical Report TR/SE-0401 Press (2004)

4. Lopes, A.T., de Aguiar, E., Oliveira-Santos, T.: A facial expression recognition system using convolutional networks. In: 28th SIBGRAPI Conference on Graphics, Patterns and Images. IEEE Press (2015). https://doi.org/10.1109/sibgrapi.2015.14

5. Baldassarri, S., Hupont, I., Abadía, D., Cerezo, E.: Affective-aware tutoring platform for interactive digital television. Multimedia Tools Appl. **74**(9), 3183–3206 (2015). https://doi.org/10.1007/s11042-013-1779-z

6. Charland, P., et al.: Assessing the multiple dimensions of engagement to characterize learning: a neurophysiological perspective. J. Vis. Exp. **101**, 52627 (2015). https://doi.org/10.3791/52627

7. Parks, C.L., Monson, K.L.: Automated facial recognition of computed tomography-derived facial images: patient privacy implications. J. Digit. Imaging **30**, 204–214 (2017). https://doi.org/10.1007/s10278-016-9932-7

8. Guo, J., Mei, X., Tang, K.: Automatic landmark annotation and dense correspondence registration for 3D human facial images. BMC Bioinform. **14**, 232 (2013). https://doi.org/10.1186/1471-2105-14-232

9. Banerjee, K., Anderson, M.: Batch Metadata Assignment To Archival Photograph Collections Using Facial Recognition Software. Library & Information Science Source Press (2013)

10. Knaus, A., et al.: Characterization of glycosylphosphatidylinositol biosynthesis defects by clinical features, flow cytometry, and automated image analysis. Genome Med. **10**, 3 (2018). https://doi.org/10.1186/s13073-017-0510-5

11. Recio, G., Schacht, A., Sommer, W.: Classification of dynamic facial expressions of emotion presented briefly. Cogn. Emot. **27**, 1486–1494 (2013). https://doi.org/10.1080/02699931.2013.794128

12. Bahreini, K., Nadolski, R., Westera, W.: Data fusion for real-time multimodal emotion recognition through webcams and microphones in e-learning. Int. J. Hum. Comput. Interact. **32**, 415–430 (2016). https://doi.org/10.1080/10447318.2016.1159799

13. Wahab, W., Ridwan, M., Kusumoputro, B.: Design and implementation of an automatic face-image data acquisition system using IP based multi camera. Int. J. Technol. **6**, 1042–1049 (2015). https://doi.org/10.14716/ijtech.v6i6.1848

14. Bueno, R., Torres, M., Gusso, H.L.: Effect of three types of feedback contents on task performance. Acta Comport. **26**(1), 53–69 (2018)

15. Benitez-Quiroz, C.F., Srinivasan, R., Martinez, A.M.: EmotioNet: an accurate, real-time algorithm for the automatic annotation of a million facial expressions in the wild. In: IEEE Conference on Computer Vision and Pattern Recognition. IEEE Press (2016). https://doi.org/10.1109/cvpr.2016.600

16. Dalton, P.S., Gonzalez Jimenez, V.H., Noussair, C.N.: Exposure to poverty and productivity. PLOS ONE **12**, 0170231 (2017). https://doi.org/10.1371/journal.pone.0170231

17. Pinto, A., Pedrini, H., Schwartz, W.R., Rocha, A.: Face spoofing detection through visual codebooks of spectral temporal cubes. IEEE Trans. Image Process. **24**, 4726–4740 (2015). https://doi.org/10.1109/TIP.2015.2466088

18. Mostafa, M., Hossein, K., Seyyed, R.H., Mohammad, M.A.: Facial emotion recognition using deep convolutional networks. In: IEEE 4th International Conference on Knowledge-Based Engineering and Innovation (KBEI). IEEE Press (2017)

19. Yitzhak, N., Giladi, N., Gurevich, T., Messinger, D.S., Prince, E.B., Martin, K., Aviezer, H.: Gently does it: humans outperform a software classifier in recognizing subtle, nonstereotypical facial expressions. Emotion **17**, 1187–1198 (2017). https://doi.org/10.1037/emo0000287

20. Carter, N.J.: Graphical passwords for older computer users. In: 28th Annual ACM · Symposium on User Interface Software and Technology, pp. 29–32. ACM Press (2015). https://doi.org/10.1145/2815585.2815593
21. Bambauer, J.: Hassle. Mich. Law Rev. **113**(4), 461 (2015)
22. Padrón-Rivera, G., Rebolledo-Mendez, G., Parra, P.P., Huerta-Pacheco, N.: Identification of action units related to affective states in a tutoring system for Mathematics. Educ. Technol. Soc. **19**(2), 77–86 (2016)
23. Cid, F., Moreno, J., Bustos, P., Núñez, P.: Muecas: A multi-sensor robotic head for affective human robot interaction and imitation. Sensors **14**, 7711–7737 (2014). https://doi.org/10.3390/s140507711
24. Gupta, R., Malandrakis, N., Xiao, B., Guha, T., Van Segbroeck, M., Black, M., Potamianos, A., Narayanan, S.: Multimodal prediction of affective dimensions and depression in human-computer interactions. In: AVEC 2014, Orlando, Florida, USA, 7 November 2014. ACM Press (2014). https://doi.org/10.1145/2661806.2661810
25. Whitelam, C., Bourlai, T.: On designing an unconstrained tri-band pupil detection system for human identification. Mach. Vis. Appl. **26**, 1007–1025 (2015). https://doi.org/10.1007/s00138-015-0700-3
26. Calvo, M.G., Avero, P., Fernández-Martín, A., Recio, G.: Recognition thresholds for static and dynamic emotional faces. Emotion **16**, 1186–1200 (2016). https://doi.org/10.1037/emo0000192
27. Chen, J., Ariki, Y., Takiguchi, T.: Robust facial expressions recognition using 3D average face and ameliorated Adaboost. In: 21st ACM International Conference on Multimedia, pp. 661–664. ACM Press (2013). https://doi.org/10.1145/2502081.2502173
28. Reeves, J., Drew, I., Shemmings, D., Ferguson, H.: Rosie 2' a child protection simulation: perspectives on neglect and the 'unconscious at work': perspectives on neglect and the 'unconscious at work'. Child Abuse Rev. **24**, 346–364 (2015). https://doi.org/10.1002/car.2362
29. Imotions: Software iMotions Neuromarketing Startup Package. https://imotions.com/neuromarketing/
30. Emotion Research Lab: Facial Action Coding System. https://emotionresearchlab.com/
31. Affectiva: Affdex. https://www.affectiva.com/product/affdex-for-market-research/
32. Mathworks: E-Prime. https://www.mathworks.com/discovery/reconocimiento-facial.html
33. Kairos: Face recognition made easy Kairo. https://www.kairos.com/features
34. Calderón, P., Tejada, M., Yerovi, E., Espinoza, M., Ortega, L.: Facial recognition: a bibliometric study of 20 years. In: Conference: I Congreso Científico Internacional, Sociedad Del Conocimiento: Retos y Perspectivas, At Guayaquil, Ecuador (2016)
35. Bazurto, L.F.G.: The neuromarketing applied to movie trailers of the years 2009 to 2013. Katharsis—ISSN 0124-7816, No. 19, pp. 265–288, Envigado, Colombia Press (2015)

Opinion Mining for Measuring the Social Perception of Infectious Diseases. An Infodemiology Approach

José Antonio García-Díaz[1](✉) ⓘ, Oscar Apolinario-Arzube[2],
José Medina-Moreira[2], José Omar Salavarria-Melo[3],
Katty Lagos-Ortiz[3], Harry Luna-Aveiga[2],
and Rafael Valencia-García[1] ⓘ

[1] Department of Informatics and Systems, Universidad de Murcia, Murcia, Spain
{joseantonio.garcia8, valencia}@um.es
[2] Facultad de Ciencias Matemáticas y Físicas, Universidad de Guayaquil,
Cdla. Universitaria Salvador Allende, Guayaquil, Ecuador
{oscar.apolinarioa, jose.medinamo,
harry.lunaa}@ug.edu.ec
[3] Facultad de Ciencias Agrarias, Universidad de Guayaquil,
Cdla. Universitaria Salvador Allende, Guayaquil, Ecuador
{jsalavarria, klagos}@uagraria.edu.ec

Abstract. Prior to the digital era, knowing the perception of society towards the health-system was done through face-to-face questionnaires and interviews. With this knowledge, governments and public organizations have designed effective action plans in order to improve our quality of life. Nowadays, as a result of the irruption of computer networks, it is possible to reach a higher number of people with a minor cost and perform automatic analysis of the collected data. Infodemiology is the research discipline oriented to the study of health information on the Internet. In this work, we explore the reliability of Opinion Mining to measure the subjective perception of people towards infectious diseases during times of high risk of contagion. In short, linguistic characteristics, among other relevant data, were extracted from tweets written in the Spanish Language by the end of 2017 in Ecuador. The built model contains the most relevant linguistics characteristics related to determine positive and negative pieces of text regarding infectious diseases. In addition, the corpus used in this analysis has been published for other researchers to use it in future experiments in this area. The results showed Support Vector Machines achieved the best results with a precision of 86.5%.

Keywords: Infoveillance · Infectious diseases · Natural Language Processing
Sentiment analysis

1 Introduction

Infodemiology consists of the use of online information for public health purposes such as (1) the prediction of epidemics of infectious diseases, (2) the development of active public health monitoring programs or (3) the development of tools that measure the

R. Valencia-García et al. (Eds.): CITI 2018, CCIS 883, pp. 229–239, 2018.
https://doi.org/10.1007/978-3-030-00940-3_17

perception of the users regarding public health concerns [1]. In this essay, we deal with the third point, that is, regarding the measurement of the perception of public health concerns.

Opinion Mining, aka Sentiment Analysis, is a major task of Natural Language Processing (NPL) related to the study of the subjective opinion of customers regarding a certain topic. Opinion Mining has demonstrated effectiveness as a complementary method for measuring public perceptions in emergencies such as outbreaks of infectious diseases [2]. International Health Regulations (IHR) has indicated surveillance systems are a strategical tool in order to schedule and coordinate strategical actions to mitigate the effects of outbreaks of infectious diseases. Moreover, recent events, such as the first case of contagion of Ebola in Spain, have highlighted the importance of these systems since due to the disproportionate, uncoordinated and non-effective measures adopted [3]. In addition, some types of virus to which humans have not yet developed any kind of immunity, affect areas with a health system not fully developed where conducting surveys is time-consuming.

In this work, we present an analysis of the efficiency of Opinion Mining applied to the healthcare domain from tweets written in the Spanish Language collected from Ecuador. The results of this experiment can be used to better understand the social behavior during outbreaks of infectious diseases.

The rest of the paper is organized as follows. In Sect. 2, background information of related works regarding the retrieval of health information from microblogging sources and opinion mining was provided. The experiment carried out to analyze the effectiveness of sentiment analysis for the Spanish Language is detailed in Sect. 3. In Sect. 4, the results and an analysis of the extracted linguistic characteristics are presented and, finally, in Sect. 5, further lines of research regarding infodemiology are discussed.

2 Related Work

In the bibliography, we found several works related to measuring the perception of the society towards public health concerns from data extracted from the Internet. These works explode two main types of sources: (1) Data queries and (2) Social Networks. On the one hand, regarding to data queries, Ginsberg et al. 2009, monitored large numbers of queries in different search engines to analyze the health-seeking behavior [4]. In [5], the authors conducted an experiment about predicting the dengue influenza by analyzing queries related to the nomenclature, symptoms and treatment of this disease. On the other hand, the earlier works regarding social networks, started by analyzing around two million of tweets related to the influenza under a Sentiment Analysis perspective. The results obtained in this experiment showed that opinion mining applied to streaming content is effective in order to evaluate the overall perception of the society [2]. Prieto et al. developed a method to identify tweets concerned to the healthcare domain by applying regular expressions and machine learning techniques for the Spanish and Portuguese languages [6].

Broadly, every textual piece of information can be categorized into facts and opinions. Whereas facts represent objective expressions about entities and their properties, opinions represent subjective sentiments and appraisals about them. Opinion Mining is a field of Natural Language Processing (NLP) used to measure the opinions and subjective attitude of users regarding some topic [7]. Therefore, Opinion Mining is a key activity to develop systems that measure automatically the public opinion regarding a specific domain.

As a first approach, every Opinion Mining finding can be expressed in a 3-tuples expressing the *author*, the *topic* and the *polarity* of his/her opinion. Modern approaches suggested the inclusion of the *time* as a fourth dimension to express when the opinion was expressed [8]. There are different ways to register the subjective polarity of the users. On the one hand, a binary classification can be used to express if the opinion is positive or negative. On the other hand, more sophisticated approaches give a numerical score to each sentiment (anger, sad, etc.) [9]. However, the most polarized systems, that is, those that allow the least range of responses, are usually the ones that offer the best results.

According to the fine-grained detail of the topic, Opinion Mining can be classified in three different ways. First, in document level, the polarity of a text is extracted as a whole. Second, in sentence level, texts are divided into sentences where each polarity is analyzed individually. Finally, the aspect level classification divides the topic in aspects and performs a more thorough analysis matching a polarity to each aspect of the topic. Aspect-level approaches are usually better to perform deep-analysis, but the identification of the aspects of the topic and tagging a polarity to each of them is complex. In [10], authors combine ontological models to solve these issues.

In order to automatically infer the most consensus sentiment labeled to a new piece of text, Sentiment Analysis offers three main approaches. On the one hand, by identifying the presence of unambiguous words within the text associated to certain sentiments. This approach is easy to use because there are already some repositories containing these words, such as Senti-Word Net. Nevertheless, due to the ambiguous nature of the natural languages, this strategy does not always offer the best results. On the other hand, it is possible to apply machine-learning algorithms to determine if there is a correlation between some of the characteristics of the texts and its subjective polarity. In this area, the study of the frequency of single or paired words can be performed using a Bag of Words model. Other strategies detect more sophisticated sociological and lexical characteristics from the texts, such as the percentage of words related to particular domains: health, food, work, leisure, etc. Linguistic Inquiry Word Counter, aka LIWC, is the de-facto tool to extract these characteristics [11] that has been tested in several domains such as satire detection [12] and Spanish reviews [13].

3 Validation

The proposed experiment consisted in the creation and validation of a sentiment analysis classifier of linguistic pieces related to the Zika, Dengue and Chinkungunya viruses. The training process started with the recollection of a labeled corpus about the infoveillance domain. The source of the corpus was the microblogging social network Twitter, because it provides information which is public, easy to obtain and, due to the limited length of their posts, easy to analyze. However, it is important to remark that

Twitter is not a magic source of data. In [14], some of the weak points of Twitter as a source of Sentiment Analysis were discussed. In particular, the major problems reside in the lack of context of the tweets and problems regarding the bias. However, its benefits weight more than its drawbacks.

For the current experiment, Twitter API was used to query about tweets written in Spanish Language containing keywords such as Dengue and Zika in the geographical area of Ecuador. In this first stage, we automatically filtered tweets with no meaningful information, composed only by mentions, links or hashtags.

Second, the tweets were normalized performing the following actions: (1) Removing the *at* sign from the Twitter usernames, (2) Links were converted into a special tag in order to make easier to detect duplicated tweets; due to the URL minification mechanism of Twitter, the same URL is encoded differently in copy-paste tweets and (3) retweets and duplicated tweets were removed from the corpus. An example of a positive tweet is shown in the Fig. 1.

Noticias Monumental
@MonumentalCR

Seguir

2017 cerrará con importante disminución en casos de dengue, zika y chikungunya
bit.ly/2A09Jy0 #NM935

3:38 - 22 nov. 2017

Fig. 1. Screen capture of a positive tweet

Thirdly, the manual classification of the corpus took place. As machine learning applied to Sentiment Analysis relies in supervised techniques, all the texts had to be labeled as positive or negative. Manual classification is a time-consuming task. In order to solve this issue some works propose automatic labeling techniques that search the presence of emoticons, hashtags in the text, or by combining manual and automatic strategies [15]. However, due to the minor number of emoticons in this corpus, a manual labeling process was decided. We counted with the collaboration of a group of twenty volunteers who every day during four weeks, labeled a set of tweets as positive, negative and out-of-domain. These volunteers performed a total of 51,127 manual classifications. It is important to remark that each tweet was revised and classified by each volunteer, so the tweets with the major consensus opinion were selected, discarding the most controversial tweets.

Figure 2 details the workflow of the manual classification. Grey color represents how many tweets were marked as out-of-domain; red and orange colors represents tweets tagged as negative or strongly negative, and yellow and green represents tweets tagged as positive or very positive.

At the end of this process, we have a balanced corpus with around 1 k positive and 1 k negative tweets. As an additional contribution of this experiment, full list

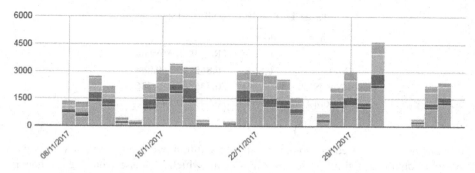

Fig. 2. Workflow of the manual classification. (color figure online)

containing all the tweets IDs is available at http://semantics.inf.um.es/joseagd/infoveillance-zika-twitter.rar

Finally, once the corpus was developed, we extracted linguistic characteristics to perform the machine learning classification. We used two approaches to compare the results: First, the frequency of each term was extracted using a Bag of Words model. Second, lexical, morphological, semantic, and emotional characteristics were extracted by using UMUTextStats [16].

4 Results

Once the linguistic characteristics of the texts were extracted, the WEKA framework [17] was used to build and measure the classification model. Different algorithms were applied, such as SMO, J48 and BayesNet. WEKA was configured with a 10-fold cross validation. This validation consists of a non-exhaustive cross-validation technique used to avoid cross-fitting that consists of splitting N times randomly the corpus into two complementary subsets, performing the analysis and the validation independently in each subset.

As regards the linguistic model, we extracted a vector with 122 linguistic characteristics for each tweet. The results obtained for each classifier applied to these linguistic characteristics are shown in the Table 1, which contains three metrics: precision, recall and f-measure. The precision of the model represents the fraction between the elements correctly classified by the total of relevant instances. The recall stands for the sensibility of the model and represents the probability of detecting true positives. F-measure is the harmonic mean of the precision and the recall.

Out of the three classifiers, the Support Vector Machine classifier (SMO) is the one that obtained the best precession with an 86.5%. This algorithm consists in searching the hyperplane that maximizes the distance between the positive and negative examples. The second algorithm that matches the best result was RandomForest with 84.5% of precision. Random forest consists in the creation of multiple decision trees and returns the mode of the class of all of them. The objective of using multiple trees with random initial values fixes the overfitting to their training set. The worst of the three algorithms was BayesNET with a precision of 73.6%. This network relies in a

Table 1. Results of UMUTextStats

Classifier	Measures		
	Precision	Recall	F-Measure
SMO	**0.865**	**0.865**	**0.864**
Bayes NET	0.736	0.736	0.736
Random Forest	0.845	0.844	0,844

probabilistic model based on acyclic graphs. In addition, we can observe that the three classifiers obtained a similar precision and recall which expresses that the method is reliable.

Figure 3 shows the linguistic characteristics with major info gain ratio, which indicates the level of uncertainty reduction of each attribute. For the sake of simplicity, we show only the 20 attributes with major info gain.

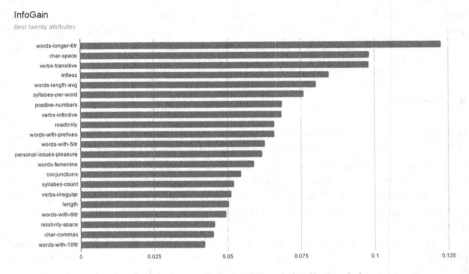

Fig. 3. Information gain of the linguistic characteristics

We can observe how linguistic characteristics related to legibility are the most discriminant in this experiment. Transitivity and the use of the infinitive are the two characteristics of the verbs with major info gain. On the one hand, transitive verbs in Spanish are verbs that need semantic context due to its broad meaning. This kind of verbs usually appear in headlines of news. For example, the verbs *aumentar* and *disminuir* are very popular in headlines as we can see in tweet "*2017 cerrará con importante disminución en casos de dengue, zika y chikungunya*". On the other hand, infinitive verbs are very common to express future events in headlines as for example: "*Destinan 26.6 mdp para prevenir el dengue*". According to sociological characteristics extracted we found the importance of words related to personal issues related to the pleasure.

The individual evaluation of the dimensions is shown in Table 2. These characteristics were grouped by their major category into different categories regarding (1) Errors (ER), (2) Grammatical elements (GE), (3) Linguistic Process (LP), (4) Socio Linguistics (SL), (5) Symbols (SY) and (6) Twitter (TW).

Table 2. Precision regarding the selected characteristics

Dimension	SMO			Random Forest			Bayes NET		
	P	R	F1	P	R	F1	P	R	F1
ER	0.502	0.809	0.620	0.498	0.733	0.593	?	0	?
GE	0.821	0.827	0.824	0.829	0.812	0.821	0.76	0.739	0.749
LP	0.793	0.749	0.771	0.777	0.716	0.745	0.716	0.64	0.676
SL	0.763	0.800	0.781	0.794	0.753	0.773	0.681	0.721	0.7
SY	0.732	0.665	0.697	0.734	0.696	0.715	0.565	0.794	0.66
TW	0.591	0.443	0.507	0.579	0.621	0.599	0.565	0.586	0.575

We can observe how the grammatical elements contain the characteristics with major precision of the model. This category is composed by linguistic characteristics such as the number of adjectives, adverbs, personal pronouns or verbs within the text. The categories of linguistic processes and symbols achieve a precision of 79.3% and 73.2% that indicates the importance of word length and legibility scores as discriminative characteristics. On the other hand, the Twitter category and the Errors category achieved the worst results because the majority of the collected tweets were headlines from news sites with few linguistic errors. As categories are combined, we reach the results showed in Table 1, but we can conclude that it is not necessary to use all the linguistics characteristics extracted and it is possible to produce a more reduced set that achieves similar result with better performance.

A deep study of the linguistic characteristics of grammatical elements is shown in Fig. 4. The grammatical elements category is composed by the elements which give structural rules to build sentences including verbs, adjectives, adverbs, etc.

In the previous figure, the grammatical elements with more info gains are: (1) transitive verbs, (2) conjunctions, (3) infinitive verbs, (4) irregular verbs and (5) numeral adjectives. As commented above, the presence of the infinitive and transitive verbs is related with the linguistic style of news headlines. This is not a surprising result, because some of the styling guides regarding headlines contain these well agreed patterns. The use of present tenses to indicate past events is a special tense called historical tense that adds dramatism and highlights foregrounding events [18]. The use of conjunctions is the second linguistic characteristic with more info gains. In this case, we observed the use of the Spanish preposition *como* (such as) in news rated as positive in headlines such as "*Cómo el cambio climático ayudará a predecir virus como el Zika y el Ébola*"; the absence of this conjunction in negative statement calls our attention. Reviewing positive and negative tweets, we observe how negative tweets should

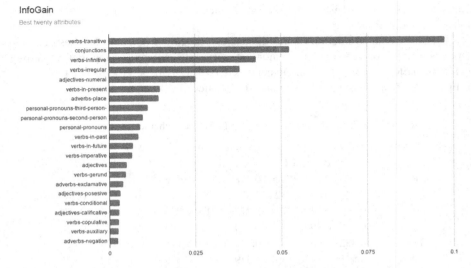

Fig. 4. Information gain of the grammatical elements category

indicate specific events to alert society such as "*OJO Virus con síntoma del zika avanza en el Zulia*" or "*Artemisa registra casos de zika en embarazada*". Numeral adjectives are the type of adjectives with more info gains because they are commonly used to report specific statistics, usually more common in headlines with negative subjective perception.

The built models based on linguistic characteristics were compared against a Bag of Words Model. A Bag of Words consists on vectors that contains the frequency of the word of a tweet in the whole corpus. Despite its simplicity, the Bag of Words model works well for different purposes. Its effectivity has been put in value in the development of spam filters [19]. Specifically, all the words of each tweet of the corpus was collected and the following filters were applied: (1) a stop-words filter, to remove all the common words in Spanish that do not add extra meaning, (2) a stemmer, to reduce words to their stem and (3) all words were converted to lowercase. However, the Bag of Words model is not very suitable for big corpus due to the large number of characteristics extracted. In addition, a major drawback of this approach is that words are treated in isolation and the context that can be extracted from the surrounding words is lost. A solution to this problem is the use of an N-gram that extracts sequences of N-words, resulting in a more powerful approach but with an excessive cost in time and memory for certain situations.

The results highlight the presence of the verbs *evitar* (to avoid), *prevenir* (to prevent), *reportar* (to report), *confirmar* (to confirm), nouns such as *niños* (children), casos (cases), *campaña* (campain), chikungunya; places as Guanajuato or Guatemala, and symptoms related to the infectious disease such as *microcefalia* and *hemorrágico* (Table 3).

The linguistic characteristics with more info-gains are shown in the Fig. 3. We can observe how linguistic characteristics related to legibility are the most discriminant in

Table 3. Results of the Bag of Words

Classifier	Measures		
	Precision	Recall	F-Measure
SMO	0.837	0.836	0.836
Bayes NET	0.730	0.730	0.729
Random Forest	**0.844**	**0.843**	**0.843**

this experiment. Transitivity and the use of the infinitive are the characteristics of the verbs with major info gain. On the one hand, transitivity verbs, in Spanish, usually need semantic context due to its broad meaning. This kind of verbs usually appear in headlines of news, which is one of types of twitter publications. For example, the verbs *aumentar* and *disminuir* are very often in headlines as we can see in tweet *"2017 cerrará con importante disminución en casos de dengue, zika y chikungunya"*. On the other hand, verbs in infinitive are very common to express future events in headlines as for example: *"Destinan 26.6 mdp para prevenir el dengue"*.

Regarding the results obtained by the Bag of Words model, it is important to remark the vector space obtained for big corpus makes very expensive the construction of machine learning classifiers. The built corpus, once stop-words were discarded and a stemmer has extracted the stems, have a total of 9,950 different words were found. The alternative proposal, based on linguistic characteristics, contains only 187 characteristics that grouped words by semantic meaning. The difference between the number of characteristics has a critical performance impact when applying some machine learning algorithms such as the Random Forest.

5   Conclusions and Future Work

In summary, an analysis of opinion mining has been performed to a balanced corpus formed by tweets written in the Spanish language collected in 2017 in Ecuador. The majority of the collected tweets were headlines from news sites; this fact has been discussed in related works such as [20], where the authors crawled Twitter in 2009 and found that the majority of the extracted tweets were news headlines.

The analysis has been performed under two different models. On the one hand, a total of 122 linguistic characteristics have been extracted from the tweets. On the other hand, the frequency of each word within the corpus has been extracted using a Bag of Words approach. Both models were compared using different machine learning algorithms such as SMO, BayesNET and Random Forest. The results showed that linguistic characteristics perform better than the Bag of Words in order to simulate the human subjective perception of headlines regarding infectious diseases. As an additional contribution of this paper, the IDs of the tweets that conform the corpus were published for further experiments regarding opinion mining.

The achieved precision of the Support Vector Machine classifier suggests that it is effective to apply opinion mining techniques to complement surveys to measure social perception regarding news related to infectious diseases. The techniques and models used in this experiment can be useful to develop systems for monitoring the social activity on the Internet. However, it is necessary to complement this approach using techniques that identify the pieces of texts that are relevant for the domain.

Despite the efforts in the filtering process to avoid duplicated items, some of them are difficult to detect. For example, some users copy other tweets modifying some words, turning from singular to plural. Similar tweets are problematic as they introduce bias to balanced corpus because the linguistic characteristics of the duplicated texts have more weight in the construction of the model. To solve this issue, some strategies such as the Levenshtein Distance are being studies. This kind of solutions have demonstrated effectiveness in the detection of duplicated web pages [21].

The precision of the learned models suggests the possibility of their use in systems capable of measuring social perception. However, the corpus set was composed specifically from tweets collected in a specific period of time and a specific geographical area. As the results suggest, some of the linguistic characteristics and words obtained are related to specific topics regarding the infectious diseases studies, so this model should achieve lower performance applied in other contexts. Further research lines should focus on reducing these drawbacks and developing techniques that seek discriminant linguistic characteristics more effectively.

In addition, it is necessary to perform a more robust validation of the UMUTextStats to ensure all the linguistic characteristics contain the minimum number of errors.

Acknowledgements. This work has been funded by the Universidad de Guayaquil (Ecuador) through the project entitled "Tecnologías inteligentes para la autogestión de la salud".

References

1. Eysenbach, G.: Infodemiology and infoveillance: framework for an emerging set of public health informatics methods to analyze search, communication and publication behavior on the Internet. J. Med. Internet Res. **11**(1), 11 (2009)
2. Chew, C., Eysenbach, G.: Pandemics in the age of Twitter: content analysis of Tweets during the 2009 H1N1 outbreak. PLoS ONE **5**(11), e14118 (2010)
3. Jamison, D.T., Breman, J.G., Measham, A.R., Alleyne, G., Claeson, M., Evans, D.B., Musgrove, P.: Disease Control Priorities in Developing Countries. World Bank Publications, Herndon (2006)
4. Ginsberg, J., Mohebbi, M.H., Patel, R.S., Brammer, L., Smolinski, M.S., Brilliant, L.: Detecting influenza epidemics using search engine query data. Nature **457**(7232), 1012 (2009)
5. Althouse, B.M., Ng, Y.Y., Cummings, D.A.: Prediction of dengue incidence using search query surveillance. PLoS Negl. Trop. Dis. **5**(8), e1258 (2011)
6. Prieto, V.M., Matos, S., Alvarez, M., Cacheda, F., Oliveira, J.L.: Twitter: a good place to detect health conditions. PLoS ONE **9**(1), e8619 (2014)
7. Pang, B., Lee, L.: Opinion mining and sentiment analysis. Found. Trends® Inf. Retr. **2**(1–2), 1–135 (2008)
8. Banerjee, D., Mondal, B., Chakraborty, S.: A new framework for sentiment analysis with six-tuples. Communications **2**, 25–29 (2015)

9. Strapparava, C., Mihalcea, R.: Learning to identify emotions in text. In: Proceedings of the 2008 ACM Symposium on Applied Computing, pp. 1556–1560. ACM (2008)
10. Salas-Zárate, M.D.P., Medina-Moreira, J., Lagos-Ortiz, K., Luna-Aveiga, H., Rodríguez-García, M.Á., Valencia-García, R.: Sentiment analysis on tweets about diabetes: an aspect-level approach. Comput. Math. Methods Med. **2017**, 9 pages (2017). Article ID 5140631. https://doi.org/10.1155/2017/5140631
11. Pennebaker, J.W., Francis, M.E., Booth, R.J.: Linguistic Inquiry and Word Count: LIWC 2001, vol. 71. Lawrence Erlbaum Associates, Mahwah (2001)
12. del Pilar Salas-Zarate, M., Paredes-Valverde, M.A., Rodriguez-García, M.A., Valencia-García, R., Alor-Hernández, G.: Automatic detection of satire in Twitter: a psycholinguistic-based approach. Knowl. Based Syst. **128**, 20–33 (2017)
13. del Pilar Salas-Zarate, M., Paredes-Valverde, M.A., Limon, J., Tlapa, D.A., Báez, Y.A.: Sentiment classification of spanish reviews: an approach based on feature selection and machine learning methods. J. UCS **22**(5), 691–708 (2016)
14. Barbosa, L., Feng, J.: Robust sentiment detection on twitter from biased and noisy data. In: Proceedings of the 23rd International Conference on Computational Linguistics: Posters, pp. 36–44. Association for Computational Linguistics (2010)
15. Liu, K.L., Li, W.J., Guo, M.: Emoticon smoothed language models for twitter sentiment analysis. In: Proceedings of the Twenty-Sixth AAAI Conference on Artificial Intelligence (2012)
16. García-Díaz, J.A., Salas-Zárate, M.P., Hernández-Alcaraz, M.L., Valencia-García, R., Gómez-Berbís, J.M.: Machine learning based sentiment analysis on Spanish Financial Tweets. In: Rocha, Á., Adeli, H., Reis, L.P., Costanzo, S. (eds.) WorldCIST'18 2018. AISC, vol. 745, pp. 305–311. Springer, Cham (2018). https://doi.org/10.1007/978-3-319-77703-0_31
17. Hall, M., Frank, E., Holmes, G., Pfahringer, B., Reutemann, P., Witten, I.H.: The WEKA data mining software: an update. ACM SIGKDD Explor. Newsl. **11**(1), 10–18 (2009)
18. Brinton, L.J.: The historical present in Charlotte Bronte's novels: some discourse functions. Style **26**, 221–244 (1992)
19. Kanaris, I., Kanaris, K., Houvardas, I., Stamatatos, E.: Words versus character n-grams for anti-spam filtering. Int. J. Artif. Intell. Tools **16**(06), 1047–1067 (2007)
20. Kwak, H., Lee, C., Park, H., Moon, S.: What is Twitter, a social network or a news media? In: Proceedings of the 19th International Conference on World Wide Web, pp. 591–600. ACM (2010)
21. Di Lucca, G.A., Di Penta, M., Fasolino, A.R.: An approach to identify duplicated web pages. In: Proceedings of 26th Annual International Computer Software and Applications Conference, COMPSAC 2002, pp. 481–486. IEEE (2002)

Early Alert Infrastructure for Earthquakes Through Mobile Technologies, Web, and Cloud Computing

Diego Terán, Joel Rivera, Adrián Mena, Freddy Tapia$^{(\boxtimes)}$,
Graciela Guerrero ⓘ, and Walter Fuertes ⓘ

Universidad de las Fuerzas Armadas, Av. General Rumiñahui w/n, P.O.BOX:
171-5-231B, Sangolquí, Ecuador
{dfterne, jariverall, almena4, fmtapia, rgguerrero,
wmfuertes}@espe.edu.ec

Abstract. During these last years, the use of mobile and Web technologies around the world has reached an increasing impact in society and people's lifestyle, including different places and social classes. Ecuador is a South American country with intense seismic and volcanic activity, where current politics and contingency plans are not optimal, making it necessary to think about a more efficient solution to mitigate this risks and consequences. Considering the growing amount of mobile device users, the reach of mobile networks and combining the risk of situation in which many countries are alike, such as Ecuador. This paper sets the design and development of an early alert infrastructure, through the use of new technologies such as Cloud computing, geolocation, pervasive computing, and Web services. The implemented architecture, and the provided Web service has the objective to improve the evacuation logistic and subsequent rescue work after the occurrence of a natural disaster. The results obtained demonstrate that the use of the system improves to a good extent of the evacuation by reaching to a safe location.

Keywords: Cloud computing · Geolocation · Mobile devices
Global Positioning System · Location Based Services

1 Introduction

Around the earth planet there are a great number of countries exposed to a variety of natural disasters which affect the population. One of the many countries that face this risk is Ecuador. Due to the fact that Ecuador is located in the Pacific Fire Ring, surrounded by many volcanoes alongside the Andes Mountains range, it is prone to lots of volcanic eruptions. Ecuador is located around a lot of tectonic faults, the most important one is the subduction of the Nazca and South American plates [1], as well as the two main faults that spread throughout the country, which are the Pallatanga Fault, and Chingual Fault, giving these places a higher risk of telluric movements, tremors or earthquakes.

© Springer Nature Switzerland AG 2018
R. Valencia-García et al. (Eds.): CITI 2018, CCIS 883, pp. 240–251, 2018.
https://doi.org/10.1007/978-3-030-00940-3_18

These are the two main causes Ecuador is at a high risk of having some big earthquakes each decade, which cause great damages, in some of them human lives are lost, and there are also economic problems for t the inhabitants of the zone and for the country.

Currently in Ecuador, the main institution in charge of regulation and control of natural disasters is the Integrated Security Service ECU-911. According to its home page, ECU 911 integrates the National Police, National Network of Health (Ministry of Health and the Ecuadorian Institute of Social Security and other agencies that provide health services) Armed Forces, Fire Brigade, National Secretariat for Risk Management, Red Cross, National Transit Commission, among others. An emergency and risk central that monitors all kinds of risks and situations which are provoked either the natural environment or the human being. However, the official notification system for natural disasters is the one provided by the Geophysical National Institute, which automatically posts seismic and eruptive data on the official Web page of the institute and on the official Twitter account.

The main aim of the present study is the design, implementation, and configuration of a system for a notification and evacuation guide through the use of technological tools such as Cloud databases, Google Maps Services, Social Networking Media, SMS and real-time Geolocation, by integrating all these services in an efficient way through a network architecture that connects a server application written in Node.js and a mobile application for Android Operating System.

Through the implementation of this system, a technological solution is proposed to face the lack of knowledge on the subject that exists in the majority of countries. By exposing these threats around the Pacific Fire Ring, an effective application that notifies the user in case of a near seismic event is presented, showing the most proximate safe locations and the most optimal route to access them. Additionally, the system also notifies to an emergency contact pre-established by the user about the event by sending an SMS with information about the user and its geographical location (i.e. latitude and longitude), helping to the rescue teams such as firefighters and paramedics in search of survivors.

It is worth mentioning that "on the 16th of April 2016, a Mw 7.8 earthquake impacted coastal Ecuador, being the most devastating registered in northern South America in this century so far" [1]. This is a convincing reason to fulfil concrete actions based on applied research.

Therefore, the main contributions included in this study are: (1) a new application service based on geolocation, assembled on a four-layer architecture, applying the Scrum agile methodology in a modular way, whose system speed results have been validated; (2) An architecture design for a distributed application composed of a Web service, API consumption, and mobile application.

The remainder of this paper is as follows: Sect. 2 describes the related work. Section 3 explains the experimental and computational method used, as well as the process of implementation. Section 4 illustrates the obtained results. Last but not least, Sect. 5 closes the paper with the conclusions and future work lines.

2 Related Work

The present research is based on the concept of ubiquitous or pervasive computing [2], which is a model of interaction with omnipresent and reliable communications in the form of services with high availability. One of the main techniques that has been used is the real-time geolocation, provided by using mobile devices, which are being increasingly used (e-Marketer [3]).

Within this context, the geolocation industry has grown in great number in the last ten years using mobile devices technology. In fact, Location Based Services (LBS) use real-time geolocation data from GPS devices available in smartphones to provide information, entertainment or security [4]. However, in addition to all the advantages provided, the field of LBS also presents itself with difficulties and challenges regarding research, industrial, and commercial interests [5].

Some concerns to be considered with LBS are the personalization, ubiquity to mobile user, security, privacy, and transmission context chaining (i.e., time, location, user profile, and other dimensions) [5]. Another problem not yet resolved and therefore one of the main objectives of this research work is the fact that diverse LBS applications running on mobile devices are developed with the use of geographic data of one of the maps services such as Google Maps, Bing Maps, Yahoo Maps, or free solutions as Open Street Maps, these have some deficiencies in terms of geographical positioning (for example, directions and specific points location), limiting the use of these services in developing countries. Particularly, a lot of routes are not yet defined nor registered. In this situation, the telecommunication, devices, and software companies in the world have invested a lot in the development of technology and the acquisition of companies that let them provide LBS [6].

Based on this context, the industry and the scientific community have been developing studies to improve the quality of life using ubiquitous computing. Outstanding examples include geolocation models [7–10], which describe a system, gadgets, and methods to display searches for network content on mobile devices.

Other topics have been the indoor location method [11–13] with the aim of providing location services in indoor environments. In addition, there are studies that apply Augmented Reality [14], with the purpose of allowing users to navigate in an area with their mobile devices and the interactive discovery of their environments.

There are also tourist guides based on geolocation [15–17] and location of mobile entities in intelligent environments, where there are proposals for different papers [18–20] that use systems based on mobile phones that explore the logical location. Finally, there is LBS to obtain geographic coordinates by providing certain information through its geographic location, such as [21–24].

3 Experimental Setup and Methodology

3.1 Experimental Topology

A mobile application has been developed for devices with Android OS due it has a greater number of users in the market. Figure 1, presents its elements integrated in an architecture that allows its optimal and efficient operation. For this, the system has been composed with a server in the Cloud, which host a developed application that uses Node JS. From here their optimal features are exploited, such as work in real-time, with the aim of being constantly listening to the publications made on the official Twitter account of the Geophysical Institute in charge, so that, when the system of it detects and notifies of the existence of a seismic or volcanic event, the service detects and downloads a file in XML format that the Geophysical Institute maintains on its official Website and updates each event. Once the service detects the publication on Twitter, it compiles an event ID published by straight from Twitter and compares it with the ID stored in one of the records of the downloaded XML file. From which it can obtain data such as the geographical location of the event, and its intensity.

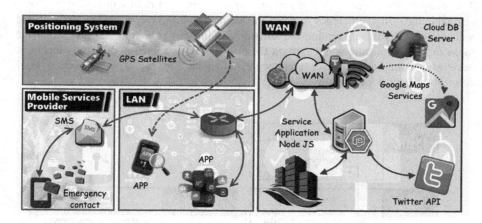

Fig. 1. Diagram of the elements in the network architecture.

Since the specific data of the last reported event has been obtained, it is sent through a PUSH notification using the notice plug-in provided by One Signal to all the devices that have the mobile application installed. The One Signal application is based on the consumption of the Cloud Messaging service provided by Google through its FireBase platform. Subsequently, the device compares its current location with the location of the event received in the notification, and based on that comparison, shows the user a message that is out of risk, or opens a map with the most optimal evacuation route.

For this, the GPS technology (Global Positioning System) [18], allows to determine a location at any point on Earth with a certain degree of precision, putting at hand a tool that allows the user to move with an accurate guide of where the user is and where the user should move to. Finally, if the user is within the risk zone of the disaster, an SMS text message is automatically sent to two telephone numbers previously configured by the user, in order to alert them of their risk situation.

The developed application allows the users to perform several important actions in relation to guarantee the safety and integrity of them during an event of a natural disaster, such as knowing the status of the event near their location, getting an evacuation route to a safe point through a mobile application, and an automated texts messages with the location of the victim of the disaster at the time of the event to two numbers previously configured.

Thanks to a connection through Twitter API it has been possible to obtain data in real-time from the moment of reading of seismic events by the equipment of the Geophysical National Institute, which in charge of reporting these events through its official account. The prototype in its Web service module allows the reading of the reported event on Twitter and the data sent to mobile applications.

3.2   System Architecture

According to Pressman [25], the software architecture is a representation that allows analyzing the design efficiency to cover the identified requirements, makes changes and reduces the risks when creating the software. Using this principle and given that the focus of LBS applications is based on the positioning of a person, our study has been developed using a four-level architecture illustrated in Fig. 2, of which a brief description is provided below.

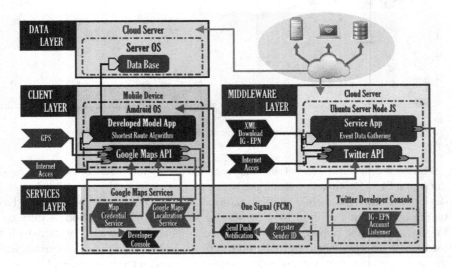

Fig. 2. Four-level architecture system.

The Data Persistence layer, where a server in the Cloud stores a relational database with all the safe points to where it is possible to evacuate according to the type of threat with its respective position, name, description and type of disaster attributes to which applies. In addition, the information of the user's name and telephone numbers to which an SMS will be sent with an alert that the user is in the risk zone at the time of the event is stored.

The Client layer, where the Android mobile application receives information from the database, the Node JS service application through One Signal, and the Google Maps address service. With this information, the Android application indicates the user's risk situation, an evacuation route to safe points and sends an SMS to two emergency contacts.

The Middleware layer, where a server in the Cloud runs a Node JS service application, which is responsible for listening, collecting, validating, and sending the information of events reported as threats automatically and in real-time to the mobile application. For this, the service uses Twitter API to listen to the publications of a specific user, read the chain in a defined format, download an updated XML file with the information of the events from the official Website of the Geophysical Institute, compares it through an event ID, and sends the pre-processed information to the mobile application through the Cloud Messaging service of One Signal Firebase Cloud Messaging.

The Services Layer, provides the system with the following functionalities: (1) Google Maps Services: Maps, Routes, Directions; (2) Twitter Developer Console: Real-time listening for a specific account posts; (3) One Signal: Multiplatform service for administration and Push notifications sending to mobile devices.

3.3   System Implementation

To implement the system, it was initially developed a database with real data obtained through an experimental research, allowing to store all the descriptive and geographic data for the safe places. In addition, name and contact telephone numbers were entered, they will receive a text message with the user's coordinates at the time of an event such as earthquakes or volcanic eruption.

Subsequently, the Node JS application has been designed as a listening service, which allows to know in real-time when there has occurred a natural disaster, event automatically published by the Geophysical Institute via twitter account. The Node JS application displays on the screen a message, announcing that the event has been raised.

On the server, the Node JS application constantly remains listening to the official twitter account of the Geophysical Institute in charge, with a text analysis algorithm written in the publication, which is responsible to identify the two main parameters.

The label in which the type of natural disaster or event that has arisen has been analyzed, it could be #SISMO or #VOLCAN, thanks to the identification of these labels it allows the server to distinguish the useful publication for the application, so that the correct notifications can be sent. Each event has an event ID, which is an alphanumeric code that allows the Geophysical Institute system to identify a unique form of occurrence.

When the service detects by means of a label that the event is of an earthquake type, is proceeded by downloading an XML file from the official Web site of the Geophysical Institute trough an event "request HttpGet". Later it evaluates trough a search in the XML file which ones are the detailed features of the event that is identified in the XML files with the same event ID that is published-on twitter. This way, the service automatically obtains the details of the seismic or volcanic event in real-time, to finally send these data through the Push notification platform "OneSignal", which is based on the FireBase Cloud Messaging platform (FCM) from Google.

The reason for the use of a push notification service in this research project is due to the efficiency of resources of this type of warnings, given that it allows the application to receive information while it is closed. All thanks to the fact that a component of notification implemented in the application that consumes very few system resources remains waiting to receive information as a background process.

Therefore, the mobile application receives the information through the notification, which allows the relative position of the user to be evaluated by means of the GPS device incorporated in the smartphone in relation to the position of the event in latitude a longitude that was received in the Push notification (Fig. 3a and b). In case the application detects that the user is not in a risk zone, it will simply show the warning alerting the user that a seismic event has arisen, and when selected by the user, it will only show a message indicating that he is not located in a dangerous area.

(a)   (b)

Fig. 3. SMS received by emergency contact (a) Route generated to nearest safe location with the option to select another secure site (b)

4   Evaluation, Results and Discussion

4.1   Efficiency of the Architecture Service

In order to quantitatively evaluate the proper and efficient functioning of the distributed software, measurements were made of the time invested by the system by notifying the user about an event, and in the same way taking time for the emergency contacts mobile phones to receive the text message with the user's location on the mobile application. The time collected is presented in the Table 1 in "seconds, thousandths of a second" and in its respective numerical value for further statistical analysis. The respective numerical values were stablished by making the transformation from the time to numerical value and multiplying it by 100, since they are extremely small values expressed in thousandths of a second. These measurements of times are demonstrated in Fig. 4.

Table 1. System notifications times (minutes, seconds and milliseconds)

	x_0	x_1	x_2	x_3	x_4	x_5	x_6	x_7	x_8	x_9
x_i	1	2	3	4	5	6	7	8	9	10
$f(x_i)$	0,0 016 169	0,0 022 836	0,0 031 157	0,0 013 831	0,0 043 368	0,0 025 382	0,0 030 544	0,0 021 609	0,0 030 949	0,0 035 903
$f(x_i)$	00: 01, 397	00: 01, 973	00: 02, 692	00: 01, 195	00: 03, 747	00: 02, 193	00: 02, 639	00: 01, 867	00: 02, 674	00: 03, 102

In order to verify the consistency of the times, and therefore the constancy of the system state despite the network conditions that could be found both on the server and on the mobile device, two fundamental statistical measures were evaluated, and they are arithmetic mean and the standard deviation, from which it has been possible to obtain a statistical measure of relative dispersion known as the coefficient of variation (C.V.), whose mathematical model is expressed like (Eq. 1):

$$C.V. = \frac{\sigma}{\mu} 100\% \tag{1}$$

Where σ is the standard deviation and μ is the arithmetic mean, both criteria are previously calculated by using the following formulas and by obtaining the values presented below (Eq. 2):

$$\mu = \frac{\sum x_i}{n} = 0.0027175; \sigma = \sqrt{\frac{\sum f(x_i - \mu)}{n}} = 0.0009019 \tag{2}$$

Finally, the C.V. is calculated by giving a value as a percentage indicating whether the measurement is constant. Furthermore, demonstrating that the implemented architecture favors the consistent functioning of the application in very short answer

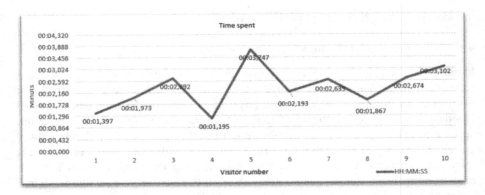

Fig. 4. Time spent in sending the push notifications

times. This value gives as a result that the application works, in a generalized way as an early warning system with notification in real-time.

4.2 Time to the Secure Location

To evaluate the efficiency of the developed system in the fulfilment of its main target, that is to safeguard people's lives by allowing them to reach a safe location in the fastest way, the time that it takes to reach the nearest safe location was also evaluated.

For this, measurements on three different routes with different starting points in two different scenarios were done: using the system, and without using it (i.e., following traditional signage). With the purpose of performing a statistical and comparative analysis of the times used in both scenarios, the calculation of the arithmetic mean was made (Table 2).

Table 2. Route data

Data	x_0	x_1	x_2	x_3	x_4	x_5	x_6	x_7	x_8	x_9
x_i	1	2	3	4	5	6	7	8	9	10
$f(x_i)$	0.0 017	0.0 028	0.0 023	0.0 031	0.0 027	0.0 014	0.0 019	0.0 025	0.0 015	0.0 027
$f(x_i)$	0:0 2:3 0	0:0 4:0 3	0:0 3:1 5	0:0 4:2 9	0:0 3:5 4	0:0 1:5 9	0:0 2:4 6	0:0 3:3 8	0:0 2:1 1	0:0 3:4 9

The data collected from the first route is shown in Table 3, and they represent an example of them. The same process of data collection and their transformation to numerical values was carried out for Route 2 and Route 3.

In addition, the C.V. has been calculated to evaluate the times in three destination routes, in which the proposed architecture has been used versus not using any architecture. From these results, it can be obtained that the use of the system improves greatly to evacuate to a safe place (Table 4).

Table 3. Calculation of the arithmetic mean and standard deviation.

Data	$R1 - \mu$	$R1 - \sigma$	$R2 - \mu$	$R2 - \sigma$	$R3 - \mu$	$R3 - \sigma$
With system	0.0023	5.9422e−04	0.0016	6.0924e−04	0.0013	4.2728e−04
Without system	0.0056	0.0012	0.0037	6.6926e−04	0.0022	5.8167e−04

Table 4. Coefficient of variation calculation.

Data	C.V. Route 1	C.V. Route 2	C.V. Route 3
With system	26.2744%	37.3055%	32.6119%
Without system	21.9044%	18.0983%	26.7607

These results demonstrate that this implementation allowed the adequate and efficient use of the available technological resources. Furthermore, it improves the overall performance of the system and taking advantage of the progress of the mobile network conditions and the services provided by Google and the advantage of obtaining information from social networks, allowing users of the same (twitter) to be part of the solution.

4.3   Discussion

After that the design and implementation of a prototype of the proposed real-time early warning system was completed, it can be verified the great contribution that it provides to users when evacuating to a safe location in the case of a natural disaster occurrence.

The implementation of a distributed application architecture with four layers allowed the adequate and efficient use of the available technological resources, improving the overall performance of the system, and taking advantage of the progress of the mobile network conditions and the services provided by Google and the advantage of obtaining information from social networks, allowing users of the same (twitter) to be part of the solution.

Regarding the development of location-based services (LBS), a system like the one presented in this project research aimed in favor of the community and safeguarding lives can be implemented in national security integrated environments such as the ECU911 in Ecuador. This integration can allow, for example, that the application reports to the ECU911 system about the exact location in coordinates of the users at the time of the natural disaster, facilitating the work of rescuers and other security entities such as paramedics, firefighters and police.

5   Conclusions and Lines of Future Work

The present of this study has been focused on the design and development of a complete and distributed infrastructure in layers for a more efficient use of technological resources, without overloading the processing, memory usage and network use of a mobile device through the use of a database hosted in the Cloud, consumption of Google API and analysis of social networks such as Twitter.

In addition to the implementation of a server that is responsible for the processing of information, so that the user is offered a light application. The results show that the prototype has met expectations, allowing to improve times of evacuation to safe sites, safeguarding user's lives in case of natural disasters. Furthermore, it was demonstrated that the implemented architecture works efficiently through the measurement of response times since an event is published on Twitter, until notification is received in the mobile application.

As a complementary study, the analysis of other means has been proposed to obtain additional data of the social network Twitter, in order to get information from other types of risk events that may occur like tornadoes or nuclear accidents.

Acknowledgements. The authors would like to express special recognition to all students and professionals of the Department of Computer Sciences of the Universidad de las Fuerzas Armadas ESPE, who participated actively during the development of this project. Our distinctive recognition to the Distributed Systems, Cybersecurity and Content (RACKLY) Research Group of that University, for their invaluable help, resources, and technical support.

References

1. Toulkeridis, T., Mato, F., Toulkeridis-Estrella, K., Pérez, J.C., Tapia, S., Fuertes, W.: Real-Time Radioactive Precursor of the April 16, 2016 MW 7.8 Earthquake and Tsunami in Ecuador. J. Sci. Tsunami Hazards **37**(1), 34–48 (2018)
2. Biljana, R., StojkoskaKire, T.: A review of internet of things for smart home: challenges and solutions. J. Clean. Prod. **140**(3), 1454–1464 (2017)
3. eMarketer: Smartphone Users and Penetration Worldwide 2013–2018, August 2015. https://www.emarketer.com/. Accessed 23 Oct 2017
4. Rao, B., Louis, M.: Evolution of mobile location-based services. Commun. ACM **43**, 61–65 (2003)
5. Schiller, J., Agnés, V.: Location-Based Services. Elsevier, Oxford (2004)
6. Vaughan-Nichols, S.: Will mobile computing's future be location, location, location? IEEE Xplore **42**, 14–17 (2009)
7. Chen, Y., Kobayashi, H.: Signal strength based indoor geolocation. In: de 2002 IEEE International Conference on Communications, Conference Proceedings, ICC 2002 (Cat. No. 02CH37333), New Jersey (2002)
8. Yang, Z.-D., Guan, M.: Research on precise geolocation model and method using satellite remote sensing. J. Remote Sens. **2**(2), 232 (2008)
9. Arth, C., Pirchheim, C., Ventura, J., Schmalstieg, D., Lepetit, V.: Instant outdoor localisation and slam initialisation from 2.5 d maps. IEEE Trans. Vis. Comput. Graph. **21**(11), 1309–1318 (2015)
10. Hamynen, K.: Displaying network objects in mobile devices based on geolocation. US Patent US8301159 B2, 30 October 2012
11. Qian, J., Ma, J., Ying, R., Liu, P., Pei, L.: An improved indoor localization method using smartphone inertial sensors. In: de International Conference on Indoor Positioning and Indoor Navigation (2013)
12. Subbu, K.P., Brandon, G., Ram, D.: Locateme: magnetic-fields-based indoor localization using smartphones. ACM Trans. Intell. Syst. Technol. (TIST) **4**(4), 7:31–73:27 (2013)

13. Kang, W., Han, Y.: SmartPDR: smartphone-based pedestrian dead reckoning for indoor localization. IEEE Sens. J. **15**(5), 2906–2916 (2015)
14. Aydın, B., Gensel, J., Calabretto, S., Tellez, B.: ARCAMA-3D – a context-aware augmented reality mobile platform for environmental discovery. In: Di Martino, S., Peron, A., Tezuka, T. (eds.) W2GIS 2012. LNCS, vol. 7236, pp. 17–26. Springer, Heidelberg (2012). https://doi.org/10.1007/978-3-642-29247-7_2
15. Noguera, J., Barranco, M., Segura, R., Martínez, L.: A mobile 3D-GIS hybrid recommender system for tourism. Inf. Sci. **215**(Suppl. C), 37–52 (2012)
16. Priandani, N., Tolle, H., Hapsani, A., Fanani, L.: Malang historical tourism guide mobile application based on geolocation. In: de Proceedings of the 6th International Conference on Software and Computer Applications, Bangkok (2017)
17. Aleksandar, P., Pletl, S., Pejic, S.: An expert system for tourists using Google Maps API. In: de 2009 7th International Symposium on Intelligent Systems and Informatics, Serbia (2009)
18. Roth, J., Tummala, M., McEachen, J. Scrofani, J., DeGabriele, R.: Maximum likelihood geolocation in LTE cellular networks using the timing advance parameter. In: 10th International Conference on Signal Processing and Communication Systems (ICSPCS), Australia (2016)
19. Coronato, A., Esposito, M., DePietro, G.: A multimodal semantic location service for intelligent environments: an application for Smart Hospitals. Pers. Ubiquit. Comput. **13**(7), 527–538 (2009)
20. Azizyan, M., Constandache, I., Choudhury, R.: SurroundSense: mobile phone localisation via ambience fingerprinting. In: de 15th Annual International Conference on Mobile Computing and Networking, New York (2009)
21. Shek, S.: Next-generation location-based services for mobile devices. Comput. Sci. Corp. 1–66 (2010)
22. Santana, J.M., Wendel, J., Trujillo, A., Suárez, J.P., Simons, A., Koch, A.: Multimodal location based services—semantic 3D city data as virtual and augmented reality. In: Gartner, G., Huang, H. (eds.) Progress in Location-Based Services 2016. LNGC, pp. 329–353. Springer, Cham (2017). https://doi.org/10.1007/978-3-319-47289-8_17
23. Jones, R., Alizadeh-Shabdiz, F., Morgan, E., Shean, M.: Techniques for computing location of a mobile device using calculated locations of wi-fi access points from a reference database. United States Patente US20170127376 A1 (2017)
24. Schiller, J., Voisard, A.: Location-Based Services, p. 273. Elsevier, Sebastopol (2004)
25. Pressman, R.: Practitioner's Approach. McGraw Hill, New York City (2007)

E-learning

Funprog: A Gamification-Based Platform for Higher Education

Mariuxi Tejada-Castro[1](✉) ⓘ, Maritza Aguirre-Munizaga[1] ⓘ,
Elke Yerovi-Ricaurte[1] ⓘ, Laura Ortega-Ponce[1] ⓘ,
Oscar Contreras-Gorotiza[1] ⓘ, and Gabriel Mantilla-Saltos[2] ⓘ

[1] School of Computer Engineering, Faculty of Agricultural Science,
Universidad Agraria del Ecuador,
Av. 25 de Julio, P.O. Box 09-04-100, Guayaquil, Ecuador
{mtejada, maguirre, eyerovi, lortega}@uagraria.edu.ec,
angeloscar21@hotmail.com
[2] Facultad de Ciencias Naturales y Matemáticas,
Escuela Superior Politécnica del Ecuador,
Km. 30,5 Vía Perimetral, Guayaquil, Ecuador
gmantill@espol.edu.ec

Abstract. Gamification is an approach that uses game design elements in nongame contexts. The gamification approach has been successfully applied to a variety of different contexts such as tourism, architecture, and education. In Colombia and Ecuador, there are several works that have generated great contributions to the gamification domain. However, in South America, and specifically in Ecuador, there are few higher education applications based on the gamification approach. In this sense, this work presents Funprog, a gamification-based platform for higher education that aims to generate an emotional and social impact on students. Funprog defines a set of game levels where students face new challenges that allow them to obtain more knowledge and improve their skills. Funprog was used by first-year students from the Agrarian University of Ecuador. Specifically, this application was focused on the teaching of the Programming Fundamentals subject. Finally, a set of surveys were conducted to know the level of acceptance of Funprog among students and teachers. The surveys' results denote a clear acceptance of this application.

Keywords: Gamification · Education

1 Introduction

Gamification is an approach that uses game design elements in nongame contexts [1]. It is suggested that "gamified" applications provide insight into novel, gameful phenomena complementary to playful phenomena. Gamification has proven to provide positive results in the education sector [2]. In Colombia and Ecuador, there are several works that have generated great contributions to the gamification domain [3]. However, in South America, and specifically in Ecuador, there are few higher education applications based on the gamification approach. On the other hand, there are several studies

© Springer Nature Switzerland AG 2018
R. Valencia-García et al. (Eds.): CITI 2018, CCIS 883, pp. 255–268, 2018.
https://doi.org/10.1007/978-3-030-00940-3_19

that show a tendency for students to use mobile applications to reinforce the content learned or introduce new knowledge [4].

Considering the above-discussed facts, this work presents Funprog, an educational platform based on gamification that aims to generate an emotional and social impact on higher education students [5]. Funprog addresses the gamification usage in higher education in Ecuador. Furthermore, the present work describes a case study about the application of Funprog in an Ecuadorian university in order to better understand how gamified system-student interaction in higher education is developed. Besides, this work describes theoretical foundations for the influence of gamification on student motivation.

The remainder of this work is structured as follows: Sect. 2 discusses a set of research efforts focused on the adoption of the gamification approach in the educational domain. Then, Sect. 3 details the components of the Funprog architecture, whereas Sect. 4 describes the case study regarding the use of Funprog in an Ecuadorian university. Section 5 presents a set of surveys conducted to know the level of acceptance of Funprog among students and teachers. Finally, Sect. 6 discusses research conclusions and future directions.

2   Related Works

The gamification approach has been successfully applied to a variety of different contexts such as tourism [6], architecture [7], socio-cognitive [8, 9], and education [10], to mention but a few. For instance, in [11], the authors propose a model for the introduction of gamification into the field of e-learning in higher education. Also, the authors mentioned that a proper integration of gamification in the field of e-learning into higher education will produce a positive impact on the learning process achieving results such as a higher satisfaction, motivation and greater engagement of students. On the other hand, in [12], the authors presented the framework GEL (Gamification for EPUB using Linked Data) which allows incorporating gamification concepts in a digital textbook, using EPUB 3 and Linked Data. Also, the authors proposed the GO (Gamification Ontology) ontology which allows discovering other gamified books, to share gamification concepts between applications and to separate the processing and representation of the gamification concepts. In [13], authors describe the added value of using gamification in project management education. In this sense, they evaluated an actual case study of a gamified PMBOK-based project management course for junior project managers in Europe. This evaluation covered training, evaluating the reactions of the participants, the level of cognitive learning, and the way actual behavior changed. In [14], the authors presented a gamification-based architecture for the Web environments and addressed its applications and challenges. Also, they present a case study concerning gamification of electronic tests and discuss how gamification can change a stressful exam environment to a joyful and yet instructive one.

In [15], the authors defined that the objective of a gamified application is to increase the comprehension of a subject through game techniques and rewards. In addition, they found that the gamification approach facilitated the learning of a programming language while improved student understanding. On the other hand, in [16], the authors concluded that a virtual environment can make students reflect with respect to the functional, formal or material quality of architectural spaces, which suggests a new educational path based on the gamification approach. Finally, some authors suggest that gamification approach can be adapted to the new ways of learning of students since it promotes the interest of individuals through activities that allow them to make decisions, be creative and achieve an objective [17]. Hence, the gamification techniques can be integrated into the curricular design model of the Ecuadorian universities [18] aiming to improve the learning environment of students and accelerate the process of skills acquisition.

2.1   Gamification in Education: A Bibliometric Analysis

This section presents a statistical analysis of written publications, such as books or articles related to the gamification approach in the educational domain. For this purpose, we performed an exhaustive analysis of 56 scientific and academic works that analyze gamification features. This task consisted of a multivariate statistical analysis focused on detecting similarities between four explanatory variables that represent the research works. These variables are the year of publication, publication modality, language, and gamification features.

Figure 1 shows the occurrence of works published in Spanish and English under the modalities of book, conference, congress, journal, repository, and symposium, from the period 2011 to 2017. As can be seen, in the years 2015 and 2017, a greater number of works related to the gamification approach was published in English under the journal modality. In addition, in 2015 a greater number of works in Spanish was published under the modalities of congress, journal, and thesis.

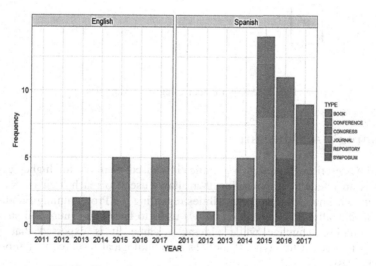

Fig. 1. Research works grouped by type and language.

Figure 2 shows the MCA (Multiple Correspondence Analysis) [19] for four categorical variables namely: year of publication, language, modality, and gamification features (dynamic, motivation, objectives, and goals). These gamification features were selected because they allow monitoring the content programmed in a Web environment. As can be seen, the dynamic feature has a major impact on works published in Spanish under the modality of "Conference" during 2012. Meanwhile, the motivation feature affects mainly works published in English under the modality of "Journal" in 2013 and 2017. The objectives feature is mainly found in works published in English under the "Symposium" modality. Finally, it can be observed that the goals feature has had a great impact since 2015.

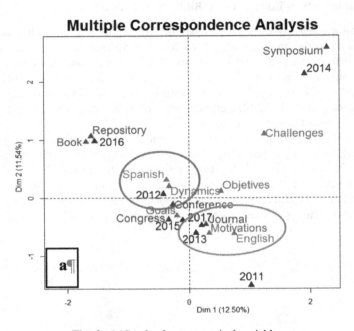

Fig. 2. MCA for four categorical variables.

3   Funprog's Architecture

This section describes Funprog, a gamification-based platform for higher education. Funprog is an interactive application that allows users to reach their objectives and strengthen their knowledge and capabilities regarding the Programming Fundamentals subject. Specifically, this application allows users to learn the syntax and structure of the programming language while playing a game. It is expected that Funprog encourages the use of this type of tools as a technological resource that supports the learning process.

The Funprog's architecture consists of five main layers namely: user interface, scenarios, game objects, application, and gamification. Each layer contains a set of

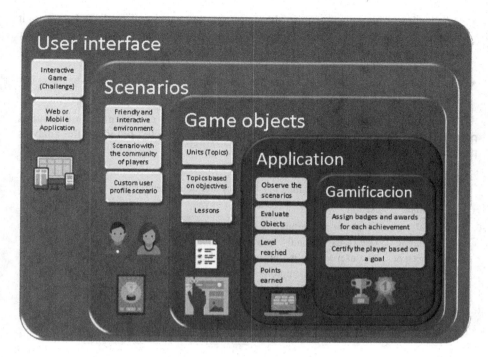

Fig. 3. Funprog's architecture.

components with different levels of interdependence. This means that the tasks and responsibilities of Funprog are distributed through all its layers and components, thus allowing for scalability and easy maintenance. The functional architecture of Funprog is presented in Fig. 3.

The layers of the Funprog's architecture are below described in detail.

- User interface. This layer consists of a multi-device application that allows higher education students to access all features and services offered by the gamified platform. That is, to play a game that provides them interactive content focused on learning the structure and syntax of a programming language.
- Scenarios. This layer provides a scenario-based learning environment that aims to promote learning by involving students in realistic problems where they are forced to consider a wide range of factors, make decisions and reflect on the outcomes and what they have learned from this.
- Game objects. This layer provides a set of game objects that are assigned to the units of study or levels of learning. These objects provide content that users must learn to achieve game objectives or awards. When the user achieves an objective, the game assigns a score. When users reach a score, the game allows them to advance level in the game. At the end of the game, the application provides users their final score and certifies their participation.

- Application. This layer refers to the way users are rated and evaluated, that is, it provides the user with a general report with the score achieved. In this way, the user can approve each module or level of the game based on the scenarios and learning objects included in it.
- Gamification. This layer is responsible for assign badges and awards to users for each goal they achieved.

The Funprog platform aims to meet with the actions and gamification features presented in Table 1. These features and actions were selected based on the analysis presented in Sect. 2.1.

Table 1. Gamification features and action analyzed.

Feature	Action
Goal	The basis of learning. (Challenge)
Dynamic	Use of user-friendly interfaces
Objective	The user knows the objective he/she intends to achieve
Motivation	To establish a compromise between the player and the game
Objective	There are different player profiles
Motivation	There is a predisposition of the user to learning through the game
Dynamic	To encourage learning through play
Goal	The objective of the game is to reach the goal

Next, each of the actions presented in Table 1 is described in detail.

- The basis of learning. This action aims to allow the establishment of goals as well as to reinforce learning competencies within the environment. For this purpose, it is necessary to use personalized learning objects.
- Use of user-friendly interfaces. This action aims to use user-friendly interfaces as a motivational and didactic strategy in the teaching-learning process. This will allows generating specific student behaviors in an attractive and motivating environment.
- The user knows the objective he/she intends to achieve. This action aims to engage users with the system, as well as to support the achievement of positive experiences that allow them to achieve meaningful learning.
- To establish a compromise between the player and the game. This action focuses on limiting the actions of the players in order to keep the game manageable and to allow everyone to participate. This action is achieved through rules that must be simple, clear, and intuitive.
- There are different player profiles. This action aims to establish multiple competencies and complexities in the game in order to allow users to know their progress, which in turn will generate credibility and reputation.
- There is a predisposition of the user to learning through the game. The user's predisposition is evidenced by the freedom to choose and make mistakes. These actions are scored at the end of the episode, and the system generates statistics on the player's performance.

- To encourage learning through play. This action helps users to explore and advance the game based on different possibilities, which motivates the competition and the feeling of achievement through rewards and goals.
- The objective of the game is to reach the goal. This action helps users understand the purpose of each activity, thus allowing directing the students' efforts towards their academic goals.

4 Case Study

As mentioned above, Funprog is a gamification-based application focused on the teaching of the Programming Fundamentals subject. This application provides elements that aim to allow students to develop logic and critical thinking skills. The Programming Fundamentals subject was chosen because it has been included in the curricula of different courses at the Agrarian University of Ecuador. Specifically, this application is aimed at first-year higher education students. Some of the topics addressed by Funprog include Programming Fundamentals, Introduction to Computing, Introduction to C programming, Control Structures, among others. In Funprog, there are two types of users who are student and teacher. These users have access to different functionalities which are described below. Finally, it must be mentioned that Funprog is available in the Google Play store[1].

Fig. 4. Teacher's interface.

---

[1] https://play.google.com/store/apps/details?id=com.artech.compilou.funandroid&hl=hu.

Figure 4 shows the teachers interface where they can create groups of students as well as obtain a detailed report of the objectives and awards achieved by the students. This report also provides information about the units and lessons completed by each student. Hence, this report can be considered as part of the evaluation of students in classroom.

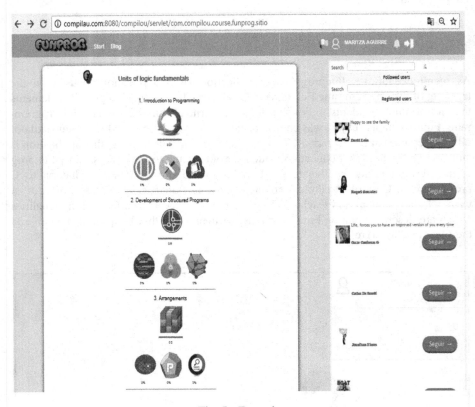

Fig. 5. Example.

Figure 5 shows the interface that presents the units and lessons to be covered during the Programming Fundamentals course. Once student complete 100% of each lesson, he/she performs an evaluation whose results determine if the student can advance to the next level or lesson.

Figure 6 shows an example of a message that is provided to the student when he/she successfully concludes a lesson, which will allow him/her to advance to the next level.

Finally, Fig. 7 presents the interface where students can customize their profile. Specifically, this interface allows them to choose an avatar, configure additional profile data, access personal performance reports, consult the awards and results obtained in each lesson. In order to create a collaborative environment, the student can create

Fig. 6. Example.

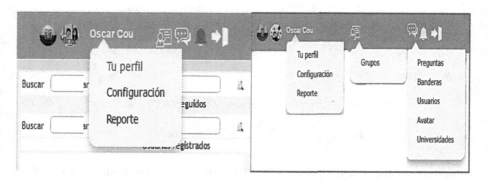

Fig. 7. Example.

groups with whom to share their achievements and exchange comments. In this way, the game becomes competitive and exciting because each student will feel motivated to be part of the game and meet the final goal, that is, to finish the game with the best score.

5 Evaluation

First, a survey was conducted with a group of 80 students from the Agrarian University of Ecuador. This group was formed by 43 men and 37 women with an age range of 17–23 years. The objective of this survey was to know how often students use mobile

Table 2. Questions asked before students were asked to use Funprog.

No.	Question
Q1	Gender
Q2	Age
Q3	How often do you use a mobile device or a PC to reinforce the knowledge acquired in the classroom?
Q4	Do you think a tool that helps to reinforce the knowledge acquired in the classroom is useful for students?
Q5	How often do you use a mobile device or a PC with Internet access?

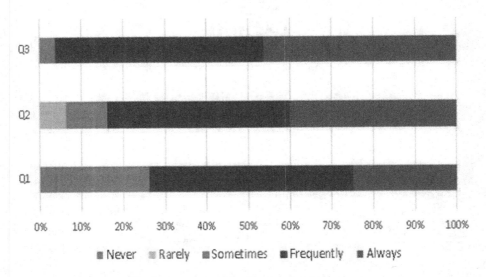

Fig. 8. Survey results prior to using the system.

applications or any other software to reinforce the knowledge acquired in the classroom. Questions used in this survey are presented in Table 2.

The students answered Q3–Q5 questions according to a scale of 1 to 5, where 1 = never, 2 = rarely, 3 = sometimes, 4 = frequently, and 5 = always. Figure 8 presents the survey results which denote a clear trend towards the use of a tool that helps students reinforce the knowledge acquired in the classroom.

Once the above-described survey was conducted, students were asked to use the application for 8 weeks. At the end of this period, a second survey was conducted aiming to know the level of acceptance of Funprog among students. Table 3 presents the set of questions asked in this survey.

The students answered questions according to a scale of 1 to 5, where 1 = strongly disagree, 2 = disagree, 3 = neutral, 4 = agree, and 5 = strongly agree. Figure 9 presents the results of the survey performed after students used Funprog. In this figure, it can be seen that most of the students (70%) rated the application with a 4 or 5, which

Table 3. Questions asked after students used Funprog.

No.	Question
Q1	The interface friendly and intuitive
Q2	Using a scale of 1 to 5, how intuitive is the interface?
Q3	I will use Funprog to reinforce the knowledge acquired in the classroom
Q4	I can solve problems that I could not before
Q5	The interface is appropriate for higher education students
Q6	The content is suitable for higher education students
Q7	Funprog meets the learning objectives of the Programming Fundamentals subject
Q8	How dynamic is Funprog?
Q9	Funprog allows reinforcing the knowledge acquired in the classroom
Q10	How customizable is the user profile?
Q11	The tests provided by Funprog allow to correctly evaluate the knowledge acquired
Q12	I would like to use Funprog to learn other subjects

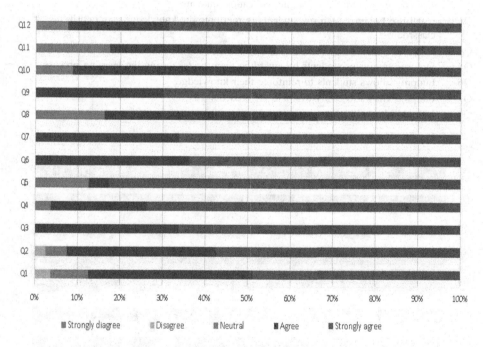

Fig. 9. Results of the survey performed after students used Funprog.

means that they agree or strongly agree with the characteristics of the application. The first two questions were focused on knowing the students' opinion regarding the intuitiveness of Funprog interface. The results of question Q1 indicate that half of the students completely agree with the fact that the Funprog interface is friendly and intuitive. Meanwhile, the results of question Q2 indicate that 54% of students rated the intuitiveness of the application with a 4 (using a scale of 1 to 5). Question Q3–Q9 were focused on knowing the student's opinion regarding the knowledge and content provided by Funprog as well as the objectives established by it. The results of these questions indicate that more than half of students (52%) agree with the knowledge acquired as well as the goals achieved through the application. Finally, questions Q10–Q12 were focused on knowing if students would like to use Funprog to learn other subjects. The results of these questions indicate that most students (71%) would like to use this application to reinforce the knowledge acquired in the classroom.

Finally, a third survey was conducted to know the level of acceptance of Funprog among teachers. Table 4 presents the set of questions asked in this survey.

Table 4. Questions asked to teachers.

No.	Question
Q1	Funprog allows to correctly evaluate the students
Q2	The content is suitable for higher education students
Q3	I will use Funprog with my students to reinforce the knowledge acquired in the classroom
Q4	Funprog helps students to interactively learn
Q5	Funprog motivates students by awarding them prizes during the learning process
Q6	Funprog allows students to reinforce their knowledge
Q7	Funprog allows to easily evaluate the students
Q8	I would like to use Funprog to teach other subjects

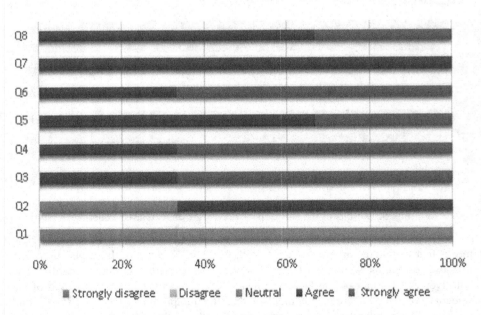

Fig. 10. Results of the survey conducted among teachers.

Like the students, teachers answered questions according to a scale of 1 to 5, where 1 = strongly disagree, 2 = disagree, 3 = neutral, 4 = agree, and 5 = strongly agree. Figure 10 presents the results of the survey conducted among teachers. Considering these results, we can conclude that most teachers consider Funprog as a tool that can help students to reinforce their knowledge as well as to make easy the evaluation of their students.

6 Conclusions and Future Work

The teachers know that there is a culture of play among young people. Therefore, higher education teachers must implement innovative teaching methods that improve the learning process of this group of students. In this work, we adopt the gamification approach as an innovative alternative that is implemented in higher education by means of attractive activities aiming to improve the learning environment of students and accelerate the process of skills acquisition [20]. The implementation of this approach will also allow that teachers create a collaborative environment where their students can creatively solve problems without fear of being wrong. Funprog encourages students to achieve their goals by awarding them prizes during the learning process. This application defines a set of game levels where students face new challenges that allow them to obtain more knowledge and improve their skills concerning the Programming Fundamentals subject. As future work, we plan to use the architecture described in this work for the development of new gamification-based mobile applications focused on different subjects and educational levels. At first instance, we plan to develop a mobile application focused on teaching programming languages. The main objective of this application will be to improve the logical reasoning of students.

References

1. Deterding, S., Dixon, D., Khaled, R., Nacke, L.: From game design elements to gamefulness. In: Proceedings of the 15th International Academic MindTrek Conference: Envisioning Future Media Environments - MindTrek 2011, p. 9. ACM Press, New York (2011)
2. van Roy, R., Zaman, B.: Why gamification fails in education and how to make it successful: introducing nine gamification heuristics based on self-determination theory. In: Ma, M., Oikonomou, A. (eds.) Serious Games and Edutainment Applications, pp. 485–509. Springer, Cham (2017). https://doi.org/10.1007/978-3-319-51645-5_22
3. Ocampo, S., Sarango, S.: Aplicación de juegos digitales en educación superior. Rev. San Gregor. **11**, 10 (2016)
4. Ortega García, A., Ruiz-Martínez, A., Valencia-García, R.: Using app inventor for creating apps to support m-learning experiences: a case study. Comput. Appl. Eng. Educ. (2017). https://doi.org/10.1002/cae.21895
5. Domínguez, A., Saenz-De-Navarrete, J., De-Marcos, L., Fernández-Sanz, L., Pagés, C., Martínez-Herráiz, J.J.: Gamifying learning experiences: practical implications and outcomes. Comput. Educ. **63**, 380–392 (2013). https://doi.org/10.1016/j.compedu.2012.12.020

6. Alčaković S (2018) Millennials and gamification – a model proposal for gamification application in Članci/papers millennials and gamification – a model proposal for gamification application in tourism destination

7. Fonseca, D., Villagrasa, S., Navarro, I., Redondo, E., Valls, F., Sánchez, A.: Urban gamification in architecture education. In: Rocha, Á., Correia, A.M., Adeli, H., Reis, L.P., Costanzo, S. (eds.) WorldCIST 2017. AISC, vol. 571, pp. 335–341. Springer, Cham (2017). https://doi.org/10.1007/978-3-319-56541-5_34

8. Szegletes, L., Koles, M., Forstner, B.: Socio-cognitive gamification: general framework for educational games. J. Multimodal User Interfaces **9**, 395–401 (2015). https://doi.org/10.1007/s12193-015-0183-6

9. Khan, A., Ahmad, F.H., Malik, M.M.: Use of digital game based learning and gamification in secondary school science: the effect on student engagement, learning and gender difference. Educ. Inf. Technol. **22**, 2767–2804 (2017). https://doi.org/10.1007/s10639-017-9622-1

10. Epema, D., Iosup, A.: An experience report on using gamification in technical higher education. In: Proceedings of the 45th ACM Technical Symposium on Computer Science Education - SIGCSE 2014, pp. 27–32 (2014)

11. Urh, M., Vukovic, G., Jereb, E., Pintar, R.: The model for introduction of gamification into e-learning in higher education. Procedia Soc. Behav. Sci. **197**, 388–397 (2015)

12. Heyvaert, P., Verborgh, R., Mannens, E., Van de Walle, R.: Linked data-enabled gamification in EPUB 3 for educational digital textbooks. In: Conole, G., Klobučar, T., Rensing, C., Konert, J., Lavoué, É. (eds.) EC-TEL 2015. LNCS, vol. 9307, pp. 587–591. Springer, Cham (2015). https://doi.org/10.1007/978-3-319-24258-3_65

13. Briers, B.: The gamification of project management. In: Proceedings of PMI Global Congress, New Orleans, Louisiana, New Orleans (2013)

14. Kardan, A.A., Arani, A.K.: A novel gamification-based architecture for web environments. In: 2016 2nd International Conference on Web Research, ICWR 2016, pp. 125–130 (2016)

15. Khaleel, F.L., Ashaari, N.S., Meriam, T.S., Wook, T., Ismail, A.: The study of gamification application architecture for programming language course. In: Proceedings of the 9th International Conference on Ubiquitous Information Management and Communication - IMCOM 2015, pp. 1–5 (2015). https://doi.org/10.1145/2701126.2701222

16. Valls, F., Redondo, E., Sánchez, A., Fonseca, D., Villagrasa, S., Navarro, I.: Simulated environments in architecture education. Improving the student motivation. In: Rocha, Á., Correia, A.M., Adeli, H., Reis, L.P., Costanzo, S. (eds.) WorldCIST 2017. AISC, vol. 571, pp. 235–243. Springer, Cham (2017). https://doi.org/10.1007/978-3-319-56541-5_24

17. Escamilla, J., Fuerte, K., Venegas, E., Fernández, K., et al.: EduTrends gamificación. Obs. Innov. Educ. 1–36 (2016)

18. Vergara, V., Lagos-Ortiz, K., Aguirre-Munizaga, M., Aviles, M., Medina-Moreira, J., Hidalgo, J., Muñoz-García, A.: Knowledge-based model for curricular design in Ecuadorian universities. In: Valencia-García, R., Lagos-Ortiz, K., Alcaraz-Mármol, G., del Cioppo, J., Vera-Lucio, N. (eds.) CITI 2016. CCIS, vol. 658, pp. 14–25. Springer, Cham (2016). https://doi.org/10.1007/978-3-319-48024-4_2

19. Husson, F., Lê, S., Pagès, J.: Exploratory multivariate analysis by example using R. Comput. Sci. Data Anal. **40**, 240 (2010). https://doi.org/10.1080/02664763.2012.657409

20. Sanchez, E., Young, S., Jouneau-Sion, C.: Classcraft: from gamification to ludicization of classroom management. Educ. Inf. Technol. **22**, 497–513 (2017)

Advanced Semantics Processing-Based Information System to Support English Learning

Rodrigo Martínez-Béjar[1,2], Alexander José Mackenzie Rivero[3(✉)],
and Edwin Joao Merchán Carreño[3]

[1] Faculty of Informatics, University of Murcia, Murcia, Spain
rodrigo.alternativa@gmail.com
[2] International Doctoral School, UNED, Madrid, Spain
[3] Faculty of Technical Sciences,
State University of Southern Manabí, Jipijapa, Ecuador
{mackenzie.alexander, joao.merchan}@unesum.edu.ec

Abstract. Our world is becomes more and more globalized. Frontiers are not what they once were, thanks to the discovery of the Internet. Knowing several languages is something that is almost essential. When we are studying a new language, we focus on learning vocabulary and all about syntax. In other words, this means we want to know how to coordinate and join words to create sentences and concepts. But language has another dimension that we usually overlook: semantics. This dimension is very important in language because it gives meaning to words. Semantics study could be as wide and complex as language to analyze itself. Therefore, in order to simplify our tasks, we have started with a finite set of terms, Specifically we have the first five levels set up by an English language academy. The objective of this research presented here was the development of a system that allows to analyze and detect semantic errors in simple sentences and syntactically correct to support English learning. Basically, the system we have developed is formed by two different components: a semantic analyzer and a web interface. The semantic analyzer has been built using the programming language Java and utilizes ontology and a reasoner over it. The use of ontologies allows the classification and categorization of different words in a language so that we can apply a reasoner to classified concepts to infer new knowledge and to detect whether a sentence makes sense or not.

Keywords: Semantic Web · OWL ontologies · English learning

1 Introduction

Knowing several languages is something that is almost essential, not just to be successful in work environments, but also to be successful in our personal lives. Thus, knowing several languages gives one a different view of the world, helps you getting to know new cultures, new ways of thinking and, definitely, makes you an open minded person. Among thousands of different languages that exist in the world, we pinpoint

© Springer Nature Switzerland AG 2018
R. Valencia-García et al. (Eds.): CITI 2018, CCIS 883, pp. 269–284, 2018.
https://doi.org/10.1007/978-3-030-00940-3_20

three of them: Mandarin Chinese, English and Spanish. Mandarin Chinese is the undeniable winner when we look for the most spoken language, due to the huge numbers of person in Asian when use this language to communicate with each other. The other languages, English and Spanish, have a similar amount of speakers, and depending on the source consulted, one is more spoken than the other one.

Unlike Mandarin Chinese, speakers of English and Spanish are not concentrated in only one region of the planet. And this is the reason why these languages are more global. However, between English and Spanish, English is the most widely used. In fact, it is almost mandatory to have a fluent level of English in order to travel to many places world wide or just to use modern technologies. When we are studying a new language, we focus on learning vocabulary and all about syntax. This means we want to know how to coordinate and join words to create sentences and concepts. But language has another dimension that we usually overlook: semantics. This dimension is very important in language because it gives meaning to words. We have created a web system that lets us analyze and detect semantic mistakes in simple and syntactically correct sentences.

In this work, a system facilitating English learning is described that has been developed around two main components: a semantic analyzer and a web application. The semantic analyzer is built using the programming language Java and utilizes ontology and a reasoner over it. The use of ontologies allows for the classification and categorization of different words, so that we can apply a reasoner to classified concepts to infer new knowledge and to detect whether a sentence makes sense or not. In our case, we used OWL (Ontology Web Language) ontologies and Protégé editor and framework. Finally, we used HermiT reasoner due to its "hypertableau" calculus properties, so providing very efficient reasoning capabilities.

This paper is organised as follows. Section 2 is devoted to give an overview about both issues semantic technologies and languages learning. In Sect. 3, the methodology followed in this work is addressed. Section 4 describes the evaluation of the system developed. Finally, in Sect. 5 the main conclusions are put forward.

2 Semantic Technologies and Languages Learning

Linguistics has always paid more attention to syntax than to other linguistic levels. This almost exclusive attention is justified by the complexity associated with the semantic analysis of language [28] the semantic process works on different parts of a sentence. If it does not exist a previous syntactic analysis, the system must identify these parts. On the other hand, if the syntactic analysis takes place, number of constituents that semantic analyzer must considered is restricted enormously, becoming more complex and less reliable. Syntactic analysis is less costly than semantic analysis in computational terms (semantic analysis requires important inferences). Therefore, if we have a syntactic analysis we can save resources and decrease system complexity.

Although we can extract the meaning of a sentence without using syntactical facts, it is not always possible.

These are the reasons that make evident that we need a good parser if we want to achieve good results in higher analysis levels.

2.1 Semantic Web

Web has changed deeply how we communicate to each other, how we negotiate and how we do our work. It is possible a low priced communication with the whole word at any time nowadays. We can carry out economic transactions by Internet. We have access to millions of resources, independently what is our language or where we are. All these factors have contributed to Web success. However, at the same time, these factors have occasioned its big problems as well: overload of information and heterogeneity of sources that causes interoperability problems. Semantic Web helps to solve these two big problems letting users to delegate tasks in software. Thanks to employment of semantic in Web, software is able to process its content, to reason with it, to combine it and to make logic conclusions to solve quotidian problems automatically. Because of this, we can consider Semantic Web as an extended web, equipped with a bigger meaning in which any Internet user will be able to find answers to any question in a faster and easier way thanks to better defined information. When equipping Web with more meaning, and thus, with more semantics, we can get solutions to habitual problems of information search thanks to we will use a common infrastructure where we can share, process and transfer information in an easy way. This extended and semantic based Web is supported by universal languages that solve problems caused by a lack of meaning Web where, sometimes, accessing to information is a hard and frustrating task [19].

To equip web with meaning, ontologies have been used. Although this concept has been used in philosophy for ages, currently, it is more identified with computer as a vocabulary that machines understand and that is specified with enough precision to distinguish related terms. With the developed system, we will contribute to semantic web by creating an analyzer which uses an ontology in order to test semantics in English sentences.

2.2 Natural Language Processing

According to [26], Natural Language Processing (NLP) is a theoretically motivated range of computational techniques for analyzing and representing naturally occurring texts at one or more levels of linguistic analysis for the purpose of achieving human-like language processing for a range of tasks or applications.

Several elements of previous definition can be further detailed: "range of computational techniques" is necessary because there are multiple methods or techniques from which to choose to accomplish a particular type of language analysis; "naturally occurring texts" can be of any language, mode, genre, etc. The texts can be oral or written. The only requirement is that they be in a language used by humans to communicate to one another. In addition, the text being analyzed should not be specifically constructed for the purpose of the analysis, but rather that the text is gathered from actual usage; the notion of "levels of linguistic analysis" refers to the fact that there are multiple types of language processing known to be at work when humans produce or comprehend language (it is thought that humans normally use all of these levels because each level conveys different types of meaning); "human-like language processing" reveals that NLP is considered a discipline within Artificial Intelligence

(AI) because it strives for human-like performance; finally, "for a range of tasks or applications" points out that NLP is not usually considered a goal in and of itself, except perhaps for AI researchers. For others, NLP is the means for accomplishing a particular task. Therefore, you have Information Retrieval (IR) systems that use NLP, as well as machine translation (MT), question-answering, etc.

Difficulty in NPL systems goes to language ambiguity [27]. A NPL system needs to determine something of the structure of text normally at least enough that it can answer "Who did what to whom?" Conventional parsing systems try to answer this question only in terms of possible structures that could be deemed grammatical for some choice of words of a certain category. For example, given a reasonable grammar, a standard NLP system will say that sentence "Our company is training workers" has 3 syntactic analyses, often called parses:

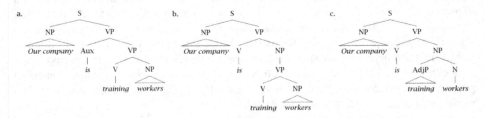

Fig. 1. Different syntactic analyses of "our company is training workers"

There is (a), the one humans perceive, where is training is the verb group, and two others with is as the main verb: in (b) the rest is a gerund (cf. Our problem is training workers), while in (c) training modifies workers (cf. Those are training wheels). The last two parses are semantically anomalous, but in most current systems semantic analysis is done only after syntactic analysis (if at all). This means that, as sentences get longer and grammars get more comprehensive, such ambiguities lead to a terrible multiplication of parses. Therefore, a practical NLP system must be good at making disambiguation decisions of word sense, word category, syntactic structure, and semantic scope.

2.3   Ontologies

As it has been previously proposed, the huge volume of information available in the Web, which has been increasing following a geometric progression over the last few years, make necessary to add meaning to the data on the Web in order to can process these data like humans do [4]. We achieve this by using ontologies.

Conceptual systems, which are typically represented by concepts and categories, can be modeled by universal constraints independently of cultural variations [11], in which case the quality of the categorizations is positively correlated with the level of simplicity of these categorizations. Ontologies, which are commonly conceived as explicit formalizations of shared conceptual systems [15], are the most widely used approach to represent knowledge, due to their properties of modularity, reuse, sharing and formalization, among others. Knowledge in ontologies has been typically formalized using, at least, five components: classes, relations, functions, axioms and instances [16]. In this sense, although there are several ontological languages, RDF and OWL have become the de facto Semantic Web standard ontology languages. Besides, ontologies provide a common vocabulary of a conceptual system and define – with different levels of formality - the meaning of the terms and the relations between them (Fig. 1).

All the above described ontological characteristics have resulted in ontologies being an essential part of several world research trends, leading to the achievement of a more intelligent web [18] or the automation of science [22, 23]. In particular, ontologies form the backbone on which to build the Semantic Web [3] and are expected to be used to provide structured vocabularies that describe the relationships between different concepts, allowing computers (and humans) to interpret their meaning flexibly yet unambiguously [24].

2.4 Languages Learning in Educative Systems

When it comes to learning a second language, the most important facet is how learners acquire vocabulary [6]. Teacher must ensure that his students receive a sufficient exposure to new vocabulary, both on and off classroom, where multiple exposures help when it is necessary to counteract forgetting effects, provided that this exposures are distributed at time intervals. The use of flashcards in the classroom in order to consolidate the new vocabulary, instead of trusting just in study at home, avoids students who do not study a lot learn less than the ones that study more. This way, new vocabulary can be used, in an effective form, in structural exercises and conversation. Students notice the success, and it leads to they feel more motivated and willing to work at home, where ICT can be used to do more written exercises with this new vocabulary and to consolidate its learning [2]. The developed system here presented is just one of this ICT tools that can be used to support second language learning.

3 Methodology

The development of this project has followed the steps that are shown in Fig. 2.

Fig. 2. Stages of the development

3.1   Extraction and Classification of English Terms: The Ontology

We have considered suitable to use terms which belong to the first five levels of learning set up by an English academy in Murcia, Spain. After knowing which terms we are going to use, in other words, the vocabulary used by the ontology, we have to classify these terms, getting father terms, son terms and relationships between them. To create this categorization, we use an ontology. According to Artificial Intelligence (AI) [14], the ontology of a program can be described by defining a set of representational terms. In such an ontology, definitions associate the names of entities in the universe of discourse (e.g., classes, relations, functions, or other objects) with human-readable text describing what the names mean, and formal axioms that constrain the interpretation and well-formed use of these terms (Fig. 3).

As some authors proposed in [7], since the inception of this concept in computing, the development of languages for modelling ontologies has been seen as a key task. The initial proposals focused on RDF and RDF Schema; however, these languages were soon found to be too limited in expressive power [24]. The World Wide Web Consortium (W3C) therefore formed the Web Ontology Working Group, whose goal was to develop an expressive language suitable for application in the Semantic Web. The result of this endeavour was the OWL Web Ontology Language, which became a W3C recommendation in February 2004. OWL is actually a family of three language variants (often called species) of increasing expressive power: OWL Lite, OWL DL, and OWL Full [34]: OWL Lite supports those users primarily needing a classification hierarchy and simple constraints. For example, while it supports cardinality constraints, it only permits cardinality values of 0 or 1.

OWL DL supports users who want the maximum expressiveness while retaining computational completeness (i.e., all conclusions are guaranteed to be computable) and decidability (i.e., all computations will finish in finite time). OWL DL includes all OWL language constructs, but they can be used only under certain restrictions (for example, while a class may be a subclass of many classes, a class cannot be an instance of another class).

OWL Full is meant for users who want maximum expressiveness and the syntactic freedom of RDF with no computational guarantees. For example, in OWL Full a class can be treated simultaneously as a collection of individuals and as an individual in its own right. OWL Full allows an ontology to augment the meaning of the pre-defined (RDF or OWL) vocabulary. It is unlikely that any reasoning software will be able to support complete reasoning for every feature of OWL Full.

Regarding this work, we have used OWL 2. This is an improved version of the first released of this language, named OWL main differences between the original language and OWL 2 are following [13]:

- New syntaxes: A new syntax, called the functional-style syntax, is the main syntax used in the OWL 2 documents. The user-friendly Manchester syntax [19] is an update of the OWL 1 abstract syntax. The OWL 2 RDF syntax is backward compatible to OWL 1. In addition, there is an XML serialisation.

- New species: OWL 2 Full and OWL 2 DL correspond roughly to OWL 1 Full and OWL 1 DL, respectively. Instead of an OWL Lite species, the OWL 2 documents specify three OWL 2 profiles [29], which are sublanguages designed for increased efficiency of reasoning.
- Changes to type separation: Type separation requirements from OWL 1 are relaxed. Some changes in the semantics accommodate this. In particular, this allows for some simple metamodeling.
- New syntactic sugar: New syntax has been introduced which essentially provides macros for some things which can be expressed in OWL 1, but only in a rather verbose way.
- Language enhancements: New syntax has been introduced which exceeds the expressivity of OWL 1.

However, this technology would not be accessible either practical if it did not exist a set of tools that make easier its creation and maintenance process. These tools will be used to visualise the knowledge with different granularity; combine and extract knowledge from ontologies; validate automatically the ontologies in search of inconsistences or concepts that cannot be satisfied; make easier different people work on the same information at the same time, and finally, they can be control versions' tools. There are a lot of these kinds of tools. In [21], the authors enumerate many of these systems classified by its architecture, knowledge representation systems, inference service, and different usability features (graphic representations, collaboration, ontologies libraries,...). To develop the ontology, we have used one of these tools: Protégé. Protégé is a free, open-source ontology editor and framework for building intelligent systems developed by University of Stanford in a medical computing setting that has a large community of developers [1]. It they been developed in Java using an extensible architecture based on plugins, which allows developing prototypes and applications very quickly. Protégé's kernel define every structure necessary to represent, visualize and handle ontologies, whereas its plugins are used to widen environment's functionality, adapting it to specific needed of each domain. Protégé platform allows two different ways to model ontologies:

Protégé-Frames [9] is an editor which allows to create ontologies using frames (Open Knowledge Base Connectivity Protocol – OKBC). In this model, an ontology consist of a set of hierarchically organised classes, a set of slots associated to classes in order to describe their properties and relations and a final set of instances or individuals that belong to one of more concepts and they set up specific values to properties.

Protégé-OWL [24] is an editor which allows to create Semantic Web ontologies using OWL language. There are various reasoners that can be included in this environment using plugins architecture of Protégé. This kind of systems make possible to get facts that are not represented in the ontology explicitly but they are logic consequence of represented knowledge. Reasoners can detect inconsistences in ontologies as well.

As it is obvious, we have used Protégé-OWL to create the ontology in its last stable version 4.3 (released in April 2013).

3.2   Implementation of the Semantic Analyzer

Next step consists of the creation of the semantic analyzer. It is necessary to analyze and design the architecture of the analyzer. In broad strokes, we know that the analyzer needs to pick up sentences and its syntactic analysis from input. Then it has to check semantics in these sentences using the information stored in the ontology. Finally, it has to show its own analysis: semantically correct sentence or semantically incorrect sentence plus correct alternatives.

Fig. 3. Stages of semantic analysis

The unified Modelling Language (UML), which allows visualizing, specifying, building and documenting artefacts of a system formed by a big amount of software. This language is suitable to model from information systems for companies to distributed web applications, and even real-time embedded systems. It is a very expressive language, which covers every view required to develop and then deploy those kinds of systems. UML was created in 1997 by Booch, James Rumbaugh e Ivar Jacobson [5]. We have used this language to lay the foundations of analysis and design by using a CASE tool (MagicDraw).

When we talk about prepare input we mean that we receive the sentence written by the user and a series of tokens created by the syntactic analyzer where it sets up, in a certain way, the main parts of the sentence. We have said in a certain way because syntactic analyzer cannot distinguish between particular kinds of adverbial, for example, "in the kitchen" or "at the weekend" are "PREPOSITION + ARTICLE THE + NOUN", and it is the semantic analyzer which has to notice that "in the kitchen" refers to a place (adverbial of place) and "at the weekend" refers to time (adverbial of time).

Now is when the semantic analyzer knows perfectly what words belong to each part of a sentence and it can use the ontology to analyze. An ontology, according to Gruber's definition, is "an explicit specification of a conceptualization", where conceptualization refers to an abstract model [18].

A reasoner is a key component for working with OWL ontologies. In fact, virtually all querying of an OWL ontology (and its imports closure) should be done using a reasoner. This is because knowledge in an ontology might not be explicit and a reasoner is required to deduce implicit knowledge so that the correct query results are obtained.

In our work we have used HermiT reasoner. HermiT, as it is described in [12] supports all features of the OWL 2 ontology language [7], including all OWL 2 datatypes [31], and it correctly performs both object and data property classification.

In addition to these standard reasoning tasks, HermiT also supports SPARQL query answering, and it uses a range of optimisations [25] to ensure efficient processing of real-world ontologies. Furthermore, HermiT supports several features that go beyond existing standards, such as DL-safe SWRL rules [19] and description graphs—an extension of OWL 2 that allows for a faithful modelling of arbitrarily connected structures. A key novel idea in HermiT is the hypertableau calculus, which allows the reasoner to avoid some of the nondeterministic behaviour exhibited by the tableau calculus used in Pellet and FaCT++—two other popular and widely used OWL reasoners. In order to further improve the performance of the calculus, HermiT employs a wide range of standard and novel optimisation techniques, including anywhere blocking, blocking signature caching, individual reuse, and core blocking [10]. HermiT also implements a novel classification algorithm [12] that greatly reduces the number of consistency tests needed to compute the class and property hierarchies. Finally, HermiT is available as an open-source Java library, and includes both a Java API and a simple command-line interface. It can process ontologies in any format handled by the OWL API, including RDF/XML, OWL Functional Syntax, KRSS, and OBO.

To access to the HermiT reasoner as well as to access to the ontology we have used the Application Programming Interface of OWL: OWL API. The OWL API is a Java API and reference implementation for creating, manipulating and serialising OWL Ontologies. The latest version of the API is focused towards OWL 2 and it has been developed primarily at the University of Manchester. It is open source and is available under either the LGPL or Apache Licenses.

A UML interaction diagram is shown Fig. 4, where we can see how every component explained previously interacts with other components.

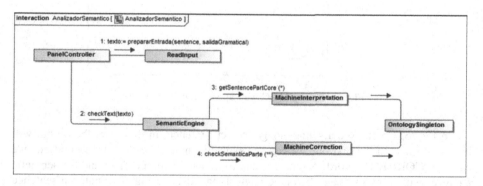

Fig. 4. Interaction diagram of semantic analyzer

3.3 Implementation of a Web Application

When it comes to creating a web application, we need to set up the features of our system: mainly, we need to know what can be done with the application and what the user interface is like. Since the application will be used to learn English, it would be a good idea that the interface uses this language. Furthermore, it will be access by different users, so that, it seems necessary a user management feature where the user can create an account with his personal data, edit this data in the future and delete his account. This leads to a home page where the user must identify himself or he can create a new account in case he has not got one. Once identified, the user will want to use the analyzer, hence, main page must show this feature. Considering that there are two different analyzers, we should use two different pages: one page would allow user to interact with the syntactic analyzer and another page would allow user to interact with the semantic analyzer. This way, we have a main idea about the features of the web application, so, it is time to create the mockups that show the final characteristics of the user interface. We have used Balsamiq as the wireframing tool to create the mockups.

Therefore, we have an idea of the user interface, but we do not know anything about how the application itself is going to be created. It is important to distinguish model features from view features and control features, so it seems that we need to use a framework that helps us in this task. Spring framework lets us differentiate these three facets in an easy way due to it provides a comprehensive programming and configuration model for modern Java-based enterprise applications – on any kind of deployment platform. The libraries necessary to use this framework are available online on Maven repository. This framework organise the code of the web application as we can see following (Fig. 5):

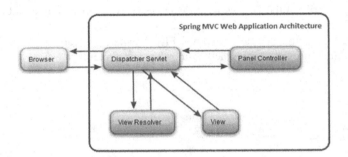

Fig. 5. Spring MVC web application architecture.

In Fig. 6, we can see a semantically correct sentence. In this case, the output will have two lines: in the first one we can see syntactic analysis and in the second one we can see "CORRECT" word. A sentence can be syntactically incorrect and the semantic analyzer will show message "Syntatic analysis failed", see Fig. 7. Finally, a sentence can be syntactically correct but semantically incorrect, see Fig. 8.

It has been used a server of the University to run the system developed. It has been set up Apache Tomcat (version 7), a widely used web server/container. It is a web server because it can manage HTTP request/reply protocol as well as it is a web container due to it can manage JEE web components as Java Servlet and Java Server Pages technologies. Furthermore, it is open source under Apache Foundation direction [8].

Fig. 6. Semantically correct.

Fig. 7. Syntactically incorrect.

Fig. 8. Semantically incorrect.

At this stage, it was important to access to the web application by different devices, so that we can test if Bootstrap adapts the elements to the screen resolution. To accomplish this, we have accessed the web application by both a laptop and a smartphone.

After reviewing every feature of the developed system, it is necessary to have this wrap up section where we will show a schema of the architecture of the system.

In previous figure (Fig. 9), we can see that user access the semantic analyzer by a web application, and this semantic analyzer uses the syntactic analyzer and the ontology to run.

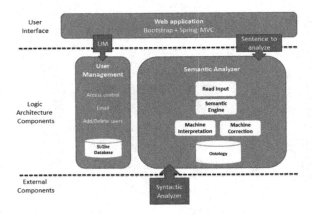

Fig. 9. System architecture

4   Testing and Evaluation of the Implemented System

After the implementation of the system above described, we proceeded to test it and evaluate it. To make this stage more automatic, we designed an automatic tester which accesses the semantic analyzer directly, without using the user interface, testing semantics of all the sentences of a file.

In order to have a set of sentences that let test every relationship, we have developed a "sentences' creator" where we set up what words can be each part of a sentence, and this "sentences' creator" choose, at random, words for each part. Some of these sentences have to be modified to avoid syntactic mistakes, because, if not, semantic analyzer will not be able to analyze semantics.

Regarding this, we used F-measure (also F1 score or F-score) to measure test's accuracy. It considers both the precision and the recall of the test to compute the score: precision (also called positive predictive value) is the fraction of retrieved instances that are relevant, while recall (also known as sensitivity) is the fraction of relevant instances that are retrieved, in other words, precision is the number of correct positive results divided by the number of all positive results whereas recall is the number of correct positive results divided by the number of positive results that should have been returned. F-measure can be interpreted as a weighted average of the precision and recall, where F-measure reaches its best value at 1 and worst score at 0.

The traditional F-measure or balanced F-score is the harmonic mean of precision and recall:

$$\text{F - measure} = 2 * \frac{\text{precision} * \text{recall}}{\text{precision} + \text{recall}}$$

Where

$$\text{precision} = \frac{|\{\text{relevant documents}\} \cap \{\text{retrieved documents}\}|}{|\{\text{retrieved documents}\}|}$$

$$\text{recall} = \frac{|\{\text{relevant documents}\} \cap \{\text{retrieved documents}\}|}{|\{\text{relevant documents}\}|}$$

In order to evaluate the system here described, we generate a data set with 1200 random sentences. With regards to correct sentences and with following data set was obtained:

- Semantically correct sentences (SCS): 569 sentences.
- SCS according to semantic analyzer: 570 sentences.
- SCS between SCS according to semantic analyzer: 549 sentences.

By applying now the above indicated formulae, it was obtained that for correct sentences, the precision = 549/570 ≈ 0.963157894, the recall = 549/569 0.964850615 and the F-Measure = (0.963157894 + 0.964850615) ≈ 0.964003511.

Regarding incorrect sentences, by proceeding in a similar manner, we got:

- Semantically incorrect sentences (SIS): 631 sentences.
- SIS according to semantic analyzer: 630 sentences.
- SIS between SCS according to semantic analyzer: 610 sentences.

So, in this case the precision = 610/630 ≈ 0.968253968, the recall = 610/631 ≈ 0.966719492 and the F-measure = 2 * (0.968253968 * 0.966719492) = (0.968253968 + 0.966719492) ≈ 0.967486121.

We can conclude that our analyzer is slightly better at detecting semantically incorrect sentences rather than detecting semantically correct sentences, but, if we take into account that a perfect analyzer would have a value 1 of F-measure, we can say that the analyzer is highly accurate.

5 Discussion and Conclusions

The work presented here aims to promote the creation and use of ontologies to structure and organize existing information in the field of languages learning. Specifically, the ontology has focused on information relating to English learning for the learning of such a language.

A web application has been developed so that when it proposes correct alternatives in order to guide users in their learning.

The use of ontologies allows for the classification and categorization of different words in a language, so that we can apply a reasoner to classified concepts to infer new knowledge and to detect whether a sentence makes sense or not. In our case, we have used OWL (Ontology Web Language) ontologies and Protégé as editor the ontology. Finally, we have used HermiT as the reasoner because, based on a novel "hyper-tableau" calculus, it provides very efficient reasoning.

It is also necessary to note that sentences analyzed semantically with our system must be syntactically correct, and this leads to another analyzer that performs before this one and this new analyzer must detect and correct sentences syntactically and grammatically, as well as, being able to identify spelling mistakes. The last feature to underline about the semantic analyzer is that when it discovers something that makes no sense, it proposes correct alternatives in order to guide users in their learning.

In this work, we developed a web system through which the user can learn a new language, in this case, English. This was achieved through the application of new artificial intelligence techniques such as ontologies and reasoners, while we used different frameworks to make the web application easy to access and to use.

The initial results with a sample of 1200 sentences, created by a builder of sentences, were positives. To measure precision and recall we utilized F-measure, obtaining for semantically correct sentences a precision indicator of 0.963157894 and a recall indicator of 0.964850615. For semantically incorrect sentences precision indicator was of 0.968253968 and recall indicator of 0.967486121. So, we can conclude that our semantic analyzer is highly accurate for basic English sentences.

Through this work, we have demonstrated the validity of the approach based on ontologies to make a semantic analyzer engine to facilitate English learning. The main advantage is simplicity of maintenance: just include new concepts in the ontology to enrich the process of the engine.

Regarding future research, we will investigate the use an ontology of concepts and an ontology of English sentence structures to obtain a flexible engine that supports concepts and sentence structures as needed, apart from testing the system with a larger corpus of sentences.

Acknowledgements. We thank Ms. Beatriz Angulo Capel for her involvement and assistance in the implementation tasks of the approach presented here.

References

1. A free, open-source ontology editor and framework for building intelligent systems. (n.d.). http://protege.stanford.edu/. Accessed 19 May 2015
2. Barcroft, J.: Second language vocabulary acquisition: a lexical input processing approach. Foreign Lang. Ann. **37**(2), 200–208 (2004)
3. Berners-Lee, T., Hendler, J.: Publishing on the semantic web. Nature **410**, 1023–10234 (2001)
4. Berners-Lee, T., Hendler, J., Lassila, O.: The semantic web. Sci. Am. **284**, 34–43 (2001)

5. Booch, G., Rumbaugh, J., Jacobson, I.: El lenguaje unificado de modelado. Addison Wesley, Boston (2001)
6. Cerezo, L., Cantos, P.: Lexical forgetfulness versus systematic repetition: an experimental approach. In: Estévez Fuertes, N., Clavel Arroitia, B. (eds.) Adquisición de segundas lenguas (L2) en el marco del nuevo milenio. Homenaje a la profesora María del Mar Martí Viaño, pp. 95–117. Universitat de València, Valencia (2013)
7. Cuenca Grau, B., Horrocks, I., Motik, B., Parsia, B., Patel-Schneider, P.F., Sattler, U.: OWL 2: the next step for OWL. J. Web Semant. 6(4), 309–322 (2008)
8. Durán, A., Medel, R.: Introducción a Apache Tomcat 5.5. Departamento de Lenguajes y Sistemas Informáticos. Escuela Técnica Superior de Ingeniería Informática. Universidad de Sevilla (2007). http://www.lsi.us.es/docencia/get.php?id=1923. Accessed 19 May 2015
9. Gennari, J.H., et al.: The evolution of protégé: an environment for knowledge-based systems development. Int. J. Hum. Comput. Stud. 58(1), 89–123 (2003)
10. Glimm, B., Horrocks, I., Motik, B.: Optimized description logic reasoning via core blocking. In: Giesl, J., Hähnle, R. (eds.) IJCAR 2010. LNCS (LNAI), vol. 6173, pp. 457–471. Springer, Heidelberg (2010). https://doi.org/10.1007/978-3-642-14203-1_39
11. Glimm, B., Horrocks, I., Motik, B., Shearer, R., Stoilos, G.: A novel approach to ontology classification. J. Web Semant. 14, 84–101 (2012)
12. Glimm, B., Horrocks, I., Motik, B., Stoilos, G., Wang, Z.: HermiT: an OWL 2 reasoner. J. Autom. Reason. 53(3), 245–269 (2014)
13. Golbreich, C., Wallace, E. (eds.): OWL 2 Web Ontology Language New Features and Rationale, 2nd edn. W3C Recommendation (2012). http://www.w3.org/TR/owl2-new-features/. Accessed 19 May 2015
14. Gruber, T.R.: A translation approach to portable ontology specifications. Knowl. Acquis. 5(2), 199–220 (1993)
15. Gruber, T.: Toward principles for the design of ontologies used for knowledge sharing. Int. J. Hum. Comput. Stud. 43, 907–928 (1995)
16. Gruber, T.R.: Nature, nurture, and knowledge acquisition. Int. J. Hum. Comput. Stud. 71(2), 191–194 (2013)
17. Guía Breve de Web Semántica. (n.d.). http://www.w3c.es/Divulgacion/GuiasBreves/WebSemantica. Accessed 19 May 2015
18. Hornby, G.S., Kurtoglu, T.: Toward a smarter web. Science 325(5938), 277–278 (2009)
19. Horrocks, I., Patel-Schneider, P.F., Boley, H., Tabet, S., Grosof, B., Dean, M.: SWRL: A Semantic Web Rule Language Combining OWL and RuleML. W3C Member Submission (2004) http://www.w3.org/Submission/SWRL/. Accessed 19 May 2015
20. Horrocks, I., Patel-Schneider, P.F., van Harmelen, F.: From SHIQ and RDF to OWL: the making of a web ontology language. J. Web Semant. Sci. Serv. Agents World Wide Web 1 (2003), 7–26 (2003)
21. Kashyap, V., Bussler, C., Moran, M.: The Semantic Web. Semantics for Data and Services on the Web, Chapter 6. Springer, Cham (2008)
22. King, R.D., et al.: Make way for robot scientists. Science 325(5943), 945 (2009)
23. King, R.D., et al.: The automation of science. Science 324(5923), 85–89 (2009)
24. Knublauch, H., Musen, M.A., Rector, A.L.: Editing description logic ontologies with the protege OWL plugin. In: Proceedings of the International Conference on Description Logics (2004)

25. Kollia, I., Glimm, B.: Optimizing SPARQL query answering over OWL ontologies. J. Artif. Intell. Res. **48**, 253–303 (2013)
26. Liddy, E.D.: Natural language processing. In: Encyclopedia of Library and Information Science, 2nd edn. Marcel Decker, Inc., New York City
27. Manning, C., Tze, H.: Foundations of Statistical Natural Language Processing. MIT Press, Cambridge (1999)
28. Reasoners. (n.d.). http://owlapi.sourceforge.net/reasoners.html. Accessed 19 May 2015

Sentiment Analysis in Education Domain: A Systematic Literature Review

Karen Mite-Baidal[1]([⊠]) [iD], Carlota Delgado-Vera[1] [iD],
Evelyn Solís-Avilés[1] [iD], Ana Herrera Espinoza[1] [iD],
Jenny Ortiz-Zambrano[2] [iD], and Eleanor Varela-Tapia[2] [iD]

[1] Facultad de Ciencias Agrarias, Universidad Agraria del Ecuador,
Av. 25 de Julio, P.O. Box 09-04-100, Guayaquil, Ecuador
{kmite,cdelgado,esolis,aherrera}@uagraria.edu.ec
[2] Facultad de Ciencias Matemáticas y Físicas, Universidad de Guayaquil,
Av. Delta, P.O. Box 471, Guayaquil, Ecuador
{jenny.ortizz,eleanor.varelat}@ug.edu.ec

Abstract. E-learning is the delivery of education through digital or electronic methods allowing students to acquire new knowledge and develop new skills. E-learning allows students to expand their knowledge whenever and wherever. Several authors consider sentiment analysis as an alternative to improve the learning process in an e-learning environment since it allows analyzing the opinions of the students in order to better understand their opinion and take more effective, better-targeted actions. In this sense, this work presents a systematic literature review about sentiment analysis in education domain. This review aims to detect the approaches and digital educational resources used in sentiment analysis as well as to identify what are the main benefits of using sentiment analysis on education domain. The results show that Naïve Bayes is the most used technique for sentiment analysis and that forums of MOOCs and social networks are the most used digital education resources to collect data needed to perform the sentiment analysis process. Finally, some of the main benefits of using sentiment analysis in education domain are the improvement of the teaching-learning process and students' performance, as well as the reduction in course abandonment.

Keywords: Sentiment analysis · Opinion mining · Education

1 Introduction

Sentiment analysis, also known as opinion mining [1], is an area of information processing that has been successfully applied in domains such as medicine. For example, there are several works that use opinion mining to analyze the emotional reaction of patients regarding different aspects of diabetes [2] and asthma [3]. The systematic review of the literature presented in this paper focuses on the use of sentiment analysis in the education domain.

Data recovery techniques [4] mainly focus on processing, searching and extracting factual information from digital education resources or learning environments [5], such

© Springer Nature Switzerland AG 2018
R. Valencia-García et al. (Eds.): CITI 2018, CCIS 883, pp. 285–297, 2018.
https://doi.org/10.1007/978-3-030-00940-3_21

as blogs, forums, and social networks. The data have an objective and subjective perspectives. On the one hand, the objective perspective is not influenced by emotions, opinions, or personal feelings, i.e., it is a perspective based in fact, in things quantifiable and measurable. On the other hand, the subjective perspective is one open to greater interpretation based on personal feelings, emotions, aesthetics, etc. Sentiment analysis focuses on analyzing the subjective perspective of data.

The sentiment analysis process is divided into four core phases: data acquisition, data preparation, review analysis, and sentiment classification. There are two main sentiment analysis approaches, namely: (1) machine learning, which is divided into supervised and unsupervised machine learning approaches, and (2) lexicon-based approach, which is divided into two categories dictionary-based and corpus-based approaches [7].

Supervised machine learning uses techniques or algorithms such as Naive Bayes [8], which is the simplest and most used classifier that calculates the posterior probability of a class based on the distribution of words in a document. This algorithm uses the Bayes Theorem to calculate the probability of a word belongs to a particular tag. SVM (Support Vector Machine) classifiers are also used in sentiment analysis. SVM are supervised learning models with associated learning algorithms that analyze data used for classification and regression analysis. On the other hand, neural networks are also used in sentiment analysis [10]. The learning process of neural networks requires a large corpus with positive, negative and neutral opinions collected from data sources such as social networks or forums. Once the training phase is completed, the network will be able to classify a new opinion as positive, negative or neutral. Finally, ME (Maximum Entropy) technique (ME) [11] calculates the probability that a text belongs to a category. To carry out this process, this technique should maximize the entropy in order to avoid introducing a bias in the system. Unlike NB, this method does not assume independence between features or terms.

The lexicon-based approach classifies a text according to the positive, negative and neutral words contained in it. This approach does not require a training phase. As was mentioned earlier, the lexicon-based approach can be divided into two categories: dictionary-based and corpus-based approaches. On the one hand, the corpus-based approach tries to find co-occurring word patterns to determine the polarity of a text. On the other hand, the dictionary-based approach uses synonyms, antonyms, and hierarchies that are found within the lexical database. The lexicon-based approach uses techniques such as specialized vocabularies [12] and dictionary construction techniques. For instance, in [13], the authors propose an emotional dictionary for sentiment analysis applied to online news. Another example of dictionary construction is presented in [14], where authors propose a dictionary for sentiment analysis based on common-sense knowledge.

E-learning is the delivery of education through digital or electronic methods allowing students to acquire new knowledge and develop new skills. E-learning allows students to expand their knowledge whenever and wherever. Kechaou [15] considers the sentiment analysis as an alternative to improve the learning process in an e-learning environment since it allows analyzing the opinions of the students in order to better understand their opinion and take more effective, better-targeted actions. Hence, it is important to analyze the use of sentiment analysis in the education domain. Despite there are currently several works that present literature reviews of sentiment analysis, there is still no proposal that presents a systematic literature review of sentiment analysis in education domain.

The remainder of this work is structured as follows: Sect. 2 presents the research methodology followed in this literature review. Section 3 describes the systematic review execution, while, Sect. 4 presents our results. Finally, our conclusions are presented in Sect. 5.

2   Systematic Review Planning

The literature review presented in this work has three main objectives: (1) to identify the techniques and classification algorithms used by sentiment analysis in education domain; (2) to identify digital educational resources or learning environments that serve as data sources for the sentiment analysis; and (3) to identify the most used techniques and data sources by the sentiment analysis in education domain.

2.1   Research Questions

For the purposes of this literature review, three research questions were defined to guide us throughout the research and help us to meet the established objectives. The research questions are listed below:

- RQ1. What is the sentiment analysis process?
- RQ2. What approaches and digital educational resources are used in sentiment analysis?
- RQ3. What are the main benefits of using sentiment analysis on education domain?

2.2   Digital Libraries

Table 1 shows the digital libraries that were used to perform the systematic literature review. Also, this table presents the type of bibliographic source, language, the period of publication, and search strategy used in this work. As can be observed, a keyword-based search strategy was used to search for research works focused on sentiment analysis in education domain. This strategy is described in detail in the next section.

2.3   Search Strategy

To answer the research questions, we use a keyword-based search strategy. For this purpose, we identified a set of keywords related to sentiment analysis in education domain as well as synonyms for the set of keywords identified. Once these terms were defined, we combined these terms with the connectors "AND" and "OR", resulting in the following search chain:

```
(sentiment analysis) AND (sentiment classification OR sentiment
analysis techniques OR opinion mining OR education domain)
AND/OR (digital educational resource) AND/OR (students)
AND/OR (university)
```

Table 1. Digital libraries.

Digital library	Type	Approach	Language	Period
IEEE Xplore	e-books, scientific journals, conferences, scientific articles	Keywords	English	2013–2018
Science Direct				
Springer Link Wiley				
Google Scholar				
ERIC Institute of Education of Science				
Elsevier				
ACM Digital Library				

Finally, it should be mentioned that only the works published in the 2013–2018 period were considered in this work, such as was specified in Table 1.

2.4 Exclusion Criteria

We discarded those papers that were not directly related with sentiment analysis and education domain. Also, we use next exclusion criteria:

- Research works not written in English.
- Master and doctoral dissertations.
- Duplicated research works obtained from Google Scholar and Web of Science.

3 Systematic Review Execution

This section presents the systematic review execution which consisted in searching for research works relates to sentiment analysis and education domain in the digital libraries selected and evaluating the obtained studies considering the inclusion and exclusion criteria. Also, this review allowed responding to the research questions presented in Sect. 2.1. These responses are discussed in next sections.

3.1 RQ1. What is the Sentiment Analysis Process?"

Sentiments
Sentiments are attitudes, thoughts or judgments triggered by sensations or mental processes. Sentiments are defined according to the experiences of each person and are generated in the subconscious. Also, sentiments are durable and recurrent since they remain in the emotional memory [16]. Sentiment analysis aims to assign a sentiment polarity to a text, in this case to texts generated by students. Sentiment polarity indicates whether the message has a positive, negative or neutral sentiment [17]. Sentiment analysis can be performed at three levels: document, sentence, and entity level.

Sentiment Analysis Process

Figure 1 shows the sentiment analysis process which is divided into four main phases: data acquisition, data preparation, review analysis, and sentiment classification. These phases are described below:

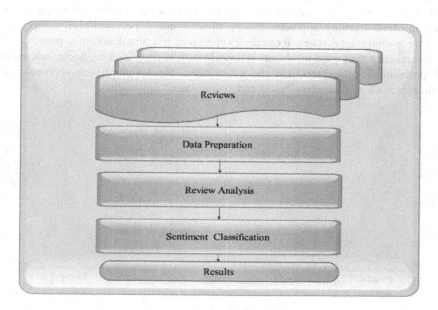

Fig. 1. Sentiment analysis process.

- Data acquisition can implement data mining techniques used in education domain [18] since data can be extracted from digital educational resources such as forums of MOOCs.
- Data preparation phase, also known as data preprocessing [19], is a necessary step for sentiment classification [20]. This phase consists of cleaning and preparing the text for classification. For instance, online texts contain usually lots of noise and uninformative parts such as HTML tags, scripts, and advertisements. In addition, on words level, many words in the text do not have an impact on the general orientation of it.
- Review analysis phase analyzes the linguistic features of reviews so that interesting information can be identified. This phase aims also to select the words that will be used in the last phase of sentiment analysis process.
- Sentiment classification phase classifies a new opinion as positive, negative or neutral based by implementing the machine learning, lexicon-based or hybrid approaches.

3.2 RQ2. What Approaches and Digital Educational Resources are Used in Sentiment Analysis?

Figure 2 shows the sentiment analysis approaches used in education domain according to the literature review performed. There are two main sentiment analysis approaches used in this domain: the machine learning and lexicon-based approaches. On the one hand, machine learning approach can be divided into supervised and unsupervised machine learning approaches. Regarding supervised machine learning approach, there are several classifiers used in education domain such as decision tree, linear, rule-based, and probabilistic classifiers. On the other hand, the lexicon-based approach uses techniques such as dictionary-based and corpus-based approaches.

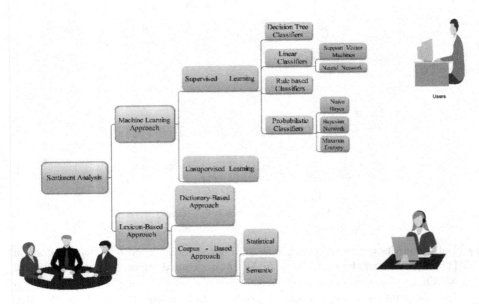

Fig. 2. Sentiment analysis approaches.

Table 2 shows the works analyzed in this literature review. This table presents the year of publication, sentiment analysis approach, classifier, and techniques used by the authors, the sentiment analysis level (document, sentence, and entity) adopted, and the precision achieved by the sentiment analysis process proposed by authors.

Japtap [22], who employed different techniques for sentiment analysis at the sentence level, concluded that it is not reliable to determine the sentiment of a user based on a brilliant or boring sentence. In this sense, the author analyzed the sentiment analysis techniques and established that each technique has a percentage of accuracy when the sentiment of a person is determined.

Table 3 present a set of the works analyzed in this literature review. This table aims to identify what are the digital educational resources most used for sentiment analysis

Table 2. Approaches, techniques and levels of sentiment analysis.

Work	Year	Approach	Classifier	Technique	Level	Precision
[22]	2013	Supervised machine learning	Probabilistic and linear classifiers	Naïve Bayes, maximum entropy, SVM	Sentence	(82.9% SVM)
[23]	2014	Supervised machine learning	Probabilistic and linear classifiers	Naïve Bayes, complement Naïve Bayes (CNB), maximum entropy, SVM	Document	(94% SVM) (84% CNB)
[24]	2016	Supervised machine learning	Linear classifiers	Linear discriminant analysis (LDA)	Entity	86%
[4]	2013	Lexicon-based	Dictionary-based approach	Dictionary-based approach	Entity	N/P
[25]	2014	Lexicon-based	Dictionary-based approach	Dictionary-based approach	Entity	90%
[26]	2013	Supervised machine learning	Probabilistic classifiers	Naïve Bayes, SVM	Document	75–86%, 77–57%
[27]	2013	Supervised machine learning	Rule-based classifiers	Sentiment fuzzy classification	Document	N/P
[28]	2013	Supervised machine learning	Linear classifiers	Hybrid approach (BLSTM neural networks and SVM)	Audio, video, document	73%

in education domain. As can be seen, the most used resources are the forums of MOOCs followed by social networks such as Facebook and Twitter.

3.3   RQ3. What are the Main Benefits of Using Sentiment Analysis on Education Domain?

Sentiment analysis in education domain [45] goes beyond just knowing what the students' sentiments are. Table 4 presents the benefits that can be provided by sentiment analysis to education domain. Some of these benefits are learning process improvement, performance improvement, reduction in course abandonment, teaching process improvement, and satisfaction with a course. Furthermore, Analytical learning refers to the collection and analysis of students' information and their context aiming to

Table 3. Education resources used for sentiment analysis.

Work	Year	Approach	Technique	Digital educational resource	Precision
[29]	2014	Hybrid (machine learning and lexicon-based approach)	SVM and dictionary-based approach	Facebook	83.27%
[30]	2014	Lexicon-based approach	Brown clustering	Forums	N/P
[31]	2013	Probabilistic classifiers	Naïve Bayes, SVM.	Twitter	84.63%
[32]	2013	Subjective classification	N/A	Learning journals	N/P
[23]	2014	Supervised machine learning	Naïve Bayes, complement Naive Bayes (CNB), maximum entropy classification, SVM	Computer texts	(94% SVM), (84% CNB)
[33]	2015	Unsupervised machine learning	Clustering	Forum of a MOOC (massive open online courses)	75.1%
[34]	2016	Supervised machine learning	Linear regression	Forum of a MOOC	56.1%
[35]	2014	Lexicon-based approach	Dictionary-based approach	Forum of a MOOC	N/P
[36]	2015	Supervised machine learning	Naïve Bayes	Forum of a MOOC	83.65%
[37]	2015	Supervised machine learning	Neural networks	Computer texts	84.8%
[38]	2016	Supervised machine learning	Decision tree classifiers	Computer program	99.7%
[39]	2013	Unsupervised machine learning	Clustering	N/P	80%
[40]	2013	Supervised machine learning	Naïve Bayes	Computer program, Facebook	87%

(*continued*)

Table 3. (*continued*)

Work	Year	Approach	Technique	Digital educational resource	Precision
[41]	2015	Lexicon-based approach	Statistical analysis	Forum of a MOOC	67.8%
[42]	2013	Lexicon-based approach	Semantic-based approach	Lexical database	75.8%
[43]	2014	Lexicon-based approach	Semantic-based approach	Lexical database	84%
[44]	2014	Supervised machine learning	Naïve Bayes	Twitter	75%
[45]	2017	Supervised machine learning	SVM	Documents	72.79%

understand and optimize the learning process and the environment in which it occurs. This information is especially important for e-learning systems, which guide students through the learning process according to their particular needs and preferences. Hence, this information is also important for teachers since it allows them to know the emotional state of their students.

Table 4. Benefits that can be provided by sentiment analysis to education domain.

Sentiment analysis advantage	Works
Learning process improvement	[37, 38, 39, 40, 42, 43, 44]
Performance improvement	[35, 36]
Reduction in course abandonment	[41]
Teaching process improvement	[23]
Satisfaction with a course	[23]

4 Results

Table 5 shows that forums of MOOCs [46] are the most used resources for sentiment analysis in education domain. In other words, in the education domain, datasets and lexicons are mainly built from forums of MOOCs. These data are provided as input to the sentiment analysis system to allow it to classify a new opinion.

Table 6 shows the most used techniques for sentiment analysis in education domain. These techniques are grouped according to the sentiment analysis approach to which they belong. According to the literature review presented in this work, the most used technique under the supervised machine learning approach is Naive Bayes, which commonly provides higher precision than other techniques used under this approach.

Table 5. Digital educational resources used in sentiment analysis on education context.

Digital educational resource	Work
Forum of a MOOC	[35, 34, 33, 36, 41]
Computer texts	[23, 37]
Learning journals	[32]
Twitter	[31, 44]
Forums	[30]
Facebook	[29, 40]
Computer programs	[38, 39]
Lexical databases	[42, 43]

Regarding lexicon-based approach, dictionary-based techniques are the most used for sentiment analysis. Finally, Table 6 also reflects that machine learning and lexicon-based approaches can be used in conjunction to perform the sentiment analysis process.

Table 6. Sentiment analysis approaches.

Approach	Work
Supervised machine learning	
Naïve Bayes	[44, 40, 36, 31, 26, 22]
SVM	[23, 31, 26, 22]
Maximum entropy	[22]
Decision tree classifiers	[38]
Neural networks	[37]
Linear regression	[34]
Sentiment fuzzy classification	[27]
Unsupervised machine learning	
Clustering	[39, 33]
Brown clustering	[30]
Lexicon-based approach	
Dictionary-based approach	[35, 25, 4]
Semantic-based approach	[43, 42]
Statistical analysis	[41]
Hybrid approaches	
SVM and dictionary-based approach	[29]
BLSTM neural networks and SVM	[28]

5   Conclusions and Future Work

The systematic literature review presented in this work revealed that there are several works that use sentiment analysis to improve different aspects of education domain such as learning process, students' performance, reduction in course abandonment, teaching process, and satisfaction with a course. This review also revealed that forums of MOOCs and social networks such as Facebook and Twitter are the most used digital education resources to collect data needed to perform the sentiment analysis process. Other educational resources used in sentiment analysis are learning journals, computer texts, software programs, lexical databases, and other electronic documents. Regarding sentiment analysis techniques, Support Vector Machine (SVM) and Naive Bayes are the most used techniques. Finally, we note that there is a trend to combine both machine learning approach and lexicon-based approach to perform the sentiment analysis process.

As future work, we plan to extend this literature review by including a wider set of digital libraries such as the Wiley Online Library. Furthermore, we plan to establish more research questions that help domain experts to obtain a better perspective on the use of sentiment analysis in education domain. This information could help experts to propose solutions that address challenges and limitations in education domain.

References

1. Vinodhini, G., Chandrasekaran, R.: Sentiment analysis and opinion mining: a survey. Int. J. Adv. Res. Comput. Sci. Softw. Eng. **2**, 282–292 (2012)
2. Salas-zárate, M.P., Medina-moreira, J., Lagos-ortiz, K., Luna-aveiga, H., Rodríguez-garcía, M.Á., Valencia-garcía, R.: Sentiment analysis on tweets about diabetes: an aspect-level approach. Hindawi Comput. Math. Methods Med. **2017**, 9 (2017)
3. Luna-Aveiga, H., et al.: Sentiment polarity detection in social networks: an approach for asthma disease management. In: Le, N.-T., Van Do, T., Nguyen, N.T., Thi, H.A.L. (eds.) ICCSAMA 2017. AISC, vol. 629, pp. 141–152. Springer, Cham (2018). https://doi.org/10. 1007/978-3-319-61911-8_13
4. Feldman, R.: Techniques and applications for sentiment analysis. Commun. ACM **56**, 82 (2013)
5. Mandinach, E.B., Cline, H.F.: Classroom Dynamics: Implementing a Technology-Based Learning Environment. Taylor & Francis, New York (2013)
6. Mayer, J.D., Salovey, P., Caruso, D.R.: Emotional intelligence: new ability or eclectic traits? Am. Psychol. **63**, 503–517 (2008)
7. Anitha, N., Anitha, B.: Sentiment classification approaches – a review. Int. J. Innov. Eng. Technol. **3**, 22–31 (2013)
8. Zhang, H.: The optimality of Naive Bayes. Am. Assoc. Artif. Intell. **19** (2004)
9. Varghese, R., Science, C.: Aspect based sentiment analysis using support vector machine classifier. In: International Conference on Advances in Computing, Communications and Informatics (ICACCI), pp. 1581–1586. IEEE (2013)
10. Tang, D., Qin, B., Liu, T.: Document modeling with gated recurrent neural network for sentiment classification. In: Proceedings of the 2015 Conference on Empirical Methods in Natural Language Processing, pp. 1422–1432 (2015)
11. Batista, F., Ribeiro, R.: Sentiment analysis and topic classification based on binary maximum entropy classifiers. Proces. del lenguaje Nat. **50**, 77–84 (2013)
12. Rice, D.R.: Corpus-based dictionaries for sentiment analysis of specialized vocabularies. In: Annual Meeting of Midwest Political Science Association (2015)
13. Rao, Y., Lei, J., Wenyin, L., Li, Q., Chen, M.: Building emotional dictionary for sentiment analysis of online news. World Wide Web **17**, 723–742 (2014)

14. Tsai, A.C.: Building a Concept-Level Sentiment on Commonsense Knowledge, pp. 22–30. IEEE Computer Society, Washington, D.C. (2013)
15. Kechaou, Z., Alimi, A.M.: Improving e-learning with sentiment analysis of users' opinions. In: IEEE Global Engineering Education Conference – Learning Environment Ecosystem for Engineering Education, pp. 1032–1038 (2011)
16. Munezero, M., Montero, C.S., Sutinen, E., Pajunen, J.: Are they different? Affect, feeling, emotion, sentiment, and opinion detection in text. IEEE Trans. Affect. Comput. **5**, 101–111 (2014)
17. Hoffmann, P., Wilson, T., Wiebe, J.: Recognizing contextual polarity: an exploration of features for phrase-level sentiment analysis. Comput. Linguist. **35**, 399–433 (2009)
18. Romero, C., Ventura, S.: Data mining in education. Wiley Interdiscip. Rev. Data Min. Knowl. Discov. **3**, 12–27 (2013)
19. Haddi, E., Liu, X., Shi, Y.: The role of text pre-processing in sentiment analysis. Procedia Comput. Sci. **17**, 26–32 (2013)
20. Ravi, K., Ravi, V.: A Survey on Opinion Mining and Sentiment Analysis: Tasks, Approaches and Applications. Elsevier B.V., New York City (2015)
21. Medhat, W., Hassan, A., Korashy, H.: Sentiment analysis algorithms and applications: a survey. Ain Shams Eng. J. **5**, 1093–1113 (2014)
22. Jagtap, V.S., Pawar, K.: Analysis of different approaches to sentence-level sentiment classification. Int. J. Sci. Eng. Technol. **2**, 164–170 (2013)
23. Altrabsheh, N., Cocea, M., Fallahkhair, S.: Learning sentiment from students' feedback for real-time interventions in classrooms. In: Bouchachia, A. (ed.) ICAIS 2014. LNCS (LNAI), vol. 8779, pp. 40–49. Springer, Cham (2014). https://doi.org/10.1007/978-3-319-11298-5_5
24. Rana, T.A., Cheah, Y., Letchmunan, S.: Topic modeling in sentiment analysis: a systematic review. J. ICT Res. Appl. **10**, 76–93 (2016)
25. Gonçalves, P., Araújo, M., Benevenuto, F., Cha, M.: Comparing and combining sentiment analysis methods. Comput. Appl. Soc. Behav. Sci. ACM. 27–37 (2014)
26. Aliandu, P.: Sentiment analysis on Indonesian tweet. In: Proceedings of International Conferences of Information, Communication, Technology, and Systems, pp. 203–208 (2013)
27. Mouthami, K., Devi, K.N., Bhaskaran, V.M.: Sentiment analysis and classification based on textual reviews. In: 2013 International Conference on Information Communication and Embedded Systems, pp. 271–276 (2013)
28. Wöllmer, M., Weninger, F., Knaup, T., Schuller, B.: YouTube movie reviews: sentiment analysis in an audio-visual context. IEEE Intell. Syst. 46–53 (2013)
29. Ortigosa, A., Martín, J.M., Carro, R.M.: Sentiment analysis in Facebook and its application to e-learning. Comput. Human Behav. **31**, 527–541 (2014)
30. Wen, M., Yang, D., Rosé, C.: Sentiment analysis in MOOC discussion forums: what does it tell us? In: Proceedings of the Educational Data Mining, pp. 1–8 (2014)
31. Neves-Silva, R., Watada, J., Phillips-Wren, G.E.: Intelligent decision technologies. In: Proceedings of the 5th KES International Conference on Intelligent Decision Technologies (KES-IDT 2013). IOS Press (2013)
32. Munezero, M., Mozgovoy, M.: Exploiting sentiment analysis to track emotions in students' learning diaries. Nat. Lang. Process. ACM. 145–152 (2013)
33. Wang, X., Yang, D., Wen, M., Koedinger, K., Rosé, C.P.: Investigating how student's cognitive behavior in MOOC discussion forums affect learning gains. In: Proceedings of the 8th International Conference on Educational Data Mining, pp. 226–233 (2015)
34. Robinson, C., Yeomans, M., Reich, J., Gehlbach, H.: Forecasting student achievement in MOOCs with natural language processing. In: LAK 2016, pp. 383–387. ACM (2016)

35. Tucker, C.S.: Mining student-generated textual data in MOOCS and quantifying their effects on student performance and learning outcomes. In: Proceedings of the 121st ASEE Annual Conference and Exposition, vol. 5 (2014)

36. Merceron, A.: Educational data mining/learning analytics: methods, tasks and current trends. In: Proceedings of the 13th e-Learning Conference of the German Computer Society (DeLFI 2015), pp. 101–109 (2015)

37. Bowman, S.R., Potts, C., Manning, C.D.: Learning distributed word representations for natural logic reasoning. In: Proceedings Knowledge Representation, Reasoning, Integration Symbolic Neural Approaches Paper from 2015 of the Association for the Advancement of Artificial Intelligence Spring Symposium (AAAI) Spring Symposium—Lea, pp. 10–13 (2015)

38. Darcy, A., Louie, A., Weiss, L.: Machine learning and the profession of medicine. Am. Med. Assoc. Innov. Heal. CARE Deliv. **5719**, 2–3 (2016)

39. Blikstein, P.: Multimodal learning analytics. In: LAK 2013, pp. 102–106. ACM (2013)

40. Troussas, C., Virvou, M., Espinosa, K.J., Llaguno, K., Caro, J.: Sentiment analysis of Facebook statuses using Naive Bayes classifier for language learning. IEEE (2013)

41. Crossley, S., Danielle, S., Baker, R., Wang, Y., Barnes, T.: Language to completion: success in an educational data mining massive open online class. In: Proceedings of 8th International Conference on Educational Data Mining Society, ERIC, pp. 8–11 (2015)

42. Chen, D., Socher, R., Manning, C.D., Ng, A.Y.: Neural tensor networks and semantic word vectors. Comput. Sci. Comput. Lang. Cornell Univ. Libr. 1–4 (2013)

43. Bowman, S.R.: Can recursive neural tensor networks learn logical reasoning? Comput. Sci. Comput. Lang. Cornell Univ. Libr. 1–10 (2014). arXiv: 1312.6192v4 [cs. CL]. Accessed 15 Feb 2014

44. Chen, X., Member, S., Vorvoreanu, M., Madhavan, K.: Mining social media data for understanding students' learning experiences. IEEE Trans. Learn. Technol. **7**, 246–259 (2014)

45. Peña-ayala, A.: Expert systems with applications educational data mining: a survey and a data mining-based analysis of recent works. Expert Syst. Appl. **5G**, 31 (2013)

46. Clow, D., Hall, W., Keynes, M.: MOOCs and the funnel of participation. In: Proceedings of the 3rd International Conference on Learning Analytics and Knowledge, pp. 185–189. ACM (2013)

Author Index

Printed in the United States
By Bookmasters